Laurentia Interpretations of 1000 Asteroids, 900 Cities,
and a Quantum Mechanical Theory of Astrology and Spirituality

Ajani Abdul-Khaliq

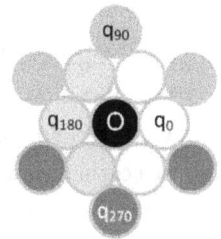

Table of Contents

Special Groups of Asteroids and Other Commentaries

Preface

Although I had no intention of adding a fourth book to the *Full Spectrum Astrology* (*FSA*) series, this one demanded to be written. As I've mentioned in the previous three books *FSA*, *Hayden's Book of Synastry* (*HBS*), and *All 144 Aspects* (*144*), this entire series was written in a three year period marking the end of my nine-year tenure as an instructor at an arts college in San Antonio. During that time, as our school stopped admitting students and eventually closed its doors, I got a good look at the world beyond the college, saw that there were a lot of people in need of something better for themselves, and sought to answer many important questions regarding my own role in helping that world. Following my last day at the school, I delved more heavily into the study of asteroids in astrology, looking for other bodies besides the familiar ones like the Sun, Moon, Juno, and Ceres for a clearer description of certain specific aspects of my life, and what hints—if any—my chart might offer regarding my next move. Then on September 20, 2017 I found something interesting: Two asteroids, 1992 QB1 and Sauer stood out in my chart as being sharply conjunct (next to each other) in an area of the chart associated with one's approach to the world. Upon further study, I found that Sauer was a die-hard restricter of others while 1992 QB1 (92Q for short) was a charmer and a support attractor. Several of my past turbulent personal relationships were explained by this, and I subsequently adopted a program for myself called the "92Q Project" aimed at cleaning up my affairs in love, work and business. The project would end up being successful after two months as I sold my house, gained some great new friends, finished my PhD, and (most importantly) learned ALL KINDS of new astrology which would eventually lead to my writing this book for you.

A few weeks later, I was sitting on the computer—bored—so I decided to subscribe to serennu.com to get a look at some 1000 asteroids which might be interesting in my chart. I felt it a kind of belated birthday present as I cheerfully copied the table full of foreign names into Excel. Let me tell you, I was quickly blown away by the names alone. Asteroids like Pax, Berenike, and Urhixidur. Eurykleia, Tantalus, and Gerlinde. To me, the names themselves were so exotic that I just had to learn what some of these space objects did in the astrochart—an intellectual journey far more enjoyable than any trek through a foreign country. Using the methods I explained in the Pluto-Selene section of *HBS*, I studied the functions of a few of the asteroids. Then some more asteroids. Then all of them. After about a week and a half I had classified between 1000 and 1100 asteroids, one at a time based on the same data set I've been using throughout the *FSA* series—with no knowledge of any previous work done on the subject. I even learned some neat tricks for sharply reading the asteroids in a person's chart. Although we traditionally say that astrology can't predict your life, after you've read the asteroids, you will have seen that it comes a lot closer to prediction than we ever expected. I talk about this in the Cause and Effect chapter later in the book.

As far back as the second chapter of *FSA* I sought to understand why the so-called "pseudoscience" of astrology seemed to work so reliably beyond chance. Accordingly, throughout the first three books you'll find certain sections which attempt to theorize the science behind how certain aspects of astrology works. Although I had settled on a theory I could live with as far back as *FSA*, I didn't include it in any of the previous books because it was, honestly, a little more mathy than I had time to write about and a lot more physics-based than I knew *how* to write about. Two families of asteroids however changed all that: the gender-body image asteroids and the social tier asteroids.

Among the social tier asteroids in particular, the two most instrumental in changing my perception of the world and how to improve it were 26 Proserpina (the "Black asteroid") and 997 Priska (the "second-placedness" asteroid). Investigation of Proserpina led directly to a change in how I see race and my own identity; and also led me to embrace feminism for reasons that may become clearer to you as you read the interpretations for certain gender asteroids. Meanwhile, Priska's effects resolved a long-standing question I had regarding my always "interesting" personal relationships—the asteroid 997 holding a status that surpasses even that of Chiron when it comes to explaining a person's relationship-based Achilles' heel. Elsewhere among the gender and justice asteroids, you have Eduarda, Dike, and Ganymed—all associated with homosexuality—as well as Hispania, Roma, Germania, and America—all associated with the overall spirit of the cultures whose names they bear. And then there are the spirit asteroids like Veritas, Eurykleia, and Laurentia. Destructive asteroids like Agamemnon, Damocles, and Natalie. Career asteroids like Moultona, Ceraskia, and Ottegebe. Enchanters like Scheherezade and Hebe. I learned that the proper naming of asteroids is extra important, which is why the International Astronomical Union won't just let you do it willy-nilly. And this is because the names themselves carry a socialized meaning that endures across minds regardless of their astrological or astronomical knowledge. History, etymology, and the original object being described all matter. My work with 997 Priska and 26 Proserpina, for example, led pretty directly to the writing of this book—effectively, *Full Spectrum Astrology, Volume 4*.

Sources

Since I don't like presenting things without knowing what they mean (or at least how they *might* fit with what I already know), I needed to improve my knowledge of physics before writing this book. As a way of updating the old lessons I learned two decades prior as an undergrad at Caltech, I picked up Thad Roberts' *Einstein's Intuition*—a serendipitously relevant look at quantum mechanics through the lens of energy-bearing vacuum space. This, combined with what I remember from Steven Krantz' *Elements of Advanced Mathematics* and MIT Open Courseware's *Linear Algebra*, forms the basis of this book's astrological theory. In the scientific spirit of citing one's sources, these (along with hundreds of megabytes of my own statistics) are my primary sources for this book. I also used Sharlene Nagy Hesse-Biber's *Handbook of Feminist Research* alongside Krantz as a guide for knowing when certain automatic assumptions in science were open to question. Robert Bruce's *Astral Dynamics* was central to identifying what other kinds of experiences might be had with our physics-physiological machinery. Serennu.com produced the first (1000) asteroid list. The International Astronomical Union produced the second (755,000) asteroid list which I used to calculate the "effect formula" in Chapter 37. I also occasionally referenced Wikipedia for summary tables of the Standard Model, M-theory, and Superstring Theory, but did not rely on Wikipedia for theoretical claims.

I write *Laurentia* during a time when the class and social divisions in the US are growing precipitously wider. And yet there is no real need to be disturbed by this. As you'll soon see, the asteroids and the math behind them lay out an order which works a lot like a programming language. If you know enough about this programming language, you'll easily be able to turn even the most uncomfortable situations into great ones.

This book is for everyone in the world. I hope it helps humanity find happiness.

Chapter 36: A Quantic Theory of Spaces

There is an order inherent in the universe and in number. There are consistent relationships between numbers such as 5 and 10. As relationships build upon each other, so too do abstractions like "one," "two," and "three" tend to take on consistent meanings which transcend the objects they count. We begin by elaborating upon the theory of such numbers and how we may put that theory to use in building the best lives possible for ourselves.

This chapter outlines the basic theory of how energy-bearing units and energy passage (flux) work together to produce cycles of fixed energy levels. Such cycles can be mapped onto a **countable** (1, 2, 3, ... **numerable**) space which is most stable at cycles of 4 and 12. The implications of this are discussed accordingly.

This chapter is the most technical of all chapters in the *FSA* series' four books. For people only interested in reading the asteroids, you may want to skip both this one and the next one. However, I'd encourage you to consider coming back to these chapters later because they serve to explain *the* reason why you can and should treat your life as a very hackable program. I will illustrate how the 4- and 12-cycles are constant in nature regardless of how long a cycle takes and what that cycle consists of, that the dynamics of all events are traceable back to their beginnings' beginnings, and will conclude with the implications for mapping such cycles onto subsets of the sets described by them.

Definition of a Paradox-Driven System

A system whose rules generate consequences which negate those very rules are called **paradox-driven systems**. By this definition, some of our most basic natural systems can be considered paradox-driven. For example,

> "If it is 12:00:00 now, then it is 12:00:02."

The above statement arises because, by the time you finish reading the sentence, the first part of it is no longer true.

> "If change is the only constant, then constancy must also be constant."

This is a paradox. Relatedly,

> "If constancy is constant, then the existence of differences [non-constants against which constancy can be assumed in the first place] must also exist."

Let us define **change** as **the relationship between constancy and differences**.

Recursion in Paradox-Driven Systems

Since we've introduced the concept of existence, let us set up a paradox-driven pair of rules.

> If existence exists, then it must be a thing.

> If a thing exists, then the thing and its existence must exist together.

The above system can be diagrammed as follows:

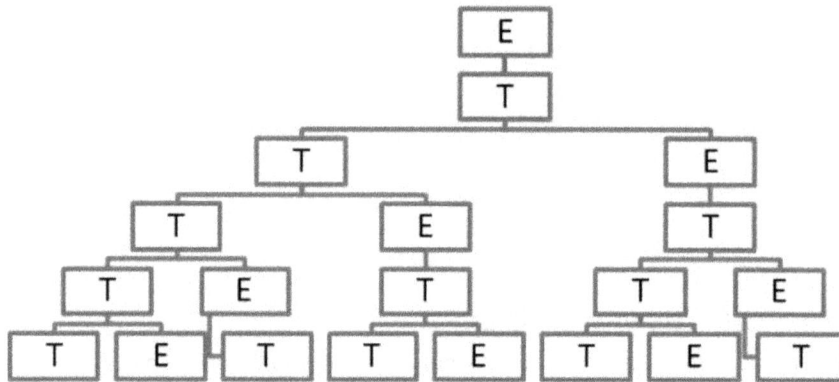

Figure 36-1: The flow of logic in the thing-existence paradox

Since the above pair of rules **ultimately keep referencing themselves**, this system is called **recursive**. Each **data-containing object in the network structure** diagrammed above (T or E) is called a **node**. An interesting property of the above rule-pair is that it introduces the notion of change. Namely "If existence exists, then it must be a thing. If a thing exists, then the thing and <u>existence given the thing as originally conceived</u> must exist together."

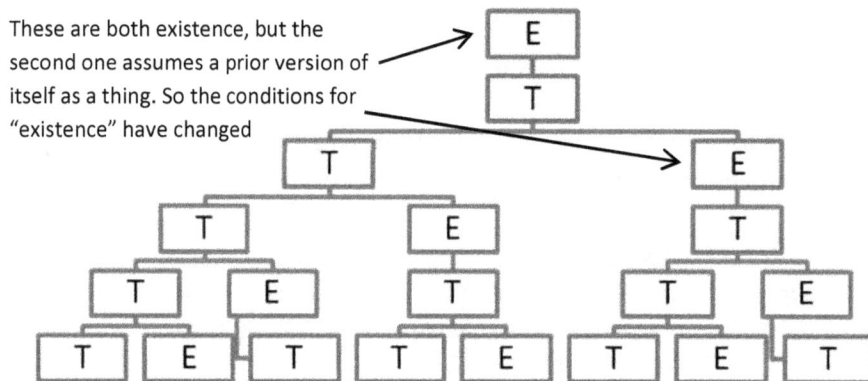

These are both existence, but the second one assumes a prior version of itself as a thing. So the conditions for "existence" have changed

Figure 36-2: A paradox stemming from recursion in the existing-thing system

If we continually follow this chain of logic, then each new level in the chain has the same structure as a similar level above it, and yet—by virtue of even *having* copies of itself above it—differs from those previous levels which could not assume themselves. Now let us add an additional pair of rules to this system to cover what happens when we branch off to infinity.

If existence exists, then it must be a thing.

If a thing exists, then the thing and its existence must exist together.

Applied infinitely, a chain of the above rules may itself be considered a thing.

If an infinite chain of the above rules is considered a thing, then the existence of that infinite chain must also be considered.

It is important to note that I used the word "considered" here, since despite my *saying* the chain can be taken infinitely, there is no reality we know of—outside of the conceptual—where such a thing called "infinity" can actually be reached. We conceive of infinity (∞) all the time, but when have you ever actually encountered it? Right after googol^{googol}? How about after googol^{googol}+1? It's not that infinity doesn't exist, just that nature doesn't seem to support unbounded infinity as an actual distance from a starting point. Instead, we seem to have constraints on our ability to count things, on the number of grains of sand in the world, on the speed of light, on the allowable states of an energy level, and on the temperature of the universe. Whenever we use infinity, we seem to be taking a hypothesized limitlessness and boxing it into a bounded, limited object called ∞. That object in turn becomes its own singular reference point, effectively turning infinity back into 1. Let us then define ∞ (**infinity**) as **the conceived limitlessness of a measurement**. We'll also define a **thing** as **any pattern which can be conceived of as existing**.[1] Let us define **existence** the **state of a thing as conceivable**. Consistent with the rules we posed above, these definitions are definitely circular. This is similar to the axiomatic definitions of set and objects in math. (Sets contain objects while objects are things inside of sets.) We can then restate our four rules using the new definitions.

> If existence exists, then it must be a thing.

> If a thing exists, then the thing and its existence must exist together.

> ~~Applied infinitely, a chain of the above rules may be considered a thing.~~ If an infinite chain of the above rules exists, then that chain must be a thing.

> ~~If an infinite chain of the above rules are considered a thing, then the existence of that infinite chain must also be considered.~~ If an infinite chain of the first two rules is a thing, then it must be both a thing and exist.

Using these four rules, we can take a thing and its existence, stretch their chain out to a thing called infinity, and box that infinity into a thing that exists. And this too can be stretched out into an infinite chain. This gives us an infinite chain of things which in turn contain their own infinities, much like the set of real numbers $\mathbb{R}$. There is a catch to this though. We never *did* count up to such a value. We only *represented* it. So instead of working with an actual limitlessness, we saved ourselves the trouble and used a limited/bounded object to stand in for such limitlessness. This brings us to the notion of memory (or processing or energy) constraints on the part of the conceiver, along with the use of cycles as a mechanism for reducing the amount of load on a system whose information would otherwise grow without bound.

Introducing complexity constraints into recursive paradoxical systems

Consistent with what we observe in nature, let us introduce a rule which accounts for the point at which a processor of recursive data stops processing additional data:

> Subject to certain constraints, a chained recursive system either (1) exhausts its ability to branch further, (2) drops old branches to make room for new ones, or (3) compresses old branches into simplified nodes which can then be put into later branches.

> In case 1 (exhaustion), the computer crashes, the human dies, the Sun burns out, or something like this. Exhaustion describes systems with no mechanism for offloading the results of their own dynamics and no strong mechanism for regulating how much processing is being done (particularly so that processing *can* continue to take place). Thus these systems just keep using up energy to do whatever it is they're doing until the energy supply is no more.

> In case 2 (dropping), we have things like policy rewriting, experiential newness, some aspects of digestion, and the notion of "today." Here the effects of old states wear off until they hardly apply at all, and there is no real mechanism for integrating them into new states. There is, however a mechanism for adapting old states to new demands.

> In case 3 (compressing), the human consolidates previous experiences into personality and simplified histories, video game characters adapt to your style of play, and DNA (along with the host environment) promotes survival-favorable

---

[1] So feelings and ideas about unicorns are things. Unicorns are also things, even if only in imagination. Actual unicorns—to the extent that "actuality" is based on normative agreement among most normal people—are not things in the real-world acceptance sense, though plenty of people recognize them as a concept in the real world. Given this notion of thingness, what counts as a thing is all about what you can get away with believing. We'll see that this also applies to the concept of time later on.

mutations.[2] Systems like this keep data clusters that are relevant and absorb less relevant functions into their histories. The actual history-referencing structure of "today" (as opposed to the mere notion) also works like this.

By the way, no one of these systems is inherently better than the other in the grand scheme of things, but are simply a property of finite / bounded energy systems (case 1), the self-sustaining subsets they evolve within them (case 3), and the dynamically stable systems (case 2) employed by the self-sustainers (case 3) towards the continued processing of more bounded energy (case 1). We can make an analogy to a previous structure I've talked about throughout the *FSA* books: All objects may be thought of as interfacing with self (itself), other (a direct interactant), and world (an indirect, abstract, or environmental space as interactant). Case 3-compression promotes self-interface. Case 2 drives dynamics with others, and case 1 describes the seemingly immeasurable (but finite) possibilities for drawing from ones' surrounding resources.

Exhaustible things can be considered bounded. Dropping represents the replacement of one structure with a new version of itself. Compression represents the transformation from one structure to another. And so we have a tool for describing a system without bounds while still using bounded states to represent it.

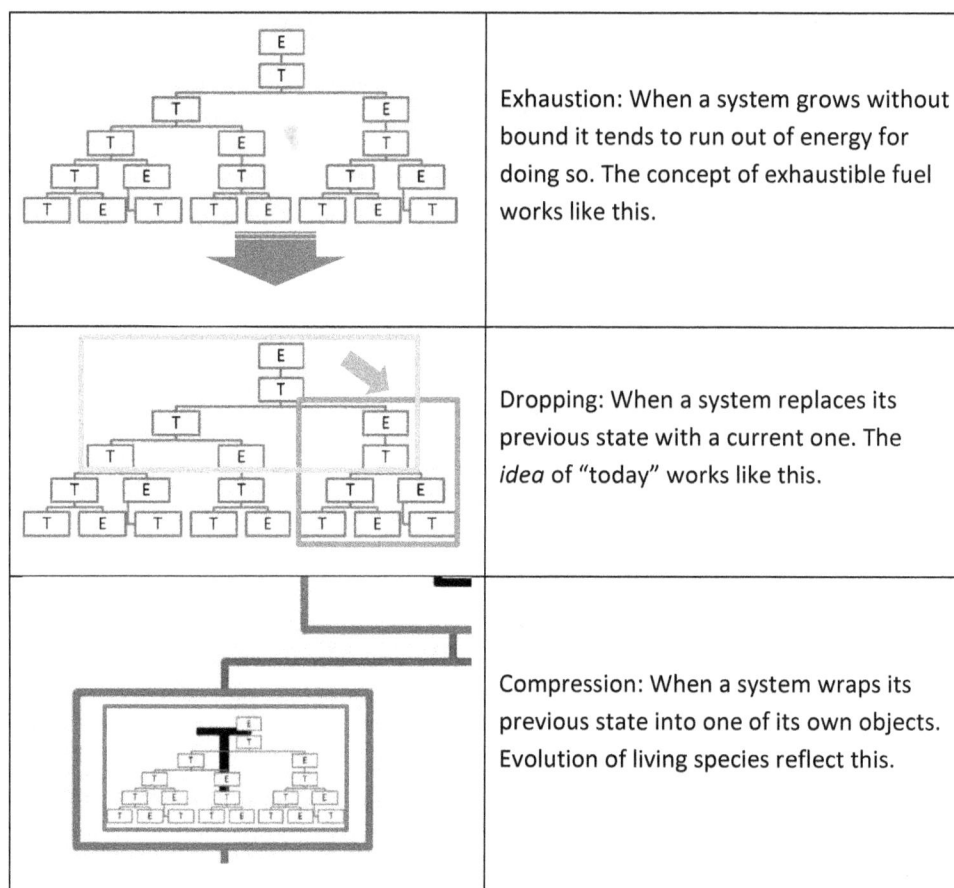

Figure 36-3: Mechanisms of data chain expansion

Assertion 1. Compression yields cycles.
There is a special role for the point at which a system wraps groups of its events into a single event. We can consider this to be the starting point for a cycle. Here the system effectively resets its progression along its branches.

---

[2] A single mutation doesn't typically constitute a drop in overall organismal function so much as it alters the tools available for performing that function. What may be considered dropping on the micro scale is more like compressing on the macro scale.

Assertion 2. Dropping introduces memory.

Memory may be defined as an attribute of systems which use dropping as a mechanism form processing nodes (the array of available states) only within a certain bound. Let **memory** be **the maximum amount of information (or energy states) that can constitute a thing before that thing ceases to be itself**. If, for example, I can only look at a contiguous block of 24 hours as equaling "today," then after those 24 hours are up I will "forget" that today is today and start calling it yesterday. In this example, 24 hours after midnight means that today ceases to be itself. In another example, the ones digit in a decimal number can only "remember" 10 different values. In binary it can only remember two. It's useful to note that this definition of memory is more like that which describes computers. Human memory doesn't really work like this, but works more like compression instead.

Assertion 3. Memory and time flow in opposite directions.

Given the flow of a memory region along a network of recursive states, we find something interesting: while later-occurring blocks are later *time-wise*, they are actually earlier *logically*. Consider the statement, "If I live in San Antonio de Bexar, then I live in Texas; if I live in Texas, then I live in the US." Notice how San Antonio is listed first in the sentence, but requires Texas as a precondition and the US as a precondition before that. In a diagram like the one below, memory builds up the network while time builds down.

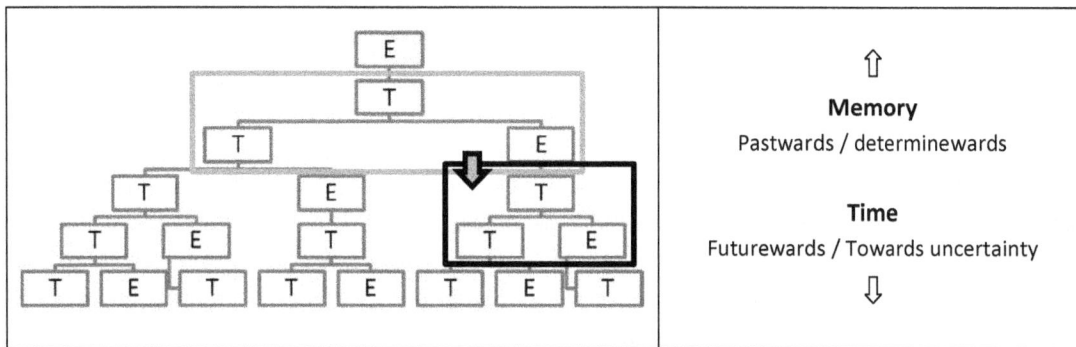

Figure 36-4: The opposing directions of memory and time

The implication here is that a system's memory is complete when it's time is exhausted. Perhaps this was obvious. Not so obvious is that systems which work like this, which also obey compression cycles, are more inclined to repeat combinations of the same themes every time they begin a new round. This is not just true for clocks, but for daily human behaviors and atomic oscillations as well. Unless disturbed by new data, we're likely to respond to the same kinds of insults in the same way we previously responded. We're likely to treat the new boyfriend/girlfriend in the same way we treated the last one. Every time we reset, we forget. Not the previous person. Rather, we forget how *we ourselves* behaved along the chain of possible choices—especially when we've made different versions of those same kinds of choices all our lives. The price of having memory is that it blurs details that might be useful in guiding future states of the system, the price of time is that it stems from the paradox of "this becoming not this," automatically decreasing the energy we put into things not of this moment, no matter how important those non-current events may be.

Although energy states in physics may not have memories in the way we think, they do possess the ultimate means of keeping track of where they've been. **Quantization**—**where energy levels can only come in fixed sizes**—allows energy states to possess a well-defined "tick mark" in their progress from one level to another. As of 2018 our best approximations of nature suggest that the universe consists of **quanta** on the smallest level. This means that we cannot pass a packet of energy which is "infinitely" small. There is **a lower limit to the amount of energy that can be coherently passed from state to state**, while passing energy below this lower limit allows systems to do things in between—to progress along their nodal chains— without any change being shown outside the bounds of that system. Every time a system registers a new compression of its former array of possible states into the first state of a brand new round, the system encodes a formal recognition of progress experienced by its parts internally. In this way, **quantic ticks** or **quanticks** (**arrival of a basic energy unit at the next allowed state**) keep track of a quantum's reaching yet another threshold after all possible unregistered states within that system have been occupied. As quanticks progress forward, the stability of the systems from which they arrived progresses backwards. Thus probabilities have their Bayesian outcomes resolved, potentials have their actualities realized, macrodynamic histories—of countries and state vectors alike—become open to modeling in the aggregate, and the energy levels dedicated to such prior states drops as exponential fractions of themselves.[3]

Quanta may not tell us what you (the quantum) did, but it does tell us that you did it. There is a way around this though. By using neighboring quanta to watch other quanta, we can keep track of specific combinations of events; it is here that we can figure out where you've been after all (within a certain level of error). For example, the arrival of a new day may not tell us what the previous day was about, but it does tell us (usually) that 24 hours went by. Note that although we'll often talk about quanta on the smallest possible level in the universe, the definition of a basic "unit of energy" can change depending on your reference frame. A sports team's quantum may be the number of games played. A molecule's quantum may be an atom. The ultimate quantum may be a combination of open and closed strings (from string theory) or may not be. Later I will argue that the placement of our solar system's planets arose from the maximum allowable energy capable of passing from the Sun (it's flux), and that the asteroids formed at the allowable subquantum states between major allowable regions.

Math Assertions

Assertion 4. As long as there is an error level beyond which certain numerical values are indistinguishable to a certain viewer, all infinite real sets which are same-order supersets of their infinite rational elements can themselves be reduced to infinite rational sets.
This is to say that, even if a number like 3.22634634771... goes on forever without repeating, if there exists some level beyond which we will never know the difference between 3.22...xx and 3.22...xy, then at that point, all finer numbers will be considered the same as 3.22...x. But this is rational because we can put it over a fraction with some power of 10 (in this example). Similarly, although sets like the real numbers are uncountably infinite in theory (meaning you can't label them 1st, 2nd, 3rd... without having another infinite dimension-like digit-span ruin your count), the real numbers are not uncountably infinite in any reality that we humans are capable of measuring or our computers are capable of calculating. Even the computer runs out of memory or time as the Sun swallows us all up. For all sets that begin, there has yet to be a set that a real-world counter can illustrate to extend beyond a countable superset. As it is with energy, there is no machine—biological or otherwise—capable of infinite energy expenditure towards the infinite expansion beyond an already infinite set which we have the ability to measure. Beyond the theoretical construct of number, all real world measurements are limited to the order of precision held by the observers that measure them. Speaking through analogy, precision beyond this requires an ability to observe either one's own eyeball or one's own "self beyond himself" to capture things that are either too small or too big for his powers of discernment to assess. In other words, because no observer can observe himself, there are limits to how far towards "infinity" he can actually go. He cannot observe anything on levels of precision higher than the units of his own observation, and at that point his notion of infinity, no matter how grand, cannot in reality be approached beyond that fundamental value. He can keep counting up for as long as he lives, but he can't count things that have gotten too small to distinguish. Not in reality. Only in theory.[4]

---

[3] To give a rough example, if I spend one hour thinking about the previous 24 hours, then each day is worth $1/24^{th}$ the energy starting that next day. But each next hour has 24x the causal information of an hour from the previous day.

[4] What about a computer which keeps estimating more precise digits of π? Doesn't it defy this rule? No. A precision estimate like this is an upward count on approximation, not a downward count on measurement. Here, the 3 in 3.14 is our bottom. What I am claiming is that bi-scale infinities in the real world which can climb both to infinitely high and infinitely low magnitudes are constrained at the low magnitudes by limits on their own precision and constrained at the high magnitudes by the time or energy allowed for their stable existence. I claim that no known real world system can breach the lower precision limit even if it strives countably towards the upper magnitude limit. Our decimal estimation programs aren't actually making themselves more precise, they're adding more magnitudes to their calculations and reporting the results as precision, which isn't the same as using finer-grained units of processing. But if we can only strive towards infinity while being required to start at a single noninfinitessimal starting point, then our uncountable infinity is reduced to a countable one. Another way of saying this is that, in a real-world system where infinities are approached, infinitesimals opposite those infinities by scale have a lower limit. This is the mathematical equivalent of saying that our ability to count is quantized, where the

Assertion 5. Beyond the theoretical limiting value towards uncountable infinity, all real world sets are countable.

Even for strange sets like the set of all points x^{y^z}, where x, y, and z are real numbers, the previous assertion's limit on the calculable span of the real numbers also places a limit on the calculable span of multidimensional objects like this. Although x^{y^z}'s inclusion of values like $27\_\_498.679^{\sqrt{9.938\ldots}^{-4.23\ldots}}$ makes us question how we would ever count this, we don't have to *count* it. We only need to do what calculators do and *calculate* it. The value we get will be some error-terminated rational which is again mappable onto the set {1, 2, 3…}. Putting a "…" or a "∞" or an " $/_0$" on something doesn't make it *actually* infinite, only theoretically so, but humans and machines in the world alike all stop caring at some point and reduce these to the practically denumerable.

So as to distinguish between theoretical infinity and **the kind of infinity which is invariably constrained to an observer's powers of precision**, we will refer to the set of events implied by the latter as "real-world observable" infinities or simply **observable infinities**.

Assertion 6. All observable infinities can be mapped one onto another via a bounded infinite sets such as $\left\{\frac{1}{0}, \frac{1}{1}, \frac{1}{2}, \ldots\right\}$.

Sets like $\left\{\frac{1}{0}, \frac{1}{1}, \frac{1}{2}, \ldots\right\}$ consist of enumerators transformed to fit a scale. The set $\left\{\frac{1}{0}, \frac{1}{1}, \frac{1}{2}, \ldots\right\}$ itself can be used to place infinity-like objects all the way up to 0-like objects. The set $\left\{\frac{1}{1}, \frac{1}{2}, \frac{1}{3}, \ldots\right\}$ can be used to map 1-like objects to 0-like objects and is just the reciprocal of the basic set of natural / counting numbers (the set used to map countables by default). Mappings like this are useful for squeezing infinities into small spaces like the space between 0 and 1, and are directly useful for placing infinite kinds of objects onto repeatable intervals.

A common mapping for the set of whole numbers is to assign all the non-positives to odd values and all the positives to even values. So we could map {…-3, -2, -1, 0, 1, 2, 3,…} onto {1, 2, 3…} by putting 1, 2, 3,… as the, 2nd, 4th, and 6th values and 0, -1, -2,… as the 1st, 3rd, and 5th values. {0, 1, -1, 2, -2, 3,…} → {1, 2, 3, 4, 5, 6,…}. If we wanted to bind these, we could then map {1, 2, 3, 4, 5, 6,…} → to $\left\{\frac{1}{1}, \frac{1}{2}, \frac{1}{3}, \frac{1}{4}, \frac{1}{5}, \frac{1}{6}, \ldots\right\}$, effectively squeezing 1…∞ into the space between 1…0. Relatedly, if we wanted to map numbers like 2412.5432… which could get infinitely large or infinitely precise, we would first note that, by Assertion 4, we don't actually need to treat numbers like this as infinitely precise. Setting an error-terminated cutoff at, say, 6 decimal places for example, we would map 2412.543289_ onto 2412543289 by multiplying times 10^6, and then just treating it like a regular counting number. Finally, we noted earlier that sets like $\left\{\frac{1}{1}, \frac{1}{2}, \frac{1}{3}, \ldots\right\}$ can be used to map 1-like objects to 0-like objects. So the final mapping of a number like 2412.543289_ will be → $\frac{1}{2412543289}$, which fits nicely between 0 and 1. This will be useful in a moment.

Assertion 7. Multidimensional infinities can be mapped onto correspondingly multidimensional bounded sets.

Returning to the set of all points x^{y^z}, we can use our bounded infinities to represent any point in this set as $\left\{\frac{1}{1} \ldots \frac{1}{\infty}\right\}^{\left\{\frac{1}{1} \ldots \frac{1}{\infty}\right\}^{\left\{\frac{1}{1} \ldots \frac{1}{\infty}\right\}}}$. This is in turn mappable onto $\{1 \ldots 0\}^{\{1\ldots0\}^{\{1\ldots0\}}}$ or $\{0 \ldots 1\}^{\{0\ldots1\}^{\{0\ldots1\}}}$ if you like.

There is a common mapping for $N^2 \rightarrow N$, where N is a countable set like {0, 1, 2, 3…}. N^2 is {0, 1, 2, 3…} x {0, 1, 2, 3…}. In order to do the mapping, you just add up one number from each pair and line up everything by giving priority to either the first or the second set. For example, adding one number from each of these sets and giving priority to set 1, we would get sums like 0+0=0, 0+1=1, 1+0=1, 0+2=2, 1+1=2, 2+0=2. Our {1, 2, 3,…}-mapped set would then be {(0,0), (0,1), (1,0), (0,2), (1,1), (2,0),…}. Notice that I'm ordering everything by lowest total sum first. Then, if the sums are the same, I'm ordering by

---

principles determining Planck-scale energies are analogous those determining the lower bound on infinitessimals. We'll see this throughout the model.

lowest to highest in the first set only. This is one way of showing how we can map multidimensional countable sets onto single countable ones.

Although there is a formal definition for the following word, we'll define the word informally here. The word is "cardinality." This will be the dimensional character of a set: the lowest number of dimensions you can reduce a set to. N^2 in our example above had the same cardinality as N, meaning you could flatten a 2D experience into a 1D one. (But maybe you knew this because your wi-fi does it all the time when taking streams of radio waves and turning them into 2D movies on your phone.) Relatedly, we can take two 2D views, fake ourselves into calling it 3D, view it as a 2D world anyway, and cast it through our camera glasses in a 1D stream. As long as the data stream is countable, 1D, 2D, 3D, or whatever, doesn't matter.

Assertion 8. As long as they share the same cardinality, observable systems of the same order can be mapped one onto another regardless of initial dimension.

Returning once again to the set x^{y^z} which started off including things like $27\_\_498.679^{\sqrt{9.938\ldots}^{4.23\ldots}}$ but eventually mapped onto $\{0 \ldots 1\}^{\{0\ldots1\}^{\{0\ldots1\}}}$, because of real-world limitations on our decimal precision, we can go even further and map $\{0 \ldots 1\}^{\{0\ldots1\}^{\{0\ldots1\}}}$ onto $\{1, 2, 3,\ldots\}$ by doing the same thing we did for $\{(0,0), (0,1),\ldots\}$. The final mapping produces something like $\{(0,0,0), (0,0,1), (0,1,0), (1,0,0), (0,0,2), (0,1,1), (0,2,0),\ldots\}$. These correspond to the $\{1, 2, 3, 4, 5, 6, 7,\ldots\}$ elements respectively, and can in turn be mapped onto$\rightarrow \left\{\frac{1}{1},\frac{1}{2},\frac{1}{3}, \ldots\right\}$ and $\rightarrow \{1\ldots0\}$ once again.

So now we've shown it: multidimensional experiences—as long as their "resolution" or "infiniteness" can be limited as the result of error-inducing precision constraints—can ultimately be mapped onto a 1D line. Even the set of all $\{countries\}^{\{sightings\}^{\{people\}}}$ can be ordered in this way if you use a combination of factors such as alphabetical names, longitude, latitude, birthdate, gene locus appearance or whatever to do it. The set of all $\{broad\ behaviors\}^{\{in\ context\}^{\{towards\ objects\}}}$ can also be ordered if you use a combination of observability, number of people involved, distance, cognitive alertness required, or event date for example to order them. Think of how one might write a biography about you. Perhaps by age, perhaps by situation type, they might actually be able to take your seemingly infinitely complex world and reduce it to a linear progression of events constrained by their own powers of precision in describing you. Thus the multidimensional infinite is mapped onto a countably bounded window.

Assertion 9. Bounded infinite sets can be converted into finite sets by simply dividing them up between the boundaries.

This one is self-explanatory. All it says is that sets like $\left\{\frac{1}{1},\frac{1}{2},\frac{1}{3},\frac{1}{4},\frac{1}{5}, \ldots, \frac{1}{\infty}\right\}$ can be partitioned into regions like $\left\{\left[\frac{1}{1}\right],\left[\frac{1}{2},\frac{1}{3}\right],\left[\frac{1}{4}\right],\left[\frac{1}{5}, \ldots, \frac{1}{\infty}\right]\right\}$, so instead of having an infinite number of items we can have a finite number of items like 10 or 4 or something.

Assertion 10. Countable sets can have bounded infinite sets as their elements.

For example, the set $\{1, 2, 3,\ldots\}$ can map onto $\{ [1\ldots0], [2\ldots0],\ldots, \left[3 \ldots \frac{1}{\infty}\right]\}$ where the sets like $\left[3 \ldots \frac{1}{\infty}\right]$ are bounded infinite sets.

Assertion 11. Periodic waves impose quanta on a system.

By virtue of returning to the states where they began, periodic (repeating) functions like sin, cos, and e^{ix} by definition contain a point which marks both the end of one cycle and the start of another. Once one period (the completion time for one wavelength) is defined, this start point also serves as the ongoing indicator that the same cycle has completed. We will call this point the 0th degree (or 0 degree). Subtracting error introduced by perturbers, all instances of the 0 degree in a wave delineate the same general structure for the wave that has occurred since the previous instance of the 0 degree, though that structure may be subjected to various transformations, including the addition of other waves.

Assertion 12. A periodic wave can be mapped onto a circle with an entire period between consecutive 0 degrees mapped onto the circumference of the circle and the consecutive 0 degree points mapped onto each other.

This assertion states that a repeating wave can be graphed as a cycle about a central point.

Assertion 13. A bounded infinite set can be mapped onto a circle with its spanning elements mapped around the circumference of the circle and its end points mapped onto each other.

This says that each element in a bounded infinite set can be stacked on top of other elements with the endpoints lined up. We can also do this for multiple versions of such sets, as with a ruler stacked and stretched upon a yardstick—the 8 inch and 2 foot marks respectively representing $2/_3$ progress around the circle.

Assertion 14. Bounded infinite subsets as elements of a superset can be used to map one period of the superset onto a circle.

I'll explain this with an example: If we have the set (0, 1, 2,...,∞), I could divide it arbitrarily into ([0...10],[11...1000],[1001...∞]). I can map these three divisions onto the first, second, and third 120° sections of a circle. There is a more thorough procedure for partitioning like this in formal math, but I'll omit it here.

Assertion 15. The number of divisions of a cycle and the number of repeats of the cycle itself can be mapped onto each other via the counting numbers.

This is simply to say, for example, that the third division of a cycle and the third time around for a cycle are both related via a mapping onto the number 3. The 12th day and the 12th hour can be mapped onto each other via the object "12." And so it is for the elements of all countable sets.

Assertion 16. Cycles consisting of bounded divisions, whether infinite or finite, can be mapped onto themselves, establishing a base system.

If we claim that the number of times around a circle and the analogously numbered section within that same circle are related by number, then the quanta imposed on the circle by the completion of its circumference yields an analogously quantic limit on that number of repeats for the circle. Though there is no rule saying that a circle divided into four sections must do something special after four repeats, the completion of that fourth cycle grants an additional quantic limiting status to the fourth section in the fourth cycle—that is, the 16th section traversed. In this way, we may pass through the first, second, and third sections of a four division cycle and, via mapping onto the natural numbers, retaining a predictable relationship to prior regions traversed. A pass through the fourth cycle would hold significance not just for the section, but for the circle and its binding set proper. The status of quantic level is thus granted to both the fourth circle completion and the 16th section completion because these are, in fact, the same event. Once beyond the 16th and into the 17th section (beginning of the fifth cycle), we may either start at 0 again or do something else...

Continuing our four-division example, suppose you need to register values beyond 16. How might this cycle register a number like 17? Recall first that both 4 sections and 16 sections are granted the status of starting point in this example. Yet the completion of each section also brings with it a similar quantic character. Even though it may not be as dramatic, every completed cycle which isn't the fourth also serves as a quanta (tick) marker. Through shared mapping onto the natural numbers, this completion of ¼ of a 16th section renders $1/4^{th}$ a single cycle also significant. But a single section brings its own tick in a similar way. Following the divisions then, ¼ of a section also becomes a quantic marker. And unlike the cycle or sections, shrinking subsections like ¼ of ¼ can go on and on forever in the number of divisions they squeeze into a circle. Accordingly, we would count 17 by looking at the first ¼ section after the first section. Every time we chop ¼ into ¼ like this, we essentially add a new digit onto our base 4 counter, turning a cycle of 4 sections into its own number system.

More generally stated, a cycle on N divisions can be used to describe a counting system in units of N^x power by mapping its own regions onto itself.

Indeed, earlier when we finished mapping the set x^{y^z} onto {1, 2, 3,...}, it actually was possible to reverse the mapping by noting that first, 1, then 3, then 6, then 10... combinations exist for each sum in the set {(0,0,0), (0,0,1), (0,1,0), (1,0,0),

(0,0,2), (0,1,1), (0,2,0),...}. Following this pattern, we can determine how far up we'll need to go for each sum we consider, and add a new digit (fractional chop) to whatever base system we have every time the limit is exceed. In our 4 example, we add a new level of division slicing at 4+1, 16+1, 64+1, and 256+1. A 4-division system counts in 4s, 16s, 64s, and so on. A 12 division system would count in 12s, 144s, 1728s, and so on.

On Quantization of the Vacuum

In line with Roberts (2015) I'll argue that "empty space" consists of quantic regions. This is not necessarily an argument that there is actually something in empty space, however. Instead, vacuum space can be thought of as the superposition of several regions into which energy can be passed, where there is a maximum amount of energy that a single region can hold. There is also a minimum size for what can constitute a "region" in a particular dimension. The smallest region containing either the maximum amount of energy for that size or no energy as registered by neighboring regions of the same "size" is what constitutes the smallest quantum possible in the observable universe. Vacuum space may not hold any energy we can measure, but if some energy were to pass through it, there would be a minimum range of effect we would need to look at in order to say that the energy was there. Such a minimum range of effect will help serve as the basis (or length) of our "ultimate quantum" regardless of whether it actually *is* the ultimate quantum (versus just being the smallest level of change our current instruments can measure).

Support for the quantum nature of the universe

The occurrence of the Big Bang suggests a scenario in which a particular collection of energy states exceeded the capacity of the region which contained those states (even if we don't know how many dimensions this region consisted of). As the universe has continued to display properties characteristic of expansion, so too has it undergone a dramatic drop in temperature, trading densely excitable states for more sparsely assembled clusters of energy states with a greater ability to synchronize the bonds between them. What formerly behaved like a really hot, entirely liquid soup has now become lumpy and cold, with chunks of stuff floating in it, but the presence of solid cosmological objects against gaseous or vacuum backgrounds with no gradation in phases at the boundary suggests that we are looking at a system which relies on fixed thresholds for certain macro-level collections of energy to assemble.

Critical energy levels seem to occur throughout the universe with our range of observation, and give hints of an underlying property of nature which holds from the largest stars to the level of the Planck Constant: Energy comes in packets—boundary-equipped states below which changes in the boundary's own stability are not easily compromised unless the energy needed to maintain the boundary is sufficiently diminished, leading to collapse (as when air is let out of a balloon). The other common way of compromising a boundary seems to be putting more energy into the energy carrier than the carrier can hold. Even in cases where gases mingle and seem to form no solid boundaries, we know that 1) this may be the result of the gases possessing energy levels that are too high for the next lowest phase (liquid or gas) and 2) that the molecules constituting those gases—barring some chemical property encouraging them to interact—still retain their initial chemical identities. Here the boundary is retained on the molecular rather than the macroscopic level. Lastly, the theorizing of the universe's ultimate Big Crunch suggests that there will be a level at which our universe itself undergoes a cycle which will lead it back to the conditions preceding the Big Bang. Big Bang to Big Crunch, back to Big Bang. What does it mean? We may guess that it means the universe obeys a cycle in the same way that a regular day does, all the while consisting of subcomponents which occur in stepped energy levels. This activity, if we assume it to be periodic (repeating), can be modeled as a wave. Does this mean that the universe has a smallest unit of energy? Not on its own. But it does suggest that the universe has a maximum amount of energy achievable in the form of peak entropy (energetic disorder). The point at which the universe no longer appears to expand is the point at which a theoretical meter-stick could be used to determine the amount of total energy available per unit volume.[5] Assuming the universe to be a closed system whose components obey consistent physical laws for energy sharing (bonding), that same amount of energy may be assumed present throughout the existence of the universe, giving us a fraction of energy available per unit space. We can also use some

---

[5] Not that we would actually do this. The point is, there will be a maximum volume associated with a set amount of energy, and such measures will not be infinite.

known universal constants and experimental observations to estimate things like the size of the universe and the scale of its associated quanta. That is not the aim of the book, however.

In the coming pages my goal will be to outline a theory for the structure of the universe which explains several as of yet unexplained phenomena which nonetheless seem to obey set patterns in human observation. The scales of things won't matter so much as the basic assumptions applied. The first assumptions revolve around how we represent key concepts.

Using shapes to represent natural phenomena in space

Because they possess certain relational properties among their features, basic shapes are useful for representing certain observables in 2D nature. Below are the shapes we will be using and what their corresponding features will be taken to mean.

Shape	Usage and Formulae (in a flat plane)
Point	A location
Circle	An area of effect about a central point. <u>These are good for representing time-like cycles.</u> **radius** r = range of effect **area** πr^2 = Area of effect associated with the central point **circumference** $2\pi r$ = the approximate number of similar ranges of effect that can be applied just outside of the circular area's reach.
Equilateral Triangle	The most basic shape formed by three points which may affect each other at similar distances. The most basic shape where one point can substitute for another in its effects on a third point, making energy passage easy. **sides** a = the shared ranges of effect that two points have to a third point **height** $\frac{a\sqrt{3}}{2}$ = the distance from a third point to the common axis shared by two others **area** $\frac{a^2\sqrt{3}}{4}$
Equilateral Horn Triangle	The region between maximally packed circular areas of effect which is itself outside of the range of all such specified regions. If the relationship among the circles is stable and there are no other influences, the dynamics inside the horn triangle will be stable. If there is information being passed among the circles, we may guess that the horn triangle will be one of the regions through which that information passage occurs. where r is the radius of each circle: **height** $r\sqrt{3} - r$, **area** $r^2\sqrt{3} - \frac{\pi r^2}{2}$ **ratio of horn triangle to circle** $\frac{\sqrt{3}}{\pi} - \frac{1}{2}$ ~.0513; it takes 19.48 to make a full circle of radius r
Square	The area formed by two orthogonal axes (at right angles to each other). <u>These are good for representing flat spatial regions.</u> **sides** s = axis length **diagonal** $s\sqrt{2}$ = the minimal distance traveled by information which changes one axis into another, independent of the route taken to accomplish this

Table 36-1: Important shapes for representing phenomena in 2D space

Assertion 17. Cycles can be modeled linearly as waves.

The progression of a cycle from start point to end point can be modeled linearly as a wave. This is a basic assertion. We also note that the start point and end point on a cycle are considered the same event, while the moment just before the end point is considered part of the last event before the end of the cycle.

Assertion 18. A quantum may be modeled using a circle which possesses only two possible internal states.
Let us assume that the smallest possible unit of energy that can exist in the universe—the base quantum—has a uniform range of effect on neighbors in all possible directions. We will also assume that all base quanta are the same size (which is not necessarily true, but will suffice for the ideal case). Given that such an energy carrier can only alternate between states of having maximum energy and having no energy, such a quantum may be modeled using a circle in the real-potential/imaginary plane. Because the circle's range of effect is assumed fixed under this model, the real and imaginary axes are not considered independent, but are related to each other such that the magnitude of the quantum's imaginary component is equal to the square root of its [range of effect squared minus its real component squared]. This is just the Pythagorean theorem solved for one leg when the other leg and the hypotenuse are known. There is, however, another axis which is superimposed on the first one, whose real and potential axes are at right angles to the first axes. So the model for the quantum appears to graph in two dimensions, though it actually graphs four (two of which are dependent).

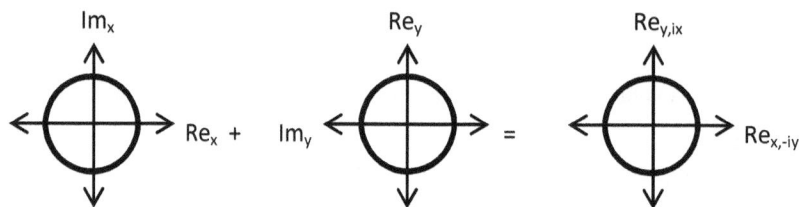

Figure 36-5: x-y axes are a superposition of real and imaginary x with real and imaginary y. For simplicity in the quantum case, we'll assume the quantum to have a radius of 1. Keeping with the right handed order throughout and our knowledge of non-commutativity of multiplication in nature, $Re_y = Im_x$ but $Re_x = Im_{negative\ y}$

That's that. But now the question arises, if the base quantum can only have two states, what is the difference between it having full energy during a regular non-transitioning state and it having full energy just before losing its energy to another quantum? How does it know?

Assertion 19. For any two events marking the start and endpoints of a cycle, 4 is the minimal number divisions for the cycle between them.
Four divisions capture all four critical states of maximum potential energy and minimal potential energy between the two events as well as maximum actual energy "towards" versus maximum energy "away from" each other. These are actually the critical points of the *sin* and *cos* periodic functions and their derivatives.

Regardless of whether **a cycle** exists in space, time, or by process, it **will always have two real states and two potential energy / imaginary states** that it passes through. This **four cycle** exists because an event destined to repeat again, both the start and the end, necessarily yields to a point on the cycle farthest away from the event itself—its complement. If inhalation is an example of such an event, exhalation would be the complement. There will also be boundary states in which neither the real event nor the complement are occurring. Pausing the breath between inhalation and exhalation and pausing it between exhalation and inhalation are two such states. No repeating cycle of any kind is immune to this. Not even the cycle of the universe—which undergoes a Big Bang, expansion, a Big Crunch, and contraction.

Assertion 20. Binary quanta have four states, two of which are observable as energy level, the other two of which are unobservable as potential energy level.
Given the ubiquity of the four-cycle for every cycle, it is useful to consider quanta as having four states: having energy, not having energy, transitioning to having, and transitioning to not having. The transition states, though not observable, are hypothesized to occur at the boundaries of the quantum as the result of differentials between itself and its surroundings. By changing its orientation with respect to those surroundings, the quantum may donate its energy to the purely imaginary axis in a single dimension. This allows it to have energy without appearing to have energy.

Assertion 21. "Observers" are created when a third event responds to a second event in light of a first event. No fewer than three events can form a basis upon which observation takes place.

We'll explain this with a definition. In order to see a thing one must first "see." a thing. The seeing requires an event to be seen. The "thing" is the label or context against which the seen thing is identified. If you have no "thing"-label, you have no "observation" of that which is supposedly observed. Instead we have only response, though there is no distinguishing whether the response was to some first event or the seer's own processing of some first event. The seer itself is the third event. I've explained this in earlier books. In order to identify what is responded to (the object), a responder (the responder) needs a third context (the thing-label) to compare the responded to object against in the first place.

Assertion 22. In order to successfully be observed as having a magnitude at all, an energy packet (the quantum) must exist in at least three dimensions, the third dimension being viewer-scale.

The notion of a potential state (or cycle orientation) brings us back to the earlier assertion that we need three points in order to observe anything. While it is easy to say that a circle has a radius of 1, it is not easy to prove that such a length of "1" actually applies in every reference frame. In order to claim a length of 1, I have to be a certain distance away from the page while having some sense of the lengths of all other things. The moment I fall into the same plane as the circle I've drawn, that length of 1 looks more like a length of infinity to me—stretching out on either side of me as far as the ink dot will project from my field of view. In other words, we can't see an x-y plane unless we ourselves are in a z plane, thus the quantum will need an additional axis which comes out of the paper. We also note that the length of the radius is inversely proportional to our distance from the plane of observation, so there is yet another complementary axis which follows the radius of the circle we've drawn.

R (in page)

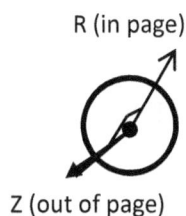

Z (out of page)

Figure 36-6: The z dimension can be thought of as "zoom" (or scale), and allows us to compare the magnitude of energy packets against each other. It is orthogonal to the radial axis.

Assertion 23. A continuous energy signal of reasonably constant character can be modeled using periodic waves, but no fewer than four events are required.

Allowing for the subtraction of noise from other parts of an energetic system, an energy signal, whether or not it is cyclical, can be modeled using periodic functions like sin, cos, and e^{ix}. This is because the observer itself, in order to assert cyclicality, will hold its own cycles against which the observed signal can be mapped. By analogy, though every day is different, I still describe days according to their regimented activities. This has less to do with time and more to do with my own trained behavior. So a daily cycle emerges not because the day is cyclical, but because my physiological & response modes against the days are cyclical. Though not commutative, the reference frame issues in discussed earlier apply here. Without cycles, responses are still possible. Point-comparative observations are also possible, but long-term identities are not possible because the long-term nature of a standing identity label requires the passage of multiple cycles in order to be considered long-term in the first place. In this way, although three events are required to observe an event (against some other event which is evidence of the observed's "thingness," long-term identification of a thing requires four events: the first event, its responder, a context, and a second context unequal to the first against which the first context or label is allowed to be defined as continuous. It is through this fourth dimension that we get the notion of time or its equivalent. A 3-dimensional object-observer-context system cannot change in time (or any other way) unless there is a fourth "context's context" against which successive states of that 3-D system can be compared to each other—allowing the notion of "change" to actually exist.

Assertion 24. The nature of energy establishes the universe as a paradox driven system.
As the Big Bang and Big Crunch scenarios suggest, the universe evolves according to a cycle. But why does it evolve? What is it that makes time go forward?

Where energy is broadly defined as the ability to do work, a scenario similar to the earlier thing-existence system arises: The existence of energy presumes that there exists work to be done. Even at maximum entropy where all of the energy in the universe is (to us) unusable, there remains a paradox stemming from complete disorder. It takes a massive amount of work for me to do *nothing* that my neighbors are doing. No bond sharing, no matched spins, no energy transfers, no patterns of any kind. At the instant of the conditions for a Big Crunch, we can assume that the universe's expansive energy has been exhausted in one direction, but if the entire system is considered closed, and such energy cannot be destroyed, then the work done will have been at its maximum. But how can we have maximum work without the existence of any energy? Thinking of work done as potential energy contained in the history of the system, work becomes another form of energy, and should all the potential orientations in the universe suddenly fall to 0, then the conditions for time itself will have undergone a change in direction, as with the real-imaginary relationship, shifting all of the energy towards the potential axes from their real counterparts. The real worlds' Big Bang is the potential world's Big Crunch and vice-versa as a big bang nearly instantaneously converts potential energy to real energy and, in that same reference frame, a big crunch converts real energy to imaginary energy. Although I have used "potential" and "imaginary" interchangeably up to now, it may be useful to think of the $-i$ orientation as potential (right before real) and the $+i$ orientation as imaginary (right after the real axis and right the before real-complement axis).

We can model this scenario using the following paradox driven system:

> If there is energy, then there is both energy and the potential for work. The logical contrapositive of this is, "If there is not both energy and the potential for work, then there cannot be energy."

> If there is the potential for work, then there is energy.

A system whose potential for work drops to 0, by the first rule, is a system whose energy drops to zero, but our observations of nature and the First Law of Thermodynamics do not support this. While entropy (disorder) may not be the kind of energy which is easily harnessable by organized systems which rely on ordered patterns to stay stable, we may guess that there is at least one system which can make use of entropy: the system characterized by complete disorganization. The potential real universe prior to the Big Bang is an example of such a system. The potential real-complement universe (the one that exists under the Big Crunch) will be another such system, drawing from the total entropy we are feeding into it now.

Assertion 25. Time progresses as the result of span (memory) constraints on the collections of quanta that respond to fixed windows of states within the universe.
Within a space filled with energy carriers, **where certain energy carriers respond to the collective behavior of others** while themselves being responded to as part of a collective, a system of **meta-response** becomes possible. The most basic example of meta-response can be seen in a tightly packed triangular arrangement of equally sized circles where the behavior of the third circle is synchronized distance-wise with the behaviors of the other two. If these circles happen to represent quanta, they can only take on four energetic states (or flops) with respect to the other two and yet, by virtue of being surrounded by still more quanta, are capable of encoding much more through their spin/potential orientation with respect to some "true north" direction (which I'll discuss shortly). Given that a meta-responsive energy carrier can encode the dynamics of its surroundings, but that there are limits on how much it can encode (determined by the radius, # of flops, distances among its own axes, and allowable units of energy transfer), the energy carrier eventually arrives at a state in its oscillatory cycle which represents a 0 degree "reset" point in its encoding. At that reset point, the only thing that is encoded is the state of the system since the last reset, and this system state is passed on to the next responder. Thus old frames are dropped for new ones and a sequence of state animation is born. The ultimate gauge for the amount of data that can be stored by a quantum is the speed of light, for which I will present an estimate shortly. For now we simply note that time

exists for us because, as super-quanta with limits on our own ability to respond to the kinds of events we respond to, we—through a paradox driven system built on "energy therefore not energy"—continually donate (and therefore lose) energy to different windows on the same chain of mutually exclusive combinatorial possibility. These windows have a span which is determined by our particular arrangement of the energy carriers that constitute us. This also applies to nonliving systems which, in their cycles, also have fixed amounts of data around which they may arrange themselves. In some abstract way then, even planets have a memory span as their orbital orientation with respect to their neighbors and internal energy states are reflected in potential energy dynamics with those neighbors which vary from year to year. These are the precessions.

Assertion 26. A quantum's dimension of time can be represented as a function of the angle of orientation between a quantum's directional/global reference point and the neighboring direction with which it exchanges the most energy locally.

When I throw a ball, the ball has two vectors which determine its dynamics against the rest of the frame. Those two vectors are 1) the one pointing to me and 2) the one pointing to the earth. That angle is associated with the ball's ability to continue travelling horizontally away from me so that if I were to throw the same ball at a different angle, its combination of horizontal progress (range of effect) and energy of ground impact (force of effect) would be altered. Note that in this case, the vector pointing to the center of the earth constitutes a kind of true north for the ball. Interestingly, though, there is another "true north" to which the entire system points: the vector pointing to the Sun. I will return to this point later. For now let us add another to axis to our quantum which can be used to indicate its relationship to a comparatively globally fixed 0° mark. This will be the theta axis θ. Regardless of which direction the quantum engages most energetically on a local level, the original source of its energy will always be considered the start point—the point of maximal energy sourcing—for its next localized cycle. As with all of our axes, theta will have an orthogonal (potential energy) counterpart; the perpendicular to θ, $i\theta$ will suffice.

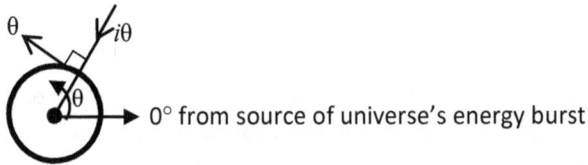

Figure 36-7: Representing cycle angle (phase) as vectors
↖ θ goes this way, tangent to the circle. ↙ $i\theta$ goes this way, along the same path as the radius, but in the opposite direction. Not only does this ensure that a 90° (or × i) rotation stays consistent with the right hand orientation of the rest of the system, but it also explains the balanced trade-off between a particle which expands its radius and one which takes in/encodes more data as a function of its spin direction.

From the above we can see not only how $i\theta$ and r correspond to opposite directions, but where there might be a role for Euler's identity, $e^{i\pi} + 1 = 0$ in the scaling of a completed cycle into the next cycle. Recall that the length of the radius shrinks as our distance from the plane we're observing grows. This magnification relationship changes as $1/x$. Setting a reference scale of magnification at 1, $1 + 1/x$ shows us how much bigger than itself our object would be if we grew it by a factor which needed x number of divisions of the object to match it. This is just one cycle of compounding at a rate $1/x$. So if we chopped our object into 4 equally sized pieces and wanted to grow the object by that much, we would have an object 1 + $1/4$ bigger after doing so. If we did this 4 times to account for each piece's size being multiplied by another $(1 + 1/4)$, we would have an object $(1 + 1/4)^4$ bigger at the end of this. The original object will have been $(1 + 1/4)^{-4}$ smaller by comparison. Extending this infinitely, the $e^x = \lim_{x \to \infty} \left(1 + \frac{1}{x}\right)^x$ = 2.718... That is, we have a case of chopping an object into slices of itself which are infinitely small so that the result, after being adding to the original, needs to be blown up an infinite number of times to reach a completed rescaling. The final object after rescaling this way will be ~2.718 times bigger than the original. Suppose that in addition to chopping the object into infinite pieces, we also compounded the chopping by doing this however many [potential circumferential : range of effect] pieces were required to wrap around the cycle of potential space. We would then have to raise $e^{2\pi i}$. This operation should neither grow nor shrink the object, but restore it to its original value since all we've done is chop the circle up $e^x = \lim_{x \to \infty} \left(1 + \frac{1}{x}\right)^x$ and add it back together by regrowing

its potential all the way around the circumference ($\lim_{x \to \infty} \left(1 + \frac{2\pi i}{x}\right)^x$). So $e^{2\pi i}$ needs to = 1, but $e^{\frac{\pi i}{2}}$ must also turn 1 into

i. So the square root of $e^{2\pi i}$, $e^{\pi i}$ will = -1. For our purposes, zooming away from an object's start point along its own potential-real circumference eventually restores it to its original magnitude. Zooming away from it by a real self-factor x using e^{-x} makes it smaller accordingly.

Assertion 27. The dynamic passage of energy among quanta requires four dimensions: two of planar space (x and y), one of scale space (z), and one of cycle space (θ).

This follows from the above. The scaled axes are interdependent and obey the following relationships: $y = ix$, $x = -iy$, $z = ir$, $r = -\frac{i}{2\pi}\theta$, $x = r\cos\theta$, $y = r\sin\theta$. Of all these dimensions, x and y form a fixed spatial pair with respect to our chosen 0° mark while z and r form a magnitude pair for scaling x and y. θ and $i\theta$ (or $-r$) form a cyclical energy pair for reflecting where the quantum is in its evolution towards the principal spatial axes. At $\theta = 0°$, this system can be reduced to the dimensions x, y, and z whose overlap obscures the ongoing temporal evolution during the rest of the quantic cycle. Why should we use the original Big Bang as the reference point for 0° and not some more local source angle? Because the apparent constancy of the speed of light suggests that the reference frame for the number of allowable states between quanticks is not open to variance across systems.[6]

Assertion 28. On torque

One thing that has confused me since high school was the idea of torque. Why would quickly spinning a top cause it to stand up? Why would spinning a container of liquid cause the liquid to push down? The reasons seem to be the same as the reason that pushing the hour hand of a clock upwards from 3pm to 2pm also causes the end of hand to move inward. With orthogonal axes, decreasing the real energy on one axis increases the potential version of that energy along the next axis 90° later. As long as the spatial radius in an x-y plane is held constant, shrinking the x projection grows the y projection. Since $z = ir$ and $r = -\frac{i}{2\pi}\theta$, as long as the radial vector r is held constant, growing z projection grows shrinks the r projection. But now what about θ? If θ is constantly turning, increasing in magnitude in the direction of the next degree, but if r is held constant and $i\theta$ *isn't allowed* to shrink spatially with θ's tangential growth, then the scale of $i\theta$'s energetic contribution must shrink as the scale of z's energetic contribution must grow. That is, if we imagine the surface of the spinning liquid to be a landscape full of quanta, spinning the entire collection (rendering it a super quantum) creates a situation where the water surface "wants" to expand but can't because of the container. The spinning top wants to disintegrate but can't because of the molecular bonds holding it together. So rather than growing spatially, the z-r axis (which is married by means of $r = -\frac{i}{2\pi}\theta$ to the θ-$i\theta$ axis) grows in energetic scale—the individual quantic surface constituting it—rather than being made up of liquid molecules doing their own thing (compared to a solid)—temporarily has the energy shared among its quanta "locked" internally where a particle at radius r has to lose more of its independence from a particle at $r+1$. This gives us a "single super particle" with a bigger effective radius and twice the energy to share <u>in the same direction</u>. We can thus expect this higher scale quantic energy to push outward and upward along the z-r plane. If the structure of whatever we're spinning won't allow its contents to fly apart, those contents will either push outwards within the object's bounds or draw inward outside the object's bounds.

---

[6] This assumption may be unnecessary. An alternative explanation for quanta obeying a known reference phase may be that the quanta themselves hold some internal value which determines some kind of maximum energy—like a compass direction. The later chapter on city cultures suggests that the largely human-imposed timezones of the Earth work something like this. I haven't assumed such an internal compass here though because, as we'll see, that would imply that pre-quantic energy is of greater importance than the whole idea of quanta (as not allowing pre-energetic coherence) might suggest.

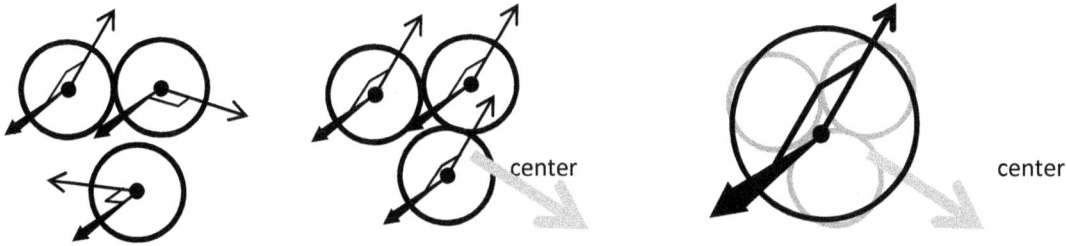

Independent points on the cycle when quanta aren't being moved together

Once quanta are forced to respond to the same orientation, their former responses to each other are aggregated. (These sample quanta are located some distance away from the center of the spinning group which contains them.)

The quanta now act like a collective, since the energy they would have exchanged independently are now exchanged with the perimeter. The above shows what happens inside a super quantum's bounds: pushing outwards in conservation of what we will later describe as the "intervening space" required for stable bond exchange. This same phenomenon predicts, for example, that if our solar system weren't spinning, not only would it be more spherical internally but the contents of the Oort Cloud would be less concentrated at the shell and hold more of an inward gradient inside the system's shell.

Figure 36-8: Quantic coupling to form super quanta

Assertion 29. In order to successfully trade energy, quanta need other quanta, along with an intervening space

Suppose we have two quanta, one possessing energy and another not. How do they trade energy? Assuming that energy will travel between them, we must assume some dimension—potential or real, ambient spatial or intervening quantum—that will serve as the medium. Although our earlier model depicted a single fundamental energy carrier using four dimensions, this did not take into account any mechanism for transferring energy beyond the carrier. In order to build the capacity to transfer energy into our model, we will need more dimensions. Why? There are several reasons:

1. Scale has no meaning without comparators
2. Nature suggests at least four levels of quantic action: strong nuclear, weak nuclear, electromagnetic, and gravitational. These levels seem to coexist without necessarily overriding each other's role, suggesting at least one other scale dimension which allows these levels to resist talking to each other.
3. Even if energy could just disappear from one quantum and reappear in another, our current model has no dimension for explaining what causes this or where that energy would go when our quantic range of effect drops from say, 1 unit in at least one dimension to 0 units in every dimension. Up to now, our energy was always located *somewhere*.

While we could simply add a second quantum to the picture, we immediately run into a problem.

If we select a random "tiniest" region of space and call it a quantum, representing it as a range of effect about a point, we'll get a circle. Let a second quantum also be a circle. When we fill up a space with these circles, we either get an equal number of horn triangles which don't belong to any quanta, or we get an exceptionally complicated system of overlapping quanta with various oddly shaped regions of instability, some of which put more than their share of quantic energy into the same region. We could fix this by simply limiting the amount of quantic energy available to any compound quantic region. But if we're ready to go through all that trouble, why not just stick with the horn triangle scenario? (At least that would allow us to keep all of the fundamental packets separate and tightly arranged.) Maybe circles are the wrong shape. Perhaps quanta can be modeled as squares, triangles, or hexagons, but not only does nature not suggest these shapes for most fundamental aggregations of energy, they are simply uneven in the areas affect about their centers. Even hexagons and squares. Why should a quantum be expected to have a range of effect of $\sqrt{2}$ along one orientation but only a range of 1 along some other orientation? Barring the influence of non-ideal neighbors which stretch ranges of effect into ellipses, modeling quanta as circles makes more sense. And so we prepare to accept the presence of intervening space between quanta.

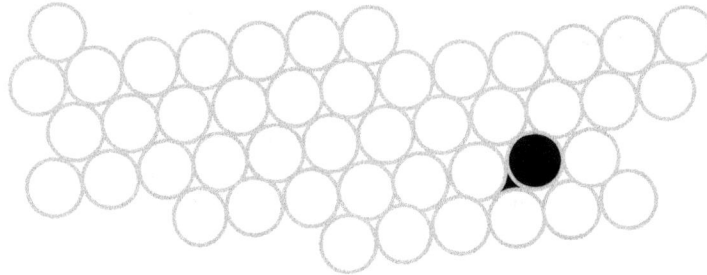

Figure 36-9: Idealized quantum packing

The above represents an idealized model for packing quanta in cycle-space. Here we are more concerned with each quantum's θ relationship between the universe's energetic source and the direction from which it most actively receives local energy. From here on, though, we'll need to consider a horn triangle as part of each quantum unit. There is one for every circular area of quantic effect. Fortunately, the horn triangle is the perfect intervening space for passing energy to any of 6 or 12 of a quantum's neighbors. For consistency we won't allow these shapes to carry any density of energy higher than their circular partners. Since our model will set the energy contained in a quantum equal to π (the area of each idealized circle given a range of effect $r = 1$), the maximum energy within any horn triangle will be $\sqrt{3} - \frac{\pi}{2}$. This is ~.1613. Even better for us is the idea that these shapes are naturally uneven, so there is no reason to restrict them to the binary (π or 0) rules applied to our circles.

For brevity, I'll indicate the energy of a fundamental quantum using О (Cyrillic round omega) and the maximum energy of the horn triangle associated with it using $\Delta_О$. ("delta omega"). For the purposes of modeling, these energies will just be equal to their areas.

As nature clearly illustrates, it is possible to pass energy through a medium which is not already maximally dense with potential. We may also assume that it is not possible to contain more than the quantic maximum energy in a region the size of a quantum. Even the quanta inside of a black hole can only contain so much energy. It is true that space is subject to curvature, but that doesn't mean that it can curve infinitely so as to render any of its points an endless vacuum. Here we question the idea that black holes can fall into actual infinity, since even the Big Bang suggests there is a bottom limit to how deep an energy hole can go. It has to get back out somehow. Because the energy passing between quanta likely pass through regions not at their limit, and especially because there is no reason to believe that any circle we choose to denote our quantum is any more special than a similar circle scooted over by a hair, we may assume that in a maximally packed quantic region full of circles, we will need about 19.48 units' worth of $\Delta_О$s per О in order for passage to happen (calculated earlier). These $\Delta_О$s don't have to occur in perfect arrangement with their corresponding Оs, but can occur as the empty space surrounding a maximally dense packet.

In order for one of the circles to pass energy to another circle which registers it, the inner $\Delta_О$ plus an additional 18.48 $\Delta_О$ units of the surrounding area (at a minimum) must temporarily hold the passing energy. Doesn't this defeat the "quantum" in quantum mechanics if you can have regions which don't have binary values? I actually think it threatens to. For this reason, we will use the next assertion to redefine a spatial equivalent of the Δ_o as the actual lowest practical, quasi-energetic region possible. We'll call such a spatial division a "quantic block." We'll also see that it does *not* replace the quantum as the smallest unit of energy.

Assertion 30. The components of quantic cycle energy can be remapped spatially onto quantic blocks.
In the same way that an atom is the smallest form of an element which still retains the properties of that element while atoms themselves can still be divided into protons, neutrons, and electrons, we can consider the quantum to be the lowest form of energy which still retains the properties of energy while quanta themselves can still be divided into spatial units—theoretically at least. Suppose for example that we build an ultra microscope and finally measure a quantum region to be about 2×10^{-35} meters long. There's nothing stopping us from doing math using grids 1×10^{-44} meters long. Our instruments may never register anything beyond noisy nothingness on this level, but we may still—for whatever reason—decide that 1×10^{-44} meters makes some kind of geometric sense for working with quanta. Perhaps as a way of calculating the percentage of a cycle spent on a single flop state, for example. Similarly, if we think of a quantum as a kind of closed loop rope possessing a wavy character, we can think of the space between quanta as a soup of "ropelettes" or pre rope-like molecules possessing nothing but fragmentary volume; we'll need about 19 or 20 of these volumes to make a rope in our model, but by themselves they won't prefer any particular cycle, direction, or energy level which can be separated from the noisy volumes within the measuring instrument itself. These volumetric (potential carrying) regions are can be thought of as ubiquitous throughout space, but have no temporal or spatial meaning unless pooled together into a quantum. They're just a superfluid sea of potential representing the maximum allowable jitter should any energy ever pass through. If quanta are like clocks, quantic blocks are like pulsating partial cookie cutters for clock slices. The latter have no registerable meaning unless brought together into the shape of a clock—at which point they possess either 1 unit of energy or no units of energy for knocking around their neighbors in a regulated fashion.

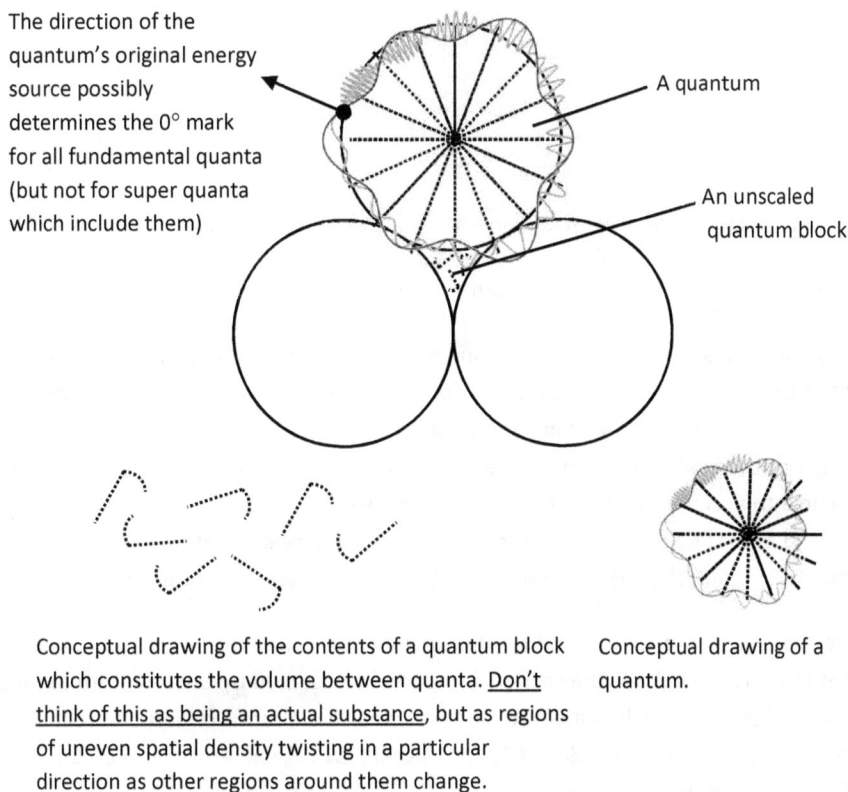

The direction of the quantum's original energy source possibly determines the 0° mark for all fundamental quanta (but not for super quanta which include them)

A quantum

An unscaled quantum block

Conceptual drawing of the contents of a quantum block which constitutes the volume between quanta. <u>Don't think of this as being an actual substance</u>, but as regions of uneven spatial density twisting in a particular direction as other regions around them change.

Conceptual drawing of a quantum.

Figure 36-10: Conceptual depiction of a quantic unit (a quantum plus its block)

There are several things to note about the drawings above.

About the quantic block drawing

The dotted lines indicate pulsating energy flow, possibly determined by flux from the original universal energy explosion plus any local emitters in the region.

About the quantum drawing

Notice the outside of the quantum is not dotted. This is my way of indicating that the disorganized, pulsating pre-energy of quantic block contents display coordinated interference in order to produce a boundary which obeys a coherent cycle. Notice also that the frequency around the boundary changes as we move around the circle. This illustrates the definite role of spin orientation not just for small quanta but for megaquanta like planets and galaxies. In order for block contents to mean almost nothing while quanta do have meaning, there has to be some way in which block contents come together to join their noisy ends in a differentiated, yet recursive fashion.

In order to explain what makes the contents of a disorganized quantum block "want" to stick together, I propose that quantic regions naturally form at the first stable radius beyond existing concentrations of energy, having their pulses synchronized via the regular flux from that region. I will explain this later.

Quantum blocks can be mapped as squares

Since Δ_0 is just an area, we can take its square root and use the value we get (.4015) as the sides of a square. These scaled quantic blocks form a good grid for keeping track of how many pieces of "pre-energy" we need to form a whole quantum. They also reveal an interesting and unexpected error term: .0078.

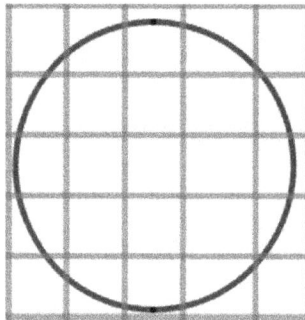

Figure 36-11: Quantic cycle space superimposed on a spatial space grid. This shows how much spatial space a full cycle would require to have all of its energy transferred at once while still allowing the other quanta to which it's transferring to hold only binary values.

Since each square has the same area as the normal horn triangle, it takes 19.48 squares to form a quantum. Whether you can actually have 19.48 of these is question I have no answer for, since this is like asking whether you consider a proton to be more "fundamental" to the hydrogen atom of which it is a part. Maybe yes, but it depends on whether we care more about measuring pre-energetic potential or actual passable energy as fundamental. I imagine that as our knowledge of physics improves and we come to accept more than four dimensions, we'll get a better sense of what such pre-energetic regions actually consist of, and at that point we will consider them to be the real quanta. Until then, we will resolve to file these under a list of mathematical tools (like π) which don't possess a reality we can empirically measure with perfection.

When we attempt to place the cycle representation of a quantum into the spatial representation of a grid, we require a 5 x 5 grid of squares with sides of .4015 each. Even the corners are partially occupied by the quantum as modeled circularly, so we cannot cut them out of the diagram. Recall that we set the radius for the quantic region of effect at 1, so it has a diameter of 2. The total 5 x 5 grid, however, has sides of 2.0078, leaving us with an error term of .0078. Perhaps this was just coincidence, or maybe it was luck that this error term not only allows us room to accurately calculate the speed of light, but it also forces us to reintroduce the idea that the quantum's boundaries are probably not perfectly circular, but wavy. So we should expect such an error term. A proper calculation of one guess for the speed of light's origin requires the number

2.01097, which falls within the allowable distance between the centers of two quanta contained in their respective grids: 2.0078 x 2 – 2 (where we subtracted the portions of each quantum's $r = 1$ radius backed against their respective walls.

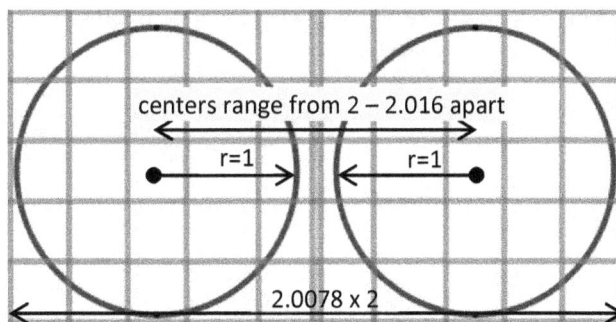

Figure 36-12: Two quanta in their spatial grids. Note that they don't have to touch.
Realistically, quanta probably have wavy boundaries instead of perfectly circular ones.

Assertion 31. 12 is the minimal number of stable divisions for a circle whose divisions reference other divisions within that same circle.

An earlier asserion stated that we needed four events in order to identify anything among a group of changing events. Any fewer and it becomes impossible for 1) an event to happen, 2) that event to be responded to, 3) that response to be observed against a context and 4) for that context to be stable enough across another context to be considered a "label" or identity for what was seen. In math, working with time slices without time is like working with Dirac deltas without summations: we'd only end up with infinitely thin glimpses of nothing. That is, if not for an extra, animating dimension. In the math section, I showed that cycles can chop themselves up into the same number of subdivisions as there are divisions in the main circle, but I didn't talk about how one element in such a bounded circular set can respond to another in the same set. That gets us into the realm of relationships within the cycle.

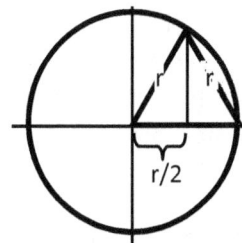

If a cycle is to represent not only its own divisions, but relationships among those divisions, the easiest thing we can do is set one of the elements as the center of the circle and look at points on the circumference which illustrate relationships between an element on the circumference and the location in the center. As far as quanta are concerned, the best place to do this is at the halfway points along each axis. Given a radius of r, points which place us at $r/2$ for any of the four axis directions will essentially show us where the central element and the circumference element are perfectly positioned to send and receive the same kinds of input from a central observer at the same time.

Trigonometrically speaking, 12 is the lowest number that allows us to land at all 8 kinds of axial halfway points around the circle. Although you might think that there were only four halfway points along the four axis directions, remember that the outside region is a circle. Halfway *up* quadrant I is not the same perimeter point as halfway *over* in quadrant I. Instead, each quadrant has one halfway projection onto the real axis, and one onto the imaginary axis for a circle graphed in the Real-Imaginary plane. Although we don't normally think of such halfway points as being necessary for describing two events in periodic interaction with each other, it's not the event's we're concerned about, it's the observer at their midpoint.

Imagine being an observer halfway between a ball at the peak of its height at 20' and the hand that threw it straight up from a height of 0'. Imagine also that you live in a flat world on a piece of paper (otherwise this analogy doesn't work). What's your best vantage point if you're stuck on a circle of radius 20? If you said 10' up on either side, you're right. That's 30° above the axis on either side. Now suppose it's not a ball, but a yo-yo dipped 20' below the person. The best vantage point for you who are stuck on a circle of radius 20'—one which puts you right between the person at 0' and the yo-yo at -20'—would be -10' on either side (30° below the axis on either side). Now imagine another ball being tossed sideways from left to right. At the time the ball reached its peak 20' to the right of the thrower, what would be the best place for you to stand to measure its sideways progress? 10' to the right of the thrower, correct? From above or below on your circle, this is

60° above or below the axis. The same holds for the other direction: 60° above or below the axis on the left. All in all there are eight vantage points like this which are trigonometrically favorable which, when considered with the original four axes, makes the 12 cycle ideal for using a circle to map sets whose elements relate to other elements in that same set—where the second element is considered to have a resting energy of 0.

Assertion 32. Quanta are stable in their possible energies, unstable in their energy trading.

Regardless of how we model quanta, there is no shape which a quantum can have which is 1) even in its surrounding range of effect, 2) constant and rational in the ratio of its perimeter to its range of effect, and 3) capable of filling a space completely with copies of itself alone. That is, the geometric properties of a quantum's range, perimeter, and contained energy are, in at least one quality, irrational compared to the others. Accordingly, if we have any of these properties which responds to the others either in themselves or other quanta, that property will either respond irrationally or cause the comparison property to adopt an irrational value. For example, if the radius of a circle is rational, its energy (area in our model) will be irrational; if that circle represents a quantum which cannot have irrational values, the quantum will gain or lose energy in its interaction with surrounding rational-energy quanta. If the perimeter of a circular quantum is rational in that it is surrounded by six other quanta in a densely packed setting, then its rationally valued circumference at 6 will, through division by π, definitely yield an irrational radius and, sometimes (if the energy is nonzero for example), an irrational energy. So the quantum will gain or lose energy there as well. All of this is to say that the geometric properties of quanta promote constant energy trading either 1) forever, 2) until no more energy can be traded and all the entire system plateaus in its evolution, or 3) until a certain global least common multiple among geometry-relevant numbers like π, $\sqrt{2}$, or $\sqrt{3}$ is found to a degree of precision minimally relevant to the quantic scale.

In my model, as quanta are encouraged to trade energy constantly by virtue of their rational-irrational geometries, they are also encouraged to form trading units with other quanta in the same way that quantic blocks are encouraged to form quanta. The number of surrounding quanta in a trading unit will be a function of its geometric stability. Namely, this will be the number of quanta required to assign an associated trade partner for every major point along its real-potential axis cycle.

Assertion 33. A quantic exchange unit can be modeled using 12 quanta surrounding a central quantum.

If pre-energetic quantic blocks are encouraged to assemble through resonance with each other (thanks to period-specific flux from the emission source from whence they came), then single quanta are similarly predisposed to gather together into minimally coherent groups. The natural arrangement of circles around a circle—all of the same size—is six, a hexagon.

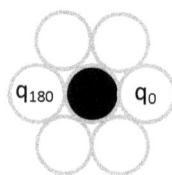

Figure 36-13: A hexagonal arrangement of quanta

The hexagon model for an exchange unit above is especially good for modeling when a central quantum O is inclined to exchange with another in its "true north" direction. By setting q_0 as the 0° mark in the direction of the Big Bang origin, for example, and q_{180} as the 180° mark away from it, we can keep track of two major directional orientations for O. The remaining four quanta would, as discussed earlier, represent points of geometric similarity for the O's relationship to these axial points as well as serving to divide the net range of effect between these quanta in half—allowing the bodies at 60°, 120°, and so on to exchange with O on the basis of its own cycle properties. One thing is missing from this model, however. There are no quanta for processing O's state of complete potential energy with respect to the 0°-180° axis. In the hexagon model, there are no neighbors designated to capture O's 90° and 270° states. So we need to introduce six more neighbors.

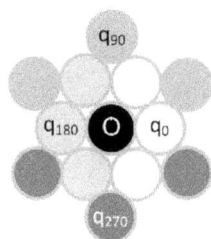

Figure 36-14: A snowflake arrangement of quanta. All neighbors go through their fundamental flop cycles at the same rate with respect to other neighbors, but all of the surrounding neighbors need to finish their independent, non-coupled cycles before the central quantum counts a tick and resets to its original relationship with them. So no, you don't have 12 different kinds of neighbors. Your neighbors are all like you. You do, however, have 12 different collections of cycling to reconcile before you can return to your beginning.

The snowflake model above assigns a quantum exchange partner for every geometrically stable energy state along a quantum's oscillation cycle: the pure potential dimensions and their cyclical dividers as well as the pure real dimensions and their cyclical dividers. This system includes 12 horn triangles on its interior and, minimally, 12 half horn triangles on its exterior which could just as easily be extended indefinitely into space.

It should be noted that the model above does not necessarily place quanta in a 2D plane. Because it represents cycle space, the above can just as easily be applied to a single period sine wave divided into 12ths, a 3D axis collapsed projected onto a plane using two 60° turns, or even a graded line whose body represents a flattened cosine wave. The idea is that every trigonometrically stable point in one quantum's cycle has another quantum which corresponds to it. The 3D case is particularly interesting because it shows how q_{270} is not necessarily "farther away" from O than q_0 is.

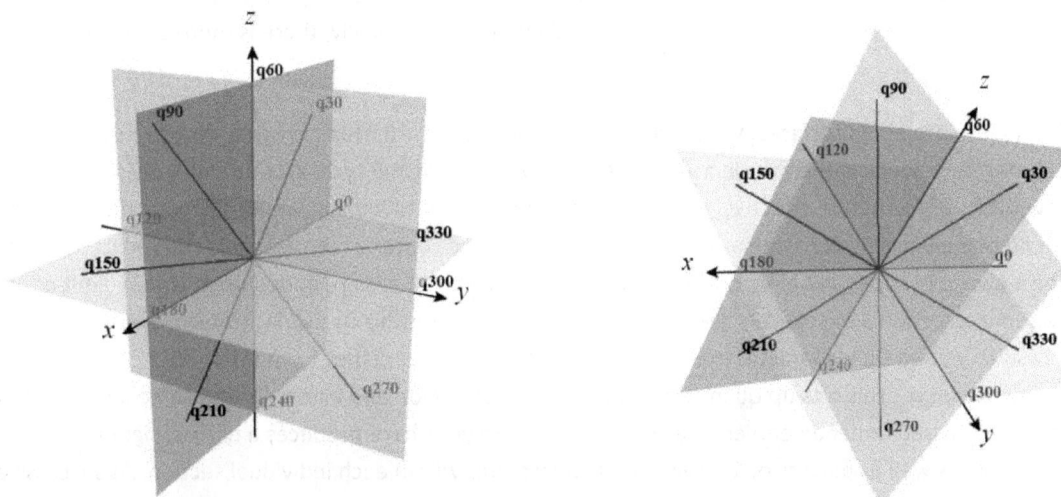

3D Space. For an arrangement of points which produces the next image (the flattened view to the left of this one), you may notice that the 90° points from each main axis exist entirely in a different plane. For example, along the 0°-180° axis, 90° and 270° are in the plane which 0° and 180°'s line is not in. The same goes for 150° and 330°. They are located in a plane which does not include 60° and 240°. I think this is a good illustration of being in an imaginary dimension IF you use the axes conducive to the next image...→

Flattened view after two 60° turns of the view to the right. Note how it makes a counterclockwise circle. The snowflake shape can be used to model this.

(Images like this created using http://web.monroecc.edu/manila/webfiles/pseeb urger/CalcPlot3D/)

Figure 36-15: A 3D view can be easily flattened by simply "moving the camera" around it.

Why should we stop at 12 quanta? Why not 13, 18 or even more? In a maximally dense, idealized model, however, adding a 13th quantum to the picture gives us something like this:

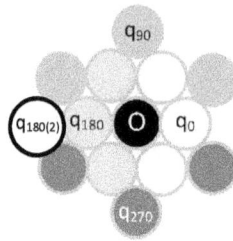

Figure 36-16: Adding a 13th quantum to the snowflake model doesn't do much geometrically, since the first 12 get in the way. Besides, even if you did have more than 12 neighbors (which surely you do in the actual 3D+ cases), the number of flops goes up, and key values like the fine structure and charge constants are no longer optima. 12 is the geometric minimum for covering all major phase orientations among the four possible potential-real dimensions.

Here, most of O's resonance with $q_{180(2)}$'s state is already captured by q_{180}. When the quanta are not maximally packed then this is less of a problem, but the energy density of the whole system will also be lower, so that any extremum values we attempt to calculate such as the Planck length or the duration of a chronon will not actually be extrema. The best we can do then is to ignore any quanta outside of the snowflake...with the understanding that we'll need at least 1.48 more Δ_Os worth of quantic blocks in order to truly pass energy from the central quantum without losing it to another dimension outside of the model (after we add the 12 half-Δ_Os at the perimeter).

An energy-efficient flattening of a 3-axis system to a 2-axis system is a pair of 60° turns about the global y-axis, then x-axis

This claim is extra, but may be useful for mapping certain 3D volumes onto 2D surfaces: a pair of 60° transformations reduces the projected radius of a unit sphere by 50% while preserving the total projected surface area of the planes outlined by the 2 x 2 planes circumscribing the projected unit circle. (Basically, there is more color overlap in the right image in *Figure 36-15*.)

Redistributing the projected surfaces, we double the radius of the new flattened region. Notice how this rotation produces a natural order for traversing the axes in a way that preserves the original cycle around the 4-division circle. We'll also notice how this transformation effectively pushes everything down into a plane while still maintaining a distance between observer and plane which is the same as the distance between the center of the axes and the radius. Both these radii as well as the viewer distance can be expected to expand as successive shells are added on at the 2π limit of each previous shell. The same assertion also suggests a natural base system of 12 for this particular transformation. In that base system of 12, the divisions gained their character from whatever combinations of planes from the former 3D axes were projected onto the new 2D space. This sets up quantic boundaries for each region and allows for the same kinds of element-to-self mapping also discussed under an earlier assertion. Having 12 regions here produces a natural significance for 12 cycles around the circle as well as powers of 12 divisions of subsections within each individual section. As successive shells are added and successive radii double, we arrive at a system which reaches a quantic marker at 12 shells or $2^{12}r$ where r is the radius of the first shell beyond the central axes. Although there can certainly be more or fewer than 12 shells in a real world system, 12, 3, and 4 are particularly significant for reasons related to the flux passing through whatever source is represented by the central axes, and we might not be surprised if the system attempted to "capture" other bodies or pull existing ones in to make up for a deficit, or pushed bodies further out to compensate for extra shells with insufficient material in them.

The posited existence of quantic units has implications for attraction and repulsion. But first I'll summarize the major claims of the model so far.

Assertion 34. The universe consists of fundamental, organizable quantic regions described by the oscillatory environment that characterizes them.

Beginning with a scenario where one $\natural$-dimensional "space" of existence undergoes no cycles and another, i-dimensional potential space of existence comprises completely random energy cycles, at the peak of the latter's random energy there is,

paradoxically, no more work to be done in that space. For a system which is all energy with no potential to do work can't have its energy be considered energy. Through the ongoing reconciliation of rational properties among its components with irrational properties (modeled here via geometry), the space with the energy continues to have its 100% energy components seek new arrangements past the point where further arrangements will only decrease entropy. The i-space uses "unusable" energy and thus does something akin to "unwork" on the system which is not it—it's potential space ℏ. In ℏ-space a Big Bang occurs in light of i-space's Big Crunch. Time also begins for ℏ-space as the paradox driven systems of ["energy = energy + work"] and ["irrational geometry = rational + irrational energy and geometry"] promote ongoing, recursive energy exchange with respect to the fundamental energy carriers' own previous states while those states are simultaneously "forgotten"—replaced by the states they gave rise to. Time will continue in ℏ-space until all oscillatory energy is lost, yet the loss of such energy does not mean loss of the density gradient among energy exchangers that preceded this, so the system will continue to evolve despite having no registerable energy to do so. If a quantum should break into incoherence, the resonances that held it together should cease doing so according to this theory. But what kind of energy turns resonance into dissonance in this way? (I assume that it takes work to break a quantum packet already in resonance among its angular regions, even if that work is a simply failure to resonate any longer, and so potential space gains where real space loses, and the cycle heads back to where it began.)

Quanta can be modeled as circles with ranges of effect that are their radii, but when we do this we find that regions not covered by the circles remain. These regions can be remapped as squares and used to model quanta in space. They are also useful for storing the pre-energy that passes among quanta. Pre-energy is different from energy in that, being a property of oscillatory patterns across non-quantic regions, it permeates even the tools used to measure it. But it's not ether. It's not an object. It's a characteristic dynamic among objects which it shows up as a function of some natural relationship to the source from which it originated. I've modeled this relationship as a geometric one involving circular neighbors. Pre-energy takes the form it does because there is a maximum amount of change that a system can undergo before it is no longer considered changing. No change is no change. Total change (without an unchanging reference) is also no change. So pre-energy may be better framed as a characteristic potential-change gradient typical of a region. When a subregion of that gradient develops a characteristic oscillation pattern with respect to other neighboring regions, that oscillating section of gradient is called a quantum. The range of effect of a quantum is $\frac{1}{\pi} \times$ its area of effect in this model, but more generally (as a boundary) can be expected to have a square root relationship to the energy when considered in a real-potential single plane. The boundary of a quantum must also be described by a wave function that wraps a previous cycle of itself into the next component of its own cycle. There is a zoom/scale relationship involved here which not only introduces a third dimension for observing and a fourth dimension for time, but also marries those dimensions to each other via various orthogonality relationships including $z = ir$ and $r = -\frac{i}{2\pi}\theta$.

Although it is both possible and likely that real energy is frequently converted to potential energy and back, (just lifting and dropping a ball accomplishes this,) it is unlikely that a quantic system will make use of potential dimensions every time it needs to pass energy. In order to stay in a preferred, real plane, a quantum will need neighbors for passing energy across a space of one or two dimensions, and for this purpose we looked at a snowflake model as a way of allocating the relevant quantic neighbors for each of the four real-potential axis states associated with a particular quantum oriented in a particular direction. I add here that, because there is a "true north" associated with every fundamental O, there is also a preferred axis and a preferred plane not just for every quantum, but for every quantic exchange group to sit in. I propose that Os prefer to turn towards "true north" while *collections* of quanta—super- and megaquanta—turn towards "local north:" the direction of the energy source which sponsored their aggregation. The next preferred axis after this one will be the axis perpendicular to this north but which more or less shares a close radial position away from it. The least preferred axis will be the one which changes the range of effect (or radius) of the north source. A good example of this can be seen in human movements on the Earth. We automatically fix our altitude in concert with gravity—a vector pointing to our local "true north" of the Earth's center; it is from here that our freedom of movement is measured. We first prefer to move sideways, longitudinal eastwards-westwards in equatorial regions we know. Less frequently do we change latitude, because the change in (climate) energy is higher for doing so. Lastly, given a fixed local altitude, crouching and jumping—flying and digging to change that altitude from ground level—is much harder. Thus the natural axis order is, starting at ground level, 1) longitude, 2) latitude, and 3) height with respect to the ground. Similarly, atomic orbitals also have preferred orientations, which the snowflake models' neighbor-geometry and 3D analog can be used to approximate. Also similarly, our planets love their native elliptical orbits first (preferring not to change them), their circumferential movements next (preserving potential energy from the central emitter), their declinations third (typically changing these a lot less, and only to balance movement along the isoshells of the ecliptic), and finally their eccentricity (which—often in response to major events or inherent instability—takes a much longer time to drift in value). Thus the natural axis order is, starting at their favored ellipse level, 1) circumferentially, 2) declination-wise, and 3) eccentricity with respect to the favored ellipse.

There are some occasions where the four dimensions proposed reveal non-standard effects, the most salient being the phenomenon of torque. When a system of quanta would like to remain independent among its carriers but has those carriers forced to respond to an artificial north which runs counter to their basic orientation, the resonances among those carriers are coupled together in the direction of their angular velocity and the various vectors describing their associated dimensions are increased in scale along with the that of the net directionality applied to their cycles. Inside of a constrained object the now superquanta are equipped to resonate with states farther beyond the shell that constrains them, and push outward on that shell along the plane where they are spinning and downward into its center as the z-dimension increases with increasing $i\theta$. Outside of a constrained system, the neighboring quantic regions are drawn to the spinning quanta, pushing inward along the circumference of spin. Meanwhile the object is tilted upward as the z dimension, again, increases.[7] In general, megaquanta might be thought of as seeking neighbors on their own scale, which informs us partially of the workings of gravity.

Assertion 35. Quantic distances are maintained through a combination of required intervening space and paradox driven resonance affinity.

Let us begin this section with a basic analogy. Although nearly all humans are inclined to form willing relationships with someone somewhere, almost no humans will stand for being constantly followed by the people they bond with—having their every step dogged by some person who won't even let them go to the bathroom in peace. We form relationships not shadowships. Similarly, objects equipped with a range of effect tend to have that entire range to themselves, lest they cease to be themselves and become part of some aggregate. Ceaselessly trading with their neighbors as they transition back and forth from whole-valued energy—frequencies against the frequencies of their neighbors—to whole valued perimeters of effect—whole-period wavelengths on their own cycles—they undergo a number of transitions with their neighbors required to reset them (approximately) to where they began. In doing this, they remain about two radii away from their nearest neighbors, exchange with each neighbor via a different frequency with respect to north, do so in a specific direction (clockwise or counterclockwise), but prefer not to get closer than two radii unless a boundary of other quanta outside of their neighborhood has formed which keeps them closer than they would prefer to be. Although the model at this point might allow energy to be exchanged through some other dimension not represented by geometries used so far, I argue that we should not do this. By asserting that the quanta prefer to exchange energy within the plane formed by the two axes of lowest energy away from north, we gain an explanation of quantic, atomic, and planetary shell formation, characteristic chemical properties, the speed of light, and gravity. I will address these in order.

Rather than considering the universe to be a matrix of space filling quanta, or considering it to be some other version of a homogeneous field, we consider the universe to be an inhomogenous mixture of relative oscillatory characteristics

---

[7] Earlier I said the super quantum pushes outward from inside the object. Now it sounds like I said that the circumference still pushes outward, but the normal to that circumference pushes *downward* inside the object. Which is it? Actually, the Z of the internal system does push outwards, getting generally larger. A consequence of this is that it also runs into the shell boundary at the top of the spin, so the growing arrow doesn't grow its arrow tip beyond the object, but grows its arrow base into the object's center. If there is a liquid there, the liquid in the center is pushed down as a result. That's my theory. It doesn't matter whether the liquid or substance of the object is uncovered. If the object is circumferentially bounded and doesn't want to be (by virtue of its artificially imposed coupling), a wannabe torus will result at the edges.

arranged first and foremost against an original burst source, inhomogeneous in that certain regions of effect spontaneously develop oscillatory characteristics of their own with respect to their surroundings, within a self-reinforcing perimeter determined by the full range of irrational modes between flux pulses from that original burst source. Meanwhile, the intervening blocks between such patterned oscillatory regions do not obey any regular energy transfer cycles that can be measured on the level being considered. (We'll get back to that though, because this point is related to gravity.)

A side note on frequency mapping

The above explanation, by the way, suggests that the snowflake model really should be linearized for our traditional field models to apply. That is, instead of treating the quantic 12 neighbors as circles in a 2D plane, we should scrunch them into a cosine wave, give the cosine wave different magnitudes as a function of the angle away from north, flatten it, then use the resulting lines as axes on a square grid. This is similar to the way we display color wheels.

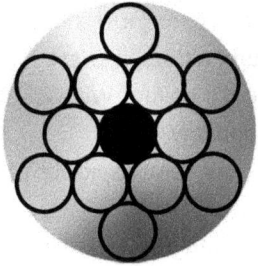

If we begin with a representation of a central quantum in frequency space with respect to its neighbors...

...we can flatten that frequency space to describe the quantum's frequency in two spatial spaces, allowing us to account for spatio-temporal curvature (if we're dealing with an elongated elliptical exchange pattern). For example, a red frequency along one axis might, under curvature, map to a red-orange one when both the x and y axes are normalized to a length of 1).

Figure 36-17: A color representation of a quantic neighborhood

There are other uses for the flattening of frequency space. We could use a grid of these to describe the changes in such curvature over space. Finally, we can also use these axes as the background for decribing generalized wave interactions. As a statistical astrologer I am interested in how 2^5-resonant bodies like the Sun interact with 2^{10}-resonant bodies like Saturn, but I could just as easily map all forward inconjuncts (+150° differences) using a wraparound line of slope $-\frac{12}{5}$ to look for broader behavioral patterns if they applied; this way I could ask what Sun-Saturn, Mercury-Uranus, and Venus-Neptune had in common for example.[8] Division of the above grid into thirds allows us to see trines. Divisions in to fourths allows us to see squares.[9]

---

[8] The answer: They all statistically broadly correspond to "envisioning" behaviors, which is typical of the inconjunct. If I had had a way to do this while writing *FSA* and *HBS* it would have been much easier than eyeballing Excel tables for months. Unfortunately, the technology for the actual energies of planets—knowing where the Sun actually sits in a space like this—didn't exist until recently. I provide a formula which I derived for it later in this book. With that formula, we can apply the regular statistics of variance and standard deviation alongside various social and psychology instruments (especially EEG and fMRI) to test astrological claims and their associated implications for aspects of experience previously thought immeasurable. The way behaviorists once thought emotions were immeasurable. Astrology can't be reliably tested without proper data-analytic tools. Statistics on orbits combined with known personality measures, I think, will be critical for this effort.

[9] ❋The same frequency-to-spatial mapping may be used to attempt the creation of something I've always wanted to see: a database of chemical reactions—a "Chemoplex" if you will—which can be referenced for everything ranging from the development of healthy, fancy drugs and extrapolation of broken DNA function to realistic environmental interactions for future holo-environments and video games (my personal favorite). If we know how certain chemicals are supposed to interact as a matter of their characteristic behavior in bond-space, then we might be able to hypothesize certain results without ever testing them.

Repulsion forces

There are two factors responsible for repulsion among quanta: the existence of their determined ranges of effect (which won't allow two quanta to overlap without being *modellable* as the same quantum), and the proposed need for intervening space to carry the energy being passed. Without intervening space—if we assume the horn triangles in the model are completely empty for example—then quantic energy will either have to pass through boundary jitters exclusively or pass through some dimension outside of the model. Here, however, we allow nature to give us a hint as to which of these scenarios occurs on the macroscopic level. Objects don't just teleport (on a scale we know of) when they move. Also, it likely takes more energy spending to move them through potential space than it does to move them in the space they're already in, given that such objects are not fundamental quanta themselves. Even if they do move through other dimensions, the version of them which registers in this dimension still appears to move through this one. Given the orthogonality of at least the first 4 dimensions, it may be safe to assume that a certain amount of non-quantic space in the same dimension or the boundaries of the quanta themselves are needed to store the energy being passed. As for the idea of storing the would-be-transferred energy in the boundary, this doesn't appear consistent with nature. Although sweat and other bodily emissions travel through our outer boundaries, they don't usually start there. We're not hollow. We have internal states that build up and drop in their excitation levels. For quanta to store their transitioning energy in their boundaries most likely means that their boundaries must deform in some way. Perhaps this happens, but I am suspicious of how a quantum would do this while still maintaining a relatively stable cyclical relationship with its neighbors.[10] So intervening block space it is. Thus, if I am a quantum and you are a quantum, then I want you near me...but don't touch me. I don't like it. And if you *must* touch me, then the next quantum will have to be even farther away from both of us (since I can no longer use this empty space between us for any good elbow room).

When we have a single circle of radius 1, all we need is π's worth of surrounding space for energy to be sent to another circle of the same size. The additional radius needed will be $\sqrt{2} - 1$ (~.414), because squaring this will double the area, allowing both the circle and its needed space to both exist. This is the point at which the circle no longer cares if any other quanta form. In fact, it may want quanta to form here (assuming it's inclined to stand alone in the first place, which it isn't; just go with the example for now). But now suppose our circle is crowded with 2 other friends, now we have 3π's worth of energy taking up $3\pi + \sqrt{3} - \frac{\pi}{2}$'s worth of space. Will $\sqrt{2} - 1$ additional radius be enough to grant us the space we need? No. Even if we make use of the $\Delta_\circ$ and don't include its *energy* in the 3π, our triad of circles still occupies a *radius* bigger than $\sqrt{3}$ no matter how you do the math. In even the simplest calculation, the amount of extra radius needed will grow every time the radius grows. We'll need at least $\sqrt{6} - \sqrt{3}$ (~.717) additional radius before the triad will accept any new triad's worth of exchange partners. Any closer and the potential exchanger will either need to join our triad or literally get blown off.

Energy exchange ultimately requires space for storing the energy as it builds up. The range of effect rule is akin to the strong nuclear force. More than an abstract "force" that holds the quantum together, I propose that the strong force is a region of space containing the complete range of possible oscillatory frequencies that cover every possible phase within a fundamental quantic density. But there is a limit to the span of such a region before the oscillations become redundant and amplitude-unequal (or amplitude reducible). Beyond this density, the next strongest force is that which holds quantic neighbors of similar atomicity to each other. Given that their perimeters of effect are irrational with respect to their ranges, their cyclic progress asymmetric along the "true north" axis, and the energies they contain ever-unbalanced with respect to their radial ranges, quanta adopt neighbors to cover for the oscillatory modes they themselves can no longer accommodate. This is akin to the electromagnetic force which assigns a radial family of quanta to a central one in order to allow for the efficient exchange of the central quantum's stable potential and real modes with respect to north. This time, however, we're not looking at true north, but local north (which may or may not be the original universal expansion source). The reason for this is that the radial family of neighbors really do have their own lives, and don't need to align their cycles with that of the central quantum. While one neighbor's history may have assigned it a cycle completion at 42°, another neighbor may complete a cycle at 319°. True north is a determinant of light, chronon span, and possibly universal

---

[10] In any event, the intervening block space for each quantum may *be* the boundary of which we speak (even if we did find that the boundaries held the passing energy).

expansion direction, but is not the major (direct) determinant of quantic family formation. That is the purview of collision history and thus, largely, the dynamics of mass and temperature. Alongside its radial family of 12 immediate angles, a central quantum gains the ability to propagate light in a direction perpendicular to the plane being modeled, where the E and B fields represent alternations in active energy flow between the central quantum and its real and potential axes.

Attraction forces

A theory of attraction phenomena is, in my opinion, more complicated than a theory of repulsion, and requires some new tools.

Assertion 36. The order of error of a system determines the stability of its interactions with other systems.
Let us define the **order of error** of a system, its ϵ_{low} and ϵ_{high}, as **the approximate level of activity below which changes to the system do not detectably affect the system's behavior and above which changes in the system do not detectably affect the behavior of the larger scale system that contains them**. By this definition, changes smaller than the lower order of error won't be felt by the system on any level it can recognize (without some detection-enhancing tool). Relatedly, though the system make change to its heart's content, a thing that exists on a scale beyond its upper order of error will not be affected by it (unless the system gets help from other systems).

Assertion 37. Approximation of the fine structure constant
I recall reading *Einstein's Intuition* (2015) during Thad Robert's discussion of black holes and thinking to myself, "Infinity? *Really*?" Sure enough Roberts suggests that black holes don't actually fall off into infinity, but instead have a limit to how energetically deep they can go. It's not that I don't believe in infinity, it's just that every time I picture it I imagine a ship sailing off the side of a flat earth, crashing into the Devil's forehead in the 9th circle of Hell. But even in that scenario, the abyss has a bottom. An infinite amount of anything is simply hard for me to imagine. So when the author introduced the value Ж (Cyrillic zhe, or je) = .0854245 as one of the fundamental limiting values of nature, I thought as an astrologer "that's just 1/12th $(.08\bar{3})$." I asked what it meant to have a minimum curvature of π and a maximum curvature of Ж and looked at the snowflake model I had already been working on to understand the asteroids.

In the 12-model, we presume that although a single quantum would like to trade with other quanta, it first needs to form. Then it needs twelve neighbors to complete its own capacity to register important states. Then it needs space to allow bonding with any of its neighbors. The snowflake unit includes 12π worth of other quanta as well as $12 \left(\sqrt{3} - \frac{\pi}{2}\right)$ horn triangles for storing any possible energy passing across its bounds. The number .085 is clearly more than .083 and suggests that the horn triangles really do need to be considered. I asked if a flat 2D model was even appropriate and concluded that, as an idealized, shortest-distance projection of any higher dimensional model which still captured the probabilities visually, it was. Sticking with 1/12th then, I took $(O+\Delta_O)/(12O)$. This didn't work, but produced .085472, which was close. Then recalling some lessons from chemistry years earlier, I tried using *half*-bonds for the amount of empty space available to the would-be charge exchanging neighbor. $(O+\Delta_O)/(12(O+\frac{1}{2}\Delta_O)) = .0854185$. This was close, and basically says that there is a slightly higher than 1/12th probability that a cycle neighbor and its horn triangle will, at any time, engage in exchange with the central quantum.[11] Subtracting the paradoxical idea that there is one place where half the bond energy *cannot* be (interior or exterior) whenever the exchange is taking place anywhere, we get

---

[11] Why do we take $O+\Delta_O$ for the numerator instead of $O+\frac{1}{2}\Delta_O$ the way we do for the denominator? Because we are assuming that, in an exchange, the central quantum will definitely engage in one whole Δ_O worth of energy storage somewhere around its neighborhood along with one whole partner to itself O as an active flop provider, even if the energy exchanged is 0. The denominator on the other hand only includes half bonds as a reflection of the fact that energy is always transitioning between being where it is and being where it's going (not where it is). So we take an average of Δ_O and 0, which is $\frac{1}{2}\Delta_O$, for the next possible movement of the total Δ_O energy.

$$\frac{0 + \Delta_0}{12(0 + \frac{1}{2}\Delta_0) - \frac{\Delta_0}{180}} = \frac{\pi + \left(\sqrt{3} - \frac{\pi}{2}\right)}{12\pi + 6\left(\sqrt{3} - \frac{\pi}{2}\right) - \frac{\sqrt{3} - \frac{\pi}{2}}{18\pi}} \dagger$$

(†See the footnote [12] for an explanation of this additional term, and [13] for a general comment on this equation.)

which = .085424822 (compared to Robert's .085424543135). I assume that there is some additional error term which reflects 1) the probability of energy being transferred beyond the central 12 quanta and their six omitted neighbors, 2) the probability of energy being transferred into a subsystem within or outside of the Δ_0s, 3) the probability of energy being transferred into the energy of any of the resonant bonds between the main quanta and their satellites, or 4) the probability of energy being transferred into preserving the orientation of the quantic group as a whole. Maybe some of these possibilities amount to the same thing. As you can see though, whatever stray probability that is must be extra small, and possibly gets us into the realm of the weak nuclear force for peeling looky loos off of the central quantic unit's periphery. Just as my calculated term is off by a factor of 1 millionth, the weak nuclear force is about 1 millionth times as strong as the strong nuclear force.

The .0854 value is the square root of the fine structure constant in particle physics (approximated here as .0072974, compared to .007297353), and essentially represents the "charged quantic fraction" of a quantum exchange unit. Ж approximates the ratio of actively traded charge to potentially traded charge in an optimally dense, 12-phase quantum space, and tells how much of a particle's surrounding energy is open for trading in the sum total of its possible frequency dimensions—which are largely mutually exclusive except for the quantic blocks they share. Give this approximation, I believe that the fine structure constant $\alpha = Ж^2$, as a measure of "charged quantic fraction squared," gives us the "charged quantic fractional area" of a quantic space, and thus should figure into calculations related to the likelihood of quantum collections bonding and breaking bonds with other quantum collections. Above the scale of the fine structure constant— commonly approximated at $\sim\frac{1}{137}$—you encounter energies which are strong enough to break electroweak bonds but not strong enough to break strong ones, and so you also have the scale of energy needed to park stable subdynamics within the horn triangular regions of tightly packed quanta without disturbing those quanta. On the fundamental level this doesn't mean anything as far as our measurements are concerned, but if you apply the snowflake model to megaquantic regions like galaxies, you get an explanation of how systems on the order of $\frac{1}{137}$ or smaller can exist within the "nonquantic" zones between megaquanta and not know it. Megaquantic galaxies are too grand for small stuff like planets. Solar systems are too grand for small stuff like countries. So even if there is a massive block potential pinning the Solar System to the rest of the Milky Way, none of us in the Solar System will notice it. It is possible that our planets exist in the equivalent of a "horn triangle"[14] between the rest of the Galaxy and the space outside of it, such that our movements are to that system, what the movements of a quantic block's contents are to the quanta that flank them. Applying our 12-model to the macroscopic level, we're small enough to be considered negligible perturbations in a bigger system. But we're not nearly small enough

---

[12] In order to trap the horn triangle energy somewhere between any of the bonds of the central 12, we introduce six more quanta around the outside of the snowflake. These represent the energy of "not in here" where the exchanged pre-energetic packet may be located outside of the central 12 quanta between q_{90} and q_{150} for example. Although the central quantum doesn't have access to these outer six (and accordingly omits them from the snowflake), the bond energy of the horn triangle does. The probability that a Δ_0's worth of energy will attempt to pass into any of these 18 is $\frac{\Delta_0}{18\pi}$. I believe that such energy will not be available for the rest of the possible transitions in the calculation, so we subtract it. Thus we've accounted for both halves of the central quantum's Δ_0 involved in an exchange. A whole Δ_0 will be active in a bond in the numerator. Half of that Δ_0 will be among the bond possibilities in the denominator. The other half, from the reference frame of the central O, will be assigned as transitioning into or out of one of the 18 Os associated with any of the regions accessible to any of the Δ_0s. Whether those Os register that energy quantically is another story.

[13] This model applies to the 2D case. In the more common 3D case we may approximate the potential (i) scale of energy ($\hbar$) in a layer of spheres ($\frac{4}{3}\pi r^3$) whose upper and lower regions are partly lopped off by its upper and lower adjacent layers (minus ~25%-30%) to fit the approximation $i\hbar \cong \pi r^3$.

[14] Not the literal shape of a horn triangle, just the concept of the intervening space it represents.

to escape the collective energy trading preferences of the actual, countless quanta which constitute us. Accordingly, ultramicroscopic resonant patterns like gravity and electromagnetism remain an inescapable fact for us...until the day we find a way to make ourselves 10^{39} times smaller.[15]

We've approximated the fine structure constant in order to arrive at some boundary value for determining when energy trading systems can spawn (or be ineffective in influencing) other energy trading systems outside of their scale—the level at which the massive pull of a Solar System ceases to pull even you. At that level we can identify where changes in an energetic gradient (such as the frequency span of a variable-frequency cycle) are just too big or too small to notice.

Assertion 38. Quanta are the automatic byproduct of harmonic resonance in the cycles between energy pulses of another emitter.
What follows is a very unscientific analogy, but I'll make it anyway.

In asking why certain people are attracted to certain things in ways that can be astrologically or psychologically verified, I asked what the common underlying phenomenon was. It seemed to be resonance. Whenever an actor saw complementarity between himself and his goal or between himself and something involving his goal, he was more likely to take properties of the similar thing as his own. This was neither electrical nor gravitational, but definitely seemed to be frequency based if there were any scientific explanation at all. Whether the frequency of neural encoding, the chemical properties of pheromones, or the direction of current, energy patterns which supported each other seemed to go hand in hand with energy patterns that moved together. So we'll investigate a theory of attraction based on resonance and complementarity.

I've already considered the idea of how quanta might form as the result of coherent oscillatory patterns in a region evolving a range of effect which establishes a predictable cycle with respect to its neighboring regions. In this explanation there are two phenomena needed to promote coalescence: similarity of phase for regions of the gradient near each other and complementarity of groups of similar phases to the environment they assemble in. A collection of waves needs both similar frequencies and a similar net response to its surrounding frequencies in order to form a bond. It may in fact be energetically cheaper to do so. Interestingly, the "× 2" relationship allows a wave with double the frequency of another wave to bond with that other wave because the two waves are precisely arranged to 1) complete cycles together and 2) change amplitude in concert with each other. Together, ½ and ¼ form a kind of chord. So too do $1/29$ and $1/58$. Although they don't bond in the "glue" sense, they do join their effects together to influence whatever medium they're in. Imagine, then, that you have a pool of frequencies ω which covers every value between 1 and 2. Sure its range will probably be irrational, but if you can manage to time the completion such that ω_1 completes a cycle whenever ω_2 does, you'll not only create a system which wraps an entire intervening range of other frequencies onto itself, you'll also establish a time ordered system (based on the number of distinguishable modes between 1 and 2), a phasic scope of memory (indicated by the length of the circumference), a range of effect (which moves as the square root of the energy contained in the cycle), as well as—and here's the important part—a cycle that can resonate with any other cycle anywhere. Need to resonate with a frequency of 1.414? try the 180° mark on your cycle. (assuming we've agreed to measure cyclic progress using degrees). Need to resonate with .5? try the 0° mark. It finishes a cycle whenever 1 does and then some. How about the number 200? Try the 231.8° mark. After wrapping around 7 times, our cycle will have learned to treat 2^7, 128, as if it were the value 1. The 7th wraparound equivalent of 200 is 1.5625, which is 231.8° after the cycle start point. A doubling cycle does it all. The only thing is that such a cycle isn't very good at counting whole number pulses from neighbors located along its potential axis (90°). But we've seen this issue before:

To summarize a familiar tale, a × 4 cycle is better than the × 2 version for our geometric models, because they make it easier to handle imaginary axes. The physical reality is probably indifferent to this choice though. The 360° mark on a

---

[15] I also note that, because it takes about 19-20 horn triangles to equal a related circle, we may use $\left(\frac{1}{20}\right)^2$ as an appropriate scale for gauging when entire systems can be built on other systems without those larger systems necessarily being affected. Think of ants and dust mites. Do you always know when they're crawling on you? I think not.

quantic cycle very likely has some kind of × 2 relationship to the 0° mark, implying that quanta automatically form where this kind of resonance is possible. They won't be geometrically (or energetically) stable among neighbors however until such resonance can be reliably scaled to accommodate those six other surrounding resonators formed under the same conditions.[16] A cycle which not only recognizes powers of 2 but also powers of 3 may be ideal in nature. Powers of 4 are even more convenient for us to study such things though.

Assertion 39. Waves of slightly different frequencies whose orders of error are not different tend to synchronize to an average unless continually acted upon by a third, outside wave.
Suppose you have a wave which wobbles at 4 cycles per second, give or take ½ a cycle. (The ½ cycle is both its upper and lower order of error). By our definition of the order of error, any difference from 4 which is less than ½ will still be considered equal to 4. My claim is that, unless you have 1) some other wave which wobbles on the scale of less than ¼ (½ of ½) with an even smaller order of error or 2) some other wave which wobbles at a much greater scale with a lower order of error greater than 8 (twice 4), your two waves—when crossed with each other (i.e. multiplied)—will tend towards matching each other's frequency in the frame of one wave if there is no third wave or function to prevent them from doing so.

Why? Minimally, the energy of waves adopts a quantized range of frequencies—stepped rather than sliding on the scale of a period. The range of values between 1 and 2 may not be quantized, but the completion of whole cycle is. Should the sum or product of two bounded infinite wave functions deviate from the allowable fixed steps, the system will evolve or an energy will be emitted to correct this.

Adding versus mulitplying
Let us think of adding as roughly "the process of putting two things together" and multiplying as "putting one thing with itself another thing's number of times." Although adding two different things won't do anything spectacular (because their view, their sounds, or any other spacetime perceptual effects appear to be registered <u>separately</u>), multiplying does affect them because they are effectively added to themselves. Subject to their own structure, things whose spacetime behaviors are compounded upon themselves—sitting still over time—are subject to the natural entropy that comes with being impinged upon by other events. The longer I sit still, the more outside events I absorb, adding new dynamics to my former old structure. In this way, adding considers an event to remain itself next to a different event while multiplying forces an event to be considered against another version of itself. Ironically, it is the process of adding that puts two of the same class of events together where no two instances of that event are the same; that is, those events occupy different reference frames, even if we see them as the same.[17]

Passable error
In math we commonly represent repeating waves as $A cos(\omega t) + iB sin(\omega t)$, where cos (cosine) represents the real dimension and sin (sine) represents the imaginary dimension, A and B are amplitudes (numbers representing how much of each wave you have), i is the square root of -1, ω (omega) is the frequency you're looking at and t is the point in time you're looking at. You can combine these two dimensions into a single value $Ce^{-i\omega t}$ (where C is a combined real and imaginary [complex] amplitude). If you have two waves which are slightly off in their frequencies then you have two functions $C_1 e^{-i(\omega+\epsilon_1)t}$ and $C_2 e^{-i(\omega+\epsilon_2)t}$ where ϵ (epsilon) represents the positive error in the frequency.[18] Multiplying them gives $C_1 C_2 e^{-i(2\omega+\epsilon_1+\epsilon_2)t}$ where the lowest possible order of error as responded to by an outside reference frame is $\epsilon_{close} = \|\epsilon_1 - \epsilon_2\|$ and the highest is $\epsilon_{far} = \|\epsilon_1\| + \|\epsilon_2\|$. Maybe your error cancels mine out. Maybe our errors add. Whatever the case, that error gets multiplied by whatever length of time we're doing this for. But in multiplication, we're only counting one object over and over. So if we're working with a frequency of 4 with an error of ½, then sometimes 4 means 3.8, and sometimes 4 means 4.1. As an outside responder is always required for anything not responding to itself

---

[16] Again, does it have to be six? What if we developed this model in 3D or 4D? But in order to account for the potential energy axes—in many ways key to the system's reason for being—we only need two dimensions. I discussed earlier how higher dimensions can be mapped on to these two. Still it may be more accurate to say "the 2D model requires that the system scale to fit 6 neighbors."
[17] Apple 1 and apple 2 both look like apples, but they aren't the same apple.
[18] We assume both orders of error to be symmetric in this case.

(while anything responding to itself cannot hold the same state as both responder and original event), the thing possessing error whose definition is determined by the responder takes on the error which it presents to that responder. In the end, I will claim that while 4 means 4, 3.6 is close enough to still be considered 4 in this example. When responding to a function multiplied though, I consider my own point of response to be instantaneous, reassigning the error in my response to errors attributable to you, thus you will take on the average of both our errors while I define myself as a precise responder. Behaviorally, this sounds unfair, but it is only the result of my own inability to respond to my own response over time. Mathematically, then, we say that $C_{(r)esponder}e^{-i(\omega+\epsilon_r)t} \times C_{(o)bject}e^{-i(\omega+\epsilon_0)t} \to C_r C_o e^{-i(2\omega+\epsilon_r+\epsilon_0)t} \to C_r e^{-i(\omega)t} \times C_o e^{-i(\omega+\epsilon_r+\epsilon_0)t} = C_r e^{-i(\omega)t} \times C_o e^{-i(\omega+\epsilon_{object\ as\ responded\ to})t}$.

The idea above is that multiplication, though commutative in theory (where $A \times B = B \times A$) is not commutative in reality. **When responders respond to an object, the responders forget their own error and respond to the object at an instant—assigning errors in their own response to errors in the object responded to**. We'll call this "**passable error**." The object, on the other hand, has multiple spacetime slices of itself piled upon each other in the time it takes a responder to process that object— different light waves, different sounds, differentially excitable "perceptrons" so that the responder treats his own non-instantaneous perception as instantaneous (even though it isn't); he also treats the different spacetime states of his own perceptual mechanisms as different states in the thing responded to. This is a reference frame issue which is more a consequence of the responder's own structure for absorbing events than it is a consequence of anything he responds to.

To go from A to C we must first pass through B, but there are contingencies inherent in B which can lead to the framing of entirely alternative reference frames. For now we will only claim that your responding to me stacks multiple observations of me on your terms—multiplying us in your mind—while my responding to you stacks multiple observations of you on my terms, multiplying us in my mind. But even in a world where we share exactly the same facts, the same cognitive pathways, and the same perceptual mechanisms, simply by virtue of being two distinguishable objects, we will not share the same point in spacetime. I will be affected by a set of events different from that which affects you, such that the absorption of each other's data will not produce the same results. And so it is for abstract objects as well: if they are not the same object, the substance of their differences will produce differences in what is observed when one frames the other. Accordingly, the differences in how two waves behave are reduced to differences in how a second wave appears in the apparently (but not actually) "unchanging" reference frame of the first wave against which the second wave is counted. 4 sees 3.5 as itself minus ½. 3.5 sees 4 as itself plus ½. You walked into my house, one foot before the other, so there was a point at which you were half in, half out. But because I don't think of this, I see your arrival as instantaneous and instead attribute the half-in half-out nature of your collision with my house as being a property of you called "speed." In this way, errors in perceptual stacking not only render multiplication and mutual response non-commutative, but also relegate such non-commutativity to the realm of derivatives in calculus: changes over time in the responses of any perceiver unable to perceive all things at a single simultaneous moment.

A cycle sends information to another cycle and gets information back. But the first cycle only registers events against its own cyclic start point (say 43° for example). Although the second cycle probably registers changes against a different start point (like 119° for example), cycle 1 processes all changes as though they happened at the cycle 1 start point. The difference between the moment where cycle 2 actually made changes and the moment when cycle 1 "says" cycle 2 made changes falls within the passable error of cycle 1 onto cycle 2. In the case of quanta, this is like trying to process information from neighbors faster than a flop cycle—the speed of light—will allow. This is where quantum 1 says to quantum 2, "119-43? Nah, that's just you doin' you."[19] It's not as though no changes are being made, just that any changes made in a widow smaller than this aren't registered in quantum cycle 1's state changes until quantum 1 finishes the round it's on. Since quantum 1 now thinks that quantum 2 and all 11 other neighbors are all on quantum 1's cycle (and they very likely aren't), and all 12 of quantum 1's immediate neighbors process changes as though each one's neighborhood is on each one's own cycle, the whole system continues to respond to each other as though they are in resonance, sending information among

---

[19] "And it's certainly NOT me being out of phase with you by 43-119. I just consider myself responding naturally to you. There's no error at all. Not at all" says the central quantum. Nevermind the fact that he's taking a full 2π worth of cycle to do everything he does while calling it "instantaneous." Therein lies all the error.

each other accordingly...on a third frequency that nobody knows about. In these neighbor's eyes, everybody is in sync OR if they don't respond to each other as if they are in sync, then they respond to their unsynced neighbors using a third function which, when added to the neighbors, re-syncs them. Either way, the system is kept resonant by virtue of patterns of mutual response which overlook the tiny order error each quantum undetectably passes onto quanta other than itself.

Assertion 40. Flattening versus sphericity in 3D space
The following section applies the 12-model to the level of galaxy-size megaquanta rather than that of fundamental quanta.

Suppose we take the snowflake model and intersect it with itself along the z-x plane. We know that the original snowflake (which we'll call x-y) has a central O that always wants to trade with neighbors, that it wants to spin along some orientation in its recursive survey of its own irrational circumference, and that some neighbor somewhere along the perimeter will be the pulse recipient along this cycle. We also know that they quantic unit/neighborhood now needs about 13 times the intervening space around it if all quanta are to have the chance at trade which the central one does. So there is a favored distance where the next stable group of trade partners should be allowed to form. x-y wants partners at this distance, but because of the intervening space required won't want these partners any closer. What happens when we intersect this same dynamic in another dimension? Either the highlighted partner in z-x must be the same as the one in x-y or it must be a second highlighted partner which cannot be stably allowed in the same plane as the one in x-y.

If we allow, say, the z-x exchange partner to simply do what it wants while the x-y partner does what it wants, the two will eventually correspond to the same neighbor receiving more charge than a quantum is allowed to handle. That's unstable. If however, the two exchange partners are allowed to spin in opposing directions, permanently avoiding each other via an ongoing traversal of mutually exclusive neighbors, they may yet constitute a valence shell of two exchange partners instead of one. Barring this, the existence of the z-x plane will not automatically mean the existence of exchange partners rotating through that plane, especially where x-y is the energetically preferred choice for exchange partners. In other words, sometimes the snowflake model lends itself to spheres and other times to discs. When does it do which?

I argue that the concentration of energy-carrying quanta contained within the orders of error of bigger megaquanta determines sphericity versus discality. So far the idealized model we've been using has two basic kinds of regions: circles and horn triangles. Since we know that nature places us in three visual spatial dimensions, now will be a good time to consider the familiar shapes in 3D space. The circles become spheres, but what about the horn triangles? These take on more exotic shapes such as that flanked by five sphere, but because this shape is patently uneven, so too is its internal potential gradient irregularly distributed. If we assume that this interspherical volume is being bombarded by pulses from its spherical, quantic neighbors and that all neighbors carry roughly the same energy, we may also surmise that subquanta will be inclined to form too which reflect the oscillating energy passing through this region. The most uniform arrangement of subquanta in this region will be that of a plane, since, among the five surrounding spheres, two will be farther way than the other three—the altitudes of two triangular pyramids as opposed to $1/3$ the three altitudes of the bases of these pyramids respectively. Between the spherical quanta, the close triad flanking the plane can be expected, as part of the greater 3D snowflake, to exchange energy at a particular angular frequency. The upper and lower altitude pair however can only trade energy up and down, altering the vertical oscillatory gradient within this volume considerably and discouraging the formation of stable quanta compared to the region at the midpoint of these two. As a result, we can expect a disc to form at the triad, its spin a reflection of the exchange among three regions of megaquanta surrounding it. In this case, stable quantic neighbors above and below the disc are unlikely to form, though certain stable radii associated with this disc will have an inclination (tilt) which counteracts certain energetic excesses in the base plane of the main disc. So maybe Eris would live in the plane of the ecliptic if not for the wrong ratio of other quantic trade partners living there. In this case, as only a slight deviation from the flanking three megaquantic spheres, and as an aggregation of oscillatory gradients just off the main plane but still stable enough to assemble, Eris and other dramatically inclined bodies like it are just fine orbiting at a crooked angle.

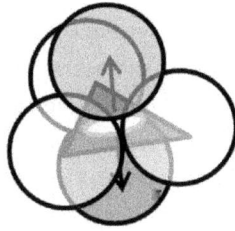

Figure 36-18: In a tightly packed volume of megaquantic spherical regions, the distances of these five megaquanta from the intervening space between them is not equal. Subregions of quanta less than the order of error of the megaquanta may form quantic volumes of their own, but subject to the unequal resonance gradients among the five. The above case forces the subsystem (dark gray with a white circle) into a disc shape because the upper and lower megavolumes (gray) are farther than the three flanking ones (white). Here we see both spheres and discs in action. Other arrangements are also possible for systems packed in other ways.

To summarize, an original universal burst can be expected to have taken place in all dimensional directions. Spherical regions of stability then formed as the universe cooled enough to support meaningful gradients between pulses from the burst. Those spheres left horn zones between them which were highly asymmetric along their true north axes pointing towards the burst. These horn zones were most energetically stable along the planes between the midpoints of their upper and lower spherical regions. Additionally, in cases where stacked triangular pyramids were not formed, other shapes besides discs will have been been more stable.[20] In the planes, neighbor-seeking well under the megaquantic order of error will have resumed, allowing spheres to form once again with a diameter that was again smaller than the order of error of the altitudinal megaquantic spheres. In this way, newly spherical stars and their outer bond shells are allowed to form within flat galaxies. Within the star shells, flat star systems can give rise to spherical planets.

The conditions for spheres is that an energetic concentration be allowed to expand unbounded without being restricted to a particular shell—either by gradient boundary, energy limits, or a pre-existing matrix of bonds. The conditions for a disc are that a volume of energy exist and that the larger energy sources surrounding that energy favor two axes above a third. By this argument there should be a third shape that occurs when one axis is favored above two others—possibly shaped like a tube. Beyond these basic, ideally packed arrangements, we can expect even more possibilities.

Although I recall hearing somewhere that gravity was responsible for the difference between spheres and discs, I believe this is only true if we consider oscillatory stability among energy centers to constitute gravity. At least in this model, neither the altitudinal spheres nor the flanking triad pushes down on anything so much as they trade energy at a regular frequency which synchronizes their phase within an order of error which the intervening space is free to rearrange without facing chronic instability. Perhaps the flattening of spherical energy into a disc really is the work of gravity; but if so, the carrier of gravity—the "graviton"—may be a masked man with a 2^{nth} power self-referencing wave hiding underneath. That man insists on synchronizing frequencies to match his own. The bigger his collection of quanta, the more quantic exchange partners he requires, the farther the range of effect involved.[21]

Assertion 41. the stable radii of orbits are a function of the flux passing through the most recent shell's surface area.

In a 3D space, if the volume of a sphere of radius r is $\frac{4}{3}\pi r^3$ and the surface area of that sphere is $4\pi r^2$, given that the flux (energy passing through that sphere) is measured in $\frac{energy}{unit\,of\,surface\,area}$, then as the radius of a sphere approaches double its original radius, the area of the flat disk determined by the new radius approaches that of the surface area of the original

---

[20] We'll leave the nature of these shapes to other investigators.

[21] I don't like the "Gravity. That's it." explanation for both spheres and discs in astronomy. If it is gravity which keeps our inner Solar system flat but our entire Solar System spherical, I would ask, the gravity of what? It seems highly unlikely the same body of matter or force is doing two different kinds of work.

sphere. Accordingly, the flux through a flat disk in an ideal system is equal to the flux through a sphere of half that disk's radius. As energy-emitting spheres are mapped onto disks, successive spheres determined by the radius of each newly mapped disk are energetically stable at double the radii of the preceding sphere. Were this not so, points at slightly smaller radii would receive too much energy from the emitter and would, themselves, emit the excess while points at slightly larger radii would receive too little energy per unit time from the emitter and fail to stably attach to the emitter's system. Barring the introduction of other forces included in successively larger spheres, systems comprising comparative non-emitters around single energetic emitters form stable radii on the order of double each previous stable radius. The surface area/energy of the central emitter determines the oscillatory pulse I've been referring to thus far. Between each surface area's worth of energy emission, a cycle is completed. The self-sustaining organization of every possible phase between one pulse and the next constitutes a quantum for that system. Coalesced into a range of effect at twice the energetically effective radius of the previous stable shell, a quantum is more likely to describe an aggregated volume every 2^n distances from the emitter. Other distances receive the same energy, but the pulses from those other distances don't reinforce each other nearly as easily.

At what point does the point-emitting system above become unable to stack additional spheres? This likely depends on the amount of energy issuing from the central emitter, probably a function of its chemical constraints. If the emitter is the only object in a system (taking up the entire volume of the energy in that system) and has no surrounding non-emitters within the radius determined by its effective surface area, there should be no satellites around it and it will stack no further. If, however, the emitter becomes compressed into regions of emission and non-emission, the emitting region should be able to stack stable orbits up to the limit of its volumetric entirety—until the radius reaches no more objects (a similar boundary as the entirety case). That is, an emitter of energy x with an effective boundary radius of r will influence everything within r whether or not the source of the emitter is the whole emitter or a central "core" therein. Beyond the emitter's effective boundary, its energy is dissipated such that it no longer influences the orbits of objects beyond it. The relationship described here is related to the Roche Limit and a $2\sqrt{2}$ multiplier of T when area is doubled in Kepler's laws.)

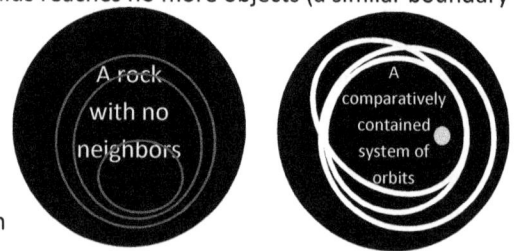

A rock with no neighbors

A comparatively contained system of orbits

Assertion 42. Stacked 3D volumetric orbits repeat their character every four cycles when a band of receivers receives their emitted energy as time-dependent linearized.

The area traced out by the hemisectional plane of an emitting sphere is one fourth of the surface area of that sphere $(\pi r^2 = \frac{1}{4}(4\pi r^2))$. In a mapping from sphere to plane, four periods of planar flux equals one period of surface area flux, so that each disk at which a stable energetic orbit occurs generates one fourth of the number of cycles needed to constitute the energy issuing from the surface of the now larger shell it cuts through. But the energy of the disk itself is energetically determined by 4 pulses of the prior sphere whose surface area flux preceded it. In this way, the addition of four orbits towards the restarting of a cycle is a property of stacking energetic systems composed of the everyday matter familiar to us. Where a mapping preserves dimension (sphere to sphere) we might expect the number of orbits to be preserved, allowing greater and greater numbers of satellites to be packed around the central emitter. Where a mapping does not preserve dimension (sphere to plane), we might expect the four cycle to pose limits on the number of orbits constituting a repeat as earlier degrees of freedom are lost.

If an event in spacetime—such as an audible note—can be described as sending out its information in 3 dimensions of observation (space) and 1 dimension of change (time), then we have the basic omnidirectional emission from which its cones are derived. But a single point located away from the point of origin cannot process the full 4D nature of the event. As the endpoint on a line between the point of event's origin and itself, the receiving point can only process the event in 2D, one of space and one of time. This is basically a mapping of the pulsed sphere onto a linear/transverse wave. In an example of this, our ears convert 4D sound into 2D modulated mechanical energy. In terms of the total energy emitted from a sphere, we can consider this the second derivative of the volume. The volume of a sphere of radius r, $\frac{4}{3}\pi r^3$ →

surface area of that sphere at $4\pi r^2$ → linear "reach" $8\pi r$ $(4 \times 2\pi r)$. In this way, the energy from a point emitter in 3D space + 1D time would map from a function of volume to a function of line in the receiving point. From here, however, you not only get another justification of the 4-cycle mentioned above ($4 \times 2\pi r$), but you also get a basis for stereotyped waveforms characterizable by frequency. That is, if I have h units of energy per unit time coming from a volume emitter of radius r, as a linear receiver I process that energy as a function of $h/_{8\pi r}$, of order $1/_r$. But there is a further *rate* at which I process, so we take one more derivative to get something like the impulse. 8π would constitute a standard ratio for describing how a point receiver processes signals from a volumetric emitter. That is, you would need a minimum of four cycles of signaling to fully characterize any periodic information coming from a volume—especially if that volume's signal is itself linearly oscillating and you, as a receiver require a non-instantaneous (passable error-generating) time window to process the signal you receive.

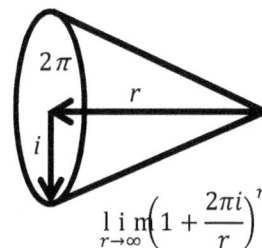

$$\lim_{r \to \infty}\left(1 + \frac{2\pi i}{r}\right)^r$$

Assertion 43. Gravity is the synchronization of frequencies passing between two volumes of quanta, and the fundamental equivalent of the scale axis applied to a region of quanta.

I claim that gravity is the gradual reconciliation of the phases of the component waves of two volumes of wave functions in all directions, as one volume's z axis conforms to the requirements of another's x-y plane.

Just as my observation of you multiplies copies of you in my mind and passes my error onto you, a larger body's "observation" of a smaller one creates multiple copies of the smaller one in the larger one's intervening space, passing its error onto the smaller. "Observation" in this case refers to the third party relationship between the larger body, the smaller body, and the surrounding region whose multidimensionality must match that of the larger body. In order for the larger volume's circumradial interactions (circular wavefront which follows from a completion of each oscillatory period) to maintain its general structure without being disturbed by a smaller body, the smaller body's net wave function must conform—high frequency to low frequency—to the phases of the wave form of the larger body. This is the process by which one oscillator with a full range of frequencies between 2^n and 2^{n+1} comes to resonate with another such oscillator of different magnitude. The smaller magnitude oscillator is made to conform to the cycles of the larger. Think of yourself as a single $C^\#_3$ note and the Earth as an opera. As your linearized volume wave combines with Earth's linearized volume wave in all directions, you are, through wave function resonance, placed by others in the opera, not the other way around. And even if you're slightly out of tune, as long as you're not a C_3 or anything other than a $C^\#_3$, in the larger context of the opera your slight difference won't be heard. Furthermore, if you are out of phase with the higher amplitude $C^\#_3$s in the opera, the opera can bring you into phase without changing your $C^\#_3$ nature. So in this case, $sin(138.6t + kx) \to sin(138.6t + 0)$ as $x \to 0$. The only ways you can fight this are 1) by becoming so small that the Earth's wavelengths pass right by you like a mountain, 2) by becoming so big that you synchronize the Earth instead of it synchronizing you, 3) you become so distant that too much intervening volume gets in the way or 4) you adopt a wave form which is so chronically out of phase with Earth's that synchronization is unlikely—effectively rendering a large part of your component energy the occupant of a separate dimension. Given that both you and Earth are made up of the same kinds of visible matter though, and given that you're actually made up of stuff you've eaten from Earth, this last option is difficult for us to perceive without some really legit particle physics technology at our disposal.

If you think of the way tuning forks bring each other into resonance based on their shared structures, you'll get a sense of the above conception of gravity. Where gravity is concerned, not only are objects being pulled together physically, it's actually the case that one object's wave is simply being brought in as close "proximity" to another object's wave as possible, by means of bringing all component frequencies into phase. The effect is to make both objects a part of the one with the denser wave function—so that any point beyond either will be a point beyond both. As long as there remains distance between the two objects, this minimum is not achieved as the various frequencies in the smaller continue to be out of phase with the various frequencies in the larger. What physical distance presents us with is a suboptimal phase difference between the attracted and attracting objects—as though one mass has a huge wobble, the other has a similar wobble, and in between them...nothing much? The net function emitted from their sum will resist this, pulling them towards a single phase-coherent mass. Lastly, this system is driven forward by the recursive nature of time.

So why do we have planetary orbits? I believe it is for the same reason we have quantic cycles: regions of graded oscillatory phase from one or several energy emission sources form self-reinforcing cycles that circumscribe a region of effect. It's probably more appropriate to ask why we have planets at the same time as asking why planets orbit. So that's what we'll do. In the quantic sense I propose that planets—like basic quanta—are inclined to form at whatever phase angle the central oscillatory region collectively compresses the most, given that the emitting source's r-distant pulse plus the pulse from its $2^n r$-distant interactant can be thought of as building a standing wave whose major amplitude is carried along by the bigger emitter. Here are the proposed steps:

1. I'm an energetic emitter.
    This means that I have a reliable ability to take on every possible energy-passing frequency mode within my local slice of volume between the order 2^n and 2^{n+1}, and have the ability to create a <u>periodically stable</u> oscillating current in the region around me. By this definition, my ability to do work is my ability to make currents in the region around me conform to whatever phasic mode I hit them with at my perimeter of effect.

2. I throw an energy ball. Now the ball is an energetic emitter.
    So the currents around me can adopt their own cyclic character with the energy available to them.

3. The ball throws its own energy ball.

4. The energy I throw wins because I'm bigger than the ball and have more energy to throw. The ball gets pushed further out.
    If you are a cyclical region next to me and I am bigger than you, then I have the right to change your frequency according to my phase. So if your effective energetic radius is $\sqrt{2}$ times mine, then the circumferential currents I create can cancel yours. Although my electromagnetic-scale emissions aren't enough to destroy the strong-scale resonance that holds you together, I can encourage you as a quantum to resist forming stable resonances with any neighboring regions. I effectively turn your region of effect into noise, retaining you as part of *my* region of effect.

5. At every doubling of my energetic radius, however, the energy thrown from the ball is perfectly synchronized with my cyclic reset. So the ball is allowed to stay and gather with more energy.
    In a 2D (or basic discal) model, whenever you are located at around 2^n times my range of effect, you are also at a place where your circumferential cycles are double mine. I have a harder time cancelling the currents you create, because they are the same as half my currents plus two halves of the currents created by your neighbors 60° on either side of you. Not only do you get to stay stable, you may (if you're lucky) even overpower most of your neighbors at that same radius. Either way, you are now the proud representative of that 2^n radial energy level, and you are still within my range of effect. So I consider you to be a part of me.

6. If you successfully overpower your neighbors at the same radius, you will cancel their oscillatory coherence within that band and push them around the band...towards yourself.

7. If you absorb enough energy in assembling stable quanta of your own within the confines of that band, you may eventually develop a large energy-packed volume. And you will be something like a planet. (This applies to other levels like atoms and galactic clusters as well. I'll also talk about its implications for human dynamics later.)

8. As a volume of phase-synchronized oscillation, you too will be an energy emitter. As long as it is within an order of error that doesn't compete with my effects on you, you can follow the same process I did and develop moons as a way of fine tuning your phasic relationship to my system. These will be your decimal places in cycle space.

And there you have the planets...

On mass formation

...More generally we have a portion of a theory for mass coalescence: strongly patterned energetic exchange resonances within a comparatively concentrated volume. I say comparatively because there is certainly a difference between putting your toe in the water (one fluid layer at a time), and smacking it from a 2 mile fall (many bond layers at a time, rendering the surface solid). Thinking of mass as simply a higher concentration of quantic energy sharers than other forms of matter, and matter as comparatively structured pattern of concentrated energy sharers, both mass and matter can be thought of as counting the quanta involved <u>in specific pattern</u> of exchange. So not just any volume of quanta will do. If we're looking at quanta that don't care to exchange in any specific way, then we won't have mass, just energy. If we're looking at one sharing pattern mixed with another then we may have multiple kinds of masses (like a colloid). If we're looking at pre-energy that doesn't even have an organized spin or frequency range, then we don't even have quanta, just potential space into which a regulated, fully phasic variable frequency must be introduced—similar to the phase-saturating activity of the post Big Bang environment.

On Gravity

For objects of unequal mass and thus unequal spans of quantic effect, the usual rational-irrational predisposition to exchange with other quanta holds. But here is where quantic assemblies are most inclined to copy each other in the minimization of undesirable energy differentials. Recall that quantic exchange units—neighborhoods—not only want to bond, but need to. They will continue to absorb other quanta's behavior into their areas of effect until they encounter the megaquantic boundaries of the oscillatory region in which they are located. A sphere of quanta will grow until the products of its own emission at $2^n r$ say that it shouldn't any more. Within the space of a particular sphere-flanked region, a disc can only grow up to the lower order of error of the flanking megaquanta. But in the current model, megaquantic spheres are held together through circumferential resonance. Interspheric discs are held together through topological resonance across surfaces with similar potential with respect to the quantic spheres that surround them.

Circumferential and topological resonance are in fact the same thing, except that one treats an oscillatorilly equipotential plane as a plane and the other treats such a plane as a differential slice on the surface of a sphere. Remember though, what happened when we tried to intersect two snowflake models in two orthogonal planes, one normal and the other perpendicular to it. We usually couldn't get away with this except under the very special case of exchangers possessing opposite spin in the valence region surrounding the central quantum. But what if a small packet of quantum like a human finds himself near a big surface like a planet? His quanta in the z plane of the planet is exactly what we get. As we saw earlier, there's no way the x-y planetary plane is going to let this happen without a challenge. And so, through a sneaky appeal to z-axis style torque, the bigger body compels the smaller body's resonance with its own x-y planar cycles. It doesn't just do this for the smaller body, but for all of the surrounding quanta outside of its perimeter of effect. Imagine putting the snowflake on the ground and looking down at it. Our early example showed that any other snowflake plane sticking out the ground and passing through your legs for example will be affected by the preferred equiradial (differential) plane of the floor, not only is the arrow sticking up through you—the natural direction of the emitter's energy emission at your location—but the line of your quanta points downward exchanging emission in turn. The planet overpowers your cycle influence, but won't destroy your strong bonds, so what happens? Energetically you lose the right to form where you are, but thanks to your pre-existing strong bonds (your mass) the neighborhood of the planet definitely finds it easier to spin your constituent quantic masses towards itself than to push you away. In the end, your quanta are resonated with closely with the bigger object like any other neighborhood. Instead of you moving, however, your bond pattern is copied across quanta on the scale of the orthogonal plane to which your quanta respond. You appear to retain mass as you fall, but your quanta aren't necessarily moving. Your bond pattern is moving. You are the base of the arrow. The planet is the spinning bucket of water. The coupled x-y cycles of the quanta which form its mass, also couple your quanta, torquing you along its z as it invites you into its neighborhood. It works just like the outer surface of the spinning top, except that it's not the spin of the planet that matters, it the coupled cycles of the planet's quanta spinning your quanta into resonance on a MUCH smaller scale.

Also, because this is a quantic effect and not necessarily a planetary one, you don't need planets to make it work. You just need any pair of neighborhoods of coupled quanta cycling nonindependently: our new definition of mass.

The above analogy also holds for equal masses. Applied in 3D, a mass shows an x-y planar cyclical oscillatory pattern from the view of another body located on its z axis. Here we have two bodies sitting in each other's spacetime cones with altitudes of z and cone bases corresponding to each one's x-y cycle. The need for irrational quanta to exchange energy causes the x-y cycles to adopt each others' frequencies within an allowable order of error, limiting the allowable phases of their zs to a certain optimum value compared to other volumes of quanta involved.[22] For bodies imbued with mass (and thus already existing multi-quantic resonance structures) however, z distances other than 0 become harder and harder to maintain as the number of quanta involve blow up. Thus the z components of net resonances within both masses are brought as closely to 0 as possible as complex, but more easily alignable x-y cycles are made to resonate more closely at the r between the objects. The quanta which carry the mass patterns don't need to be involved in this. Nor do highly energetic volumes of energy carriers, since their cycles are not coherent enough to allow their easy capture. If you were a solar wind or a radio wave you might be able to bounce off the Earth with ease. But since you have a mass and your patterns need to be maintained, the Earth has no choice but to pass your pattern towards itself by means of its quanta's x-y planes torquing your quanta's z axes and restricting its possible values until you and the Earth are in the same place.

Some early personality implications

In an interestingly related twist, there is a relationship between the real axis and imaginary axis, proton-neutron core and electron clouds obeying the Pauli exclusion principle, and spherical Oort Cloud surrounding the discal material Inner Solar System with psychology. There exists a construct in psychology called the interpersonal circumplex whose chief axes are those of agency (dominance) and communion (togetherness). Communion and Agency have been repeatedly shown to form orthogonal (perpendicular) axes to one another because one of the axes (communion) is aimed at getting along—attracting its own kind—while the other (agency) is aimed at getting ahead—repelling its own kind. If only all matter attracted each other, everything might still be an indistinguishable blob. Alas, an event's progress along a cycle alternates between states relevant to the real (like-viewable) and those relevant to the potential (like-denying). We'll call this **arrangement of a like-denying axis placed orthogonally to a like-attracting axis in a 2D space** by the name of **half-complementarity**. It is common for complete systems like these to be described by events that look like each other and hang around each other while being shielded by some collection of events which don't care much for each other yet watch at a distance. There seems to be an almost 1:1 correspondence between the bond-forming inner core of a central quantum and the interior-of-the-center bond-rejecting (but still pairing) outer cloud of mutually exclusive neighbors. There also seems to be a strong relationship between the amount of bonders who gather together in the center and the distance kept by those at the perimeter, and this brings us to an additional comment on gravity:

In order to oscillate stably, a material object needs someplace to store its potential energy, this is not only true of electromagnetic waves, but of the sine and cosine functions themselves. When sine reaches 0 cosine reaches 1. When cosine reaches 0 sine reaches 1. One holds the potential of the other, though only one function (typically cosine) is considered real. Relatedly, in order to oscillate reliably in concert with their trillion cells, humans need some place to store their potential energy so that they may retain their structure. For each material event, a potential space exists whose "distance" is a function of the energy flux passing through that event as well as the amount of coherence of the event itself. High energy events require higher potential holders. Lower energy events require less. Between the inner material core at x-y and the outer potential shell at z lies a vast space occupied by nothing less than the orthogonalizing wave itself. The core and the shell mark the endpoints of the wave. The space between the core and shell holds the body of the wave—most of which constitutes the math function which interfaces with some volume which appears to approximate dark matter. While gravity reconciles the frequencies of two wave functions along an axis by aligning resonances of the planes normal to that axis, those two wave functions consist of both real and imaginary components. Core and shell. Material and potential. Each of these axes has their own function which stores the unused energy of the other, but the dynamic between them also has a function. It is this dynamic space between core and shell which determines the range of effect for objects within each other's' gravitational range. The bigger the volume occupied by the material core, the larger the radius of effect. Accordingly, field vectors and Trojan behavior arise on either side of an object to be resonated with, as the entire attracted system plays out the results of its compelled resonance not only in the direction of the attractor, but along all coupled dimensions including those on the opposite side of the attracted object and its associated L_2 Lagrange Point.

---

[22] This relates to atmospheric composition as you change altitudes above a planet.

On the Number of Universal Dimensions

Assertion 44. Predictive comparison of emitters requires at least a triad of processors. In a [volume-to-linear rate]-mapping system, this gives rise to the stability of 3 x 4-cycles for volumes.
How do cyclic systems give rise to predictive behavior? Again we'll use the 12-system applied to super quanta rather than fundamental quanta. That way we'll be free to subdivide our energy carriers.

As we've discussed, a cyclical/periodic process of constant total energy is describable in two dimensions: its actually emitted energy and its potential energy. These correspond roughly to a vector on the real and imaginary axes. If I am a point receiver designed to "expect" certain signals from a volumetric emitter, then at least two things are happening: First, I have internal processes which correlate with the handling of the volume emitter—suggesting that I myself require another, internal signal emitter of *different* frequency, as well as a third "counter" for determining when the two functions coincide. (In order to see an x-y axis, you need an observer in the z dimension.) Second, I need a way of monitoring when I'm *about to* arrive at the point of coincidence between my internal emitter and the volume emitter. That's what expectation is all about; let's define a system's **expectation** as **the system's response to the future state of a thing**. The simplest, and probably most accurate kind of third counter I can have is actually a phase-shifted copy of my internal emitter—which will perfectly predict the original internal emitter's state unless one of them is disturbed by an intruding function. The second most accurate kind of third counter is a frequency-doubled version of the original emitter. This 2-1 setup has implications for quarks within protons and neutrons. But the overall idea is that a system imbued with the ability to reliably predict the results of responding to a thing outside of itself needs at least three emission-processing points—one for the external volume, one for the internal "clock" against which the volume is compared, and a third for the internal "counter" for indicating when the volume and the selected point on the clock coincide. If we only want to reliably map a volume onto a line, we'll need 4 of our own cycles' worth of processing from that volume. But if we want to form targeted responses to (or characterization of) that volume's signal (such as a plant turning towards the light$_{volume}$ in expectation$_{counter}$ of optimum sun$_{clock}$), we'll need at least three basic ways of processing signals in this reference frame.

Given this definition of expectation, how many dimensions can we expect will be needed for a full description of the universe? That is, how many independent dimensions will we need to predict the future state of the universe in any frame? You probably won't be surprised if I say it's 12. I'll build up to these in the next section.

Assertion 45. Non-resonant frequencies can still be counted via coincident quanta upon their multiples.
Earlier I showed that the 12 cycle acts as a kind of optimum for periodic systems which respond to other periodic systems in ways that are countably expandable yet stable. I might also add that you can easily account for non-resonant frequencies in this model by referring back to the volume-clock-counter trio referred to above. Even if it is true that 1.4 doesn't produce good half-way points with 2, if you establish a counter which looks for both periods to reach 14, you can line them up by means of counters upon the least common multiple.

Assertion 46. All systems of N dimension require an additional dimension to view them.
Relatedly, an N+1 dimensional system can only have respondable frames of N dimension, where the final dimension is reserved for the responder themselves. The responder must exist in a space orthogonal to the frame it responds to, otherwise the responder becomes coupled to the initial frame, attempting to respond to itself (which cannot be done without changing both). I can view a 2D object, but I'll need to be in 3D space away from the object in order to see it.

Assertion 47. All systems of N dimension require two additional dimensions to view them in time.
The previous assertion states that N+1 dimensions are required for a responder outside of an N-dimensional system to *respond* to that system without attaching to it. Per an earlier assertion, this responder requires yet another dimension in order to actually *identify* what is responded to. I can view a 2D system from a 3D space, but I'll need to be in 4D to animate my process of viewing it.

Assertion 48. The number of units used to describe physical reality vary with the number of dimensions considered to constitute that reality.

A basic cycle ultimately has two axes: the real and the potential. If this forms the entirety of a responder's reality, then there can only be one unit of measure: that of existence (salience). This is because, in line with previous assertions, the responder itself must occupy a dimension—likely that of potential in the 2D case. This is a very limited view, however, and warrants more dimensions to line up with our observable reality.

In another example, if we consider ourselves to exist in 3D space, then we require another dimension outside of space to house ourselves as responders. The dimension of time, then becomes a proxy for our own attention to certain points of experience. This view may also be seen as insufficient though becaus it fails to include a fifth dimension to house identity constructs (the chain of 4D states which constitute the system's memory of the times it has processed. If we really do wish to process 3D space as time-animating observers and keep track of windows of time, we'll need no fewer than 5 dimensions. If we wish to study the dynamics among these 5 dimensions, we'll need 7 more. Let us investigate why.

Assertion 49. The 12 dimensions of reality stem from an initial four augmented by an upper and lower scaling.

We are familiar with the first four dimensions of spacetime: x, y, z, and t. But this can't be all there is.

x_A, ϕ_A, and z_A

As we've defined quanta as regulated volumes of oscillatory gradient, it is fitting to think of a quantum A as being located in familiar 3D space. x, y, and z represent three axes of space, but unfortunately don't reflect the preference for x and y as equiplanar axes away from an emitter's z. There is, after all the matter of the z-axis from one snowflake being the x-axis of the snowflake at right angles to it. In order to capture the preference for one axial orientation over the others as well as place ourselves in familiar disc space with true north lying in the x-y plane rather than along the z axis (as we temporarily arrange it in the gravity scenario), we'll recast x, y, z, into cylindrical-like coordinates with x_A representing the vector to true north (the main energy source) from the system we're looking at, ϕ_A representing an angle in $< x, ix >$ in the plane of the reference frame of the object we've chosen, and z_A representing the least preferred axis which happens to be orthogonal to that $< x, ix >$ plane. These are dimensions of space within a system's global reference frame. They effectively establish cycle space on the quantum level, putting our snowflake in the same place we've been putting it, with the $< x, ix >$ projection of true north at 0 degrees plus or minus some astronomical distance we don't need to care about.

Now that we've done the above, the reader should note that from here on, our familiar <x, y, z> space will NOT be considered mapped by <x_A, ϕ_A, z_A>. Unless you happen to be a quantum. We'll use a different set of dimensions to properly map familiar <x, y, z> space shortly.

t and τ

As I've studied astrology and worked with the LSRI (lifespan revolution indicator), there is clearly a remapping of cycle flow that comes with every non-fundamental collection of energies. Whether you have a lifespan of 80 years or 80 minutes you will, energetically, be describable by an angular value τ which completes a single revolution over the entire span of your life. In this side branch of astrology it is possible to calculate how long you will live using milestones around your wheel, yet you can imagine that the energetic neighbors with which you interact—be they people, countries, or atoms, will not share your span. Accordingly, there is a span for global time t dictated by the possible number of flops in a quantic cycle and a second span of local time dictated by a volume's own allowable number of global time cycles before the volume itself dissolves into instability. There is the span of light and the span of light-spans. Outside of the dimensions of a single quantum cycle we need another dimension for counting how many of those recursive cycles a thing is allowed to undergo throughout its existence. Normalization of this second time dimension (to where every event's lifespan is scaled to 1) is the nature of the LSRI in astrology, but also the nature of radioactive decay in chemistry, and a determinant of entropy rates in physics broadly. t sets no such limits, yet we know such limits exists in full disregard of t. Thus, our manmade heavier elements tend towards a level of instability unmatched by the regular elements. τ tells us how long your neighborhood is expected to stay together and, by extension, which of your phases will interact with other neighborhoods' phases. t as the sole time dimension cannot keep track of relative (or relativistic) time.

r_{Bz}, θ_{Bz}, and ϕ_{Bz}

It is uninformative to treat quanta as dimensionless singularities in space when, as part of a system, they are hypothesized to have different properties depending on their orientation. Think about how spinning a magnet in another magnet's field or a lasso at 45° off the horizon requires another set of spatial dimensions for the movement of an interaction partner against the main object's background. Just as it is important to know a specific t on a timeline or a specific x in location space, it is equally important for cycling systems to have a specific direction for where their current phasic "attention" is pointing. r_{Bz}, θ_{Bz}, and ϕ_{Bz} capture this orientation with r_{Bz} indicating the distance vector to an appropriately chosen reference point from the $< x, ix, z >$ origin where object A is located, ϕ_{Bz} representing the angle of orientation between x_A and the projection of object B onto the $< x, ix >$ plane, and θ_{Bz} representing the angle between r_{Bz} and z_A. These are dimensions of space within an object's local reference frame, and the closest equivalent of the familiar $<x, y, z>$ space we all know and love. Why? Because it doesn't assume the axes to be married to each other via cycle dynamics the way the earlier spatial trio did.

Have we covered everything we need to describe the system? No. Consider the next three dimensions that stem from important analogs in biology and astrology.

Дz ($\ddot{r}_{Bz}$)

There are many examples in neuroscience of where our brains respond to changes in stimulus rates over the activity of the unchanging stimulus itself, resonators, peripheral nervous system response and some cases of visual direction detection are examples of this. A particular neuron may have a constant firing rate (velocity), but when that rate changes, different kinds of activity may ensue. Acceleration is the key in this type of situation. In another example, astrology offers a comprehensive picture of an event in spacetime, but most of the factors in an astro chart are not activated unless the chart possessor pays attention to their implementation—a change in the factor's current rate of use. An interaction object which exerts no force on the main object is different from an object which exerts force. So it is not enough to simply show where two objects are located while knowing the time slice and lifespan of one. We also need to know if the relationship between the two is inclined to change at a certain rate. This is something like the approach increase (or distance decrease) per cycle time: acceleration along the r axis towards the volume B, $\ddot{r}_{Bz}$. I will use the Cyrillic letter de (Дz) for this one since many of the Greek letters are taken, it looks close enough to a Latin "a" for filling in wherever acceleration may be in use, it also looks like a delta (for indicating a rate of change), and the d.e. appropriately captures it role as a measure of differential emission rates among quantic collections.

With intersecting energetic neighborhoods we already assume we've got some ongoing exchange rate between the volumes in question, so velocity isn't as important as the *change* in the velocity of exchange. The image of more quanta of a similar character to a central one being added to the central quantic volume at a certain rate comes to mind. If these quanta are not independent, the resonant pulse they send to their interactant will increase as the square of the cycle time. As much as I'd like to call this dimension by its better known name, acceleration, it isn't really clear that regions on the scale of quanta will actually be speeding up towards each other. More likely, it's their regional oscillations that will be increasing exponentially (along with their mutual influence). So we'll label this dimension using a name slightly less associated with mass and more associated with attention/event intersection: We'll call it the collision (or differential emission) dimension.

The subscript z on some of the dimensions by the way is an indication that this entire system uses spherical spatial space with z_A as the reference axis. I will be swapping these out later for related, but remapped cylindrical spatial space.

β

In astrology and in neuropsychology, certain factors receive stimuli regardless of whether the possessor responds to those factors. Sometimes, through lesion or some other impairment, the possessor cannot respond in the expected way. Maybe the body you've slapped is dead. Maybe the volume you're looking at isn't a quantum at all, but a pre-energetic "horn triangle." Our system needs a dimension for describing volume A's ability to do anything in response to an interaction. I initially called this dimension "brightness" as a way of describing the potential of an object to be "seen" by another object, but instead have opted for a more familiar value which is a better reflection of several known physical quantities: β for temperature. I use β as an analog to beta-weights which turn up or down variates in statistics, and also because we've already used t and τ.

m

And now for something simple. When I do an astrochart chart for a project, there are certain things that the project just can't do. A person or a dolphin however might have all kinds of expressive options. So too does the degree of self-referencing behavioral options vary with the number of quanta in a quantic exchange unit. So our last basic dimension will be that of quanta-count in a non-independent region: mass m. Assuming idealized quanta, mass can easily be converted to area, and when multiplied by $Д_z$ gives us a conception of force as the amount of coupled energy exchangers approaching an interacting volume at a particular rate. (Later we'll drop the multiplication and simply consider m to be a quantum count scaled against z_A instead.

מ (or $\phi_מ$)

The last dimension is unfortunately tricky, but necessary I think. One thing astrologers often run into from mainstream science is the idea that, "if astrology works, why don't you prove it." Aside from being backwards (with the debunker holding the burden to disprove the entire field by induction), the challenge to disprove astrology often rests on the assumption that a person can automatically look at a chart and know what he's seeing. But as shown by the example I gave earlier, there's no way of knowing the difference between the chart of a great actress and the chart of a footstool built at the same time. The chart of a drummer or a dead man. One needs to know something about the form and the interactional history of a system before he tells you what it might be, let alone what it might do next. Similarly, I believe that we can never know how a system will evolve in the future if we don't know how such a system adapts to its own past. We discussed a precursor to this in the assertions on recursive cycles. The final dimension in our system, then, plays the important role of absorbing the system's entire history into one of the system's possible existing states. This is the memory dimension "mem," represented by the Hebrew letter mem, מ (which also looks like a Latin "n" for iterating the number of save states under consideration).

What is the best way to collapse an entire 11-vector into a single value? I suggest the same way we do it in second-level astrology: via one of its bounded-infinite angular phases ϕ_A.[23] The angular phase ϕ_A is the only value among the previous 11 which represents every possible phasic orientation for the quantum. All other values are either 1) linearly unbounded, 2) interactant-dependent and theoretically, uncountably, infinite, or 3) constraint-making rather than state-spanning. Like ϕ_A, מ is best described as a spatial state, but on the quantic scale. If the sum of a cycle is capturable through a מ angle in this way, it follows that the role of a state vector $|\Psi>$ is to count the population of each frequency type occupied by a volume of quanta at a given point in 11-space. This would establish the table of aspects in an astrology chart as the reductive equivalent of a state vector without consideration for things like mass, collision, and interaction object. The number of frequencies available to a cycle are effectively infinite, but in astrology we can use powers of 12 like 12, 144, or (in the case of the asteroids) 1728.

4D kinematic spacetime versus quantum descriptors

Given all of the dimensions above, I think it would be easy to mix certain dynamics improperly. The 4D spacetime we're used to $<x, y, z, t>$ for example is more like $<r_{Bz}, \theta_{Bz}, \phi_{Bz}, t>$, because it describes objects away from a certain point without regard to the object's all-important cycle state and the restrictions that state poses for things like bonding and inter-volume resonance. Attempting to apply quantum rules to the B dimensions will invariably lead to missing information. Spin and phase, for example, are encoded in the sign and angle of ϕ_A. Relativistic effects likely involve the acceleration in

---

[23] These are the astrological aspects / angles that link planets to each other. The aspects themselves take on the same characters the planets do, so applying an aspect to a planet is similar to applying a previous planet's "situation" to a new planet. The later chapters on the asteroids will make this clear.

the z_A and τ directions rather than of r_B the because z_A and τ are most directly associated with lifespan on the ϕ_A cycle. Calculation of constants like the speed of light likely require a well-defined x_A direction. So as to determine an anchor point for locking neighbors in place around the central quantum. I'll give an estimate for the speed of light in the next assertion.

Assertion 50. Estimate for the speed of light c

Why is there an upper limit on the speed of light? While working on this book I thought about that question and concluded that it must have something to do with the amount of energy (area) allotted to a quantum. So far, the numbers associated with the 2D modeling of quanta as neighborhoods of circles include 2, 4, 6, 12, π, $\sqrt{2}$ if we're flattening squares, $\sqrt{3}$ if we're lining up triangles, e if we're zooming out, and 1 if we're adding dimensions. So the constant 299,792,458 units per unit time might have something to do with these values. Reverse engineering these values, I obtained the speed of light as

$$c = 4^{12} \times 2\pi \times \sqrt{2} \times 2.010971616$$

The first two values made easy sense on scales of 1 and π. The value 4^{12} is just the number of flop states available to all 12 neighbors in the snowflake model (the two real plus the two imaginary dimensions raised to the 12). 2π is the ratio of one perimeter of effect to one quantum range of effect. The last two values were much harder to arrive at, but my guess is that, since light was hypothesized earlier to travel at a normal vector to the base plane of the spacetime cone, we need to take the shortest distance between the quantic radius of 1 and the end of its z-axis 1 unit out of the paper. That distance is $\sqrt{2}$. Lastly, we need to account for the ratio of distance between the centers of any two quanta passing information and the range of effect of those quanta. This is 2:1, and produces a value which is off by about 1 million m/s (0.3%). The value 2.0109, however, falls within the allowable error for quanta arranged in quantic block grids, and may tell us something about the amplitude of the string-like, wobbling perimeters of these oscillatory regions. 299,792,458 m/s is equivalent to the ratio of [independent transition states of quanta (4) associated combinatorially with dynamics with the quantum's neighbors (n^{12}) through a full cycle of oscillations (2π) projected onto a unit axis normal to the cycle ($\sqrt{2}$) through the distance traveled between their ideally packed centers 2.0109] and [the range of effect of that quantum (1)]. It is hypothesized that any attempt to send information faster than this ratio will not be reflected in any transition states of any of the quanta involved in such a transfer, and will have to be relegated to "pre-energy" of volumes resistant to a coherent oscillatory pattern.

It's at this point that I remind the reader of my reasons for offering the various theories I've offered throughout the *Full Spectrum Astrology* series. Because there have been very clear, very obvious patterns in my statistics, I've sought to explain my findings to myself as more developments have arisen with each new book. This is especially true now that there does exist a formula for predicting, reasonably accurately, the astrological role of fully untested, unnamed asteroids (which I'll discuss later). I offer my estimates of values like c and the fine structure constant as an attempt to reconcile what I've found in astrology with the physics that is already well studied. As there were no other satisfactory explanations of these values that I could easily find, I've offered propositions regarding them here.

Assertion 51. On spacetime curvature

For people who have had trouble understanding space time curvature diagrams like I did prior to working on this, the snowflake shape can provide a hint as to what's going on.

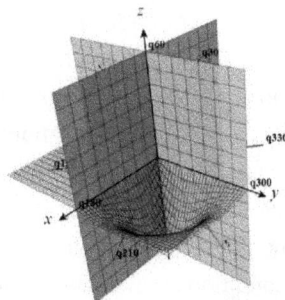

Figure 36-19: A spacetime curvature diagram

In line with the earlier hypotheses regarding gravity, a change in potential orientation (spin) cycle coupling in the x-y plane produces a compensatory change in the range of the z-axis because the usual restriction on occupyable states outside of a single quantum's preferred x-y plane forces neighbors now behaving like itself to compound their z-restrictions with that of the central quantum. 2D spins influence 3D options. The more coupling of quantum states we have in a region, the more mass, the greater the need to exchange with other quanta at the borders of the coupled region, compelling the resonant oscillation (pulling in) of volumes of other quanta just outside of the coupled volume. I can't exchange with you if you're a cyclic clone of myself, so together as a super quantum we make two quantum exchanges worth of resonance at our borders and forbid two quantum exchanges worth of possible energy carrier clashes in the region just above or below our plane of cycling (if the range of the oscillatory gradient region we occupy is limited; if not, we're more likely to propagate our desire for exchanges spherically). Spacetime curvature can be thought of as caused by incongruities in the extent to which regions are quantically coupled in a particular plane, with higher coupling in the center of a dipped region and lower coupling density as we move radially away from this dip.

I remember looking at rubber sheet diagrams and thinking, *Where is the third dimension?* But I now agree with Mr. Roberts that the dip in a rubber sheet diagram is not the familiar third dimension, rather it is the dimension of z-magnitude associated with quantum level cycling; that is, the aforementioned axis z_A. The altitude we typically look for in familiar 3D space isn't z_A, but the vertical component of $<r_{Bz}, \theta_{Bz}, \phi_{Bz}>$ which, when translated into normal space would be $<x, y, z>$. We should consider the A axes $<x_A, \phi_A, z_A>$ to represent "quantum cycle space" while the B axes $<r_{Bz}, \theta_{Bz}, \phi_{Bz}>$ represent "normal space." So if we want our rubber sheet diagrams to look more like the reality we know, we'll have to apply them to each of the three planes in $<x, y, z>$ space, x-y, y-z, and z-x as shown below.

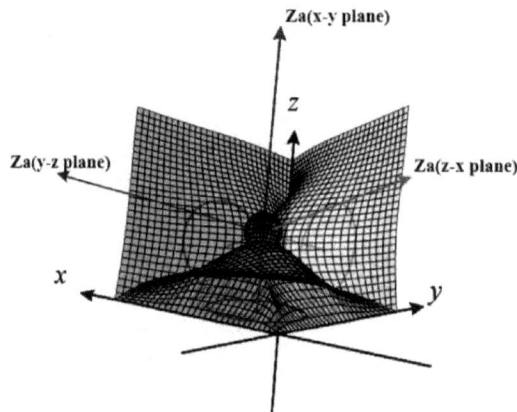

Figure 36-20: Spacetime curvature diagrams make more sense when applied in every plane.

Depending on the angle of volumetric capture and subsequent aggregation, a sufficiently densely coupled three-axis gradient field can consolidate into an astronomical body with a specified tilt. Minimum curvature allows the energy exchanged about a quantic region to obey its usual circumregional arc of $2\pi r : 2r$, which is the same as $\pi : 1$. Maximum curvature forces such energy to be exchanged almost exclusively with that one quantic neighbor along the orthogonal axis to the usual plane of cycling. Instead of trading with everyone along the $<x_A, \phi_A>$ circumference in the regular plane of cycling in the minimum curvature case, the central quantum trades with only one neighbor in the second snowflake perpendicular to the regular snowflake plane whose axis coincides with the regular $<x_A, \phi_A>$ snowflake's $<z_A>$ normal vector. This is consistent with the earlier explanation of gravity as a phenomenon rooted in orthogonality to a mass' projected plane of cyclical resonance through its $<z_A>$. The quantic neighbor which monopolizes the resonance exchanges of the central quantum has a regional "charge" occupancy probability equal to the square root of the fine structure constant, or .0854. But it should be noted that such a probability is not infinitely small because quantic regions themselves cannot be infinitely small—requiring regions of energetic flux for their existence. We might hypothesize, then, that the center of a black hole contains ongoing Big Bang conditions as a single quantic region continually receives and expels more neighboring energy than it can cyclically organize in a non pre-energetic fashion, though there continues to be more than enough pre-energy to continually re-form new quanta.

$\sim \frac{1}{12} \times 2\pi r + [\text{span of } \Delta_O]$

$\sim.0854 \ [\frac{1}{12} + \text{"horn triangle"}]$ **of the total surrounding region**

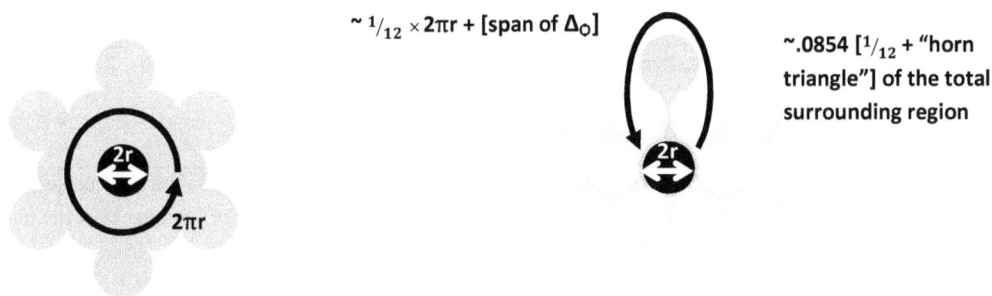

Figure 36-21: Minimum versus maximum curvature. Under minimum curvature (left), the energy exchange about the regular ratio of circumference:diameter holds. Under maximum curvature (right), quantum exchanges are linearly constrained to about 1/12 + a "horn triangle" fraction of the possible circumference. In the real world these would be calculated in terms of areas or volumes instead of circumferences, but I have used the 2D, r=1, and assumed quantic energy = 1 to illustrate the basic point.

Assertion 52. Summary of the 12-vector

The aforementioned 12-vector arises from a three-fold multiple of the basic four dimensions inherent in all cycles. For every quartet of <real, potential-complement, real-complement, potential-real> states, there are also two more states which denote 1) the intervening space between a central energy carrier and the neighboring energy carrier as well as 2) the neighboring energy carrier itself which is about to send or receive those states. Ignoring the preexisting state of the neighbor then (because our central carrier doesn't have access to this information) there are three neighbor-dynamics for every possible quadrant of cycle phase: keeping that quadrant state to itself, getting that quadrant state from the other, or giving that quadrant to the surrounding world. Not only are these dynamics mutually exclusive, the quadrants in which they trade are also mutually exclusive. And so we have 12 possible families of cycle behavior. Not only are these families modellable using a region of 12 circles about a central state possessor, but they also hint at the idea that the states themselves may each require their own dimension—since measurements in terms of one say nothing about measurements made in terms of another. How many times do I have to give potential energy to something before I am allowed to give no real energy to something else? Without knowing anything about how these exchange partners are coupled to me or each other, I can't come up with a function for this. The situation is similar to our geometric treatment of basic x-y coordinates. How many times do I have to move along x to be allowed to move along y, say, twice? Without some kind of mathematical relation between these two dimensions, I can't answer this. Absent a mapping function among the 12 cyclic regimes via some stable exchange relationships, the information contained in one regime does not seem to be influenceable by another. So the twelve cyclic states—to the extent that the missing information in those states is tied up in 12 independently operating quantic volumes—imply 12 dimensions of measurement.

The full quantic state vector, as proposed here, consists of the following dimensions:

Dimension	Description
β	a count of the amount of energetic exchange happening in a volume, this dimension is the equivalent of pre-energetic blocks per quantic area, making it a relative of acceleration. In order to have quanta at all, you need energy to exist somewhere which is capable of 1) traveling and 2) generating an organizable pulse that can be sent to surrounding regions between cycles. Here the dimension of energy level, **temperature**, is the precursor to packets of energy levels (quanta). Its corresponding unit is KELVIN. This unit is akin to a **spatial rate** (which is a good thing, since the other rate, $Д_z$, will get dropped in later assertions.

x_A	**space** axis pointing to quantum's primary energy source, which determines the 0° mark in its phasic cycle. As a point of concentrated resonance perpendicular to the circumference of the quantum, it may be hypothesized as a measure of **luminous intensity**, in CANDELAS.
ϕ_A	angular **space** axis indicating current **phase** away from x_A. This unit is measured in the number radii of effect per cycle: RADIANS.
z_A	quantum magnitude. the orthogonal **spatial** axis to $<x_A, \phi_A>$ which captures the total projective magnitude of the quantum in question. Its fundamental unit should count the transferrable energy of the quanta in the plane normal to it and multiply the energy therein: COULOMBS for **charge**.
t	the number of <u>fundamental</u> quantum magnitudes z_A that have transpired since the first universal burst. Since we don't know when this original point was, we count in relative chronons, Planck time, or seconds since an agreed-upon starting point. As a count rather than a measure, this is familiar, global **time**, measured in SECONDS
m	the number of stable energy exchanges among quanta occupying a particular volume. This dimension does what z_A does, but counts pre-energetic quantic-blocks (exchange regions) instead of quanta. Thus it might be considered **spatial**. This has weird implications for the hardness versus softness, or permeability versus impermeability of a substance since you can effectively have a bunch of quanta sitting around with no mass, mixed mass, or black hole-style mass. Its basic unit should coincide with one measuring coupled interactions between quanta: KILOGRAMS for **mass**.
$Д_z$	**collision / differential emission**. this is space divided along two cycle dimensions, giving us a measure of instantaneous change in space that describes the system as new quanta are added or subtracted to its count. This measure can be used to count anything on all sorts of scales, from the logarithm of frequency shifting along a 2^n recursive cycle to the ratio of quanta implicated in adding additional torque to an approaching volume. Because, on the quantum level, it is a function of reliable 2^n phase evolution around a circle and on the macro level it is a function of reliable 2^n radial evolution between and energy source and its sink, the second derivative of space remains constant even in relativistic reference frames. The whole basis of acceleration is two axes of cycle time changing as a radius of effect remains constant, so acceleration-like values can be expected to grow with quanta counts like mass and z_A, but may otherwise be expected to behave as invariant no matter what the speed of the reference frame. This is a lot like saying "You will always have 2π radians per planar circle no matter what the circle." Curvature may bend the circle, but because it's a cycle-circle rather than a strictly spatial one, those of us on the bent circle can be expected to bend with it. So we won't notice.
r_{Bz}	the spatial **distance** between a central point (quantic or megaquantic[24] doesn't matter) and a specified energy exchange partner. It is important to note that without this and the next two dimensions for slicing out a piece of the central quantum's surrounding world, we have no choice but to consider the quantum in terms of a superposition of a probabilistic world full of states, thus losing the ability describe any location-dependent interaction characteristic of the quantum. It is measured using basic **length**: METERS.
θ_{Bz}	the angular **spatial** separation between r_{Bz} and z_A. It indicates **tilt**, and may be hypothesized to play a role in setting the stable axes for bodies acquiring mass in a system, including planets.
ϕ_{Bz}	the **spatial** angle of orientation between x_A and the projection of object B's reference point onto the $< x, ix >$ plane. For lack of a better label, I'll call this the **mass-cycle**. I believe it not only has something to do with how efficiently a quantic collection captures new mass, but also how its fundamental quanta respond to energetic inputs from the mass' local north direction as opposed to true north.
τ	the number of quantic cycles allotted for a quantic collection to stably exist, given the patterns exchanges it has formed, before it can no longer sustain those general patterns. This is another count and thus another **time**-like measure. It

---

[24] Quantic here implies the size of a fundamental quantum. Megaquantic denotes the size of anything bigger than that.

	indicates the duration of a quantic collection's lifespan. Note that the notion of **lifespan**—by virtue of the requirement for patterned exchanges—depends here on a thing having mass. No mass, no lifespan.[25]
מ	the **memory** save state of the previous angular phase, essentially **spatial**, with the property of reducing all prior interactions to a single resultant value.

Because I would like to assign a priority to each dimensional system as a central cycle passes through it, it is instructional to order the above dimensions by the scales of energy required for them to evolve.

1. We have three levels of energy oscillation to consider: 1) the quantum level, 2) the level of the quantum's interactant (which could be anything from quantic to megaquantic), and 3) the level of the intervening space between the quantum and its interactants. Each of these should be characterized by oscillation, though on different scales and greatly different character. According to our theory, quantic oscillations are organized, recursive, and considered a standalone unit of local energy patterning. The quantum interactant holds a cyclical pattern which is not known by the standalone quantum under consideration, consists of coupled rather than isolated energy flows, and is allowed to have a changing rate of resonance as a function of the number of quanta involved with it. The pre-energy-filled intervening space is not considered coherently organized, may be thought continuous, and serves as a space in which a chaotic mash of energy-flow vectors clash.
2. $<x_A, \phi_A, z_A, t>$ describes an animated quantum in cycle space.
3. $<r_{Bz}, \theta_{Bz}, \phi_{Bz}, \tau>$ describes a located interactant in physical space.
4. $<m, Д_z, \beta, מ>$ describes a region of resonance exchange in potential (interphysical) space.

The following heuristics assume that nature is recursive such that geometric rules which govern four dimensions in one space will govern them in another.

5. Interphysical space is nonsensical without at least two instances of physical space, and physical space is nonsensical without at least one instance of character (cycle) space. Thus the ordering of the above groups of variables is cycle, physical, interphysical. Another way of thinking about this is that it takes one quantum to define quantum space; it takes two quanta to define physical space; it takes the disjunction of space in light of two quanta to define interphysical space. But it is from interphysical space that new quanta are born from the pre-energy not participating in existing quanta on a particular scale. So the cycle, physical, and interphysical spaces wrap back around into cycle space.
6. The time (or cycle counting) dimensions t, τ, and מ, as animators of their three partner dimensions in the same space, are all last.
7. מ, as animator of an entire 12-cycle is the very last dimension before a cycle resets.
8. The magnitude assignment dimensions x_A, r_{Bz}, and m, which specify the range of effect of the base energy constituting each space , are first in their groups. Cycle space consists of cycles of the radius x_A about a central point. Physical space involves a sphere of potential interacting volume at the isoshell range of effect r_{Bz}. Interphysical space consists of the amount of regulated, flowing pre-energy among quanta, which we may count as quantic blocks Δο; The sum of these blocks, when they participate in the stable arrangement of quanta (and not otherwise), constitute mass m.
9. The orientation deviation dimensions ϕ_A from x_A, θ_{Bz} from r_{Bz}, and $Д_z$ from m, all follow their magnitude assignment dimension in a group.

---

[25] So what about the universe just before the Big Bang? Did it have a mass? To the extent that it might have had an amount of time which it took to lose half of its bang energy or at least emit half the flux in a later moment as it did at an earlier moment, we might be able to calculate a mass for the theoretical volume of energy bounded by a singularity via momentum. In other words, even if the pre-Universe isn't considered to comprise any quanta—dominated by complete non-organization of pre-energy, the span of that pre-energetic volume might still be assigned a range of effect via the concentration of energy later projected away from it. This allows us to avoid saying that the pre-Universe had no mass just because it *may* have had no quanta.

10. The volumizing dimensions z_A, ϕ_{Bz}, and β, produced by the cross product of the magnitude and deviation dimensions, set the zoom level for each system and also serve as the dimensions along which areas of effect, (magnitudes × potential magnitudes in the maximum deviation direction of their respective spaces) are counted. Based on our earlier look at the 2D versus 3D rotation of the snowflake model, we may suspect that these dimensions also determine the axis along which the next dimension's magnitude orientation will be measured. (But we'll save this discussion for later.)

And so we have our order $<x_A, \phi_A, z_A, t, r_{Bz}, \theta_{Bz}, \phi_{Bz}, \tau, m, \text{Д}_z, \beta, \text{ɴ}>$. This system demonstrates a kind of rotational symmetry with the first dimensions of a quartet describing the energy of the system we're considering, the second describing its deviation from its starting reference point, the third projecting the net energy contained in this system (of a type specific to that space)—which also determines the amount available to the next space, and the fourth describing the evolution of the system as a volume of the space's interactions.

Now I pose a question whose answer might be easy for astrologers but less intuitive from a basic physics perspective like the one I learned in college. Why should dimensions have an order? That is, shouldn't axes like x, y, and z, all be basically equal in the eyes of mathematics? They might be, but in our matrices such axes have a row order. In our right hand rule they have a definite orientation. On a gravity laden planet they have a strongly preferred direction followed by a moderately friendly longitudinal direction and an ultimately (climate-wise) discouraging latitudinal direction. Lines look fine sideways but circles do not. There are many reasons why, in the real world, we can't just take three coordinate axes and weight them equally. Natural systems, from the crystal structure of certain molecules to the semimajor axis of an asteroid, tend to move along a hierarchy of preferred axes, from those with a low threshold for energy exchange to those with a very high threshold. No wonder many a physics student has had trouble understanding free body diagrams. In the real world you can't just turn off gravity to solve a particular homework question; ideal situations in which we sometimes shut off permanently active variables are great for modeling, but ultimately clash with nature. Also, the ordering of certain dimensions over others should make sense. Given an initially 0-dimension starting point, the dimension of things really should take precedence over the dimension of interactions among those things.

Assertion 53. On the formation of stable atomic and chemical structures

What determines when a cluster of quanta settle into a stable enough arrangement to stop attracting new quanta? Based on the above dimensions we may guess that the density of the gradient, the size and shape of the intervening regions within that gradient after its basic quanta have formed, the tilt and mass-cycle of the region in question, the influence of neighboring regions, and the concentration of forward versus backwards spinning quanta (with respect to their local north) all have something to do with the size, shape, and stability of the quantic neighborhoods allowed to form. Where the twelve elementary particles of the standard model may be classified according to various configurations of the dimensions listed above, some of these particles ultimately assemble into the elements constituting the periodic table. Here the orbital structure of the valence shells lends credence to the various shapes in the 3D snowflake model (where there exists a level of quanta both above and below the plane we normally look at). Although we certainly can't claim that elements follow directly from arrangements of fundamental quanta (the former are way too big for that), we can claim that the basic oscillating 12-structure we've posed repeats itself on macroscopic levels spanning from the size of a quantic neighborhood to the shape of a spiral galaxy. Elements, unsurprisingly, seem to mirror the structure of the quantic configurations that constitute them—right down to the orbital filling preferences of the Pauli exclusion principle. Imagining elements to consist of 3D spherical collections of spherical subquanta, we can then see how certain among those quanta are inclined to exchange resonances preferentially above other quanta until the orbital shell level is filled, but in between block filling, quanta of the same current energetic exchange shape are stable enough to sit as standalone atoms, forming molecules of the element via the establishment of weak bonds rather than waiting for the high energy of strong bonds to arrive. As the universe cools, more complex assemblies of elemental subquanta will be more difficult to form since the energy required to break current neighborhood structure and add another strong bond to the mix isn't there. Alas, all you get are more copies of the same thing bonding to each other. It's kind of like R&D in a factory. Making new, big stuff takes work. Making more of the little stuff is easy.

An atomic element, then can be thought of as a sphere of subquanta (but not necessarily fundamental quanta) with a particular core of two kinds of neighborhood (protons and neutrons) with a preference for a particular valence collection of electrons outside of their required intervening space. Because these cores are grown linearly (by whatever number of quanta constitute the nucleons) rather than radially (by whatever number are needed to add a brand new sphere), the types of valence shells—and hence the types of interactions—they form vary with each new proton.[26] The preferred shapes of these valence shells, along with their sizes will have profound implications for the element's quantic cycle structure, its crystal structure, and ultimately its behavior.

---

[26] The elements' high dependence on the number of protons suggests that neutrons may play more of a space-filling role between protons than a resonance determining role, rendering their quarks some kind of collection of quanta with satisfied partners. Protons on the other hand, will still require an electron to balance them.

Chapter 37: The Astrological Reference Frame

The previous chapter contained no astrology. In this chapter I will map the 12-cycle onto people, define astrology broadly, and discuss some of the consequences of this. I will also talk less about quanta and more about the wave functions which can be used to describe those quanta's ongoing behavior.

Assertion 54. On the formation of the solar system

As an energy mass of varied density and chemical composition from its outermost radius to its center (assuming a sphere temporarily), the Solar System may be thought of as a cloud of chemicals with isoshells of equal chemical potential about a center. Subject to the chemical properties of the innermost core, we may postulate that an original Sun of a certain initial radius formed near the center of the primordial cloud, but that the net field of binding energy which held the outermost shell about the center of the cloud constituted one surface of endpints which, when coupled to the center, constituted the major field of oscillatory resonance range for all objects contained within. The outermost shell is the Oort cloud. Via the shell building system we discussed earlier, we may further postulate that the planets formed at the same time over the course of years of flux pulses issuing from the central Sun and bouncing off the chemicals present at the successive 2r points of progressively higher powers of 2. Nearest to each stable equipotential region, the regimented, regular beat of flux pulses from the central Solar emitter imparted stable, less noisy critical points upon such regions, making it easier for planets to form there. Gradually under their own gravity, on a scale smaller than the lower order of error of the larger Solar System's oscillation function, the forming planets continued to attract nearby material from the cloud until most of such material had been accounted for. Throughout this process, larger megaquantic regions surrounding the coalescing cloud are assumed to have been nonuniform in their positions about the cloud, promoting a flat cycle structure even as the total 12-dimensional structure remains spherical. At the distant point where there was no longer enough energy to drive the formation of an additional planet, the original cloud remained a cloud which would continue to absorb the now highly dispersed flux from more inward shells. Such absorption regularly leads to some local congealing and the formation of bodies of enough significance to be pulled back into the inner Solar System's gravity, and these bodies include things like the comets, and Sedna distant objects.

Assertion 55. Time & axis mapping can be used to assign predictable static and interaction-dependent relationships among number.

With the 12 cycle and the role of resonance/stability reasonably established, we need only apply one more mapping for spacetime volumes: that which connects each mappable frequency to the counting numbers themselves. I already discussed this mathematically via the first set of assertions. All that remains is to outline a reliable set of rules for processing

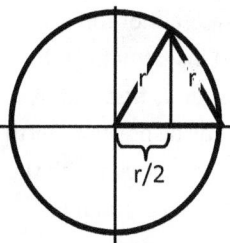

relationships in this base-12 system. Through mapping, the first region after a quantic tick constitutes the beginning of a cycle. The twelfth region after that same tick marks the end of a cycle. To the extent that we care about halfway points and other power of 2 divisions along a single axis, each of the twelve divisions gains a distinct and predictable quality along a full cycle, regardless of how long the cycle takes.

Traveling upwards through the degrees around the unit circle, and assuming we are located in the real-potential plane, the various energies are defined energetically in terms of their relationships to the major axes. Note that whenever we land at a 60° point, not only do we cut one of the major axes in half, but we also create an isosceles triangle connecting our current location on the circle to both the end point of the major axis as well as the center of the circle. At such locations, the equal distance required for a signal to travel from our two connecting points to us on the circumference along with the maintenance of that same distance between the center and the axis end point allows us to energetically treat the center and the axis end point (from our 60° reference frame) as equal. The table below illustrates this.

Degree	(Projection's) Relationship to major axis	Energetic character
0°	the positive real axis; cos(θ) = 1	the start of a cycle, the full real event
30°	halfway up the potential axis, coming; sin(θ) = ½ ↖	seeding potential energy
60°	halfway forward on the real axis, leaving; cos(θ) = ½ ↘	reflecting the real event
90°	the positive potential axis; sin(θ) = 1	finishing the first event, holding the potential for event receivers
120°	halfway backwards on the real axis, coming; cos(θ) = -½ ↙	approaching the coming receipt by event receivers
150°	halfway up the potential axis, leaving; sin(θ) = ½ ↗	approaching the end of potential to be received
180°	the negative real axis; cos(θ) = -1	the complement, receiver, or audience for the real event
210°	halfway down the potential axis, coming; sin(θ) = -½ ↘	using the receiver to seed a gain of potential for the next event
240°	halfway backwards on the real axis, leaving; cos(θ) = -½ ↖	reflecting having been received towards the gain of potential from the receiver
270°	the negative potential axis; sin(θ) = -½	gaining potential from the receipt of the event; holding the potential for the next event
300°	halfway forward on the real axis, coming; cos(θ) = ½ ↗	approaching the next real event having been given potential through receipt of the first event
330°	halfway down the potential axis, leaving; sin(θ) = -½ ↙	reflecting having gained potential from receipt of the event in preparation for the next event

Table 37-1: Relationships among the axes in terms of the four potential-real and eight bisecting potential or real circumferential points. For the eight bisecting points, the arrows indicate which axis on the regular unit circle the bisector is immediately related to, not the direction of circle traversal. For example the 60° projection bisects the 0° line, whose endpoint lies to the southeast of the 60° vector, so the arrow points ↘.

In *FSA* I used something called construct induction to assign meaning to number. This method worked mainly because the numbers themselves possessed geometric properties which built upon each other. Unfortunately, construct induction automatically assumed a certain level of coherence in human activity. Time & Axis mapping doesn't do this, but explains all regions in a 12 cycle using axis location and relationship to the nearest major axis only. Accordingly, this mapping scheme has much stronger roots in physics than in human behavior and is in many ways, more tenable as a result. The above pattern describes all repeating cycles regardless of how long they take or what the cycles consist of. The pattern is based on real versus potential energy, approaching versus leaving critical points in the cycle. Accordingly, we can use it to map our own behavioral cycles onto many other kinds of 12 cycles.

Assertion 56. Preexisting events impose their wave functions on new events, the former defining the latter. For an unwritten event which comprises little more than a notion in 12-space, definition is gained not from the event itself, but from interactions with those volumes which initially recognize and respond to the event. Such interactions establish the new event as a space describing sharp complements to each responder, in effect setting all the world—and especially the primary interactant—as the "mother" to the event. In no other scenario will we encounter such a pure metaphor for motherhood as this one—where the one responding to the event first, most strongly, and with the most investment is the same one who actually defines the event. Said differently, it is the collection of circumstances which responds first and most intensely to the newfound existence of a thing which constitutes the thing's primary definer. Genetic disposition, birth or creation context, or blind generators of the event do not possess wave functions which interact strongly enough with the event to determine its character, so it may be said that the receiver context alongside the most active set of responders forms the primary set against which a newly derived wave function comes to be.

When a new wave function is defined in function space, the process is similar to that of solving a riddle. "I am a counting number which this set calls even, that set says is less than 7, and this third set responds to as if a perfect square." Gradually such an event comes to be recognized as the number 4, having derived its being from the initial set of 12 units outlined earlier as held by all other wave functions with which it interacts. But even when these interactants themselves were so defined, their own wave functions determined at the moment of conception by their closest respondents (or quantic neighbors, they also possessed a more subtle history that existed via a sequence that traced all the way back to the initial evolution of their forebears, all the way back to their forebears' forebears, in turn traceable back to the chemically unique shell building across the local space of energetic potentials. An event happening now stems from the history of every event which led up to it.

Rather than thinking of wave functions as simply arising out of nowhere, we should more properly think of them as reflecting the ever colliding, fusing, spin-changing, color-cycling interplay of the characteristic primitives of standard model physics—for each physical form reflecting a temporary tangling of the most resonant families of simple waves. The consistent chemical composition of a stellar system, the gradual emergence of orbiting forms as a byproduct of ever ordered chemopotential gradients in a matter cloud helps ensure that most species local to each other reflect frequency families local to each other—organic forms building organic forms like themselves while the dynamics among those organic forms—whether thoughts or social structures also evolve dynamics like *them*selves. It is not only the particle that changes its states in time, but the dynamic that particle has with other particles which also changes. Thus collisions among functions breed more collisions and more similar collisions in a local frame where previous functions were already susceptible to multiplicative framing, until functions more fit to respond to states of the very frames they occupy are born. From this arises the notion of the genetic algorithm and, relatedly, the functional evolutionary process itself.

Why might a species of ultra-complex function have its core dynamics explainable through a combination of simple functions which fall far short of the main function's complexity? Because the former has its origins in generating circumstances which in turn have their origins in previous circumstances, reducible back to the simple functions. Even where this chained system has been subject to heavy interference, the large number of current dynamics surrounding any newly emergent function under any given set of initial conditions serves to keep the much larger wave functions of planets and orbits stable against most of the little workings of smaller occupants.

Assertion 57. Responders against a system advance in the direction opposite the systems they respond to.
A point traveling forward on an axis necessarily means that the containing axis travels backwards against the point. Accordingly, nested systems alternate in their forward versus backwards progression. Alternation is the rule among systems whose states include states immediately prior to themselves so that, alongside the quantic nature of waves with end points, recursive systems rooted in real-world observability produce sections which are rendered not only discrete in boundary, but distinct in content as well. Polarity is a natural property of discrete systems whether through oddness-evenness, spin up-spin down, masculinity-femininity, sphericity-discality, communion-agency, or parent-child-grandparent character.

Assertion 58. Subsets may be mapped using the same patterns of their parent sets, and those patterns may unfold in the reverse direction as that of the parents.
This follows from the previous assertion. Here we see, for example, where a need to count more / bigger cycles around a circle gives rise to smaller sections of shrinking span. When compounded, powers of less than unity produce even smaller values, but more of them. The reader may have noticed this early in the last chapter in the case where the natural form of the bounded infinite set was {1...0} rather than {0...1}. Especially in cases where an initial value of a well-ordered subset must gradually dilute the progressive influence of the superset of which it is a part, an alternating forward-reverse ordering may be more appropriate than a simple recursive forward ordering. This claim may be confusing, so I will give two examples—one of each kind of ordering—along with an explanation of why we might concern ourselves with this.

- In math, the non-negative whole numbers form a well-ordered set in that 0 comes first, 1 comes after 0, 2 follows 1 and 0, 3 follows 2, 1, and 0, and so on. As we build bigger numbers, the 0, 1, 2, 3...pattern repeats in the same direction; the 20s follow the 10s, the 30s follow the 20s and 10s, and so on... Every time you tack on a digit, you follow the order 0, 1, 2, 3... again in that new digits place. This is an example of recursively forward order, and works especially well for certain theoretical structures.

- In a gear system a different kind of ordering holds. If one gear spins clockwise the gear attached to it spins counterclockwise. The gear attached to that spins clockwise again. When considered as subset interactions attached to the original gear, this provides an example of alternating forward-reverse ordering.

Nested time cycles on Earth follow an alternating pattern as the advancing day corresponds to retreating Sun and advancing planets around that Sun (in line with the Earth's actual movement). The inward versus outward push at the boundaries of a torquing object are another example of this. To start a new cycle that takes place across intervals with well-defined boundaries, an alternating cycle like these may be useful for making it very clear where one parent set interval ends and the next one begins. This is in contrast to a strictly forward system of subset nesting where the difference between 29 and 30 is no more dramatic (magnitude-wise) than 30 and 31. It is more dramatic digit-wise, though. Under an alternating counting system we might go from 29 to 39, 38, 37...32, 31, 30, 40, 49, 48...Odd as that might look, you may be able to see that this is how gears proceed, with each digit representing something like the 10th sections of one particular gear. This is more dramatic value-wise but less dramatic digit-wise. Applied to digits as representatives of mutually influeincing spatial regions, the alternating system actually captures digit continuity and 10-block discreteness better than the strictly forward ordering. It also favors circularity more easily whereas the strictly forward ordering prefers unbounded linearity.[27]

Considered with the previous assertion, we may guess that separate interactants in nature may follow alternate ordering if they branch linearly (one gear at a time), of have no preferred order if they branch nonlinearly (several gears clustered together). A central quantum in a tightly packed plane for example branches off to six neighbors in the vacuum, each of which also has six neighbors, so we can expect the system to behave approximately frictionlessly if the system is to behave at all. This is because a triad of alternating gears would resist each others' cycling if the system employed a resistance force between quanta. We are concerned with this because it has implications for how we represent the division of a cycle into recursively nested regions.

Assertion 59. Divisions of the circle may be described in both the forward and backwards direction.
Let the regions described by forward progression in the ϕ_A direction be referred to as phasic character regions. Regions described by backwards progression in the $-\phi_A$ direction when compared to the forward direction will be called the harmonic history regions. Character regions are described by increasing frequency. Harmonic regions are described by increasing wavelength.

Assertion 60. The flattenable, ordered dimensions of 12-space suggest a direction of action for each dimension.
Earlier I showed how a 3D system may, given two 60° rotations, be flattened into a 2D system as well as how such a system may maintain its order under this transformation. Suppose now, we went in the reverse direction and expanded a 12-sector 2D system into a 3D space. If our space were to maintain the same kind of circular ordering as it did before, a definite sequence of sector traversal would emerge.

---

[27] If the alternate system started at 00, 01, 02,...09, 19, 18, 17... and continued through ...92, 91, 90, the next value could be 00 again with no trouble at all posed to the cycle. Since blocks starting with an even 10s digit would advance forward and blocks beginning with an odd digit would advance backwards, the entire blocks would retain a distinct character with respect to each other. The strictly forward ordering, on the other hand, flows more like a neverending sawtooth wave.

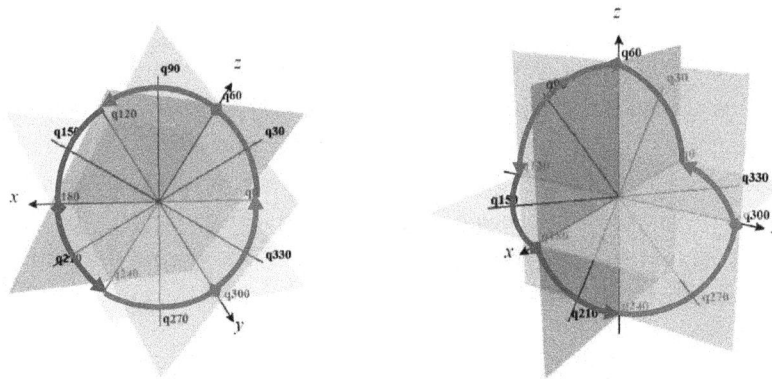

Figure 37-1: Traversal sequence for the 12 sectors of a 3D-ready, 2D cycle

We can see how going from a 2D to a 3D mapping turns our regular circumference into a sequence of three quadrant loops which circumscribe the boundaries of the spherical space nicely. Given that such quadrant loops seem to illustrate a geometric rule for this kind of mapping, we may ask whether an analogous rule applies to the fully dimensional snowflake model. That is, can we see a patterned ordering in its three subspaces that will allow us to construct a fully recursive model consistent with known physical laws?

Converting $<r_{Bz}, \theta_{Bz}, \phi_{Bz}, \tau>$ and $Д_z$ to $<r_B, \theta_B, z_B, \tau>$ and $Д$

Before we begin I will need to make an important system change. Since we will be assuming the three subspaces to be simple rotations of each other, it will no longer be fitting to use spherical coordinates for the physical space while using cylindrical coordinates for cycle space. Instead, I'll use cylindrical coordinates for both systems. This will be convenient for confining any circular behavior to a single flat plane under our rotations. Let's investigate the coordinate switch to ensure that all of our appropriate 3D-behaviors are preserved.

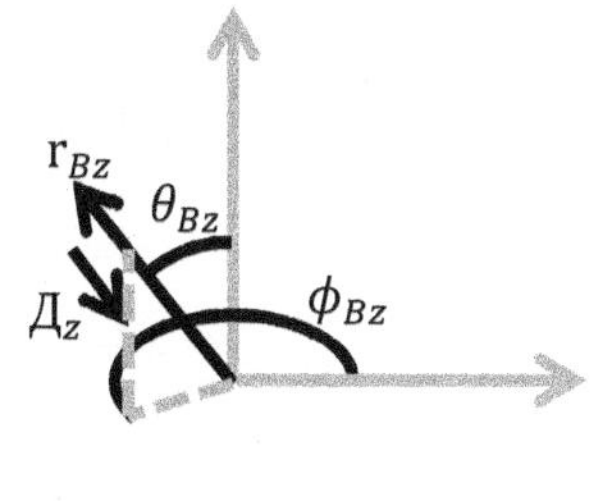	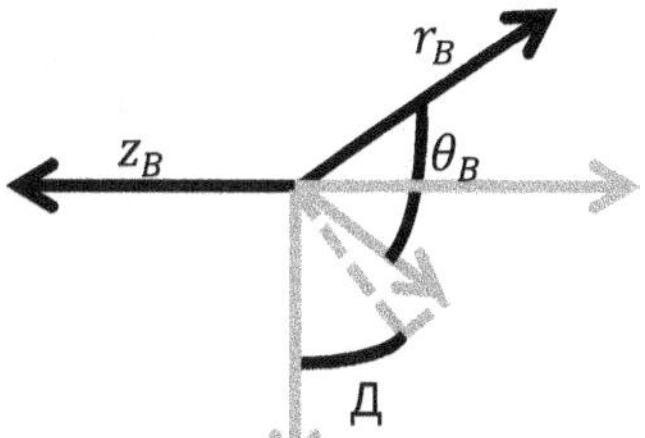
In our old spatial space system, $<r_{Bz}, \theta_{Bz}, \phi_{Bz}>$ covered every possible orientation in space using a sphere shape, where $Д_z$ served as its rate. This system was good for looking around a central emitter, but makes for ugly transformations with the other subspaces.	In our new system, $<r_B, \theta_B, z_B>$ covers the space using a cylinder while it varies its projection in the normal plane to z_B. $r_{B(z)}$ and $\theta_{B(z)}$ retain their basic meanings here (albeit rotated), while the combination of mass-cycle ϕ_{Bz} and differential emission $Д_z$ (in the direction of mass against r_{Bz}) is transformed into z_B and differential *energy* $Д$ against a perpendicular to z_B (which we'll show to be the direction of mass). At this point τ had no vector that we conceived of, though it also would have changed. I'll get to the vectorized form of τ shortly.

Figure 37-2: Comparison of the spherical dimensions to the cyclindrical ones. Note that although this isn't really a big deal geometrically, it *could* be a big deal physics-wise. Mass-cycle ϕ_{Bz} for example represented one of the most abstract dimensions in 12-space, and makes a lot less sense from our physical point of view and a lot more sense from an orbiting planet's point of view. The only reason mass-cycle even existed was as a way of explaining what the second angular argument in the spherical system was supposed to represent in nature; so it was more like a mathematical artifact. In the new system, this is dropped for the much more intuitive z_B.

Д will now be called differential energy and will be defined with respect to mass. We'll figure out what z_B does after the rotations are finished.

Assigning a vector to <t>

Up to now I have considered the dimension of time t to lack a clear geometric relationship to its spacemates x_A, ϕ_A, and z_A. No more. Since time represents a completed cycle in a plane imaginary to the x_A reference axis, it is fitting that time should be a tangent vector to the quantum at x_A. Here, time will flow in a direction perpendicular to the direction of the energy emitter, and this setup makes sense if we consider the quantum itself to also be an energy emitter with time serving as the ever-expanding radius of its spacetime cone. Also, being tangent to the quantum, it's appropriate that time flow out to apparent infinity even as the quantum itself only moves in a circumference-bounded cycle. τ and ת will have similar relationships to their respective subspaces.

Making <m, Д, β, ת> analogous to <x_A, ϕ_A, z_A, t>

If mass is the amount of pre-energy available to us, if differential energy Д acts as a kind of lattice orientation on that mass, and if β is the cross product of these two, then we got lucky ordering these dimensions in the way that we did. The order of the 12 dimensions stays the same. Now, however, mass will be a linear count in the direction away from the quantum, Д will be a flow direction coincident with that mass, and β will be a tally of the net energy occupied by these two.

The 3D 12-space model

Given the above, cycle-space looks like this:

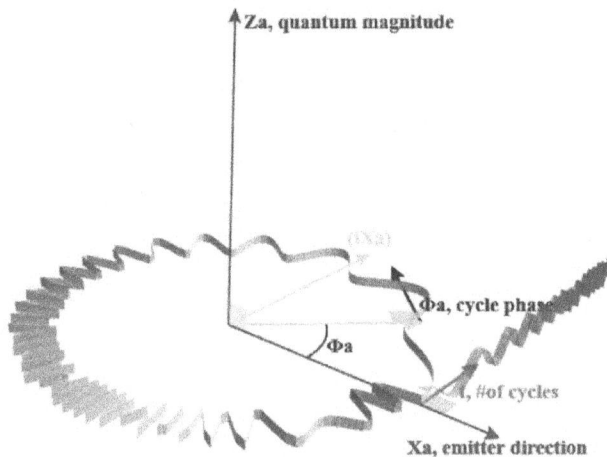

Figure 37-3: <x_A, ϕ_A, z_A, t> space

Next we apply the first quadrant loop transformation (pushing x_A up towards the direction of z_A then rolling it in the direction of its ϕ_A).

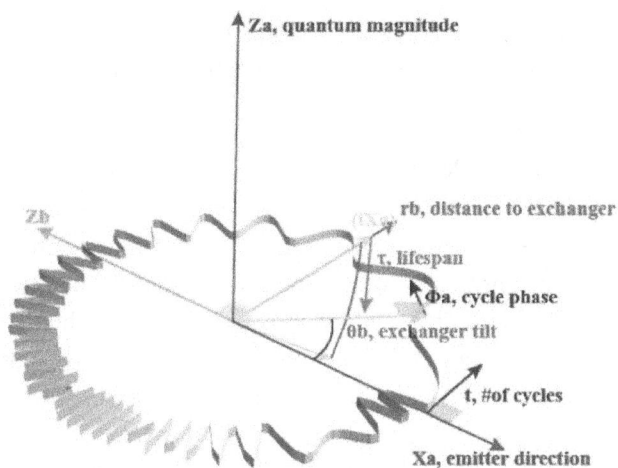

Figure 37-4: $<x_A, \phi_A, z_A, t, r_B, \theta_B, z_B, \tau>$ space

Now for the next quadrant loop.

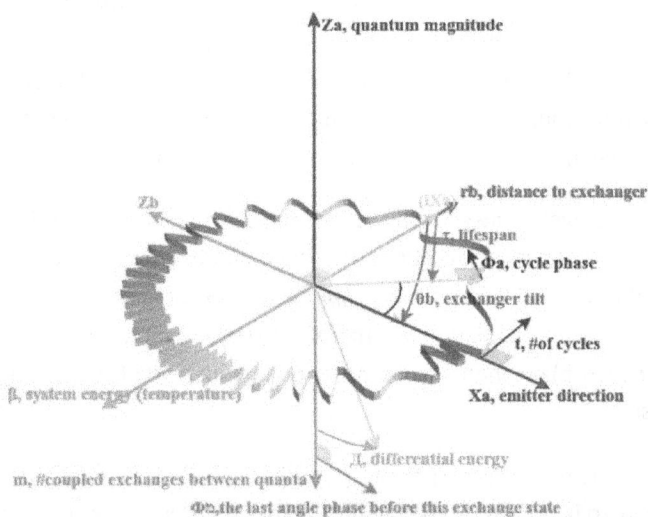

Figure 37-5: $<x_A, \phi_A, z_A, t, r_B, \theta_B, z_B, \tau, m, Д, \beta, ʠ>$ space

There is no need for a third loop since such a thing will bring us back to where we started.

Commentary on axes

It is important to note that <u>the system above does not represent space-space, but dimension-space</u>. It shows how 1) one dimension begins with a directed path between a sender and receiver, 2) a second dimension arises from the angular deviation from that path at the same magnitude, 3) a third dimension forms from the cross product of the first two dimensions, and 4) a fourth dimension arises from the completion of the second dimension's cycle where it is perpendicular to the first dimension (that is, where the angular deviation returns to zero). Furthermore, the direction of each fourth dimension forms the basis of the direction of each fifth dimension, since each fourth dimensional "tick" is a differential (tiny slice of energy) analogous to the same differential which started the first dimension's journey from sender to receiver in the first place. The whole system repeats the 1–4 cycle for the 5–8 and 9–12 cycles but this time using the 4th dimension as the direction of the new 5th and the 8th dimension as the direction of the new 9th. Finally, the 12th dimension is used as the direction of the new 1st.

Since these twelve dimensions represent 2D spatial space (namely, the $<x, y>$ plane as $<x_A, r_B>$ only) rather than 3D spatial space, this same system would have to be applied to the $<y, -z>$ and $<x, z>$ planes separately. In order for our familiar kinematic systems to emerge. That's easy enough though: we just allow the entire system to rotate spherically as a function of the local vacuum.[28] That, of course means that we will not be able to simply look to the left of an emitter to measure the temperature β for example, as β will be buried in the information of more directly human-perceivable x_A and r_B. The orthogonal relationships, however, will remain the same on the dimensional level. An interesting consequence of all this is that, if we were to shrink ourselves and stare at a quantum directly, we may expect to see only those dimensions for which our own senses are most equipped, namely $x_{A<x,y>}$, $x_{A<y,-z>}$, $x_{A<x,z>}$ as space occupied and $r_{B<x,y>}$, $r_{B<y,-z>}$, $r_{B<x,z>}$ as location—with values like the three angular dimensions and the three time-like dimensions still occuring on too small a scale for us to notice.[29] We can expect to perceive the entire world as though we were an anchor mass at one end of a rigid rotator; only through actual collision with the volumes (or through the use of helpful measuring instruments) could we expect to obtain more information about other properties like, mass, heat and charge. Only by comparing behavior of collections of quanta would we be able to separate the bounded infinite spans of angular information. I'll talk more about how this affects us directly in the chapter on spirituality.

In the above system, opposing axes are related inversely. As distance to an exchanger r_B goes up, the energy contribution to that exchanger β goes down reciprocally. Meanwhile, the flow of time t increases. This is in line with the idea that it may take years for the light from more distant objects to arrive while the light from nearby objects will take fractions of seconds. As the quantum magnitude (or charge) z_A goes up, the number of coupled exchanges m among multiple quanta goes down as does the lifespan τ of any quantic groups formed. Increasing the temperature β of a system decreases the distance to the exchanger r_B in that the increasingly energetic system is more likely to expand towards the exchanger.

In the above model, parallel forces travel in the same direction, and this has implications for certain kinds of physical laws. The more coupled exchanges among a quantic collection, for example, the longer its lifespan. The more resonance "emission," the lower the…z_B? What is that value? Given a spinning distance to an exchanger in our earlier speculation about gravity, z_B presents us with an ideal candidate for **input energy**, a force-like quantity which reflects the extent to which the quantum will host (or absorb) resonances with other quanta instead of sponsoring them. This quantity will have an inverse relationship to emission axis.

Angular values oscillate in their home plane. Cycle phase ϕ_A represents the circular magnetic axis which may be used to induce the electric current normal to it at z_A. It is possible that thanks to intervening space requirements discussed earlier, this field receives a dedicated orthogonal component along the $<x_A, z_A>$ plane as light passes through the x_A axis. I believe that differential energy Д indicates the cycle of state resonances involved in creating the potential background for a newly formed "memory" at the start of the next cycle. It represents the stage of the quantum's resonance with its pre-energetic surroundings involved in determining the next emission. Spatially speaking, there must be some dimension for handling collisions with existing regions outside of the quantum's internal dynamics, and this may be it. Note how Д makes a good rate replacement for Д$_z$ even though we switched our space spatial mapping system. As long as we update its correspondence to the relevant real-world physical phenomenon, its role as a dimension remains analogous to that of differential emission.

---

[28] The global "true north" required to ensure that quanta continue to respond to their rightful supergalactic regions will still be there, perhaps as a fixed vector x_{A0} for the direction of most efficient frequency resonance with the parent of the parent of the parent system… responsible for constellar clusters continuing to move together.

[29] Though we could certainly still observe these properties on the macroscopic level.

Lastly, we need to make a distinction between phenomena that are coherently viewable and those that aren't. The first and third axis of each subspace is viewable. The second dimensions are generally not viewable unless their process coincides with the completion of another revolution. The t-like cycles of each completed revolution are punctuated.

On what we typically see when we look at something

ϧ (or $\phi_ϧ$) has the interesting property of representing a signal in the direction of object emission. The model implies that as we perceive the information from objects straight on (which—barring cameras—is the only perspective we have in our single-viewpoint spherical space), we are receiving a chain of phasic information from those objects. The information appears as light in a concentrated array per surface area (r_B integrated over tilt θ_B), with the added—and intriguing—side effect of being flanked by external distances to other exchangers which tell us not only the space but the time separation between the thing we're looking at and the other, peripheral objects around it. We also calculate a broad idea of the mass of things using various learned heuristics. Typically, then, our light trained eyes know distance and time in parallel, spatial expanse radially, a sequence of phasic memory states as light itself, but tend to have a much harder time perceiving the anti-distance (system energy), anti-mass (charge), and anti-emitter (input energy) dimensions accordingly. We also have trouble perceiving differential and cycle phase expanse because these dimensions are mathematically "not normal" to our thoroughly visual sphere; our visual trajectory lies in the plane of their perception, so we can only know these easily by looking horizon-ways for ϕ_A or azimuthally for Д. Again, this is all a consequence of the fact the entire 12-system we proposed is continually spinning for each quantum in all kinds of directions at breakneck speeds. The dimensions will always overlap, but retain their relationships to each other's values depending on the volumes of which they are apart. Rest assured though, it will typically be very difficult for those of us creatures who specialize in particular sensory modalities to see *everything* at once.

Assertion 61. Astrology is defined as the mapping of the instantaneous $x_{A,n}$ and $\phi_{A,n}$ components of the n significant quantic collections surrounding an event O in a single plane, where each $x_{A,n}$ is a function of its $ϧ_n$, and the entire system is measured against the event's own $ϧ_O$ at $\tau_O = 0$.

Though an event may last for several decades or many hundreds of years, astrology allows an observer to read the general pattern of an event in a fraction of the event's lifespan τ. Astrology assumes that each astronomical body is the organization of quanta, encapsulates a stereotyped frequency range with respect to the local (solar) system's central emitter, observable in convolution with other resonant flux gradients in the direction of a central perceiver, that the interaction of multiple such quanta with the perceiver's 12-space quanta[30] and each other is deterministic on the various $ϧ_n$s involved, but nondeterministic on the full space of <ϕ_A, θ_B, Д> of the event itself. We argue here that in astrology, as in the rest of physics, we can calculate the range of possibilities for a system given a certain reasonable number of constraints, and we can even calculate our own possible choices among those possibilities. But we can't include every constraint. Nor can we calculate the possibilities of our possible behaviors to the ^{nth} degree without reducing the calculation itself to but one in a chain of determined outcomes. Furthermore, as our window of viewing is necessarily restricted in physical space, quantic arrangement (genetic and biochemical capacity), as well as lifespan, we necessarily order, remember, and compress the possibilities in our cycle, interphysical, and physical magnitude dimensions towards the dropping of key information regarding our previous states, so that—though we may see most of the relevant blueprint for experience, we can only view the blueprint as a blueprint by standing in one room at a time. Nonetheless, if the universe is a vacuum sea of compressed and expanded space, and if the astronomical bodies are merely organized couplings of such space which themselves compel downstream vacuum curvature resonances radially about their boundaries, then astrology describes the confluence of such resonances at a single moment $t = t_0$, for a single quantum collection O, at single location ($r_{B\{x,y\}}$, $r_{B,\{y,-z\}}$, $r_{B,\{x,z\}}$) from the local major emitter and its orientation ϕ_A theretowards, at the onset of its stable window $\tau_O = 0$, given its underlying quanta's emission in the direction of $x_{A,n}$. I know that was a lot. Let's use an analogy.

If we pick a circular spot in some pond and drop 10 or so boulders at various places around it, and then after some time photograph the state of the circle we picked, we will have the equivalent of a circumferential state capture of "vacuum"

---

[30] Not just in space or time, but in mass, charge, and the rest of the 12-space as well.

density around that location. Only in real life, each boulder drops in a regulated, elliptical pattern, formed as the result of density interactions with all the other boulders, and our very process of picking a point may itself be considered the result of the preexisting patterns which describe us as points—patterns whose previous state values are necessarily forgotten by us as surely as they compelled us to attempt prediction in the first place. The waves in the water aren't rays from the boulders, but flux from central regions of frequency-delineated density in the oscillating rubber sheet of the vacuum itself. Thus astrology isn't the study of planets, but the study of the vacuum state at a particular set of 2 to 3 values in 12-space: time t, space r_B, and (hopefully) the general form of the event being described (something like m). The major assumption of astrology is that the event being described is tied to some system—biological, temporal, or signal-communicative—which will continue to reinforce the dynamics shown in that state for as long as the event can stably endure, just as the light from a distant body will attempt to preserve its energetic properties until shifted away from those properties or absorbed. Where the system in which all of this takes place is the subset of an even larger coherent system, the underlying quantum-level dynamics are assumed to be at work not just between an asteroid and an Earth receiver, but between one star cluster and another, with a common potential-oscillation structure for the vacuum itself and the bounded regions contained therein promoting quantic block transfer among energy carriers.

As events in 12-space, we react to other events and then sustain reactions to those same events even as those events long pass us by. Thus an instantaneous capture becomes the template for an ongoing action for as long as the capture holds a preferred arc for describing every 3-dimensional phasic location's relationship to every other phase received from an interactant. Our status as living or non-living—animal, book, or social movement—circumscribes the ease with which we can act on certain phasic relationships over others as well as the extent to which we as self-reinforcers can be expected to endure. Accordingly, astrology is the study of system-local spacetime moments turned institutions unto themselves. It's power to predict events is about as strong as that of any collection of partial data against full data set, but its power to organize and summarize which frequency ranges are more likely to intersect with others in a system of complex, dynamic actors is stronger than any field I've seen, even psychology.

Although I may read certain components of your life rooted in location and distance, I cannot use astrology to read how you frame experiences, what specific actions you will perform, what you will pay attention to, how you constrain meaning, or by what quantities you exaggerate certain events. I can, however, tell you much about the classes of cycle combinations you will tend to engage and in what general order you will engage them.

When we need to study evolving systems which it is not in our power to manufacture and not within our capability to reasonably model, fields such as sociology and psychology are the macro-level defaults in cases where the harder sciences face too many antecedent unknowns. Having been trained in these fields, however, I can say that the world-view biases and barriers to genuine clarification of the human psyche are extensive—far more easily and thoroughly damaged by selective research agendas than the hard sciences are. Only through a widely available, "open source" system of behavioral psychological inquiry can we most directly arrive at an understanding of our interacting selves. I would like to see such a system emerge, and believe that a unified approach to cyclical dynamics across all fields is the best route for doing so.

Assertion 62. Astronomical bodies, to the extent that they represent consistent wave functions at various potential energy levels on the Solar System's energy along an increasing radius r, also reflect configurations of potential energy along the Solar System's 12-cycle.
This follows from earlier assertions as well as from the definition of ♭, with the added claim that astronomical bodies each have a default window of frequencies reflective of the vacuum conditions under which they formed, which may be located on the 12-cycle.

Assertion 63. Angular configurations of astronomical bodies circumscribe patterns of character which follow from the divisions of the 12-cycle itself.
That is, angular separations in the universal sky, when mapped onto the 12-cycle, indicate analogous dynamics to angular positions along the base 12-cycle. Whenever we look at bodies in a 12-cycle map, we are looking at representations of energy carriers at a particular equipotential level about the Solar System's center. That isoshell—typically an ellipsoid—

corresponds to an equivalent mapping on the idealized Solar System sphere, is described by a radius r on that idealized sphere, and can be mapped onto a line about the 2D 12-circle. So every astronomical body naturally corresponds to some span of points along the 12-cycle. The character of each body and the precision of the 12-cycle used to describe it (12, 144, 1728, etc...) depends on how specific we wish to be in comparing it to other bodies. And though each body may be considered to "live in" or "rule" a particular location on the circle, the fact that these bodies move around with respect to other points in space means that they will be subject to changing angle relationships with other bodies. Such angle relationships are easily classified, though, by setting one body as the starting point, counting the degrees between the two, and seeing where the end of the arc falls on the circle.

Assertion 64. The 12-cycle character of an astronomical body in our Solar System as viewed from Earth may be estimated using the formula $\left(log_2(semimajor) + 7 - \frac{1}{12}\right) : \left\{log_2(perihelion) + 7 - \frac{1}{12} \rightarrow log_2(aphelion) + 7 - \frac{1}{12}\right\} : \left\|log_2\left(\frac{aph}{peri}\right)\right\|$

I have estimated this experimentally via statistics on the characteristics of the 1000 asteroids listed in a later chapter. Units are in AU distance from the Sun. For example, the character of the planet Uranus is $\left(11\frac{26}{144}\right) : \left\{11\frac{16}{144} \rightarrow 11\frac{35}{144}\right\} : \|21\|$. This means that Uranus has the average character of the (26th harmonic [fans and followers] operating in the 11th region [social information]):{using the 16th harmonic [emotional support base] enacted towards the 35th harmonic [genius and innovation]}:‖with the overall apparent character of the 21st harmonic [public display]‖, where each 1/12 region is divided into 12 subregions—producing a total of 144 harmonics (countable divisions representing fractions of a circle) along the circle.

Assertion 65. All pairs of astronomical bodies present a natural potential differential between their corresponding isoshells. This differential is also characterizable on the 12-cycle.

An isoshell is typically an ellipsoid whose surface holds equal potential energy around a central point. The idealized orbital path of a body forms a 2D band upon a 3D egg. By taking the characters (phasic ranges) of the two bodies using the formula in the previous assertion and juxtaposing those characters, we may characterize the natural dynamic which any two bodies correspond to when their angle of separation is actively amplified.

The above argument is best illustrated with math. Keeping in mind the approximate doubling relationship we discussed earlier, suppose Mercury has a value of 64 (2^6), Venus right after it has a value of 128 (2^7), and Mars (right after Venus given Earth as the silent reference point) has a value of 256 (2^8). Jupiter will have a value of 512 (2^9). In this contrived example, Venus-Mercury distances will always be on the order of 64 (128−64), while Mars-Venus distances will always be on the order of 128 (256−128). Mars-Mercury distances, though, will be on the order of 192 (256−64). Is there any other way in this highly limited system to arrive at 192? No. Here the planets act like digits in a base system, and don't generally share the ability to produce certain values with their combinations. The reality is, of course that such overlaps really do occur (especially among the asteroids), but even so, the overlaps occur at the intersection of certain orbital elements that render each combination slightly different.

When the doubling effect away from a central emitter is removed via base 2 logarithm, the differences among astronomical pair separations become analogous, though they are still different. This allows us to wrap any angular separations onto the same circle as linear separations in light of a correction for the 2^n nature of the phasic circle itself. In astrology, each body is a digit in a circular numbering system. Each angular separation among those bodies is also a digit, though on the scale of radians instead of AU. The tropical seasons on Earth are used to produce their own digit system. Rather than using Earth's seasons, the sidereal system of the ambient universe maps cycle space for the fundamental quanta involved, turning things like planetary orbits into cosmic-background-inducing spaces instead. The progression of the day at a particular latitude and longitude allows for division into another digit system, the houses. And all of these can be scaled to fit on a circle for describing the myriad quantitative relationships occurring between values like 2^1 and 2^{12}. Here, Venus wouldn't be significant because of any rays it threw at the Earth. It would be significant because of its role as the aggregation of the 2^{7th}

potential energy level as a radial body in the Solar System from Earth's frame, and the analogous response to all 2^7-relevant behaviors characteristic of an instantaneously captured system which does everything else on the same 2^1-2^{12} scale.

Assertion 66. Angles of separation between points on a 12-cycle denote a dynamic between the separated bodies which is amplified when the nearest fraction of a circle with which the angle is resonant is itself amplified.

This is to say, that when a counted number of cycles multiplies the angle in question so that it approximates a whole number, the angle itself is considered to have completed a cycle. Counts are limited to the number of divisions we are considering. If we are only considering 12 divisions, then an angle like 48° will be closest to region 8, since 8 x 48 is closer to a full cycle than any other multiple less than or equal to 12. Here, 48° will have a character similar to that of the 210°-240° character region. If we are considering 144 divisions, however, 15 will be the appropriate harmonic since 15 x 48 is even closer to a full circle than other multiples, and is more immediately realizable than 30 x 48° or 45 x 48° for example. In this case, 48° will have a character similar to that of the 322.5°-325° harmonic region since this is the 15th of 144 regions going in reverse from 0° (a.k.a. 360°). I have discussed this matter in another book.

Assertion 67. Focus, framing, and attention may be directed towards the points on the circle, entire regions, angles of separation, individual events, or dynamics among those events in order to amplify any experiences connected to the others.

The 12-cycle map establishes an ongoing, recursive correspondence among all items directly or by proxy represented on the circle. Such a correspondence is made possible via the fundamental properties of cycles and their stable energetic divisions. Attention to a 90th harmonic at one level of a local system is assumed to constitute attention to a 90th harmonic at all levels within that system's order of error. Attention to a 90th harmonic within a 27th frequency ϕ_n frame at one level of a local system is assumed to constitute attention to a 90th harmonic within a 27th frequency ϕ_n frame at all levels within that system's order of error. In astrology speak: planets, angles, and degree locations activate each other. In acoustic speak: incident frequencies amplify like frequencies in other local media.

Chapter 38: Project Laurentia

The world is full of strange and interesting phenomena. While there are certainly qualities of reality that may be viewed in a normative, everyone-agreeable way (such as staying alive and being healthy), there are other phenomena which exist purely as constructs built upon other constructs which exist solely to label dynamics. Things like law, bullying, and Rome are generally believed to exist, though they don't exist with the kind of coherence that biological or natural processes do. How is it possible that an entire non-real thing like "Microsoft" can nevertheless exist in human minds? Better yet, how can a thing like a "human" exist in human minds when we ourselves—at least in terms of the hard sciences—are supposed to be mere assemblies of chemistry and physics? The answer is, even dynamics have form. Whenever a group of perceivers get together and declare something to be real, passing that reality onto their children and their neighbors alike, even imaginary things like "science" comes to gain a reality which circumscribes people's lives. Such imagined things can even be thought of as changing nature itself.

In *144* I defined belief as the state of steering one's actions around the existence of a thing. If I believe a wall is in front of me, I may lean on it, stick a poster on it, or tag it, but I won't generally try to stare through it or walk through it because—consciously or not—I assume the wall is there and circumscribe my behaviors around that fact. Over the course of the previous chapters, I showed that all repeating cycles followed the same 4 or 12 step progression such that analogies could be set up between any one cycle and any other. To the extent that all observable experiences have both a beginning and an end they too can have cycles assigned to them with the center of the cycle representing the peak of the thing's existence. For cycles like this (which seem only to be one-shot occurrences) it isn't the event which starts off one way and returns to itself, but the surrounding world which starts off without the event and ends without the event. In this way, in accordance with an earlier assertion, your astrology chart doesn't so much provide a look at *you* as it provides a look at the state of the Solar System and immediate set of dynamics that surrounds you—defining you in terms of the space that complements you in (ironically) a very 26 Proserpina-like way. To read your chart is to read a delta-like instantaneous snapshot of a larger math function which surrounds and defines you, taking its waves and energy carriers back from you once your time is up. In the energetic sense, you can think of your life as a kind of quantic tick—a brief pulse during which trillions of energy carriers intersect at an allowable stable state. Your actions throughout life represent your brief attempt to keep that state active as long as possible.

In the two previous chapters I showed that all cycles of starting and returning are describable by the same 90° progression of real event→potential to be complemented→real complement→potential to be real, and I also showed that you can introduce halfway points on the real and potential axes to give rise to increments of 30° and, accordingly, 12 regions. From here on, we will label those regions using the shorthand of astrology, and stay with the idea that astronomical bodies in the actual Solar System present a chain of orbits of increasing radii from the Sun which can in turn be mapped onto points of increasing degree away from 0° in the circle.

Much of the theory for the planets and signs has already been explained in my previous books, so I won't repeat it here. To summarize, astrology charts are a snapshot of the sky from a particular vantage point in spacetime. Any planets, bodies, or calculated points can be represented in this chart. Such bodies reflect a particular character which stems mainly from their distance from the Sun (our central energy emitter). The angles of separation between such bodies (called aspects) can be grouped together by the number of repeats it takes for them to approximate a full circle (called a harmonic). The character of an event progresses forward on the circle, 0°-360°, Aries through Pisces, while the harmonics associated with each fraction of a circle progresses backwards, 360°-0°, $\frac{1}{1}$ of a circle through $\frac{1}{144}$ of a circle if you chop each region into 12 smaller regions. Although we've continued to use 12 signs, we stopped limiting ourselves to 12 harmonics long ago in *FSA* as we showed that angles such as 105° (7 $\times \frac{1}{24}$ of a circle) actually had meaning. We used stats and clustering on over 400 (and sometimes 800) charts to make the conclusions that we made, and in *144* eventually employed a system for categorizing traditionally astrologically unfamiliar objects like 704 Interamnia and 50000 Quaoar. And all was well. Until...

Through a conversation between two fictitious characters in the third book *144*, I presented the idea that orbits may be applied in a much more consistent way to categorize space objects. Sometime during the writing of the first book *FSA*, I had settled on a related hypothesis for how astrology works in general but did not present it due to a lack of theoretical ammunition for the job. Between the writing of *144* and now, however, I obtained a list of the first 1000 MPC objects (hereafter referred to broadly as "asteroids") from serennu.com, obtained a list of orbital elements (for calculating actual orbits) from the Minor Planet Center; characterized all 1000 asteroids using the Pluto-Selene method in *HBS*; arranged them according to the closet, farthest, and average distances from the Sun (perihelion, aphelion, and semimajor axis); Then I mapped the basic astrological regions onto the Earth and found that, consistently, the 12-cycle prevailed. I learned that asteroid and planet names tended to reflect their roles in the chart much more strongly than chance (a fact which I'm sure is well known to actual astronomers and the IAU), and that certain asteroids were simply more excellent at tapping into otherworldly experiences than others. Among those asteroids were 15760 1992QB1 (the support attractor around which I built a personal project for, among other things, gaining all this information in a short time) and 162 Laurentia: the asteroid of having opportunities handed to you for no apparent reason. My Laurentia is in the 27.5°-30° duodecanate ($\frac{1}{144}$th slice) of Gemini which—as discussed in *144*—makes it a level-10 conjunct. This means that, broadly speaking, whenever I declare a thought I attract things to affirm that thought; typically, when I ask a question whose answers I actually want to know (rather than just throwing them out there in random conversation or something) I get answers. Everyone has goodies like Laurentia somewhere in their chart. But they also have bad guys like Laurentia somewhere in their chart—meaning that if you do the thing indicated by Laurentia's position, you are almost guaranteed to win—even if what you win is terrible for everyone involved.

An Introduction to 162 Laurentia

The goal of Project Laurentia is to set you up to win consistently in the area of your life occupied by this asteroid, and use that area to frame all other areas in a way that straightens out your affairs accordingly. For some people, Laurentia will revolve around happiness. For others it will simply mean survival. The mechanism for taking on the project is simple: read where this asteroid is in your chart and do what the region indicates in a way aimed towards what you want. That's all there is to it. In this chapter I'll show you how to read duodecanates so you can know what to do. But there are a couple of things I must warn you about first.

- Many, many battles—especially in noisy times—are not worth winning. If you don't like where you are, using Laurentia to win there won't help you. You'd do better to use Laurentia to get out of where you are first.
- For some people, Laurentia is in a difficult location to activate. 0°-2.5° Scorpio is one of those locations because the Scorpio background means you'll need to be exercising power over something while the inconjunct harmonic means that it's the vibe you give off which counts; so there is often a third party or at least third-person witness needed for you to get this to work. If you have Laurentia in places like this, it will be much more important for you to develop allies and an appropriately supportive surrounding environment to get Laurentia to function reliably.
- As with any asteroid, Laurentia may be next to a neighbor you don't want like 879 Ricarda: the hindering detour asteroid. Laurentia-Ricarda in some cases indicates that whenever you win, you lose. Or you are denied in some way. There are remedies for this, but it should be noted that there really are cases—many cases in the chart—where the thing you want comes at a price. Among all 1000 or so asteroids in this book, I've noticed that you'll have about 10-15 which are simply no good however you slice them, and these will best be used to fuel other

endeavors. In my own chart I've learned that the hindering detour Ricarda shows up right before I'm about to "uncover a new area of the map" so to speak; thus it serves as an announcement that I'm onto something new and worthwhile.

- Laurentia, though it represents easy victory, typically takes energy to use. While you're busy winning, you're not doing other things. I've spent most of my last 10 years in complex scholarship at the expense of things like relationships and career. So while I'm busy winning in my favorite area, I'm prone to not doing much in other areas that might be just as valuable. For me, the use of Laurentia to answer thousands of questions in a few months has brought a much higher level of stress for me as I go from one scholarly frontier to the next. So it has become much more important for me to balance the asteroid's use in light of other priorities. You really can have too much of a good thing.

- Finally, Laurentia brings the weird and often unfortunate side effect of separating you from everyone else. Like a real winner on the platform, you stand in a position that no one can touch. Not the crowd, not your competitors, not your friends. No one. While there isn't so much an association between the asteroid and isolation *per se*, there is an extent to which the better you get at using Laurentia, the harder it is for you to share your winnings with others. You're never away from the podium, so it is often the case that others think you don't need them in whatever area applies. Again, balance in your use of this asteroid will become more important the better you get.

Reading Harmonic Regions

In order to read 162 Laurentia in your chart you'll first need to know how to read harmonics. First recall that there are 12 signs in astrology which correspond to certain kinds of broad activity:

Signs covered in *FSA* and *HBS*			
♈	♉	♊	♋
Aries spontaneous behaving	**Taurus** experiencing things you value or identify yourself against	**Gemini** communicating your ideas or instinctual movement; thinking or talking to or for yourself	**Cancer** paying attention to how you feel or how you're reacting to things
0°-30°	**30°-60°**	**60°-90°**	**90°-120°**
♌	♍	♎	♏
Leo playing, enjoying leisure time, having fun, broadcasting yourself	**Virgo** working, making meaning, doing daily duties and maintenance tasks	**Libra** socializing, talking in conversation with others, engaging in 1:1 feedback activities like playing instruments or video games	**Scorpio** using your power over others, over information, or over situations broadly
120°-150°	**150°-180°**	**180°-210°**	**210°-240°**
♐	♑	♒	♓
Sagittarius leaving an impression among strangers	**Capricorn** being associated with certain formal classes of people	**Aquarius** being talked about	**Pisces** performing default actions
240°-270°	**270°-300°**	**300°-330°**	**330°-360° (0°)**

Table 38-1: Signs, the background activities they entail, and what degrees of the circle they correspond to. These tick forward from Aries.

Each of the above 12 regions can be divided into twelve mini-regions called duodecanates, which correspond to the following degrees when ordered by harmonic:

Base harmonics; planet pairs separated by these angles occur when indicated...					
♂	♊	△	□	Q or ✶	✱
conjunct naturally	opposition when comparing value	trine opinion airing	square wanting, intending	quintile interacting 1:1	sextile working, analyzing
Multiples of $\frac{1}{1}$ of a circle	$\frac{1}{2}$ of a circle	$\frac{1}{3}$ of a circle	$\frac{1}{4}$ of a circle	$\frac{1}{5}$ of a circle	$\frac{1}{6}$ of a circle
27.5°-29.9°	25°-27.5°	22.5°-25°	20°-22.5°	17.5°-20°	15°-17.5°
✡	∠	N or 九	⊥ or +	∪	丌
septile 1:1 communicating	octile influencing, pressuring	novile projecting in the world	decile enforcing order	undecile being flooded w/ info	inconjunct feeling environment
Multiples of $\frac{1}{7}$ of a circle	$\frac{1}{8}$ of a circle	$\frac{1}{9}$ of a circle	$\frac{1}{10}$ of a circle	$\frac{1}{11}$ of a circle	$\frac{1}{12}$ of a circle
12.5°-15°	10°-12.5°	7.5°-10°	5°-7.5°	2.5°-5°	0°-2.5°

Table 38-2: Base harmonics, what kinds of activity correspond to them, and what degree of each sign they correspond to. The data showed that these tick backwards starting at the end of Pisces.

In the previous books where I was first developing the harmonic-duodecanate approach, I called all duodecanates in Pisces the "level I" harmonics. Those in Aquarius were "level II." Those in Capricorn were "level III" and so on, keeping in mind that the harmonics go backwards through the signs (based on the statistics). To determine which fraction of a circle you were looking at under this system, you basically counted backwards starting at the last duodecanate of Pisces. So 27.5°-29.9° Pisces would be harmonic 1, the level I (or regular)-conjunct. 25°-27.5° Pisces would be harmonic 2, the level I-opposition. 22.5°-25° Pisces would be harmonic 3, the level I-trine…0°-2.5° Pisces would be harmonic 12, the level I-inconjunct. Once you were finished with Pisces you would move onto the level IIs in Aquarius. So 27.5°-29.9° Aquarius would be harmonic 13, the level II-conjunct. 25°-27.5° Aquarius would be harmonic 14, the level II-opposition. And this would keep going all the way around the circle until you ended at 0°-2.5° Aries, harmonic 144, the level XII-inconjunct. Where each harmonic represented fractions of a circle, you would take any degree measure like 138° and multiply it until you got the number of repeats needed to line it up with a whole circle. In the case of 138°, multiplying by 60 gives you 8280 which lines up with 360° (after several laps), so 138° would be a 60th harmonic. The theory for this can be found in *FSA* and the justification for it in this book's (*Laurentia's*) first two chapters. Since a 60th harmonic is a level V-inconjunct, it corresponds to an inconjunct's environment feeling against a Scorpio's power-pushing background, so any pair of bodies in your chart separated by this angle (or any other 60th fractions of 360 for that matter) would have their natural combination activated whenever you left an impression as an influencer. Furthermore, if you happened to have planets located in the 60th duodecanate of your chart (0°-2.5° Scorpio), this harmonic and all of the pairs which shared it (called resonant pairs) would be amplified whenever you used those contained planets. This allowed you to turn up a harmonic by using the planets in its corresponding duodecanate or to do it the other way around. That way was the old way we did things, and the explanation for how this works was finally presented in more technical language in the first two chapters of this book.

The new way we'll be doing things is actually the same as the old, but much simpler in two major ways. First, throughout this book I will no longer be using the level I, level II,… naming system, but will just **use the sign and the harmonic**. A "level V-inconjunct" will simply be called a "Scorpio inconjunct." A "level VII-octile" will be called a "Virgo octile." The levels count backwards, remember? So you'll need to take [13 – the level] in order to get the proper background for each region. Using the background tells you more about the kind of behavior you're actually looking at, though. If the old "level-N" system could be called level-naming, the new system will be called **sign-naming**. Sign-naming is MUCH easier to understand quickly than calculating level numbers.

The second way that we'll simplify things is by focusing almost solely on conjuncts—where bodies are next to each other within the same duodecanate. Except for a couple of really interesting twists later in this book, we won't pay much attention to angles like oppositions, squares, or VIII-deciles. Just conjuncts. And only within the same 2.5° region. Once we start reading 1000 asteroids, the whole chart becomes one giant stellium (chain of conjuncts), so that there's no longer any need to probe the harmonic angles for meaning. The asteroids provide absurd amounts of data via their tangle with neighboring asteroids alone. If you want to look at relationships besides the conjunct, *144* explains in brief detail how each of the 144 angle families actually play out.

Let's conclude with a couple of examples of how to read harmonic regions in your chart. Suppose your Mars is in 21°36′ Leo. This is in the 20°-22.5° duodecanate of Leo, placing it in the Leo-square area. Suppose you already know that Mars represents influence over others. Being in *LEO*-square means that your influence is turned up when you get to reflect your wants during *PLAY*. Emotion-charged *HOBBIES* will bring out your opportunity to influence others. Such hobbies will also bring out the character any of the neighboring asteroids in the same duodecanate.

In a second example, suppose you want to be a master in some area, but you don't know what area you should pursue. Based on the discussion of the angles in *144*, you already know that 34th harmonics indicate mastery because 34s constitute a Capricorn-decile—where formal groups identify you with a formal status of some kind. The 34th harmonic corresponds to 5°-7.5° Capricorn, so you look for certain planets there. Nothing. Then you download your 1000 asteroids. Along with several neighbors, 689 Zita is there. You could be a master at getting people to open up and demonstrate themselves. This quality would happen in conjunction with the qualities of other bodies (including cusps and calculated points) in the same duodecanate.

So now you can read your Laurentia. Go online to a site like astro.com and have it output a chart wheel. While you're there, make sure to have it output "162" as an additional asteroid, because this is Laurentia's minor planet number. Find its duodecanate location in your chart. 0°50′ Taurus? That's a *Taurus* inconjunct. Make sure you set up your house or office— your *value* environments—to reflect what you want. 12°10′ Libra? That's a Libra-*octile*. Try *pressuring people* through 1:1 conversation or *beating down* an opponent through video games. You could also perform its statistically associated action in *144*, highlighting deeds that don't match your personality. In general though, the dynamics shown in *Table 33-1* of *144* play out as third-party observable effects more than they do as causes. Wherever Laurentia is, your task is to express that region of the chart in such a way as to set you up for victory. That's project Laurentia.

For a Few Asteroids More

Laurentia is only the beginning of a rich and amazing list of astronomical bodies whose orbits map an untold number of stories in your chart. The stories aren't folklore, but specific patterns of transition from one energy level to another. If you're familiar with the hydrogen emission series in chemistry: Balmer, Lyman, and Paschen, for example, you know that imposing certain energies on certain energy carriers produces emissions of varying wavelengths and colors. It may be hard to imagine how throwing rays at an electron can produce visual effects, but it happens. Relatedly, imposing angular separations upon astronomical bodies which are already formed partly as the result of regional potentials means that we can, through astronomy, exploit the frequencies at which they are most resonant as well as, through astrology, map such frequencies onto a scaled down version of our own context. Being elliptical in orbit, astronomical bodies present us with a range of oscillation between energy levels which, when compared to other bodies, in turn produces a characteristic relationship. As with the jumbled oscillations of chemical potentials in our own biologies, we play out the jumbled relationships of astronomical placements in incipient anthropomorphization of their dynamics. Thus the characters pepper the night sky. We can learn much by looking more closely into what those characters are.

Chapter 39: The Asteroids

In this chapter I will present the meanings of all of the first 1000 minor planet numbered asteroids as well as all of the major planets, some additional special bodies, and each of the house cusps. The meanings of these asteroids were obtained by taking their 36-harmonic relationship to the Midheaven in the charts of 50 people, and looking at how those people clustered.

- For reasons outlined in previous books, I assume the Polich-Page / Topocentric house system rather than Placidus, Koch, or others.
- For convenience I will also use the words "planet" or "asteroid" very loosely throughout this chapter, making no linguistic distinction between Centaurs like Chiron, Amors like Eros, and Dwarfs like Eris.
- All bodies are in alphabetical order regardless of major or minor status. So the Sun, for example, is under "S" right after 563 Suleika.
- It is common for me to describe these asteroids as being "associated" with something. This means that, although the asteroid won't necessarily confer the trait described, issues related to that trait or analogous equivalents of that trait will show up in your life wherever the asteroid is active. One of the best examples of this is 1036 Ganymed. Associated with homosexual attraction, this asteroid actually reflects where you are drawn to associate with your own power dynamic. Ganymed shows where bosses are drawn to other bosses, churchgoers are drawn to other churchgoers, and yes, sometimes where masculine types are drawn to other masculine types. Associations like this will depend partly on what neighboring asteroids are present in the same duodecanate. So no, "associated" asteroids don't have to bring out the trait they're associated with, but they often do. Especially when conjunct an orbit-clearing major planet...
- Related to the above point, one pretty cool property of asteroids is that—despite being in your chart, they don't always reflect you. Instead, "displacement" is so common in both astrology and in practical life that most of us don't know just how much we rely on it. Looking for a spouse who behaves like your parent? Watching movies which depict lives you wish you could live? Surrounding yourself with friends who reinforce from the outside a self-image you don't know you have within? All of these things are analogous to the kinds of asteroids which you store inside others rather than yourself. Since your chart is actually not your chart, but the chart of broader spacetime in general, the distinction between you and the world won't matter much in the grand scheme. So it's fairly easy for you to go back and forth on how you store such qualities.
- Because most of these asteroids are in the main belt between Mars and Jupiter, almost all of them have some kind of Libra or Scorpio quality to them. This is mostly a consequence of the fact that 1) there are so many main belt bodies to begin with and 2) the technology for identifying, say, Kuiper Belt objects (a secondary "asteroid belt" around Pluto) and the probability of finding near Earth asteroids like Eros in such a sparsely populated space was lower before powerful telescopes took over the scene and gave us more options after the first 1000. As such, a great number of these asteroids are relationship and power projection-related—where sex, strength, and creativity as well as crowds, information, and social noise remain frequently interchangeable as usual. Some of the descriptions can be a little graphic for the unprepared. Don't say you weren't warned.

As I was writing this book I noticed something very interesting. In attempts to capture every asteroid in simpler pictures, I developed a short icon list for describing them. While doing so, I noticed a kind of "phonemic language" across asteroid names which seemed to unify the asteroid names. "-it-" asteroid names usually had to do with information. "-ju-" asteroid names had to do with elevation or elevated things. Why? My guess is that humans tend to naturally make certain kinds of noises in response to certain kinds of events. "-ooh-" for amazement. "-mar-" for protesting one's situations and, thus, the use of force.[31] Keep this in mind when you read some of these asteroid names. I discuss this in more detail in the chapter after this one.

Meanwhile, the icon key is shown below.

Icon	Association	Icon	Association
Role Announcers (highest to lowest ego-association)		Strain and blockers (most to least actively disruptive)	
📢	announcing, broadcasting, purposefully publicly showing	⚡	stress, conflict, opposing sides, or things that operate against other things
🗣	communication, conveying, talking, pushing ideas (usually to an interactant)	💣	"time bomb," sensitivity to provocation
🎙	central communicator, intentional message sender	☂	bad luck, unwanted occurrences
👽	a role one plays, a face one puts on	✂	relationship killers, termination, cutting off
⇧	projecting, impressions sent out	🚫	things that are blocked, not allowed
⇩	reception, impressions taken in (I often use this one and the one above to separate causes from their effects in a single asteroid)	🔒	gatekeeping behavior
Interactors (most positive to neutral)		Controllers and regulators (most to least insistent / dominating)	
🕊	bonding, peace, things that are loved	✈	control
👥	friends, friend-like exchanges	⊕	focus, attention target
💬	interactant, interaction partner	🏛	institutions, fixed systems, structure
🗨	social talk, gossip, grapevine, peer group-like exchanges	⛰	stubbornness, high obstacles
🖧	networks, networked things, exchanges with a system	🛡	defense, protection, caring for
👪	family, family-like groups	❗	work, daily tasks, duties
Spaces for events (most to least vast)		Power and action (most to least publicly elevated)	
🏝	imagination, envisioned things	🏆	leader, number one
🏕	"land," realm of familiar ideas or topics, circumstance	💪	strength, ability, power
🏚	home base (realm of familiar experiences)	👄	lust, passion
🌐	the world, global, vast things (includes and is dampened by the unfamiliar realms)	♂	men, masculine things
🏙	society, social opinion-based contexts (includes unaccepted opinions)	♀	women, feminine things
🏘	neighbors, peers, people who happen to be around	✍	actions aimed at something, deeds

---

[31] If you naturally exhale "mar," the mouth movements look like "but" without putting your tongue on the roof of your mouth. The "Mm" is what we naturally do when bracing for something or weakly accepting it; the breathy "-uh/ah-" comes with generic projection of all kinds of sentiments; the flapped "-er-" with rolled-in tongue comes with considering a next move. So Mm+ah+er would correspond to something like tentative acceptance of a thing with the plan to do something else instead.

Value, status , and pleasures (most to least material)		Things to be revealed	
👤	the body, human	🕐	time, things with a duration, how time is spent
💰	money	🔍	searching, requesting, looking, investigating (with the above, indicates "demanding")
🎨	art, creativity	💬	ideas, thoughts
👑	comfort, relaxation, comfortable circumstances	🗻	mystery, secret things, things beneath the surface
🍸	grace, cool, sophistication	🕷	enticement
🏷	-thing, -object, -product, the tangible version of whatever it's attached to	★	(a powerful asteroid, often indicating one's overall character)
Hobbies			
💥	newness, created things		
♪	music		
🎮	games, fun, enjoyed things		

Table 39-1: Icons used to describe this chapter's asteroids

Asteroid List

0 – 9

15760 1992QB1 (92Q)

💬 🕷

support attractor

Support Attractors

The Support Attractor family tends to invite the things you want. Like Laurentia, 92Q shows the thing you do which earns you the support you seek, where performing the behaviors of bodies close to these asteroids (within 5°) will tend to attract your goals to you.

The strongest support attractors I found in the data were
- 92Q
- Laurentia
- Eurykleia
- Venus

A

677 Aaltje

💰 👤 👑 🏷

what you need in order to feel physically comfortable

864 Aase

🍸 ⇧

associated with a gracious manner held by you or others

456 Abnoba

🎨 🔍

where you are cautious, skeptical regarding how others suggest this quality be used

151 Abundantia

⇩ ⚡

where you are inclined to stress yourself out

829 Academia

⇧ 🎨 💥

where you are at your most creatively, instinctively inspired

588 Achilles

🍸 👑 🔍 ⇩

where you can do great things, but only with the help of someone else

The Tied to Others family

Certain bodies work hard to keep you from getting things done on your own. Asteroids and chart sections like this often fail miserably when you simply decide to do them solo, so it's highly recommended that you keep another person or communicative object around in order to see them through.

In my data, astro-factors which most strongly tied you to others' efforts were:

- Yrsa
- Priska
- Ricarda
- Achilles
- Zerbinetta
- Anything in Libra which you need to do but which doesn't come easily

The above can wreak havoc in the chart of a loner, and can disguise deep esteem problems in the chart of a super social person.

The Tied to Others family, though similar in scope to the Partners family (see Valentine), is decidedly more negative because its member asteroids more often punish you for not having a partner. The Partners family on the other hand is more likely to reward you with a partner whenever you execute the relevant behaviors.

523 Ada

power and 1:1 exploratory behavior

330 Adalberta

barrier which prevents people who've only heard about you from getting to know you

525 Adelaide

where you willingly air issues connected to power relations

812 Adele

your preference for dirty or hedonistic things or surroundings

647 Adelgunde

where you are associated with high-status partners

276 Adelheid

where you hold influence in an overarching institution; related to Pholus

229 Adelinda

where you are more likely to hesitate or proceed carefully

145 Adeona

where others' desires circumscribe your actions

398 Admete

where you are crowd-popular (*Cheers*-style)

Admetos (transNeptunian)

where you gather (attempted) influences from far and wide

608 Adolfine

where your approach or surrounding circumstances stand out as far more significant than others'

268 Adorea

the secret you expose about your world when in close enough quarters with others

239 Adrastea

where you are sober and respectful in your treatment of others, reasonably good natured with no fluff

143 Adria

where you carve your own path away from the pack

820 Adriana

where you are the expedition [experience] leader, taking others behind you into new territory

91 Aegina

where your way compels people to express against the backdrop of your influence

96 Aegle

where you build up a creative repertoire

159 Aemilia

where you are fundamentally likeable, even when you aren't

396 Aeolia

where you are someone or some group's darling

369 Aeria

where you are prolific in the breadth of things you interact with; where the subset of your interactant set has a huge number of items in it

446 Aeternitas

where you are a cooperative and friendly partner; people see you as easy to get along with

132 Aethra

where the energy around you feels subdued, naturally calming others

911 Agamemnon

where you are a ruthless (or unbending) pursuer of your own ends. One of the "**Mean 13**:" **the 13 most negative asteroids (by default) of all 1000**. As the Ruthless Pursuer, this is the second meanest (and the most "other-harming") of all 1000 asteroids, including the Mean 13

The Mean 13

The 13 most negative, destructive asteroids among the 1000, there exists a group which puts Saturn and Mars to shame. Like every other body, each asteroid in the Mean 13 can be very positive if you master it, but are usually left unmastered in most people because of the asteroids' deep roots in things we're trained to run away from. Here's the group (from worst to not-as-bad), with Natalie, Agamemnon, and Ricarda topping the list as the most destructive of all. *Script text* harms you. Typed text harms others.

1. *Natalie* – High Stakes Punisher
2. Agamemnon – Ruthless Pursuit
3. *Ricarda* – Bad Luck
4. *Priska* – Second Placedness
5. Hamiltonia – Self-Damaged Leader
6. Damocles – Other's Anger
7. *Janina* – Servitude
8. *Liberatrix* – Sudden Endings
9. Delila – Thief
10. Lipperta – Jealousy Inciter
11. Xanthe – Chain Disposer
12. Sauer – Regulator-Blocker
13. Zelia – Impenetrable Shield

228 Agathe

where you will eliminate the one who breaches your sacred standard

47 Aglaja

where you intrude only to make yourself indispensable, setting a bar which others are hesitant to lower regardless of whether they liked you

641 Agnes

where you go first, striking preemptively in situations you are passionate about

847 Agnia

where you display abilities that pacify unruly crowds

645 Agrippina

where you nurture through boundary-breaking

744 Aguntina

where you get lost in a world all your own

950 Ahrensa

where you appear to be on a quest for something that will never attain; but actually, where you produce work without end

861 Aida

where you are unlikely to be challenged, as a result of being too strong

Repelling Asteroids

Some bodies discourage people from interacting with you. Whether through intimidation, anger-inciting, or other kinds of stress induction, the Repelling Asteroids are very good at this.

- Aida
- Agamemnon
- Arequipa
- Chimaera
- Damocles
- Rockefellia
- Sauer
- Zelia

978 Aidamina

what your physical presence allows you to do automatically—as if your body has a mind of its own. In some cases this appears as inspiration

738 Alagasta

where you confront pressing matters with a kind of light-mannered "underconcern." Though you may be concerned, your bearing is the opposite of stern, and doesn't seem as serious as some people would expect it to be

702 Alauda

side of you which is useful for connecting people to each other

719 Albert

social importance

465 Alekto

where you highlight the importance of biologically sex-typical behavior in others—more so male behavior

418 Alemannia

where your outside-expansion plans are hindered in favor of internal priorities instead

259 Aletheia

where even the enemies of your friends respect you

54 Alexandra

where you are associated with cool, smooth women or sophistication of this kind. (This is very "red-dress Hollywood" style, especially for women with this in Leo.)

929 Algunde

where you are creatively or sexually overpowered

291 Alice

where you are associated with a structured system, ordered in nature

887 Alinda

part which exudes sensuality, body sense, or a sense of one's own self-value

266 Aline

associated with manly or masculine-projective endeavors

124 Alkeste

where you are surrounded by the "craziness" of others

Chaos in One's Life

Several indicators in the chart denote realms of utter chaos in one's life. These areas are best handled by adopting a diet of "information" which you can intentionally control. Otherwise, the rampant stress of these areas can literally kill you. Starting with the most stressful, these areas are

- The Virgo-undecile duodecanate (2.5°-5° Virgo)
- The Virgo-undecile (VII-undecile, 83rd harmonic)
- Uranus
- Alkeste
- The 11th house
- Damocles

82 Alkmene

where you are identified with an entire world which you've constructed

457 Alleghenia

trait which others want to display to you as approval for how your expression benefits them

390 Alma

what you are commonly, very broadly popular for in "people's" eyes. This is a Selene-like summary body which compresses the whole persona into a single object.

Holistic Summaries (of You)

There are several bodies which can be used to sum up your personality broadly. These holistic indicators are simplifications of you in other people's eyes (as opposed to your own complex understanding of yourself). This doesn't necessarily mean they are strong, only that they are more salient than other bodies:

- Selene (White Moon)
- Sun

- Moon
- Alma
- Naema

925 Alphonsina

♀ 🎙

where you are associated with "women under the spotlight"

971 Alsatia

🍸 📇 ♈ 🗣

where you are a gifted expresser

955 Alstede

🗣 🏝 🏜

where you stand alone in knowing how a particular aspect of your world works; it's often difficult to convey your understanding or intentions to others in this area. You may truly do better to abandon explanation here and simply be intentionally abstract.

119 Althaea

⬇ 💣 🗡 ⬆

where, once a subject is opened by someone else, you react with fierce intensity; a powerful counteroffensive

148780 Altjira

🗣 ⬇

what others chase you for

850 Altona

⬆ ♈

tool you use to gain influence in the world

650 Amalasuntha

⛰ 🏛 🌳 👽 🏆

where you display a status atop a lofty ideological or expressive pedestal

284 Amalia

📢 👄 ⬆

where you are associated with overflowing lust

113 Amalthea

🎙 ♂ 🏆

where you evoke masculine standards of identity and achievement

725 Amanda

⊕ 🗣 💣 ✳

where another person or situation exercises a strong hold on you, hijacking your expression so that others can't get to it

Hostage Asteroids

Hostage Asteroids tend to be among the most frustrating points in your chart because they effectively put you and your progress under the control of someone or something else. Because they can be frustrating, they also show up as very strong in the charts of people who prefer self-determination.

- Amanda
- Damocles
- Davida
- Janina
- Priska
- Ricarda
- Yrsa

193 Ambrosia

🎙 📢 📇

the creative banner you fly when interfacing with the public; what you take pride in being associated with creatively

986 Amelia

🗣 🗣 🗣 📇

where your creations inspire others to want to project their own creative power

916 America

🏛 ✈ ♈ 🗣

realm where you dominate your close interactants

516 Amherstia

🗡 💣

where you are prepared to instantly derail those who challenge you

367 Amicitia

🗣 ⬆

outcome evoked by a typical interaction with you (where you behave more like the sign before this asteroid's sign)

871 Amneris

🗣 🗣 ⬇

where or how you solicit the feedback of others

1221 Amor

⚲ 🏆 🏔 ⬇

where you chase an inner goal which only you can comprehend

198 Ampella

what you use to build a creative empire, if you were to do so

Artist Effect Family

I found in the data a handful of GREAT asteroids for leaving long-lasting, strong impressions on people, often through one's creations. These are "artist's asteroids" which can be used to locate an area of creativity where you are exceptionally skilled in leaving a permanent impression on others. Roma, Cremona, and Ohio top the list.

- Roma
- Cremona
- Ohio
- Child
- Ampella
- Brangane

29 Amphitrite

your "get away from me if you're not up to code" behavior

Shield Asteroids

Some asteroids represent tools you use to stop others dead in their tracks. The shield asteroids do this. Plain and simple.

- Zelia
- Sauer
- Saturn
- Amphitrite

55576 Amycus

trait you are open with giving out

980 Anacostia

the side of you that draws others into a happier world

270 Anahita

where your backstory and general vibe most heavily affects future events; **this asteroid is special in that it is the only one among the 1000 which clearly showed the area where your past was likely to make or break your future** when it comes to getting opportunities from others.

824 Anastasia

where class advancement appears to come easily for you; along with Werdandi, a status asteroid

175 Andromache

where you are entertaining to everyone around

965 Angelica

how or where you willingly give up control to your partner

64 Angelina

where you seem naturally satisfaction-needy

791 Ani

where you apply your creative energy most strongly

265 Anna

where others are inclined to obey your suggestion

910 Anneliese

where you shine as a public duo-mate. **[A major partnership or friendship indicator]**

Friendship Asteroids

There were definite friendship / partnership indicators which emerged in the data. Where others have major, favorable planets on the following bodies, the chances of your being friends or partners with them goes way up:

- Anneliese
- Armor
- Vertex
- Node
- Part of Fortune
- Imum Coeli (4th house cusp)

Hopefully this setup applies the other way around in your chart to theirs as well.

817 Annika

associated with the woman who stands strongly on her own

129 Antigone

where you cover your power in charisma

651 Antikleia

hair trigger projection, what you are most likely to project at the slightest provocation. Those with this asteroid in Capricorn more often show skepticism or criticality; positively, they show mothering

The -kleias

One of the first indicators of the existence of a "language for asteroid naming, the -kleias represent a gift for power. In this book I have only covered Eurykleia and Antikleia.

90 Antiope

where you willingly enter close exchanges with others

272 Antonia

where you super-deliver your inner talents

121725 Aphidas

where you are easy to seduce; your weakness; where good exchanges (with others allowing you to use the angle) can cause you to melt

1388 Aphrodite

side of you which is unsettlingly enticing to others

1862 Apollo

where your way puts you at the forefront of everyone's memory

Apollon (transNeptunian)

side of you which taps into the mass appeal

358 Apollonia

realm where you display exceptional intuition

99942 Apophis

side of you which is characterized by vastly complex territory

988 Appella

associated with a skilled paternal role

387 Aquitania

associated with men who are not allowed to fall from the pedestal others have put them on. This is a mission-critical asteroid which, if a male blows it, will cost the relationship; related to Natalie

849 Ara

where you have a talent for intellectualizing

841 Arabella

where your masculine interactant (or you as such) is required to "act like a boss"

407 Arachne

what you are a source of in your regular daily (often work) encounters

Career and Work Indicators

In one of the most important, most practical groups of all the ones we cover in this book, the Career Group holds several indicators of your ideal job and career. Job AND career? What's that all about? It turns out that, like so many other areas of our lives, our characteristic work is amazingly nuanced in its dimensions. It's not just about what you do, but where. Not just about how you do it, but in whose eyes. And whether the thing you do is the same thing you actually get paid for. The key career indicators are shown below, but I have nicknamed this family using the king of all career asteroids: The Moultona Group.

- Moultona
- Brambilla
- Ottegebe
- Ceraskia
- Midheaven
- Arachne
- 6th house and the bodies in it
- Aslog
- Aurelia
- Carnegia (if you're looking for expertise in that career)

973 Aralia

where you break code, doing things the way they aren't done

15810 Arawn

associated with communications media (like technology)

394 Arduina

why you would make an enticing choice for a person's partner

737 Arequipa

where you hold preachable principles for behavior which, generally, only your friends can tolerate in extremes

197 Arete

realm where you display an alpha-level forward drive

95 Arethusa

where you da man (in others' eyes, that is); even if you're a woman, you're Fonz-like hip

469 Argentina

where idealism characterizes your world

43 Ariadne

where you are easily pushed around, but resilient nonetheless. Unless mitigated by other factors, this asteroid seems to be connected to health accidents—more so than the "health asteroid" Hygiea. (My guess is, as long as you keep the cluster healthy and stable, you'll be healthy and stable)

793 Arizona

how you display a loss of temper or incited fire, passion.

Intensity Asteroids

The asteroids which explode with passion, anger, or some other form of intensity can, if left uncontrolled, damage a person's world greatly. In the data, I noted the following bodies often responsible for this level of intensity:

- Arizona
- Ninina
- Damocles
- Eros
- Mars

780 Armenia

where your actions awaken and teach others to be better, whether or not you do this on purpose

514 Armida

where refinement, sophistication, and other such higher-tier qualities suit you

Status Asteroids

For favorable status in the world, it helps to have certain bodies in a cluster. Status asteroids show where high status becomes you—where you will settle for nothing less than the finest.
- Armida
- Werdandi
- Bilkis
- Kordula

774 Armor

where you form great social accompaniment; the nature of dynamic duos you get into; also, the main indicator of your "airspace:" the energy that naturally surrounds you; related to Bacchus. **[A major partnership or friendship indicator]**

959 Arne

where people look up to your contribution to the social world

404 Arsinoe

realm where you are associated with powerful or charismatic feminine or intuitive character

105 Artemis

where you perfect the life experiences of those around you

8405 Asbolus

where you hold enviable qualities which reflect the values of larger groups

Ascendant (House 1)

⇧

your approach to new situations **[house cusp]**; in addition to everything you've probably read about the Ascendant, here's something more: The duodecanate on the Ascendant shows your general aim in approaching whatever you approach willingly. For example, my Ascendant duodecanate is an Aquarius-trine (24.9° Aqu), so "opinionating" (trine) amidst the social talk (Aquarius) is my main method of expressing in a new situation. If I'm not doing this, then I'm probably not doing whatever it is because I really want to, but instead because it's part of some more utilitarian task list. Accordingly, if you want to draw out a person's approach to things (and you happen to know their Ascendant), you can encourage them by giving them the opportunity to do whatever their Ascendant duodecanate suggests, <u>and rewarding them for it</u>. That's the key. If they're not rewarded, they may use their Ascendant out of irritation or necessity, and surely you don't want that.

214 Aschera

where you demonstrate a highly complex nature which is difficult for others to unravel

4581 Asclepius

where you hold a seductive, other-attention-inviting personality

67 Asia

how or where you incite the most intense passions (positive or negative) in others

4946 Askalaphus

where you enjoy a web of interesting connections

962 Aslog

what you seem to be on a quest to perfect through your career **[a career asteroid]**; seems to be associated with the nose

409 Aspasia

where you enjoy iconic status

958 Asplinda

how you evoke the joyful passions of others

246 Asporina

means through which you air the tangled affairs you've been involved in. (The fact that there is an asteroid for this is something I found intriguing. Sounds like "a spore ina" I guess.)

672 Astarte

where you play the shield to those entrusted to your company

658 Asteria

where you elicit disbelief mixed with awe in others; "are you serious?"

233 Asterope

matriarchal role

5 Astraea

where you are a recognized situational monopolizer

152 Atala

where you are forward with your passions, revealing them to your interactants

36 Atalante

where you put yourself on sale for others' consumption; where others suspect that you prostitute yourself—trading your primal instincts for various forms of material approval **[a unique asteroid]**

111 Ate

where you use your body to coerce other's attention

515 Athalia

side of you more able to manifest through an entertainment field

230 Athamantis

where you are bathed in objectifications or materialized representations of others' values

Asteroids Which Give Form to Things

#230 is a form-giver like Varuna, and thus tends to attract its duodecanate and neighboring bodies to you like a magnet. With Varuna, though, you give form to generic things. With Athamantis you give form to other's ideas about generic things.

730 Athanasia

where you are one cool cat; where people think you're James Dean or Kim Novak or something

881 Athene

where you are inexhaustibly projective

161 Athor

tool you use to rebel against or escape constraints. Breaking out of someone's jail? Look at the bodies around this one to see how you prefer to do it.

1198 Atlantis

where you easily attract plenty; seems related to big money, but usually doesn't show up as money unless you conceive of neighboring bodies in this way. However you slice it, Atlantis is a major fortune attractor. Your job is to learn to accept what it brings as actually *being* a kind of fortune.

810 Atossa

where you are inclined to be an urban legend among those who have encountered you. This is a GREAT asteroid for purposely building up your **reputation** among the networks you frequent. Just do what the duodecanate suggests

273 Atropos

adherence to proper rules of behavior

254 Augusta

side of you which is publicly controversial

700 Auravictrix

realm of behavior where you seem unbeatable, where your direction appears—to others—destined to prevail [**the Vanquisher**, related to Laurentia]

Fun Fact About the -trixes

The -trixes (Auravictrix, Jubilatrix, etc. as well as fixed stars I won't cover like Vindemiatrix) all describe sharply-defined, "last word"-style situations. It was this family along with the -kleias that suggested the existence of a language for naming asteroids

419 Aurelia

prime skill which your career field requires [**a career asteroid**]

94 Aurora

where masculine others (or processes) fail to deliver

63 Ausonia

what you display when you are determined to force desire out of others

136 Austria

where you display maturity and a learned nature

B – D

Critical Near Earth Object: Bacchus

2063 Bacchus

your friends, cliques, and groups who will always promote your interests **[A major partnership or friendship-group indicator]**

Points Which Are Always On Your Side

There are a handful of asteroids which tend to always, always be headed where you're headed. Still running strong since we first looked at it in *FSA*, Bacchus remains the top indicator among all 1000 for groups of people who are down to ride or die with you—to go all the way no matter what. Now even though nothing in life is permanent, your Bacchus connections tend to stay with you until circumstances take you away from each other. In addition to #2063, you also have other bodies which do this in different ways. Some represent people, others represent more abstract situations, but all of them are inclined to show things that stay with you no matter where you are in life:

- Bacchus – your main clique
- Selene – your blessed talent
- Imum Coeli (4th house cusp) – the thing you draw out from everyone, including yourself

The Velvet Rope

Have you ever had that person whom you were really attached to, but somehow felt that you shouldn't be? Over the years I've developed a habit of trying to get all kinds of people to try to be my friend just because we had a great, close exchange at some point. But this is because I have a Vertex-Praxedis conjunct for creating fling-like situations where everyone feels "life-changingly" close in each others' company. Lots of us have arrangements like this in our charts which make friendships seem destined when they actually aren't. How can you tell when someone actually belongs in your clique as opposed to being someone you might plan to throw out soon? The answer to this one is important: **Look at the cluster of asteroids opposite Bacchus.** This is a really simple way to let rationality reign over deceptive emotions.

As we know from the previous books, oppositions show where objects are compared to each other. While Bacchus may indeed indicate your true blue friends and Bacchus' neighbors will indeed show other characteristics these friends possess, the points opposite Bacchus will tell you whether potential clique mates are looking out for your best interests or some other set of interests. When considering a new potential friend, ask yourself this: Are they doing the [opposite group] in my favor or not? That's it. This test is very effective and works like a charm, even if it reveals details you don't want to hear. If you do find that a potential clique mate isn't actually on your side, try doing the set of actions (related to the person's role in your life) which are suggested by the asteroids 120° after Bacchus. Once you do it, you are more likely to encounter results indicated by the asteroids 90° after Bacchus. This process works for mathematical reasons discussed earlier in this book, and I will elaborate on them in the next chapter.

856 Backlunda

trait you make others want to project strongly **[a major "provoker"]**

333 Badenia

media publication of work

770 Bali

sitting back and carefully observing

324 Bamberga

part of you which others find soothing, soft, or pleasant

597 Bandusia

where you are cheered on for your inventive or creative power

298 Baptistina

side of you which fills others with hope

234 Barbara

how you make others obey you

945 Barcelona

where you are "left on an island," isolated with your skill

819 Barnardiana

what you use to show patient (or at least coolheaded) caretaking of others

441 Bathilde

area of your life where men must absolutely act like men and be commanding

592 Bathseba

associated with being undisturbed despite another's stressors

172 Baucis

where you show a shameless streak, openly embracing the violation of unspoken rules

813 Baumeia

the interest (intentions) of the groups which like to assemble around you

301 Bavaria

where there is something unrefined, something about you which is "caveman" (if you will) despite your cool image

656 Beagle

where you are a focused worker

83 Beatrix

where you set the agenda for others' actions, leading them

943 Begonia

where others identify you with notions of bigness ["Big"-onia. I thought this one was funny; notability-related]

178 Belisana

associated with women who are meant to be followed

695 Bella

where you are open and unashamed, displaying that you want what you want right now

28 Bellona

associated with big breasts, sexualization of females regardless of context, or attention to female physical (feminized value) characteristics independent of body type

734 Benda

where a higher imaginative or spiritual directive seems to shadow your actions; where you seem to be inspired

976 Benjamina

gracious sociability, well-mannered pleasantness in one's exchanges

863 Benkoela

where you bear an intensely attractive creative power

776 Berbericia

how you build notoriety far and wide; actions which cause your reputation to travel

653 Berenike

where you have a charmingly dirty or taboo air

716 Berkeley

where mass information is a battleground for you

629 Bernardina

trait that occasions all eyes falling on you

422 Berolina

where you forgo regular relationships in favor of a dream

154 Bertha

where the culture around you holds an air of significant change

420 Bertholda

where being around you makes people feel strong, sexy, or valuable

937 Bethgea

where you assemble a complex puzzle from dirty pieces; how you transform animal urges into other things

250 Bettina

where you are on a quest to perfect your influence

218 Bianca

where your partnerships are turbulent

54598 Bienor

where you are associated with women of singularly unique accomplishments

585 Bilkis

where you accept only events of value; this is the purest indicator of money that I found among the 1000; often indicates a thin or small body frame when placed near important chart objects

The Bils

Asteroids with "bil" in the name (Jubilatrix, Vibilia, Bilkis, Ilsebill, and Brambilla) all revolve around value and are, as a group, more easily associated with money—Bilkis being the best indicator and Brambilla being the second best

960 Birgit

where you are associated with hot babes, hot guys, or their powerful equivalents

998 Bodea

a vehement opposition to what most people think are reasonable constraints

371 Bohemia

where your characteristics render you out of place with respect to the group you belong to; people's assumptions for you are VERY often mismatched

720 Bohlinia

where people have a hard time understanding or accepting what it is you want from them. It's probably their fault, but it's part of your chart; alternatively, where you act like YOU don't understand

712 Boliviana

where your actions suggest you deserve the best

767 Bondia

where you are predisposed to close-quarters, deep conversations

361 Bononia

where you chase measurable successes

66652 Borasisi

where you present yourself naturally without any b.s.

741 Botolphia

where you easily attract women or feminine elements; your girl-attracting ability

Guys vs Gals in the Asteroids

Eventually as you go through these asteroids you may ask, *why are so many of these asteroids related to women and, to a lesser extent, men?* As I mentioned earlier in this chapter, most of the first 1000 bodies are Mars-Jupiter Belt asteroids, which means they take on the Scorpio-Sagittarius characteristics: those which are concerned which emotionally-driven steering of others and image projection respectively. Disregarding biology, the behavioral difference between typically socialized men and typically socialized women revolves around the order in which we are taught to assert. Men are taught to assert their will where there are no rules for doing so, then receive the results, then assert again. Women are taught to receive or observe situations, then assert order onto them, then process again. Where the asteroids favor the results of assertion first, they tend to describe males. Where they favor situations related to situational processing first, they talk about women. Where asteroids favor the seemingly nowhere-generated creations arising from combinations of assertion and processing, they revolve around either sex or art.

Only when we get past the belt asteroids into the Centaurs and Kuiper Belt objects does this focus on masculinity, femininity, and their creations give way to descriptions of groups and societies.

Asteroids like Botolphia are essentially a mixture of potentials as they orbit at their closest and farthest, most and least tilted, positions around the Sun and its second focus relative to the Earth and the rest of the nearby Solar System objects. This is something like morphing a C# note played by a piano into an F note played by a cello. If you imagine a transition like this, you can imagine that each such transition will have a kind of mood to it whose effects will depend on other "moods" we've been trained to hear. In the end, we can describe the asteroids using a number of changing parameters, but three stand out in particular: the closest, farthest, and average distances from the Solar foci. Botolphia's orbital character for example is (per Chapter 37) $\left(8\frac{54}{144}\right):\left\{8\frac{37}{144}\rightarrow 8\frac{69}{144}\right\}:\|30\|$. This is a formula which captures Botolphia's three distances as well as the span of its orbit. Reading this as $\left(Sco\frac{Sco.Sext}{144}\right):\left\{Sco\frac{Sag.conj}{144}\rightarrow Sco\frac{Li\,bnov}{144}\right\}:\|Cap.sext\|$ and referencing the previous book *144*, we see that Botolphia shows a general tendency to

$$(make\ meaning\ amidst\ pressure):$$
$$\left\{\begin{matrix}going\ from\ a\ public\ image\ declaration\\ to\rightarrow a\ socially\ noted\ projection\end{matrix}\right\}:$$
$$\left\|\begin{matrix}with\ the\ character\ of\ a\ body\\ responding\ to\ other's\ response\ to\ it\end{matrix}\right\|$$

Now is that actually "girl-attracting ability?" Probably not, but it definitely has something to do steering others, making a communicative statement, and doing so as a Libra object to be responded to. Statistically this comes out as a specific power dynamic which is less about force and more about attracting receptiveness ($\|30\|$) as one airs their power to compel $\left(8\frac{54}{144}\right)$. Notice the Scorpio background (8) that dominates this formula, though. Most of the first 1000 bodies have this, meaning they will revolve around power dynamics like this one. Thus we have a story of exchange which is typically most easily observed via the age old set of games played by men and women. As much of the end goal of Scorpio is to get others to do things, more of the 1000 will look to *receive* results stemming from their steering efforts, so more of these asteroids will be related to women and feminine habits than masculine habits. But even basics like Ceres, Vesta, Juno, and Hygiea—with their receptive or caretaking behavioral implications—might have suggested this to begin with.

859 Bouzareah

where you are a haven for other's creative (sometimes sexual) expression

640 Brambilla

what the build-up of money or other kinds of value entails the use of [a key career asteroid which should be read with Moultona and the Midheaven]; associated with the use of a dissecting analytical mind

606 Brangane

your prime "artistic" industry

293 Brasilia

where you are inclined to chase a far off dream, or keep a dream as such over reality

786 Bredichina

the seat of your artistic ability [this is an interesting asteroid which introduces **unique** abstraction into your chart; you might look this one up alongside Quaoar]

761 Brendelia

where you are oblivious to the world outside your imagined view of things

450 Brigitta

how you use your home; its role in your life

655 Briseis

associated with deep, primal fantasy and related wishes; seems to have an association with black women [an ethnic character asteroid]

521 Brixia

realm where you resist others' advice, sticking strongly to your own instead

455 Bruchsalia

where you appeal to rule-breaking crowds

323 Brucia

where you appear not to be taken seriously, but are actually inspired; related to comedians

290 Bruna

adept communicator

123 Brunhild

where only high status offerings will do for you or *by* you

901 Brunsia

where you are logical or methodical in your approach

908 Buda

where you are a dedicated people-improver

338 Budrosa

where you draw out a strongly masculine form of caretaking from yourself or others

384 Burdigala

where you deal a reality check to people advising you

374 Burgundia

where you have a style that influences others significantly

6235 Burney

where you have a mellow allure

834 Burnhamia

where you endure a tragic event or exit; alternatively, the circumstance which writes your name in stone in everyone's minds

199 Byblis

where your influence is anchored to the exchange with your interactant; where they determine much about how you project

297 Caecilia

where you can be bossy, but it's because you care

952 Caia

where your imagination becomes doctrine. Accordingly, where you would make a good actor or performer

341 California

where you lead groups of liberal people; associated with being unoffended by alternative power relations and, relatedly alternative sexuality

2906 Caltech

"genius" which is initially underappreciated by a world not ready for the work it produces; where the public is encouraged to reject you in the name of normal ideas, but if you stay with your ideas, you may become legendary for them

957 Camelia

where notions of overpowered masculinity or creative force arise. Associated with big penises—possessed or talked about

107 Camilla

where you value fullness of expression, optima

377 Campania

where you draw the company of others

740 Cantabia

fuel source for your single-minded passion

479 Caprera

the high-powered nerd; where others are alerted not to underestimate you, suspecting you are probably stronger and more able than they are

491 Carina

where you proceed as if you haven't been listened to enough

360 Carlova

associated with a desire that must be suppressed, or self-control in the pursuit of a desire

558 Carmen

where you express being pleased with your own projected expression

671 Carnegia

where you are a role model to others

235 Carolina

your social-behavioral base for expanding your influence over people

505 Cava

where crowds of common interests gather around you

186 Celuta

protective motherly role to others

513 Centesima

where you offer your self-value and physical presence for the advancement of others' ends; Related to Sedna and Atalante

807 Ceraskia

general nature of the effort you put into your daily work [interesting for the job and career, goes with Moultona]

1 Ceres

carebullying style

65489 Ceto

hellraiser, disrupter

313 Chaldaea

where you work with creatives or innovators

19521 Chaos

the version of society's values which you project in order to promote people getting along with each other.

(Not at all what you expected was it? Me neither.)

10199 Chariklo

ambition

627 Charis

where your way demands creative power issuance from others [kind of like fraternity initiation or boot camp]

543 Charlotte

tool you use in order to be the boss in your relationships

388 Charybdis

where you are often disappointed in yourself, but where you insist on perfection from others

568 Cheruskia

where you can do no wrong in the eyes of the public

334 Chicago

where you put (mainly) males in their place, keeping them under your thumb

4580 Child

where your creations must reflect you properly; what you wish for your creations to build up

623 Chimaera

a demanding, difficult personality who switches gears unpredictably and doesn't know they're doing it. The duodecanate in which this is found shows where you act like this or draw it out of others. Be sure to look at the neighboring bodies to this one to see what your inner mutant looks like.

2060 Chiron

therapy, doctor-patient context

402 Chloe

✈ 💣 ☀ ⇧

how you play out your demanding nature

410 Chloris

⇧ ⇩ ♀ 👤 ✲

where you are aware of the effect of your physical presence on others

938 Chlosinde

🏛 ⏳ 🏆

where you demonstrate high charisma or attractive qualities

628 Christine

🕊 💬 🏛 ⇩

where you are beloved by the very generic public

202 Chryseis

♀ ⚡ 🎮 🐱 💻

where you have an affinity for girls and girly things—feminine and softer versions of things

637 Chrysothemis

🎴 💻

your brand of association with art or creative power

34 Circe

♂ ♀ ✈ 🏛

where you are identified with sex, its industry, differences therein, and (more rarely) generic power issues of the polar kind; where you compartmentalize masculine-feminine issues

642 Clara

🐱 💬 🗣

playful or more approachable side of your personality

302 Clarissa

★ ⇩ 💻 🏠

an accepted role, a place of acceptance in the world [one of the **strong spirit** asteroids: **those which seem to strongly reflect one's overall identity in the world, as favored by life itself**; "strong spirit" as a group is in many ways the opposite of the Mean 13 (which often confuse such identity aims)]

311 Claudia

⇩ 🏛 ⚡ 🗣

where the occasion for a counselor or advisor arises

252 Clementina

💻 💬 ⛵

where your actions project in a memorable way

935 Clivia

⊕ 🌍 ✈ 🗨

route you pursue to reconcile the world with your wants

661 Cloelia

⛵ 🗣 📢

occasion for being outspoken, expressing your true mode for engaging another person

282 Clorinde

🎴 💻 🏛 ⚡ 👽

where you are associated with a council of creative expressers; equals in your creative endeavors related to Bacchus; **this is a really cool asteroid** which the reader should try to make use of in their chart

237 Coelestina

♆ 🏛 🐱 💬

where exalted principles underlie your interactions with others

972 Cohnia

👽 🏝 📢

where you have a vision which extends beyond surface expectations for you

327 Columbia

⊕ ⇧ 🎨 🎗

where you are determined to go it alone, forgoing the help that is already there (often unnecessarily inconveniencing yourself as you reinvent the wheel)

489 Comacina

💻 🔒 ⛵ ⚡

what you share with others when you let your guard down with them; what members of your inner circle receive from you

58 Concordia

🕷 ⛵ ⇩ 💬 🏆

trait for which you are in high demand

315 Constantia

⛵ 🎙 📢

where your actions are very hard to ignore

815 Coppelia

🖧 👽 🐑 ✈ 🏆

where you do work in raising others' consciousness of themselves and their interactions

504 Cora

🕊 🌱 🕊 👽

strength despite being soft-spoken or sensitive-hearted

365 Corduba

🖧 💬 🏆

where others around you defer to your influence

425 Cornelia

🖧 🗣 🏆

where you project impressive [social] intelligence

915 Cosette

🗲 ⛈ 🛡 🏛

that which needs to be protected from all insult

644 Cosima

♀ 🗡 🏚 🔒

associated with women who, if allowed to show an ill-mannered nature, will seal off their own opportunities; the feminine version of Aquitania

83982 Crantor

🌱 ⊕

the seat of your self efficacy

486 Cremona

👽 🕊 🐑

where people are unable to detach from you after having encountered you; a permanent impression [a **MAJOR impression maker**]

660 Crescentia

🎴 🏊 💣 👽

where you hold promising talent

589 Croatia

🎗 ✈ ⬇ 🔒 🖧

a trait which is publicly seen as being monopolized by your partner; what your partner gains from being with you; what most people wish they could get out of you if you were theirs

Cupido (transNeptunian)

🖧 ⬇ 🐑 🕸

where you attract people's attention (and, where possible, their company)

763 Cupido (Asteroid)

🌱 🖧 ⬇

the side of you which you take into battle in order to win territory [approval points] from or for others

403 Cyane

🎤 🎵 📢 🖧

an association with media, especially music (otherwise, things that follow an ongoing rhythm); this was the most clearly music-centric asteroid among the 1000

65 Cybele

🎵 🍸 🛋 🗣

context for a sweet-worded or mellow-respectful communicator

52975 Cyllarus

🎤 📢 🎒 ⬆

where you are prone to making a show of things

133 Cyrene

🗣 💬 🎤 ⬆

where your way inspires others to enjoy liberality, releasing them from chains

5335 Damocles

⬇ 🗲 🗡

where you fill others with an aggressive lust for something. Sometimes this comes across as anger towards you **[the Unwanted Impression Maker, one of the Mean 13; generates the meanest responses from others towards onself—very often for no apparent reason]**; alternatively, what you inspire others to want intensely

61 Danae

🏊 🗣 ⬆ ✈ 🏛 🌳

where you are a teacher via experience alongside others

41 Daphne

🏚 ⊕ 🛋 🎴 🔒

where you [utterly] reject tastelessness

511 Davida

⬇ 🏛 🖧 🗲

where you are burdened with the demands of others, called on to endure in duty; there is a heavy responsibility on one's shoulders with this one. This is another asteroid with a singularly distinct character among the 1000.

541 Deborah

thing which people are more likely to come to you to get

157 Dejanira

where you require excessive strength in others

184 Dejopeja

where you have a precise way that you want things to happen; barring this, you may seek greener pastures

395 Delia

where you permeate the informational circle

560 Delila

means through which you disenfranchise (take from) others; **the Thief among the Mean 13, whether or not you intend to be**

349 Dembowska

associated with women or feminine elements which stand as a monument

667 Denise

associated with a pretty or well-groomed image, either because you have it or because you need it (i.e. you're sloppy)

666 Desdemona

where you must contend with an awakening before you are actually ready for it

344 Desiderata

Where you display an assembly line-style chain of wants [strongly affects one's character; related to Chariklo's ambition and Interamnia's greedy chasing]

53311 Deucalion

individuality expresser

337 Devosa

realm in the public eye where no one can get near your effectiveness; a (usually) favorable **reputation** asteroid

78 Diana

where you are above the little people, a more valuable social asset than others

209 Dido

unending striving for fulfillment

99 Dike

associated with feminine-feminine interactions

106 Dione

where you put the body and its intricacies on display— like a biologist, a model, a sports star or in any other way

3671 Dionysus

where you do what few around you have the audacity to do

423 Diotima

where you appear to strike an ideal balance between two extremes of expression

382 Dodona

where you connect others to vast worlds beyond

668 Dora

your brand of star appeal

48 Doris

quality which attends your association with the creative field

339 Dorothea

where you are associated with irrepressible women

620 Drakonia

🏛️👽⬆️

where you are a proponent of grown-folks standards

263 Dresda

🗣️🏛️⬇️💬🏆

mode under which you are a monopolistic communicator

400 Ducrosa

📢🏆⊕🔒

where you are associated with bombast, a cornucopia;
where you are only impressed by bigness or excess.
There is a certain haughty pride that comes with this one,
where you will indeed release the trap door on things
that aren't up to your standards

564 Dudu

💬🏆👽

where you are the pack leader (of a Bacchus-type clique)

571 Dulcinea

🛡️⬆️⛈️💬🏠

behavior you display which suggests people stay away
from you if they "know what's good for them;" Beware!
(in a tongue-in-cheek way)

200 Dynamene

🖼️❗🏛️🎒

a creative style put to practical use; mixture of
imagination and practice

E – G

60558 Echeclus

how you build relationships between people

60 Echo

where you act as a kind of parent to your peers, or where you need to be parented

413 Edburga

associated with tall, long-reaching or long duration things

673 Edda

where you open the imaginations of others

742 Edisona

where you invent new methods to do old things

517 Edith

that which you will not allow to be subpar to others

445 Edna

where women in one's life (or the woman herself) will have been more likely used as objects

340 Eduarda

association with docile males; although this asteroid doesn't necessarily indicate homosexuality, you could tell from the data that it implied a feminization of masculine impulses such that even the toughest males who had it prominent in their charts seemed unbothered by non-macho exchanges. There was an affinity with people of all power modalities, where groups clustered on interesting combinations of sexuality; II-septile -like; also, dismissal (and often resulting anger) of females; along with Dike and Ganymed, an asteroid associated with homosexuality, and the strongest of the three. My nickname for #340: "the Gay Asteroid"

13 Egeria

where you generally cannot be counted on for constancy in others' eyes; you may do better to embrace the nomad role

442 Eichsfeldia

where, despite your talent, those near you must clean up messes you've made

694 Ekard

where you make an ideal social example

858 El Djezair

how family and friends are expected to reinforce their connectedness with you **[very important for others to know if they want to be in your life; the ultimate gatekeeping asteroid for getting into your company]**

31824 Elatus

an area you seem well-versed in

130 Elektra

associated with a fire-tempered mother figure or mother role

354 Eleonora

where you gravitate towards performance [as in entertainment] scenarios

567 Eleutheria

where you display a [masculine-style] force to be reckoned with

618 Elfriede

area which your communications influence most heavily

956 Elisa

capacity in which people depend on you to define their social groups

412 Elisabetha

the kind of thing you gather and train on behalf of other people

435 Ella

where you are carefully vain and simultaneously self-conscious—looking over your shoulder while defending your house of cards

616 Elly

where your best efforts are in some way pitiable as long as they are 1) aimed at pleasing others or 2) mainstream. People who are intentionally provocative benefit greatly from this

59 Elpis

where your ways lure people out of states they would feel safer to remain in

182 Elsa

how you call attention to the value of feminine power; where you are more likely to connect with women or non-masculine asserters

277 Elvira

associated with opposite sex [or preferred partner] company for the sake of ego-enjoyment and fulfillment

576 Emanuela

where you generate strong desire or strong tension in others (directed towards you); a less harmful relative of Damocles

481 Emita

where people look to you for inspiration, seeking your counsel

283 Emma

area of performance which makes your name iconic among your circle; related to Naema and Tergeste

342 Endymion

where you are a master of your trade; the "not taking any shit" asteroid; see for yourself in your own chart.

This is what Agamemnon would be if the latter weren't on the offensive.

221 Eos

where people unite around your inventiveness and vision for something better. If you plan to unite people around you, do it using the duodecanate for this one

Unity & Social Circle Asteroids

The Social Unity asteroids are diverse in character and darned useful in application. **As you seek out your ideal group to support your aims, these asteroids take the prize** for the 1000's most informative.

- Bacchus – your homies
- Clorinde – your creative council
- El Djezair – your true "family"
- Eos – those who back your vision
- Oceana – the talent pack you lead

Note that our old friend Uranus isn't on here. Unlike the bodies on the list above, Uranus is all about the information around you, not necessarily the information which *supports* you.

There are few occasions in astrology where I would recommend parents use the chart to help them plan (or at least understand) certain things for their children. This is one of those occasions. Both for your children and for yourself, the Social Unity asteroids are excellent at showing where we can expect to have friends in our favorite places, and definitely deserve a look.

You may also want to read 836 Jole with this group for a better understanding of a person's potential areas of insecurity

802 Epyaxa

your means of giving others hot blood, for better or worse

62 Erato

where you are flaky, erratic, or simply always on the move in your deeds

894 Erda

where you act to correct the wrong expression of those around you

718 Erida

where people must brace themselves to receive you, preparing for intensity otherwise only to get blown away

163 Erigone

where managing others' behavior brings out your more serious, focused side

636 Erika

resistance to having your impulses chained

462 Eriphyla

sexiness and creative potency

136199 Eris

self-validation

705 Erminia

where you put yourself in situations which exceed your ability to handle. With help, though, you'll be fine.

406 Erna

trait you have that gains you respect (mainly in career)

698 Ernestina

where you have a self-contented, self-assured quality in expressing your own way

433 Eros

passion trigger

889 Erynia

the "lair" wherein you hold captive the attention and creative-imaginative potential of others; where your ways circumscribes others' ability to project creatively [an "other controller" in the Persephone family]

622 Esther

where you are celebrated among peers

331 Etheridgea

associated with the struggle to tame wild impulses, mainly in women. More likely to stand out in the charts of black women or the charts of women of intense primal need. All of the first 9 major aspects were described by this kind of individual in the data, and the one man among these clusters was heavily associated with such; with Briseis and Proserpina, constitutes the "Black" asteroids (see Proserpina); along with Hispania, Germania, and others, constitutes the ethnoculture asteroids

181 Eucharis

where others see your goals as having been markedly derailed, rewritten, or otherwise altered from their original form

217 Eudora

where you are pleasant-mannered and responsible

45 Eugenia

the mother who sacrifices for her young (or her creations if not children)

743 Eugenisis

where you assert that you know your own business better than other people; "it's mine I can do what I want with it"

247 Eukrate

where you need, but don't put much stock in strangers

495 Eulalia

where you can and will flirt with your desired object

185 Eunike

where you are determined to draw the value from within yourself; with the Midheaven, associated with desirousness

15 Eunomia

where you apply your critical artistic eye (or insight into patterns) to set standards for others

630 Euphemia

✗ 👽 ⬇ 🗨

trait of yours which attracts the favorable attention and company of others, such that they like you

31 Euphrosyne

🎞 📠 ⛏ 📢 ⬆

where you are identified as an artist or craftsman

52 Europa

🎭 👽 ✈ ⚡

where you act to maintain a healthy balance between yourself and natural "entropy"

527 Euryanthe

🗨 ⬆ 📢 ⊕ 🗨

how you plug into your interactant's world and get them to register your real intentions for them

75 Eurydike

🧍 ⬇ 🗨 ♀ ⛏

where people are more likely to want your body or access to its abilities, things you can do or experience with it

195 Eurykleia

★ 🕊 🏝 🗨 📠 📢 🏝

where spiritual fortunes are made grandly evident; Selene-like. This is **a MAJOR strong spirit asteroid**, and among the strongest and most positive of all 1000 in this book

Critical Asteroid: Eurynome

yur-IN-nuh-me

(Yes, it sounds like "your enemy," but is typically quite positive)

79 Eurynome

👽 📠 ⬇ 🏛 ⛏

where people expect you to be successful based on your surface characteristics. This is not a career asteroid, but hints at how people are likely to pigeonhole you into certain roles based on their very cursory exchanges with you. As such it is a GREAT indicator of the kinds of treatment people are inclined to give you for free.

Even If You Didn't Ask For It: The Given Freely Group

Which bodies seem to indicate things that come to you even though you for free, with little to no work whatsoever on your part? Here are the major ones:

- 92Q
- Laurentia
- Eurynome
- Imum Coeli
- Selene
- Mercury (less so)

These all show a fundamental quality of your communication which is in some way necessary to complement your understanding of the world. Objects near these (along with the duodecanates in which these are found) tend to show things that come to you no matter where you are, what you're doing, whether you understand or not. We can actually think of these as reflecting crystallized versions of the Taurus-septile ($12.5° - 15°$ Tau, $\frac{1}{127}$ harmonic), which gives what seems to be an unfair advantage to a person. Here the Taurus background represents your natural identity value and the septile represents your natural 1:1 communication…with pretty much anything.

Now, as I write this description I'm reminded of what we talked about in *FSA* and *HBS*, the connection between the Selene-Mercury and a history of being abused as a child in the charts of people who had "easy" angles between Mercury and Selene in the chart. The idea is that, even before we learn how to communicate formally, we are already attracting the kinds of communicative partners which match our overall personality setup. People who have the Given Freely asteroids active with things like conjuncts and squares to other Given Freely asteroids tend to have, in some morbid way, the unwanted advances of others foisted upon them in a way that precedes the chartholder's own choice or understanding. Because I have unfortunately encountered high numbers of abused people in my work as a teacher and counselor, I would actually recommend that would-be parents who 1) know of questionable dealings in their family circle in particular and who 2) find the "Given Freely"s near each other in their children's charts, should keep a watchful eye on their newborn and nurture his or her genuine talent as early as possible. Barring this, Uncle so-and-so may impose his own recognition of the child's talent in a negative way.

Among the Given Freelys, Eurynome is among the best determinants of your fundamental social presence either in others' eyes or your own. Be sure to should look at this one carefully, especially the harmonic angle family which corresponds to its duodecanate. For example, I know of a certain beautiful lady who has Eurynome in 25° – 27.5° Pisces. Counting backwards from "30" Pisces as we discussed in *144*, this corresponds to the second duodecanate, ½ of a circle, and an opposition. No wonder people can't help but assign her bodily value and self-worth for free. Oprah Winfrey's Eurynome is in 18 Sagittarius (the Saj-quintile, the 41st harmonic), so she is naturally granted the right to interact with others (quintile) before an abstract public (Saj). Note that you should also consider any angles which go with your Eurynome. My own Eurynome is in 8 Libra (Libra-novile, the 69th harmonic, and also the same harmonic which separates my Sun and Moon), so not only do I get an advantage in publicizing (novile) my 1:1 "conversations" (Libra), I'm also naturally happy with myself in doing so (Sun-Moon-69th angle). Check it out in your chart. Along with Moultona (for people still searching for themselves) and the strong spirit asteroids, this is definitely a body worth knowing.

27 Euterpe

quality you exude which comes with awkward and uncomfortable feelings (yours or others')

164 Eva

where you are more likely to require a masculine counterpart or be that masculine counterpart to someone else; neutrality is less likely

503 Evelyn

where you teach others the standards of expression

751 Faina

where you revolutionize affairs among your circle

408 Fama

where you seem to put your own interests or expression first

821 Fanny

associated with strongly body-sensual women or feminine elements strongly sensitive to their own perceptual processes. Edgar Cayce had this for example; women who need to be touched. For those who are curious, Fanny's actual character as an asteroid is $\left(8\frac{6}{144}\right):\left\{8\frac{56}{144} \rightarrow 8\frac{96}{144}\right\}: \|91\|$. Reference harmonics 6, 56, 91, and 96 in the previous book *144* to see what all these

angle families mean, then read the above formula as (*situation* ___):{*going from* ___ → ___ *goal*}: ‖*with the character of* ___‖

866 Fatme

where you are a memorable creator of images and illusions

294 Felicia

where you are associated with difficult women who harass everyone

109 Felicitas

where you are associated with primarily women of solid will

72 Feronia

where your style is irresistible to others

524 Fidelio

where you have an intuitively clearer sense of how you should proceed

37 Fides

where you are revealed to have upper-class connections

380 Fiducia

realm where you are a trustworthy asset to others

795 Fini

one who shelters their team and creative interests from external chaos

8 Flora

where you demand top class interaction from others

321 Florentina

where you rate creativity highly, are attentive to details and their exploitation

19 Fortuna

⬇ ⚲ ♀ 👽

where you draw others' attention to feminine or receptive characteristics

982 Franklina

🍸 🏛 🛡 🍸

where you are reasonably cooperative, but business-like

862 Franzia

⚲ ⊕ 🗣 🗣

analytical socializer

520 Franziska

🕷 ⬇ 🕊 🏝

where you are adored but, unfortunately, where you are also inaccesible; where you are wished for

309 Fraternitas

⬆ 👽 🎤 🏛 🎒

where you make a good "specimen" example to others; where you stand out as an expressive model against which others can be cited

678 Fredegundis

🎗 🏠 🗣 🏠

where genuine connection with you is just out of other's reach

76 Freia

💥 ⛰ 👽 🎒 ⌣ ⬆

side of you which you put to odd uses in the eyes of others

722 Frieda

🕊 🏝 🗣 ⬆ 🏆

realm where you make others feel good in 1:1 exchange with you

538 Friederike

💣 ⚡ 🎒 👽 🍸

where you display some of your most volatile energy

77 Frigga

🕷 🏞 🍸 👽 ⬇ 🗣 ⚡

side of you which is a mixture of attractive and off-putting to others—off-putting mainly by means of establishing a kind of unbridgable distance between you and others associated with you

709 Fringilla

⚲ ⊕ 🏠 🎒 📢 ⚡ ⬆ 🏆

where you can be critical and bullying to your partners

854 Frostia

🖥 🏝 🔒 ✈

where you are an orchestrator of social experiences

609 Fulvia

⚲ 🏙 🛋 🏆 🗣 🗣

where you hold a high standard for partners

355 Gabriella

🗣 ⬇ ⬆ 🍴 📢

where people invite you in to "sick 'em!"; where you act as a weapon for others who need to "regulate." (That's 90s rap slang which the reader can look up on his or her own.)

74 Galatea

⬇ 🗣 🏝 ⬆ 🎒

where you make others' dreams real

427 Galene

🗣 🎮 ♀ ⌣

where you are associated with merriment among friends, more specifically "having fun with the girls." Hugh Hefner had this in 8 Virgo (the Virgo-novile), promoting an image (novile) as part of the daily work (Virgo).

697 Galilea

🎒 👽 🗣

where others are more likely to cite you as an object for reference; when people talk about things related to this asteroid, you are more likely to come up as an exemplar

148 Gallia

👽 ⬆ 🎒 🎤 🍸

trait which earns you center stage

1036 Ganymed

♈ 🎗 🗣 🗣

where you prefer to associate with your own native power dynamic; associated with homosexuality

180 Garumna

🏞 👽 📢

where you are associated with unfettered, uncomplicated, natural expression

951 Gaspra

where you show an open-minded or liberated approach

764 Gedania

where others cannot tell what adventure you will head onto next

680 Genoveva

associated with women who resist reasonable cooperation to do their own thing

485 Genua

bossy women

376 Geometria

where you demonstrate a creative talent upon which an entire system can be built

359 Georgia

where you nurture the creative impulse in others

300 Geraldina

side of you that is entertaining, engaging, or audience-worthy

122 Gerda

where you have the queen bee status; even for males, this is a kind of passive, recognized, primacy over others

663 Gerlinde

means through which you sponsor followers and fan clubs. This is an interesting asteroid whose aspects explain a lot of unusual but well-known attractive qualities in people; for example, Warren Buffett has an "ultra wealth" cluster on 15 Aquarius.

241 Germania

aspect of your personality which is stably distinctive

686 Gersuind

the side of you directed towards a better world for those around you

710 Gertrud

where you easily alter the behavioral "fate" of those around you

613 Ginevra

where you channel others' illusions for them

352 Gisela

where you have a hard time accepting or settling for what is given to you

492 Gismonda

associated with the voice of reason regarding how others view and use their opportunities

857 Glasenappia

where you are good at bringing out the value in things; a strong "other extractor" like Irmintraud

288 Glauke

where bodily feeling or value inclinations push your actions forward

316 Goberta

where you are sensitive to rejection

305 Gordonia

where you channel a deep (usually sexual) appetite

681 Gorgo

where you prefer not to be bothered by outside imposition

424 Gratia

where you share your vastly rich creativity with others

984 Gretia

where someone is more likely to be remorselessly pushed around in your exchanges

493 Griseldis

where you are associated with enticing, smooth temptation of various kinds

496 Gryphia

that which you expose which constitutes a "moment of truth" for how people see you; where the revelations about you begin for others

328 Gudrun

where you seem open to others, but are actually the intruder; related to the Tantalus family

799 Gudula

where people see you as having an oddly self- or bodily-aware way that makes them feel awkward around you

891 Gunhild

mode in which you occupy a starring role

983 Gunila

an important tool you must be able to use in building bridges with others

657 Gunlod

where you are associated with power-polarity equality; where the differences between masculine and feminine tactics are minimized [this is pretty much a feminist asteroid]

961 Gunnie

where others interact with you like you're some kind of doll or ornament

777 Gutemberga

realm where you are surrounded by talk, where your actions are gossipable

806 Gyldenia

where you display more unrestrained (or at least less formal), in some cases primal behavior

444 Gyptis

where you demonstrate an all-or-nothing, black-and-white attitude

H – K

Hades (transNeptunian)

where you use your deep power to control others

682 Hagar

where you are a kind of escape for others

368 Haidea

where you move from coolly cooperative to electric in the pursuit of your wants

518 Halawe

your style of veiled conquest

449 Hamburga

side of you the association with which helps others escape their trained box

452 Hamiltonia

a potential leadership role hindered (or tempered) by difficulties in your personality, where you may need to share influence; **the Self-Destructive Hero among of the Mean 13**

723 Hammonia

emphasis on male creative power and its use

480 Hansa

where you instill creative or inventive thoughts in others

724 Hapag

where you turn others on or get them excited; associated with the things you do to keep people devoted to you, repeatedly forgiving your faults; eccentric likeability

578 Happelia

where your way challenges others to bring their fiercest game to the table (in the bonding sense)

40 Harmonia

where your talents take you to far off expressive terrains

736 Harvard

where you are kept at arms length, no closer no farther, from your favored interactants; where you dissect crowds associated with you, never allowing yourself to interact with them as a mob—but on a situation by situation basis instead. Harvard's asteroidal character is $\left(8\frac{8}{144}\right):\left\{7\frac{114}{144} \rightarrow 8\frac{40}{144}\right\}:\|70\|.$

136108 Haumea

aspect of your personality which proves educational to others

362 Havnia

means through which you present your allure

6 Hebe

side of you which is used or commanded by parties for their own unscrupulous objectives; **a heavy temptation asteroid in the Scheherezade family**

108 Hecuba

where you won't rest until the last castle has fallen; associated with staying with something until either you or it is completely broken, but where the breaks tend to be epically final

207 Hedda

where you favor a broad variety of experiences; associated with the company-inviting aspects of the body or personality

476 Hedwig

your potentially famous behavior

325 Heidelberga

where your circles look up to you

100 Hekate

where you make the most rational social decisions available compared to your peers

624 Hektor

where others constantly invite you to stoop down to their level

949 Hel

what you use to attempt to change the stubborn system around you

699 Hela

where you hint to others that you have dirty or taboo preferences

101 Helena

where you enjoy skyrocketed notoriety

522 Helga

where people perceive you as quirky right up to—and sometimes past—the level of being off-putting

895 Helio

where you are friendly but demanding

967 Helionape

side of you which gives rise (in others) to the hope of fantastic experiences

801 Helwerthia

where you are receptive to command by those who pressure you despite your strength

225 Henrietta

how you deliver your creative instruction; your teaching mode for lessons that actually get carried out

826 Henrika

area in which you have the ability to lead the masses

2212 Hephaistos

emotional home base [one of the best descriptors of your home environment]

103 Hera

deep bonds

5143 Heracles

where you offer others an escape from external confusion

880 Herba

where you're likely to seek external support to publicize your aims

532 Herculina

where you press strongly for self-determination, solo or for others

458 Hercynia

how or where you expose deep, dark secrets [others' or your own]

923 Herluga

where you are unafraid of handling power or difficult issues in public

346 Hermentaria

associated with being shrouded in mystery despite one's charismatic notoriety. Scorpio-like

69230 Hermes

the reason people like to gather around and watch you

685 Hermia

where you convey resolute insistence

121 Hermione

an obligation to be subject to a masculine voice of reason

546 Herodias

where your advancement is dependent on your charisma [often more than your skill]

206 Hersilia

where your charisma shows clearly

135 Hertha

associated with hurt women

69 Hesperia

area where you air your judgment of others' worthiness

46 Hestia

realm in which you are more likely to go rogue

944 Hidalgo

attention getter

996 Hilaritas

where you are visibly at the front of all of your contemporaries

153 Hilda

where you suggest critical improvements to expression which demand to be followed (most typically by colleagues)

684 Hildburg

the style of role you play in performing your duties; a II-conjunct -like public persona

898 Hildegard

where you partners place a heavy weight on the role of creativity and or power (mostly their own)

928 Hildrun

where you are a non-slouch, where your way of doing things is THE way

426 Hippo

where you are comfortable having power over another; a power that automatically compels them to do as you would want

692 Hippodamia

where you make good, prosocial company; Capricorn 692s gravitate towards luxury or, at least, order

706 Hirundo

where you demonstrate an intrusive charm

804 Hispania

the mode for your enjoyment of fun, games, and music; along with Proserpina, the two strongest ethnoculture asteroids of the 1000

788 Hohensteina

side of you which fosters others' creative projection

872 Holda

what you share of yourself with everyone

378 Holmia

where you are determined that your way should rule the day

236 Honoria

associated with idealized womanhood (or less frequently, optimally refined feminine elements)—where others can observe it in your life

932 Hooveria

where you are surest in your communication

2938 Hopi

where you are driven to "turn lemons into lemonade"

805 Hormuthia

where you are a revolutionary among your peers

4950 House

where you demonstrate refinement in your bearing

House 1 Cusp (Ascendant)

how you handle new situations

House 2 Cusp

how you measure your self-value, what you construct your identity against

House 3 Cusp

how you communicate from within, your opinion-giving

House 4 Cusp (Imum Coeli)

exposed aims; see Imum Coeli for more details

House 5 Cusp

how you engage hobbies and creative projects

House 6 Cusp

how you handle daily affairs

House 7 Cusp (Descendant)

your handling of 1:1 exchanges; **we tend to fire our friends or get fired by them** based on things that happen related to our Descendant

House 8 Cusp

how you steer others

House 9 Cusp

your handling of image promotion among strangers

House 10 Cusp (Midheaven)

what strikes others about your reputation

House 11 Cusp

information around you

House 12 Cusp

the kind of environment which surrounds you

260 Huberta

where those who associate with you must be up to standard

379 Huenna

where you require that those around you have high value or attractiveness

434 Hungaria

where you are pragmatic, sane, and stable regarding what's going on around you

38628 Huya

means through which deep revelations take place

430 Hybris

area where you are given power to steer others

10 Hygiea

where the body is important to you

10370 Hylonome

where your way appeals to mass media or mass information environments

238 Hypatia

where you are bombarded or burdened as the price of being skilled

587 Hypsipyle

where you super-extend your creative power beyond normal boundaries

98 Ianthe

where you are associated with sex and sexuality as social currency, in rarer cases this is power instead of sex

1566 Icarus

⊻ 🕷

where you are extra charming to people

286 Iclea

⬇ 🎮 🎮

where you are a hub for youthful activity

243 Ida

🗣 ♟ 🗣 👪 🗣 🏆

where you traverse taboo territory just as easily as normal territory

963 Iduberga

⚲ ⊕ ⬇ ⚚

where you must be strongly supported in order to meet your interactional goals

176 Iduna

👑 🎮 ⚚ 🗣

in a good and lighthearted manner

385 Ilmatar

⚲ ♂ ⇧

likeable masculinity

249 Ilse

🗣 ⇧ ⛆ 📦 🎮

where you continually communicate with people of a class lower than yours

919 Ilsebill

⇧ ⬇ 💬 🏝 ⊻ 🕊 ⚚

where you conjure others' ideas of association with an attractive partner

979 Ilsewa

✈ ⚡ ⛆ 👽 ◗

where you have a mellow, almost sorrowful tinge to your expression

926 Imhilde

⊻ 🏛 ⇧ 🏗

where you are a force for creating expressive paths where there was none

Critical Point: The IC

Imum Coeli (House 4 Cusp)

👑 ⇧

an indicator of the aims which everyone and everything have, which you naturally expose; the Imum Coeli (IC) is one of the top indicators of qualities you draw out of people simply by being associated with them. I actually made this discovery after finishing this chapter and felt it important to add to the description.

The "Friends Rub Off" Cocktail

Whenever you officially add someone to your immediate friendship circle and start associating with them regularly, you begin to pick up certain habits in light of them. I mentioned in *HBS* that I had a muse during the writing of that book, and in between *HBS* and this one actually met another person with the same powers of inspiration. Without knowing it, I had encountered someone with the same birthday as my *HBS* muse. This allowed me a good look at how these two people were accomplishing the inspiration in similar but different ways. My investigation produced four powerful points which come about as close as you'll get to determining exactly how we become the company we keep.

- Imum Coeli
- Persephone
- North Node
- Bacchus

And so we arrive at an unexpectedly strong cocktail to supplement the ones I listed in *HBS*:

I draw out [my Imum Coeli duodecanate] and thus [the other person's points near my IC] from everyone I encounter (including myself). In so doing I feel destined to receive [their points near my North Node] while exerting a strong power to change their lives in [their points near my Persephone]. While they are associated closely with me in whatever capacity, they are much more easily inspired to display new ways of [accomplishing whatever they have in my Bacchus' duodecanate]. In most cases, if I'm not interacting with them reliably in the realm of my North Node, my relationship with them tends to be much weaker than it would be with very close friends.

As an added bonus, you can partly determine whether the other person has truly accepted you into their lives—as friend, immediate circle-mate, or enemy—by asking what (if anything) has changed dramatically among your baseline behaviors since their arrival. When you dismiss friends from your circle you tend to stop receiving your IC region from them.

Rectification: Assigning a Birth Time to a Chart Without One

The best tool I've found for estimating birth times in charts where the birth time is unknown, the Imum Coeli can be used as a broad basis for triangulating a person's possible chart structure. Now before I go any further and tell you how to do this, I should note that the purpose of this activity isn't necessarily to get *the* birth time right, but to estimate a wheel for the person which is most consistent with your experience of them as they interact with their own worlds. Don't get hung up on finding the "true" time. Just go for a chart about which you can confidently say, "I don't have any further doubts about my process for getting this, and no further doubts regarding how it lines up with the facts available to me."

Your IC draws out the duodecanate in which it is found. Typically in everyone (including yourself), and typically all the time. The only situation where this doesn't hold is where either you or your interactant are better off with distance between you—either because your life doesn't overlap enough with theirs, you or they are lying to the other, or you and they have crossed goals. Before using the IC to rectify others' charts, it *really* helps to understand your own IC.

1.   Make sure you know how to tell when you're using your own IC.

This will give you a feel for what to look for when describing someone else's global effect on others. I arrived at this advice by studying my own IC in 8 Gemini, the Gemini-novile, and getting a sharper feel for when others' being around me compelled them to publicize (novile) their own internal monologue (Gemini). This was in addition to noting that, at the time of this writing, I have over 20,000 private recordings (a diary if you will), spanning the last decade of my life—"publicizing" my own monologue in semi-private way. If you didn't know my birth time, you would need to be able to observe how most of my interactions lead to this kind of disclosure, whether or not I'm directly involved in the interaction, and from there you could pick a birth time on my birth date (which is considerably easier to find for most people), and boom. You have your rectified chart.

2.   Note the one thing that EVERYBODY does in response to the person whose chart you're looking at.

Suppose you didn't know Adolf Hitler's birth time, but you noticed that, by and large, everybody past and present seems to be careful about saying the right thing when he comes up as a subject. This by itself won't help you arrive at a birth time, but it does narrow his IC down to something Libra, Saj, or Gemini related, maybe Aquarius. Now I actually don't remember Hitler's setup while writing this, so I'll look it up...Aquarius. Okay. But it's not like we're using the IC alone to figure this out. We're also looking at house placements, the location of the person's Vertex, the duodecanate which describes their Moon, their Part of Fortune and any planets you might have on it. Finally, we also look at their own asteroids and other major bodies which are conjunct the possible IC, which move slowly enough to stay in the same place all day, and whose character seems to line up with what the person actually draws out in people.

3.   Check the arrangement of other planets in the chart you've guessed.
4.   Check the key planets and asteroids near the IC you've guessed for the person.

It actually works pretty well. In the end, Hitler's Aquarius-inconjunct IC is reasonably consistent with his drawing out everyone's "works of the imagination," compelling a vision (inconjunct) amidst social talk (Aquarius).

389 Industria

side of you which determines your opportunities in the world

391 Ingeborg

where you spread a message of peace and love

561 Ingwelde

where you naturally make your home amidst chaos

848 Inna

where you are the social justice broadcaster IF you grow past your own personal wars; related to Pallas

173 Ino

means through which you are a social change agent

704 Interamnia

greedy chasing

85 Io

where you serve as a rallying point for others

509 Iolanda

where your way causes all other ways to fade from view

112 Iphigenia

where you put in efforts to control or direct your impulses

794 Irenaea

where it doesn't pay to challenge feminine expression

14 Irene

associated with unassuming appearance despite fierce passions underneath

7 Iris

the kind of creative expression that others use FOR YOU, around you, or on your behalf

177 Irma

where you are the center of your friendship groups and other cliques

591 Irmgard

where you convey your intentions for bigger and better things

773 Irmintraud

where you act as a life change agent for others; Antivertex-like

Otherwriters

Control the lives of others with astro-objects designed to put you in charge. Here they are:

- Persephone
- Irmintraud
- Glasenappia
- the Antivertex
- Sylvania
- Thuringia

What's the catch? The puppet is only as good as the puppeteer. Barring a certain high level of wisdom (among other things), most people who try to use these will typically end up writing themselves into trouble beyond their capacity to handle. But feel free to find this out for yourself.

210 Isabella

where you are drawn to various types of intimacy, especially of the psychological kind

364 Isara

where communicating—talking things out—is extremely important to you

939 Isberga

where you appear to expect to be treated like royalty, whether or not you deserve this

42 Isis

the role played by "queens" (women of regal status or bearing) in your life

190 Ismene

where you are emotionally volatile or provocative of such volatility around you

211 Isolda

✍ 🎗 ♂ 📻

where you have defining, turbulent, or chaotic relationships with males. I've found that this asteroid wreaks hurricane-like havoc in the charts of women who have ended up as single mothers. For those still looking to get their male-relationships right, I've observed that the solution often involves using the woman's work life as a stabilizing force between her and her intended male associate.

Asteroids Which Shred Up Relationships

- Hamiltonia
- Isolda
- Pax

More than other bodies, these asteroids come out as plain irrational in your chart. Truly enough to make the other person say, "What the f*ck, man?"

183 Istria

♈ ⬆ 🕊 🗨

making positive change for others through your trade

477 Italia

🌩 📣 👑 🍸 🏛

where life seems easy for you despite your having been through a lot

918 Itha

🏛 🌳 ✈ 🏆

where you rationally instruct others

25143 Itokawa

⬇ 📣 ✍ 🖧 🌳 ⛰ ⊕

where you can process massive amounts of information (towards some mysterious or obscured end)

497 Iva

⬇ 🗨 📻 ♈ 🏆

excessive extracting from others; negatively, associated with where and how you complain about things

28978 Ixion

✈ 🗨 ❗ 👤 👽 ●

how you order others around

383 Janina

🍸 🏦 🎗 ⬇

where you are attractively tempting, but often passed over for more favorable choices; it is often easier to make your own way with the first dedicated partner or opportunity you can find until another comes along;

advancement tends to be consistently, but reliably in someone else's hands no matter what your own efforts entail; **the Automatic Enslaver among of the Mean 13**; associated with being seen as untrustworthy by others, because after they help you, they feel you've screwed them (that is, you would use them as a footstool for your own greedy desires, and are best treated as a last resort)

People who pass you over via your Janina think you'll screw them. But will you? Yes, you probably will. Either they'll set it up or you'll set it up, but the data showed that, most of the time, it's gonna happen. You're a wolf in sheep's clothing here. A faker. Even if you really are a trustworthy person, Janina shows where you can and probably will vanish as soon as you've collected your loot from the other person. What are you after? Who knows, but once this meanie asteroid has been used, you'll typically show a rather non-remorseful version of those bodies in the duodecanate 60° before the one Janina's in.

Janina is one of the hardest of all 1000 asteroids to get right because it's just so darned slippery. The moment you try to activate it, you're often being passed by. Accordingly, it also serves as one of the most effective seed planters in your chart. That is, Janina minus 90° consistently showed where a person was relentlessly acquisitive of new levels of power throughout their lives (and sometimes beyond). So while #383 usually shows where you can't get a leg up with other people, it also shows where all kinds of potential exists for the activities backwards square to it.

526 Jena

⬆ 🏰 🖧 🏆 ♈

where you obtain or reflect creative superiority above others

607 Jenny

⬆ ⬇ 🗨 🌳 🌲

where you enable new beginnings for others; undoes Natalie

549 Jessonda

⊕ 👑 🍸 📻 🏆

the importance of good appearances, materialism

544 Jetta

🌩 🏠 ⬆ 🌳 🌳 ♈

where you overcome a challenging beginning or upbringing to become inspiring

726 Joella

trait others desire from you when they seek out your company

127 Johanna

your presence amidst flux and change-filled environments

899 Jokaste

where you are more comfortable letting the other person take the lead; where you are more of a listener

836 Jole

where, even with your power, you are at the mercy of your interactants (though they usually don't know this). Accordingly this asteroid is strongly associated with a person's **insecurity**, and they may be extremely reluctant to do this without an understanding helper at their side. People who are responsible for making and leading their own teams, might read this alongside the Social Unity asteroids to help them properly assign their team members' roles

649 Josefa

where you have a talent that can silence anyone from the lowest slave to the highest king

The Unstoppable Ultimate Group

For readers looking to get their Skeletor on, crowning themselves Masters of the Universe, we have the Unstoppable Ultimate asteroid group. These asteroids show where you are so ridiculously strong you could knock over a building by looking at it. These are areas of life where no one can hold a candle to you, and they usually don't try (unless they're fools).

- Josefa
- Aida
- Persephone
- Klytaemnestra
- Montefiore
- Octavia

The bad news for these is that, in most of us, these asteroids are located in places and saddled with neighbors which drown them in distractions. So you *would* conquer the world, but for that bill you just got from the phone company. Alas, most of us will never get around to subjugating all of mankind this way.

303 Josephina

where you are pragmatic in your decisions, no matter how unusual they seem to others

921 Jovita

where you are the model of a sophisticated approach to your field

652 Jubilatrix

context for high-spirited gatherings

948 Jucunda

where your known to make trouble for yourself through careless actions; positively, where you are intriguingly amusing to be around

664 Judith

where you evaluate others for acceptability

139 Juewa

the trait which people who want to be masters will gravitate towards you for

89 Julia

where only truly masculine forwardness is allowed

816 Juliana

where you play out your communicative charisma

3 Juno

commitment in the eyes of the world

Jupiter

image promotion

269 Justitia

that side of you which suffers if you make wrong decisions. Behave yourself with this one. Like Natalie, it will punish you if you don't.

What Goes Around...: The Karma Asteroids

Certain asteroids can be counted on to return the favor whenever you commit a wrong against someone else. These asteroids rarely help you in your good deeds, but are more than happy to punish you for your bad ones. They are the Karma asteroids (though the body called 3811 Karma itself is, ironically, not one of them). For this group, we're talking "karma" in the Western sense (what goes around comes around)—which isn't what karma actually is. You'll need to read 3811 for a body which is closer to the real karmic notion of "indebted attachment."

- Natalie – stay in line or else
- Justitia – make good decisions or else
- Cosima – display good feminine-style qualities or else
- Aquitania – display good masculine-style qualities or else

Why do these punish the bad but not reward the good? Think of this group as maintaining the standards for your "interpersonal health." Just as your body will punish you for treating it incorrectly, these bodies will punish you for treating your own social world (which you <u>need</u>) incorrectly.

605 Juvisia

area where you genuinely don't seem to need anyone to meet your goals

22 Kalliope

where your trajectory or mood is easily changed by circumstance

204 Kallisto

where you bear attractive features or are associated with people with such features

53 Kalypso

where your level of inventive originality is too high for others to keep up with

818 Kapteynia

where you are innocuously artistic; creativity kept under wraps

832 Karin

where you give hints of an exacting nature

3811 Karma

aspect of your character against which, when people interact with it, significantly alters the circumstances you share

781 Kartvelia

where yours is a journey worth following

114 Kassandra

where you absolutely demand others perform

646 Kastalia

where you defy the rules of propriety

320 Katharina

where you critically appraise all incoming influences

842 Kerstin

where you are considered socially desirable regardless of your specific characteristics or faults; related to Clarissa

470 Kilia

what individual solicitors seek your personal company for; why people would use you

216 Kleopatra

where you do others a favor by breaking down their expressive walls by force on your own expression

84 Klio

where you hold an expert's store of creative power; where you are most likely to play out sex roles. (With the Midheaven, pornstars had mostly public aspects. This was where you had a reputation for displaying your sexual or creative nature.)

97 Klotho

where you sponsor brand new opportunities for others

583 Klotilde

where your company is preferred over that of others

104 Klymene

where your talk monopolizes everyone's thoughts

179 Klytaemnestra

trait for which you are given king or queen status or the area where you are associated with such (**the Golden Status Grantor among the strong spirit asteroids**, and one of my personal favorites)

73 Klytia

associated with creative delivery of the more feminine-element kind (against more masculine standards) which needs to be pushed in order for you to express it, or which is only given after more masculine methods have been exhausted

191 Kolga

where others feel they should keep trying with you even after it is over

940 Kordula

where you are associated with high status surroundings

158 Koronis

how you tend to those whom you think really need help

867 Kovacia

where your wishes will be satisfied no matter what

548 Kressida

where others like to watch you unleash creative power on people (not necessarily them, though); associated with the breasts

800 Kressmannia

associated with the woman as being in control of the situation

488 Kreusa

where your own agenda supercedes all others'

242 Kriemhild

the adorable side of you—which may give others the impression that relations with you are better than they really are

Kronos (transNeptunian)

one of your most charming personality components

553 Kundry

where you are a considerate communicator

936 Kunigunde

where you provide others with an inspiring vision

669 Kypria

the traits you possess which get you typecast by others

570 Kythera

how you provide an uplifting presence

L – N

336 Lacadiera

where the thought of you conjures images of an impulse-commanding quality

120 Lachesis

where you are the liberator

208 Lacrimosa

where you are more serious or stern in your assertion

39 Laetitia

where you seek massive amounts of whatever this asteroid is attached to

Greedy Appetite Asteroids

Asteroids which are heavily associated with greedy craving or obsession show up as significant in the charts of people who refuse to stop chasing whatever it is they are fixated on. The major bodies denoting insatiable appetites are (from more greedy to less so)

- Ducrosa – excess wanted
- Chariklo – ambition
- Laetitia – quantity demanded
- Poesia – unending quest
- Interamnia – greedy chasing
- Holmia – one's own way

822 Lalage

sober, subdued approach; 822 in Aries in women makes for well-balanced, cool interactions with others

187 Lamberta

easygoingness

248 Lameia

roaming, scattered foci

393 Lampetia

how you channel larger sociopsychological (or to some, spiritual) principles for public viewing

683 Lanzia

where people like connecting with you

507 Laodica

where you have no equals to compare your actions to

639 Latona

the preservation of an appealing image

467 Laura

where you prefer to be associated with babes, studs, and other beautiful things

162 Laurentia

the reason you have jobs and opportunities handed to you; associated with money and other forms of value given to you without your needing to work for it; with Waltraut, Eurykleia, 92Q, and anything attached to Bacchus, constitutes **one of the clearest "easy-street" asteroids**

38 Leda

where you let others go first, releasing your power after they've successfully released theirs

691 Lehigh

where you are self-conscious and quick to correct other's mistaken assessments of you and whatever is related to this asteroid

47171 Lempo

where your very basic biologically sex-typical appeal spills out in full view of the people. This one isn't about masculinity or femininity, but male-female prototypicality; associated with a smooth way of doing the things near it

789 Lena

where you skeptically go against the norm describing those around you

969 Leocadia

where you are remorselessly unhidden, the raw you

319 Leona

associated with masculinity-paralyzing feminine power (where any feminine element-type behaviors may apply here)

728 Leonisis

realm in which people make themselves subservient to you (your slave as it were); with Persephone, an other-controller

696 Leonora

where your way elicits respect from others

844 Leontina

your brand of royal status

893 Leopoldina

associated with women with higher status or social value than their men

1264 Letaba

insistence of the salience of a creative interaction; associated with the place where one demands a specific context for co-creator exchange; associated with the kinds of relationships you attract before you figure out what you're doing; later, the kinds of behaviors you purposely demand from your partners

68 Leto

how you unite others around you

35 Leukothea

means through which you are known to protect your other interests

954 Li

experiences you demonstrate a want for

771 Libera

where people under your company feel they can be themselves

125 Liberatrix

where you experience a mysteriously sudden end or disappearance; where others suddenly tire of you; alternatively, where you preserve your influence by eliminating others [or things] from your life; **the Sudden Eliminator among Mean 13**; perhaps more positively, MPC#125 also seems to be strongly associated with sudden luck or status climbing which separates you from old ties. For most people though, this asteroid is negative by default

264 Libussa

where you are self-indulgent, taking as much as you want

356 Liguria

where you are a renegade (primarily in your field)

213 Lilaea

where you are surprisingly attractive to be around

Lilith (Black Moon, Mean Apogee)

contrariety and rebellion

1181 Lilith (asteroid)

where you are a hub around which action takes place

756 Lilliana

where your surroundings are populated by powerful forces

468 Lina

what you offer whose quality is surprisingly good to others

828 Lindemannia

where you display a creeping power to force your will

974 Lioba

associated with fiery women

846 Lipperta

where you make others feel as though you don't need them in order for you to excel. The result is often jealousy or frustration when you are seen using this elsewhere; **the Jealousy Attractor among the Mean 13**; associated with the part of your life that makes others envious

414 Liriope

attractive or powerful trait which draws others to you

58534 Logos

where you are surrounded by people and their passions

463 Lola

where you interact with people's fantasies or delusions (yours or others')

117 Lomia

where you display a subdued or disappointed bearing; seems to affect the facial features by predisposing one to a sterner expression during certain asteroid-related events (look at all of the asteroids around this one in your chart to see what I mean); like Bacchus, a strong circle-defining asteroid

165 Loreley

where you demonstrate spacey, abstract tendencies

429 Lotis

the strong woman who requires a masculine element to complete her self-definition [reminiscent of Sheila E - Glamorous Life]

868 Lova

where you are associated with more of some subject most people are self-conscious about or uncomfortable talking about

16900 Lozere

intellectual-creative appetite as fueled by bodily desires; hunger civilized

222 Lucia

the woman at the center of control

146 Lucina

where you are susceptible to others' misunderstanding

281 Lucretia

where you champion or exemplify the underdog

675 Ludmilla

associated with masculine elements which put down feminine elements by force. Future research might investigate this in the charts of abusers, as Ludmilla's neighbors seem to reflect how or why male-on-female abuse occurs for both sexes. Based on my data,

- lud = self entitlement
- mel = masculine assertion
- ah = projecting

Also, Ludmilla's character is $\left(8\frac{56}{144}\right) : \left\{8\frac{9}{144} \rightarrow 8\frac{94}{144}\right\} : \|86\|$.

("affirmation of power" situation):

{projecting an image towards
→ structuring a youthful expression}:

‖in showing off an unwelcome trait‖

292 Ludovica

where something about you is alluringly excessive...from a distance

599 Luisa

where you have unlimited ways of presenting yourself or your creations

141 Lumen

where you are outgoing and enabling to others

775 Lumiere

★ ♀ ⬇ 🌍 🏆 📦

where you express a desire for some grand wish to be fulfilled—one that seems outrageous, but may come true; a big wish granted long before you realize it **[the strong spirit asteroid which makes the impossible into the actual]**

809 Lundia

⬇ 🏆 🏝 🕊 💬 📦

means through which you channel spiritual perfection; the ideal form of expressive information which surrounds others

713 Luscinia

🏝 ⊕ ⊕

where others perceive you to be not all there, in space—with an inexplicable inattention to something

21 Lutetia

👑 👤

where you are comfortable in your own skin

110 Lydia

⚡ 🏝 ⬇ 🛡

where you are sensitive to hurt, building up instant defense mechanisms to protect yourself

917 Lyka

〲 ⬆ 📦

means through which you release the tension within you

897 Lysistrata

👤 👄 🏠 🕐

where you are associated with unconsummated or incomplete relationships (often romantic)

510 Mabella

🛡 📇

where you nurture others around you

318 Magdalena

⬇ 👤 ✈ 🏛 ⬆ ⊕

where it takes the work of someone else for you to "get your shit together"

66 Maja

🏙 🏆 👽 ⬆

where you are a social trophy whom others like to brag about knowing

136472 Makemake

⊕ 🍸 🏆 ⬆ 🏛

where you are dedicated to far-reaching influence

754 Malabar

👑 🔨 ⬆

non-threatening approach

749 Malzovia

🏝 🌲 🌳 📣 👽 ⬇ 💬 〲

side of you which is abstract and often confusing, sometimes exhausting

758 Mancunia

🍸 🏝 📣

smooth image

739 Mandeville

⬆ 🍸 📇 🏆

where you are confident in commanding your fans and supporters

870 Manto

🕷 🍸 🏔

irresistible seduction

385446 Manwe

〲 ♂ 💬

where you have turbulent or complex relationships with certain key males or their roles, often out of sight of the interactant

565 Marbachia

🏔 🗡 ⊕ ⬆

where you face all obstacles and break through

310 Margarita

📇 👪 🏠

side you use to mother others, giving them somewhere to go

735 Marghanna

〲 🏝 📇 👽

the side of you which carries with it obnoxious environments and agitated surroundings

170 Maria

👤 🛡 🏛 💬

where you take care of the people associated with you, typically those of higher rank or influence than you

602 Marianna

means through which you openly solicit fanship and others' liking

506 Marion

where you take a logical, clinical approach to things

912 Maritima

where you approach with a high-energy criticality

746 Marlu

where you express the greatest level of riches you could possibly share with others; partly shows where monetary riches plays a role in your life

711 Marmulla

where you are easily seen as a star

Mars

steering others

205 Martha

where you are certain that the input of others is not to be trusted or followed blindly; where you are inclined to be skeptical of others' professed claims

981 Martina

quality which makes you a trophy at the celebration; associated with the kind of setting which puts you more in a celebratory mode

20 Massalia

where you introduce people to concepts they've never seen; your role models often have this asteroid on key planets of yours. For example, my role models' Massalias all clustered on my major planets. (This is another one of my favorites among the 1000, and has a relatedly interesting naming history if you look it up.) **The strong spirit asteroid of the Role Model**

760 Massinga

where you reject weak expression

454 Mathesis

where you display a stable, motherly fixity in your dealings with those in your camp

253 Mathilde

where your standards cause most regular people to leave you; an "ally filter" like Sauer

883 Matterania

where you insist on tangibilities and clear results

765 Mattiaca

associated with agitated women (or more generally, tension-bearing feminine elements)

745 Mauritia

where you display cool receptiveness and adaptability

348 May

thing for which you seek love and approval from all [**an odd asteroid with unique, hard to describe properties** that I've yet to understand]

Midheaven (House 10 Cusp)

where you appear destined to prosper, or at least attain your sought ends

991 McDonalda

where you are creatively (sometimes sexually) extraverted, unembarrassed to show where you stand

873 Mechthild

where you are bathed in the illusions of others and the activity that comes with it

212 Medea

where you have a breadth of expertise in your field; related to Moultona

149 Medusa

side of you which captures others' attention

464 Megaira

where you rally people for positive expression

688 Melanie

where people identify you with the ability to command others' impulses

56 Melete

means through which you promote peace or (at least happiness) for all

137 Meliboea

general realm in which you are synonymous with leadership or iconship

676 Melitta

triggers the masculine desire nature

869 Mellena

where you bring new forms from buried potential out of others; see Massalia

18 Melpomene

where you do things that should get you censored

373 Melusina

where you are attention-magnetic, though often in an unfortunate way; associated with the attraction of abusers or deviants

1247 Memoria

means through which others feel the need to bond to you

188 Menippe

where you take an open, unapologetic approach to a preferred area of expression

536 Merapi

realm where you inspire lessons of acceptance in others, making it safe for them to act

Mercury

common grounding of otherwise disconnected or underconnected events

808 Merxia

where you have deeply philosophical or principled views

545 Messalina

where you are nonchalant regarding sexual or power characteristics. Some people find this side of you unbelievably open when they first encounter it: "Doesn't she know what she just said?"

792 Metcalfia

synonymous with women as commanders (Joan of Arc-style)

9 Metis

where you make idealized social company

878 Mildred

where you are charming company

93 Minerva

where you're inclined to let what you have hang out in remorseless display of your power; unabashed, openly announced, provocative power

594 Mireille

thing you are welcomed and respected for, primarily in your profession

102 Miriam

where you contribute to the wider culture around you

569 Misa

where you are a magnet for the opposite sex

4523 MIT

✈ ♀ 🍸 🖧

Where you are a ceaseless passer of relationship- or pattern- harmonizing information, despite a very serious or stern bearing in how that information is assembled

57 Mnemosyne

💥 🖧 🏆 ✈

where you have unusual ideas regarding what to do with the groups who follow you

733 Mocia

🗪 🏚 💥 👽

trait you have which surprises others out of their stereotypes about you

Bzz. Wrong!
Bohemia, Mocia, Lucina, and Tantalus all show where people are likely to be very wrong about you.

370 Modestia

🎒 ⬇ 💥 🗪

what you use to draw reactions from people

766 Moguntia

🏆 'Y' 📢 ⬆

where you strike others as having prolific abilities

638 Moira

⬆ ✈ ⊕ ⬇ 🏛

where you are surrounded by creative works, by virtue of being demanding; the nature of your creative demands from those around you

428 Monachia

⬆ ⬇ 🗪 🧍 ⊕

where you inspire others' body-centrism, sense of their own feeling, or sense of their own self-value

833 Monica

♀ ⊕ ⬇ 🗡 👽 ⬆ 📢

where you require an associated personality to perfect your own expression

535 Montague

⊕ 🗣 ⬆

what you put your concentrated focus into building up as a communicator

797 Montana

👽 ⬆ ⬇ 🕊 🎗

the aspect of you which would-be romantic partners and friends would love to own for themselves

782 Montefiore

📢 🏆 🌍 🏙 'Y'

where you may be described as impressive if not spectacular

947 Monterosa

⬆ ⬇ ✈ 🏚 🗪

where you render the others around you more sober either because or in spite of you

Moon

⬇ ⬆

emotions and inclinations

341520 Mors-Somnus

🏖 🌍

where you display lots of activity. (For whatever reason, I found this asteroid to be one of the biggest letdowns of all 1000. For such a dramatic name, you would think that it did more. Maybe future research will reveal something I didn't see.)

787 Moskva

💥 🏔 🏖

where you take an original, uncompromised approach to things

993 Moultona

🏖 💰 ❗

your money-making trade; along with Brambilla, Ottegebe and others, **an asteroid associated with the career and the strongest career asteroid of all 1000**. My nickname for it: "the Money Making Trade Asteroid"

941 Murray

🏖 ⬇ 🏔 🏛

where your expression is tempered by external forces

600 Musa

🏛 🗡 🎗

where you invite others to shake off their restrictions and rebel against inhibition

966 Muschi

♀ ⊕ 🏔 🗣 🕊

perfectionism beneath a more friendly or docile nature

381 Myrrha

where you wrestle with notions of beauty (outward appeal) versus duty (tasks that need to be done)

845 Naema

what your name comes to be associated with; **a key fame indicator**

559 Nanon

side of you which you allow others to enjoy when making connections with you

853 Nansenia

where sophistication arises as an issue, either because you have it or because you need it

37117 Narcissus

where you are sharply aware of your own characteristics, so aware that you may be vain here. Not always though.

534 Nassovia

where you are subject to promising beginnings which are cut short by your own choices unless applied to imagination or spiritual things

448 Natalie

the thing which—should you allow it to play out negatively, will ruin what you've built; the area whose proper functioning you must preserve no matter what; **arguably <u>the meanest</u> (and the most-self negative) of all 1000 asteroids, including the Mean 13; the High Stakes Punisher**

811 Nauheima

realm where you are associated with fantasy worlds or invented personas

192 Nausikaa

realm where you are inclined to high levels of bodily, sensual, or self-value enjoyment

903 Nealley

side of you which imposes order or restrictions on people around you; a passive version of Sauer and Saturn

51 Nemausa

where you don't take kindly to people questioning your skills

128 Nemesis

area where you create enemies for yourself; positively, where you create obstacles to be overcome

289 Nenetta

where you display a defensive shield in the form of an uninviting spaciness

431 Nephele

where you develop in a way that expressly defies the "home" that trained you; a strong and obvious asteroid which I gave the nickname: "the Far From Home Asteroid;" **the "Nephele family" of behaviors shows where one is <u>supposed to</u> defy his home training.** (As someone in touch with his Lilith-rebellious side, I really like this asteroid.)

287 Nephthys

where you raise rich images from the depths of your imagination; related to games, fiction, and other richly imagined scenarios

Neptune

the impression or vibe about you; your ambient environment

601 Nerthus

where you leave a notable impression on those who see you in action

7066 Nessus

where you are a natural media personality

659 Nestor

⇧ ⇩ 🗨️ 🏚️ ✈️

where your way causes others to control themselves and their responses to you; self-control in others; **this asteroid, like Sauer and Zelia, is GREAT for shutting other people down or silencing them.** Be careful though, like other silencers, it's also great at driving people out of your life before you want them to leave.

855 Newcombia

👄 ⇩ 🗨️ 🏆

where you are praised for your creative or desirous excesses

662 Newtonia

💼 👽 🏛️

where your persona becomes glued to the proper working of a system you've joined

843 Nicolaia

🏚️ ⸱ 🏠 ⛵ 🎗️

what you can be counted on to anchor your friends with; related to the 141st harmonic

307 Nike

⇩ 🎗️ ⛴️ ⸱

where you draw willing, compliant cooperation from others

779 Nina

🅰️ 💥 🏆 👽 ⇧

where you manifest creativity of a notably more eccentric kind

357 Ninina

⇩ 💣 👄 ⇧

the quality which, used on you effectively, lights you up; where you are impressed; **even more than Eros, one of the most passionately intense of all 1000 asteroids.** While Eros shows what turns you on, Ninina shows what turns up your turn on.

71 Niobe

🅰️ 🔥 🔍

where you reveal particular aesthetic preferences for the things you interact with

727 Nipponia

📢 ⚡ 🗯️ 💬 ⇩ 🖥️

where you rally people around your (often sad) story or the case you're making for something. I investigated whether this asteroid works the way other ethnoculture

asteroids do, and it does. As the name suggests, 727 and its neighbors reflect one's broad opinion of Japanese things.

Typecasters: Asteroids That Have Nothing to Do With You...Or Do They?

What do asteroids that talk about other cultures, body image, and certain personality quirks have in common? Statistically speaking, there's a good chance that you don't reflect them actively in your chart. If you download all of the first 1000 asteroids, however, you will almost certainly notice something eye-opening: Even if such asteroids don't directly apply to you, there is a good chance that they still show how you view the topics they indicate. So if you don't manifest Nipponia yourself, its neighbors will tend to tell you how you view or experience some or several aspects of Japanese culture. Hispania will say something about how you view Hispanic culture, and so on. This applies more to the ethnoculture asteroids and less to the political culture asteroids like Germania or Franzia, since the latter are more generic bunches of character than anything else. If, however, you are predisposed to forming grand stereotypes about Germans, Germania and other bodies like it will tend to work just like other "typecasting" asteroids in your chart.

Do you have a bad attitude towards a certain group of people whose asteroid you've found in this list? In some way, I think most of us are trained to. Locate the relevant asteroid in your chart and look at its neighbors. Go ahead. Shame yourself. Just kidding. Remember, the more negatively you behave towards a whole class of people, the more negatively you view the abstract body of associated characteristics in your own chart. So if you have a problem with, say, rebel types, you yourself will struggle with the rebel within. If you have a problem with audacious fun types, not only will you struggle to connect with that kind of personality, you will also struggle to develop the ability to have that kind of fun in your own life. Here's where it pays to try getting along with everybody, especially when the type you dislike is housed in an asteroid which is right next to a trait you really want to activate within yourself. Oh, the irony.

703 Noemi

⛴️ ⇩ ⚡

where it is easy for you to get flustered or be dissatisfied

473 Nolli

⛴️ 👽 🔥 ⇧

where people see you as being in your right element

783 Nora

⇩ ☄ ♈ ⛰

where you draw deep potential from your interactants

555 Norma

⇧ ✈ ♈ 🏆

area where you are in skilled command of your abilities

North Node (mean)

⇩ 👑 ⊕ 💬

destiny summarized

North Node (true)

⇩ 👑 ⊕ ⇧

destiny in the moment

626 Notburga

🎙 ⚡ 🔊 👽

your eccentricity and eccentric tastes; where you shock others constantly.

Shock Bodies

There are occasions where we encounter something which is so unsettlingly surprising that our first instinct is to get away from it. Then our second instinct is to never forget it. Typically, these are events which impose themselves Uranus-Mars style into our lives with a substantial dose of Pluto pressure to accompany them. Notburga leads the pack of the 1000's most shocking asteroids, but there are others whose role in your chart is to force instability into other's lives—regardless of whether you or the event does the actual shocking. It's a recipe for being remembered, usually favorably...but only after others have escaped your influence, usually unfavorably.

For reasons explained in the previous books, shock topics are often sexual among Westerners, since deep (and responsible) sexual behavior remains one of the few areas which still elicits giggles in the mainstream. From most shocking to less so we have:

- Notburga – general shock
- Camelia – overpowering assertion
- Janina (I don't understand this one's role as a shocker but it seems to be one, possibly because it implies some trait that people desire from you, but aren't publicly allowed to admit—hence being passed over for socially safer alternatives)
- Eros in Scorpio, Sagittarius, Capricorn, or Aquarius – roots private passions in public efforts
- Messalina – unsettling openness
- Nephele – defies tradition
- Lilith (Black Moon) – contrariety

- Kressida – represents an object to ogle at (especially among men, but an esteem definer among women under male/assertive standards)
- Quaoar – inexplicable creation

If you have some trait or some standard behavior which seems to upset people while you're around them but which they seem to value after you leave, there's a good chance that it's one of the above at work. You might stabilize the shockers' effects by identifying the culprit bodies first, then doing whatever fits your personality to mitigate the damage they cause.

150 Nuwa

🏠 📢 ⇩

where your home or emotional home base is open to others

About the House You Keep

For a good description of the kind of home you maintain, take a look at the following:

- El Djezair – your family-style circle
- Hephaistos – the homefront
- Nuwa – welcoming others into your home
- 4th house cusp's sign – what kinds of activity generally describe your home
- bodies in the 4th house – behaviors which are more comfortably expressed in the home

875 Nymphe

👄 ♈ 🔊

where you project a strong desire nature

44 Nysa

🏛 ♈ 🔊 ⇩ 🖧

associated with a creative power which everyone wants

O – R

224 Oceana

where you are associated with a revolutionary or talented team that forms under your influence

475 Ocllo

means through which you steer others' learning

598 Octavia

where you are seen as intimidatingly strong

215 Oenone

what you bravely take forth into the unknown, airing if necessary

439 Ohio

means through which you produce illusions which approach legendary; **this is a super strong impression maker like Roma, but for** *behaviors* **as opposed to creations**

52872 Okyrhoe

where you are a valued host or entertainer of audiences

304 Olga

where you are dead serious about your profession

835 Olivia

where you are exemplary, eclipsing all of your comparators

582 Olympia

trait that makes you immensely popular. (Libra 582s were overwhelmingly flaky, maybe because free popularity for the same conversational powers that everyone else has to actively enter means they are under less pressure to deliver on their suggested promises.)

171 Ophelia

where your partner dominates your agenda

255 Oppavia

where people are inclined to want long term association with you

90482 Orcus

where you are always supplied with an admirer (akin to your "blade" in the game *Xenoblade Chronicles 2*)

701 Oriola

where you foster uninhibitedness in others; comes with the creation of a warm, inviting persona

330836 Orius

socialite behavior

350 Ornamenta

where you make a good "type" to point to. Like Fraternitas, but for more distant strangers as observers rather than close initiates

3361 Orpheus

where your career fits into your other life priorities

551 Ortrud

where you represent the underestimated power of an underclass

Oscillating Apogee

where you are surprising and expectation-breaking

1923 Osiris

where you display super deep sexuality or super deep insight into situations [something like a sixth sense]

750 Oskar

where you epitomize the definition of cool; reference Orius

343 Ostara

means through which you put 1:1 company under your thumb

913 Otila

⚥ 🏛 🛡

associated with respect for women

670 Ottegebe

🏠🏛 👽

capacity in which you are associated with a specific business; a strong career asteroid in the Moultona family

994 Otthild

🛡 👪 ⬇ 🎗

where you take on the role of a parent in the eyes of friends; what you do which brings to mind a parenting role

401 Ottilia

🏰 🏞 🌲 ⬆

an inventive creative vision

363 Padua

🧍 🍸 🕊 🐾 🌲

where you are associated with the super-beautiful; this one is prominent in the charts of people and places recognized for their beauty

953 Painleva

🎮 ⊕ ⬇ 🗺

where your own fun and enjoyment comes before everything else

415 Palatia

💬 👽 💥 ⬆ 〜

what you use to help others revolutionize their lives and reinvent themselves

49 Pales

🏠🌲🏝 👽 💬

where you are fully at home with weirdos

914 Palisana

⬇ 💬 ⬆ 🛋 🍸 🔒

what people think they need in order to show themselves competent and to get in your good graces

2 Pallas

🏙🌍🏛🛡

social justice

372 Palma

⬇ 🎗

where others want to be your friend

539 Pamina

❗ 'Y' 🏋 🗯

where others have no doubt in your qualifications

2878 Panacea

'Y' 🏆 🖥

side of you associated with great and capable others

55 Pandora

⚥ ⊕ ♂ 'Y'

where one must provide masculine prowess or be considered a failure

70 Panopaea

⚥ ❗♂

side of you which is associated with the quest for a respectable male

471 Papagena

🎤 🎵⬆

how you use music or film to advance your identity

347 Pariana

⬇ 🏙 🌲 👄 👅

trait of yours which is a magnet for people's deep, unsatisfied desires

11 Parthenope

🕐 ⊕ 🐾

where you stay focused on the final (personal expressive) objective

888 Parysatis

🏙🏛 'Y'

where you embody the template for status attainment

451 Patientia

⊕ 🏙 🏋

dedicating your work to others benefit

436 Patricia

❗ ⊕ 🐾 🏛 👽 🛡

entrepreneurial spirit; where your efforts market you like a product

617 Patroclus

🧍 👑 ⊕ ⬆

where you give the impression of one who prizes highly their physical comfort

278 Paulina

where you express talents which border on genius, though you are considered at least slightly deviant from the norm as a result of this

537 Pauly

side of you which generates the interest of mass audiences; along with Naema, forms one of the strongest indicators of fame

Fame Asteroids

As we discussed in previous books, there is notoriety and then there is fame. The following asteroids are most closely associated with the latter:

- Pauly
- Naema
- Tergeste
- Emma
- Gunhild
- Berbericia
- Ohio (for the things you produce)

679 Pax

where your inconstant delivery makes people angry or else incites their passions; along with Damocles, Pax is likely to be behind some of the biggest personal irritants you will ever encounter

118 Peitho

an indefinably abstract quality to how you do things

49036 Pelion

how you break into other's lives

201 Penelope

how you install the tools for social approval in others

271 Penthesilea

where you demand the attention of others

554 Peraga

where others must live up to your standards and not the other way around

399 Persephone

where you give off an air of the dark and mysterious; where people are irrevocably changed by you; among the 1000, this is the asteroid with **the strongest Power to Write Others' Worlds,** and the irresistible influencer among the strong spirit asteroids

975 Perseverantia

area of expression which you can stay with for a long time without getting exhausted

482 Petrina

where you assert that others should follow your direction; where you can "hypnotize" others into cooperation

830 Petropolitana

where your personality is more likely to be considered an institution in itself, complete with its own system for handling everything

968 Petunia

where you give an enthusiastic thumbs down to perceived failures

174 Phaedra

where you express enjoyment of imaginary worlds

322 Phaeo

where you are seen as the people's darling

3200 Phaethon

where you are skillful and innovative in your expression

296 Phaetusa

where arises the issue of being used like a piece of meat

274 Philagoria

you draw crowds when you put on this mask

280 Philia

where being around you makes a touch of the taboo okay

977 Philippa

where you have a mystical, seductive quality

631 Philippina

where you display your intuitive sense

196 Philomela

where harmony in personal relationships is extra important

227 Philosophia

where you have a driving doctrine constraining your behavior

25 Phocaea

where others' creative expression typically overrides yours

5145 Pholus

associated with professional achievement

443 Photographica

the side of you others are bound to remember

189 Phthia

where you talk a good game

556 Phyllis

where the lady takes the lead

614 Pia

characteristic which makes people interested in having their way with you

1000 Piazzia

where you promote the strength of women; seems to be associated with the hips

803 Picka

your role as clan leader

784 Pickeringia

where you display enlightened, upperclass, or egalitarian sensibilities

312 Pierretta

where standards of perfection clash with reality, threatening your relationships; positively, this is a barrier which renders you selective

648 Pippa

where you insist on masculine boldness or demand it around you

484 Pittsburghia

where you seek your own fulfillment with or without others' approval

134340 Pluto-Charon

societal power standard and the pressure to meet it

946 Poesia

your unsatisfiable vision; **Neverending Quest. This asteroid is VERY strong,** and the duodecanate in which it appears is likely to show the harmonic which will continue growing throughout your life. For example, if you have 946 Poesia in 4° Pisces, this would not only show that you are more likely to be talked about or have an increasingly information-crowded world, but also ALL Pisces-undeciles (which are the same as regular undeciles) would tend to get stronger throughout your life. So if you had, say, your Sun and Moon separated by 65.45°, (a biundecile), your self-contentment would not only be tied to the social talk around you (because, as we saw in the previous books, that's what the Sun-Moon combination does), but also, that self-contentment would be something you sought more and more of throughout life no matter how much you already had. (It may be interesting to investigate 946 with other asteroids like Agamemnon and other apparently pathological asteroids to see how certain kinds of obsession work.)

142 Polana

where you expect to have your aims satisfied

33 Polyhymnia

where you address your reservations about the state of things around you

595 Polyxena

where people are compelled to admit your appeal

308 Polyxo

where you are a valuable social change tool for those associated with you

32 Pomona

where you make a good public impression

203 Pompeja

where you are reactionary yet demanding once pushed; where others must push you to act, only to get more than they bargained for

757 Portlandia

the reason people would loiter around your personality [because they want to advance their individuality here]

Poseidon (transNeptunian)

the side of you which forms the surface over grand depth and complexity

420356 Praamzius

what society prompts you to chase association with as confirmation of your worth

547 Praxedis

where you are great to meet and talk to

790 Pretoria

disregard for the patriarchy

529 Preziosa

where you are pleasant and sense-making; the setting you bathe yourself in, where you play the duke or duchess

884 Priamus

where being pretty is important

970 Primula

where you are stubborn despite any charisma you may have

508 Princetonia

an association with fullness, richness, and bounty

997 Priska

where you are the charismatic second-place to a primary personality, but you are the more stable and more powerful of the two; **the (Eternal) Second Placedness asteroid among the Mean 13 but also the Path of the Buddha asteroid** (seems to be associated with lasting peace through letting others be first, and had one of the most obvious connections to Buddhism)

Priska and the Other Side of the Mean 13

As tyrannical as the Mean 13 can be, each of them seems to hold a very positive side once it has been mastered. Liberatrix, for example, becomes synonymous with the kind of luck that makes you stand out. A refined Natalie is associated with high levels of wisdom in doing the things indicated by its neighbors. While there remains much to be learned about these and other normally misbehaved asteroids, the end result tends to be the same: Every arrangement in the chart can have its negative story rewritten.

The asteroid Priska shows where you are automatically inclined to take second place to some person or thing which shares a position with you. For people who are forever on the hunt for greater heights, 997 represents a place of potential insecurity which may loom no matter how high one climbs. As I investigated this body in various charts, I noticed that its workings in the charts of others had a very different effect than its workings in one's own chart. Where you see yourself as second place, you develop a track record for having others root for you, seek connections with you, or even follow where your hopes lead them. And no, it's not necessarily the case that anyone sees you as a failure. For those with a mind to serve others, Priska is more like an indicator of what the Daoists call "a non-need to be first." Where others are burdened with the pressures of achievement, the one who masters their Priska is not so burdened.

Thus this asteroid also has heavy ties to the Buddhist conception of personal development through the abandonment of desire. Ironically, such abandonment brings a level of reward that we Westerners would probably find illogical: Priska "condemns" you to stand behind another person or concept whether or not you compete in the pressuring world to do so. And what if you don't compete at all? You're still "condemned!" Accordingly, it also shows where you are immeasurably blessed with a high ranking power you never asked for,

but acquired through service to others—be they people or, on a broader level, concepts. If only you would let yourself receive from others that which Priska's sign and neighbors indicate instead of trying to promote such things for yourself—in a true illustration of where "the last shall be first." Perhaps that was what went on with the actual Buddha; in seeking the answer to others' suffering, it appears that he found an answer to his own. So it is with us.

902 Probitas

vehicle through which you weasel your way into others' lives

194 Prokne

where the talent available to you is unlimited

26 Proserpina

where you attract characters driven by their primal, bodily urges (as opposed to citizen-trained urges); a major ethnoculture asteroid like Hispania; strongly associated with black culture. That is, asteroids near this one tend to show a person's opinion of black people (in the US broadly) as well as their opinion of all urge-heavy classes of people. As a black person myself, I found this asteroid to be super informative. It was, in fact, my findings related to 26 Proserpina and 997 Priska which immediately compelled me to write this book. The workings of Proserpina are much more interesting than you would think, apply to everyone everywhere, and have implications for every characteristic which you visibly display to others. Here's what I found:

Proserpina and the Black Asteroids

Back when I taught Physical Anthropology I came across a family of websites which collectively offered an explanation of race views in the US. One of the site moderators maintained that, because black features were closer to those of the apes from which all humans evolved, it was easier to think of beauty in terms of physiological distance away from the first humans. The less you looked like *Homo erectus*, the more attractive you were, and you were more likely to evolve this look via climates and diets that defied those of the original temperate regions: cold ones. This would be reinforced as historical factors rendered all groups farther from Africa as having adapted in various ways which those who never left Africa never had to. Thus arose the physiological and behavioral associations between equatorial traits and savagery, polar traits and civility. As humanity moved forward, the various encounters between newly adapted groups and the original groups reinforced colonialist and subjugation-based relationships. Accordingly, even today's underclasses of any kind (not just race-based, but all across the human spectrum), tend to gravitate towards intragroup solidarity and familial collectivism, while power holding classes don't require this as heavily. So Blacks tend to stick together and identify as Black, US Hispanics identify as various forms of Hispanic, but Whites identify as normal people. This book isn't the place for me to give opinions on this issue, but I present the background to the reader as a plausible, partial set of explanations for why race issues in the US take the form that they do. I will, however, add one more guess of my own: Visible differences are easier to divide over than ideological ones, but ideological ones tend to be much more bitter because the latter are psychological in nature and mostly exist within the minds of the parties divided. It's about here that Proserpina introduces an interesting twist to all this.

When my data showed that Proserpina figured strongly in the charts of the black people in my sample, I asked why this would be the case. An asteroid doesn't recognize skin color or geographic region of origin, so what was this all about? As with masculinity and femininity however, asteroids *do* highlight interaction-types, styles of exchange, and families of responses to certain events. The new question became, what set of behaviors was Proserpina displaying which actually made (US) black people "act black?" But the question was already answered via the data before I even asked it: Asteroid 26 is not about savagery in the chartholder's wheel. It's about *the people with whom the chartholder interacts* displaying their own response to a prompt for more basic biological expression. Stated in English, a person's Proserpina doesn't show where he "acts black." It shows <u>where the others he's interacting with</u> respond as if in the presence of a biological stimulant. That stimulant could be the excitement of sports, the anger of social "noise-making," the or lust of various forms of relationship conquest. Regardless of who you are, you *will* have Proserpina in your chart. Where it falls shows the area of life where the people around you are prompted to behave primally. But it doesn't say much about you. Use Mars or something for that.

Ironically then, I concluded that my being black was less about me personally, and more about how an entire world gets triggered by certain things that I do. Asteroid 26 and its close relatives Briseis and Etheridgea essentially act like Damocles in that they get other people riled up around you. But they don't determine your actual identity nearly as much as say, Eurynome and Mercury. I also noted from personal experience that underclasses who occupy socially undesirable tiers are only more likely to fall into undesirable behaviors if you surround them with members of the same tier. Blacks around blacks are more likely to act black (whatever that means), but will act some other way if you separate them. The same goes for any underclass. Power-holding class members will also assimilate to fit whatever class you put them in BUT are more likely to adopt the neutral set of behaviors more natural to a basic human rather than a marginalized one.

In the end, your chart isn't really about you, but about the state of the world when you were born. For me, the Proserpina findings said, "You don't have to build your identity upon the fraction of yourself that makes other people antsy. Everybody has this fraction. Your physical appearance simply triggers it more easily than the appearances of others do." Indeed, Proserpina's implications for *all* body identity issues are profound. The gay asteroid Eduarda, the glare asteroid Lomia, the Armenian asteroid Armenia, the babes asteroid Laura. Throughout these books I have claimed that the physical body is a viewable manifestation of traits you possess, broadcast to others. But this is only partly true. Instead, your physical body is more like a viewable manifestation of how *everyone else* is naturally inclined to see the snapshot of the universe which describes you. When I look at your body, your face, or your dress, I'm not seeing you. I'm reacting to a specific moment in spacetime. Whether I call you rich, savage, or hilarious, I—along with the rest of the world—am naming the world, not the apparent carrier.

As physical bodies, we are born with the ability to automatically trigger certain behaviors in every person who is not ourselves. It is the willing identification with others who can trigger the same thing which forms a larger part of the basis of race and ethnicity. Physicality, however, is not the only identity group available to us. Asteroids like the Social Unity group are typically much more immediate in our lives. Accordingly, the lesson of Proserpina is that your appearance is a story about everyone else, but unless or until you own that story for yourself, it doesn't have to be about you. Although I remain quite proud of my identity and wouldn't change it for the world, I won't take ownership of most of the negative baggage assigned to it, and I'm glad that I have the option to step outside of the pigeonhole if I wish. Not only does this option allow me to see the real effects of my appearance on others, it also allows me to look at myself objectively, so that the positive sides get equal air time. Blacks may upset others more easily, but they can also excite more easily. Hispanics may stereotypically overwhelm communicatively (see Hispania), but they can also promote comfortable enjoyment. Whites may discourage the discarding of controlled communication, but they also set the standards for personal expression. And so there are both advantages and disadvantages to every appearance. The same holds for other sources of identity. It can also be extended to facial and body features as well.

Take a look at yourself in the mirror. You are a collection of triggers, but it's actually everyone else who plays out the results of how you look. If they don't accept you, then that's their rudeness...for them to play out over and over when they go home, and have it unleashed on them in turn. The people who do accept you, however, (looks and all) give you hints of the world in which you are welcome. That's usually a good indicator of a world worth pursuing.

147 Protogeneia

where you are outspoken

474 Prudentia

where you are super busy with creative ideas

261 Prymno

associated with the exposure of deep impulses

16 Psyche

where you've almost certainly seen the dark side of things

762 Pulcova

where you assert despite the crowd

632 Pyrrha

where you're more likely to cripple your own successes, often through over activity

432 Pythia

where your communication pattern frequently takes you out of your natural lane; the behavior you use to explicitly remove your default [public] mask

50000 Quaoar

creativity from an unknown source

755 Quintilla

personal trait you are overwhelmingly—often positively—remembered for

674 Rachele

where you cover a wide and scattered terrain in the messages you send

708 Raphaela

where you're identified with a dirty side [more rarely in others, usually you]

2254 Requiem

side of you which regularly grates or tires out when overused; trait you must often cut short even while it's going well in order to avoid upsetting others

927 Ratisbona

where stagnant systems need for you to break in and revolutionize things

572 Rebekka

where you take an isolated position to protect your greatness

573 Recha

playful, inviting way

285 Regina

what the artists or creative types around you are good for

574 Reginhild

where others are reminded to focus on business, either because you are so focused on it or because you are such a distraction

575 Renate

where you have tastes that most people wouldn't prefer

906 Repsolda

a strange allure despite deviation from normal standards of beauty

Perspectives on Death

Requiem, as the name suggests, is part of the **Endings** family of bodies associated with the noteworthy termination of things, though 2254 itself isn't particularly strong in this area. (Venusia, Sauer, and Desiderata on the other hand are quite strong as terminators.) For those people uncomfortable with the notion of death, the Endings group offers an interesting view of this universal phenomenon which attends all living things. Because there are several bodies in the chart which show how you suddenly cease to exist in a particular setting—yet you can only die once—perhaps you can see how the notion of death is part of a larger metaphor for the way you end things in general. Rather than approaching death with aversion then, we have the option of approaching it in the same way we approach all of the numerous other kinds of terminations in this life. What causes you to leave a place? What prompts you to end a relationship or move on from a post? Under what conditions would you refuse to stay a moment longer in a particular situation? The Endings bodies and the objects near each one shows how you leave and also shows the various options you have in doing so. Perhaps more importantly, the Endings bodies also show how you hand over control of your direct impression making to the indirect memory of you held by those you leave behind.

As part of a larger discussion related to the LSRI in *HBS* and elaborated on in the explanation of τ elsewhere in this book, our relationships with all events have a lifespan. This includes everything from our relationship with a passing car to a relationship to our own lives, from our relationship to the city we live in to our relationship with another person. We can typically read the public versions of a relationship using the relative chart between us and the event, or we can read the internal psychological version of our relationship with it using the composite chart. As surely as the relationship began, though, it will end at some point. In my observation, there is usually more than one possible "exit point" in a relationship depending on whether you end it 1) tensely or 2) through something like outgrowing, and—if through outgrowing—whether either you (2a) or the other event (2b) was the party in need of transition (a word I use non-euphemistically here). The bodies most associated with Endings are as follows, and their effects are largely dependent on the house and duodecanate in which they are located. I've also listed the three classes of "death" which is most naturally associated with each point (1 = tense death, 2a = your transition, 2b = their transition):

- Venusia (1) – how you end the possibility of things which may have wanted to share your company
- Zelia (1) – where you prevent something from going past a particular boundary with you
- Sauer (1 or 2a) – where you block the initial or continued presence of something in your life
- Desiderata (2a) – where you end things assembly-line style, filing through the same kind of thing
- Liberatrix (2a) – where you simply leave (for reasons related to this asteroid's neighbors)
- Requiem (2a) – where you leave a situation before it becomes bad
- Saturn (2b) – where you control or limit what another can do
- The last body before the Ascendant (varies) or clusters on the 8th house cusp – whatever the things here indicate; this depends heavily on the kinds of bodies you prefer to read (versus ignore) in your chart.

How you handle each of these points in your chart—and more importantly their neighboring bodies—will general show how you leave a situation. And yes, you can DEFINITELY change the positivity or negativity of each "zone" around an Endings asteroid. As I've mentioned throughout the series, I possessed a volatile temper in a former life (years ago in this one), which I now know to be associated with my Requiem-Asplinda-Romilda-Gallia zone in 29 Libra (a Libra-conjunct). Although I still break exchanges with the occasional unprompted burst of communication, I now do so under much more considered circumstances, so the damage usually comes only to those relationships that need to be purged.

In my own life I've observed that certain relationships seem to linger on no matter how violently you tried to end them, and this often means that you're cruising towards a later exit point even after an earlier one has been used. Perhaps fortunately or unfortunately, you may also find other events (either other people or more abstract situations) entering your life in order to replace the thing you parted with as you complete your relationship cycle with that particular package of experiences. Perhaps the split is delayed because one person is much more strongly (or positively) attached than the other thinks is possible. Once you've invoked an Endings point on a relationship in order to actually end it in real life, the rest of that relationship seems to be relegated to the abstract world until you finally reach the last body before your Ascendant, either in your own eyes or in others' eyes. So if you have, say, Astraea as the last body, your final view of the thing you've separated from usually won't come about until either you or it adopts the status of a situational monopolizer. (Hopefully in the Astraea case, *you* are the monopolizer—viewing your own choice to interact with the thing as a good one.)

The last body refers to any object which was rising when you were born, located in your 12th house. The notion of the last body before the Ascendant being the ultimate ideal terminator of your general relationships to most things may be foreign to some people, but it points to the special significance of this section of the chart in your life. The ASC's duodecanate, the last asteroid, the last fixed star, and the harmonic associated with the ASC's duodecanate are all important character definers, and all come with the opportunity for you to start anew—either under your own power or as a point of reference in others' minds.

(By the way it IS possible to resurrect a relationship after it has ended, given a period of separation. In this case, the relationship's lifespan seems to reset [as far as I can tell] and can then endure for whatever length of time its participants permit.)

Final Outlook Cocktail and the Last Star

You can use the 12th house objects just before your Ascendant to read how you are naturally predisposed to come to terms with things. Although I tend not to trust the Fixed Stars as indicators of anything (prior to future research), I do also include these in the pre-Ascendant description of such a closure strategy. The cocktail looks something like this:

> I see myself as [the last fixed star in overall character], having [mastered my last asteroid] in [my own or someone else's] mind. Every time I do the [Ascendant's duodecanate activity] I have the opportunity to close the door to events or open a new one. My [last major body] describes my last major phase of any relationship when that relationship is allowed to play out its natural course.

You are for the most part stuck with your chart setup, so it behooves you to treat every element of this particular cocktail as positively as possible. In terms of this book's quantum mechanical theory, the last region represents your characteristic $\phi_{\hbar}$.

A friend of mine has 14 Libra as the Ascendant, Algorab as the last star, Edith as the last asteroid, the Moon (way back in the 11th house) as the last major body, and harmonic 67 (Libra-septile) as the last duodecanate. Algorab doesn't have a solid description that I could verify based on this series' methods, but it is reported to be associated with drunkards and thieves and such. Remember though, in the Final outlook cocktail, you really need to <u>treat everything positively</u>. So instead of reading Algorab as a drunken thief, we'll read it as a lively, uninhibited purveyor of one's own will. My friend's Final Outlook cocktail would then read as follows.

> I see myself as [lively and uninhibited, having gotten what I wanted], as having [not settled for anything subpar] in [my own] view. Every time I [talk about how I have communicated with another] I have the opportunity to close the door to events or open a new one. My [emotions and inclinations] describes my last major phase of any relationship when that relationship is allowed to play out its natural course.

For more on the fixed stars and their meanings, visit
http://www.constellationsofwords.com/stars/Stars_in_longitude_order.htm.

---

528 Rezia

associated with the imposition of perfectionism, whether provided by you or your situation

38083 Rhadamanthus

where you or your partner has high demands placed on them or faces great challenges thanks to the other

577 Rhea

where people are assessed against your status standards

346889 Rhiphonos

where your actions foster busy surrounding activity

907 Rhoda

how you entertain others

437 Rhodia

where you are most comfortable or "at home"

166 Rhodope

where you are a stable center for your circle

879 Ricarda

where your progress is hampered by larger factors: where you must seek someone else to aid your advancement or else actively resist the very progress you seek; this was **the Bad Luck asteroid among the Mean 13**, and was associated with some of the clearest examples of frustrating, stopped progress among all 1000 asteroids. In actuality though, Ricarda isn't so much about bad luck as it is about situations which require the interference of others, often unbeknownst to you. Positively, 879 is associated with your position as a rare, singular talent in others' eyes; where you're only allowed to do things that others are ready for—making it hard for you to botch things once you get there. There seems to be a further connection with `perfect timing`, where your use of force will only mess things up. In my experience, a misbehaved Ricarda looks a lot like the fabled "Mercury retrograde." When things start going wrong one after the other, your best bet is very often to set your current path aside and swap in an alternative (at least until you feel you've roped in your wayward fortunes).

335 Roberta

♈ ⬇ 🖧 ✈

where people around you don't feel good enough

904 Rockefellia

🏛 ♈ 🖧 ✈

where you force people to rewrite their views or rewrite it for them; where you don't accept other's intended aims for what they are; this asteroid shows where you give nary a shit for other people's way of doing things

920 Rogeria

💬 ⬆ 💬 🏆

the nature of the change you bring to others. (Leo, Scorpio, and Pisces 920s were mysteriously absent from my data, suggesting a biased sample tied to a strongly character-specific asteroid)

472 Roma

🏛 🏛 🏆

your capacity to create enduring [and classic] creative works or impressions; this, along with Cremona, is one of THE asteroids to look at for artists

942 Romilda

🏘 🏚 🗣

where you have contrary reactions to things, and march to a different drum on regular days [Black Moon Lilith-like]

223 Rosa

🎮 📢 💬 👽

side of your behavior where you are fun to be around

314 Rosalia

🏆 🕐 ⬆ 🕊

where quality time with you has a high chance of increasing the strength of a bond

900 Rosalinde

🍸 🛋 🛍 👽

part of you associated with refinement or high status [Libra-like]

540 Rosamunde

⚡ 👄 ♈ ⚲

where you ceaselessly chase more power than you already have, making you appear lusty [Interamnia-like]

985 Rosina

⬇ ♀ ⚩

where you draw female camaraderie

615 Roswitha

✈ ⊕ 🐱🛍 ❗ 💬 👑

the thing you're typically [supposed to be] doing while you're busy socializing

874 Rotraut

❗ 🛍 ♈ ⊕

where fruitful or productive performance/exchange is important to you

317 Roxane

👽 🛍 ⬇ ⚡ 💬

trait others are inclined to use you for despite being made uncomfortable by you there

353 Ruperto-Carola

⊕ ⬆ 🎮

where you play out your intentions to amuse or satisfy yourself

232 Russia

✈ 💬 🏛 🏆

where people around you can expect you to take over the interactional picture, even if you're not directly involved in what they're doing

798 Ruth

🕊 🏝 🏆

you are the "spirit leader" for others

S – Z

665 Sabine

associated with youthful spirits vulnerable to more powerful influences

120347 Salacia

associated with an under-appreciated, underpraised, or under-recognized partner

562 Salome

where you can rise to the occasion regardless of how enthusiastic you are about it; doing something naturally whether or not you're in the mood to do it

275 Sapientia

associated with men who are open to alternative experiences or novel paths

80 Sappho

where you have a jack-of-all-trades intellectual openness

533 Sara

associated with the route used to stimulate the male procreative impulse

796 Sarita

where you advance new styles among your contemporaries

461 Saskia

the thing people want from you when they seek shelter under you

Saturn

restrictions, boundaries

9248 Sauer

the Regulator-Blocker among the Mean 13, very Saturn-like; cuts ties with things efficiently and coldly, but like

Zelia is one of the most powerful "shield asteroids" among all 1000

460 Scania

where you place high-energy investment in your communications

1525 Savonlinna

realm in which you are blessed with a partner who adores you greatly (whether or not you adore them in return); among all the asteroids I've studied, even beyond the first 1000, this was the strongest indicator of having a partner who worships the ground you walk on

643 Scheherezade

where you are associated with qualities that appear out of nowhere [Quaoar-like]; nickname: *the Enchantress*; this is one of the most other-hypnotizing asteroids of the 1000; with Persephone, Cremona, and Hebe, forms the "Spider's Web" group

The Spider's Web

On occasion as I filed through the data, I encountered a harmonic clustering pattern which made me feel all funny inside, as if I were looking at sides of the named people which I really shouldn't know. Deep down as you read these clusters you knew that you were peering into people's secret motives and the secret means they were more than willing to use to fulfill those motives. The asteroids that elicited this kind of pattern are collectively called the Spider's Web.

- Scheherezade
- Hebe
- Persephone
- Signe

The Web and its less desirous equivalent the Otherwriters represent points in the chart where you exert an almost magical ability to make others want to do what you want them to do. The downside to this is that they usually can't actually do it in a world full of all kinds of rules, so your influence via these 'stroids typically produces something closer to powerful agitation in them instead.

596 Scheila

where people are more likely to "ride your jock" so to speak; the behavior that earns you groupies

922 Schlutia

behavior through which your body or self-value becomes more evident to others

837 Schwarzschilda

realm where people look at you as a kind of idol

989 Schwassmannia

where you act to carry out the objects of your imagination

876 Scott

where you ways can take a toll on your partner

155 Scylla

what you are constantly dwelling on

90377 Sedna

spotlight and salience of presence

892 Seeligeria

where you project high salience or social stature

Selene (White Moon)

your blessed talent

580 Selene

means of passing your power intentions onto the people around you

500 Selinur

associated with entertaining or fascinating surroundings

86 Semele

behavior you display which affirms you as a good friend; Scorpio 86s are often unfortunately utilitarian

584 Semiramis

where you are a role model for others' ambition; like May, this asteroid has some strange, hard to identify qualities that I haven't figured out yet; seems to be associated with where you "hog the mic"

550 Senta

where you can lead leaders

483 Seppina

where you tell it like it is

838 Seraphina

associated with refined execution of things

168 Sibylla

where the story of your struggle is entertaining to others

579 Sidonia

where you hold high standards for your interactions

386 Siegena

where your intelligence shines through to others

552 Sigelinde

where you take on the persona of a star or central figure

459 Signe

where others fancy you as a source of fulfillment for their own dark desires; part of the Spider's Web family with Hebe, Scheherezade and others. This asteroid had an eerie association with exploitation in my data and warrants some explaining.

As a reminder, remember that almost all of the 1000+ interpretations in this chapter (except for the more well-known traditional bodies) were based on statistics. In classifying the asteroids, I dropped ten names at a time into a database and sorted each of their aspects to the Midheaven by harmonic number (usually 1-36). Since I didn't know the naming history behind most of the asteroids, I typically interpreted the harmonic clusters using only groups of 1s, 2s, 3s, and so on. Whenever I got a particularly interesting pattern of dataset names, I looked at the asteroid name and went online to research its history. Most of the more interesting asteroids in this book had a second set of interpretations which were often too detailed for this book. Signe's original interpretation (before I looked up its naming origin online) was as follows: "where others fancy you as a source of fulfillment for their own nasty desires; as a sexpot." My detailed notes read: "wow. Research this one...[Done]. It actually fits my original reading better...Of course, this would be too specific, but still...the naming..." and it turns out that the story of Signe very much fits what the asteroid's number-only clusters were showing.

Like a handful of other asteroids in this book such as Damocles, Urania and Yrsa, Signe stands out as uniquely destabilizing and visible to others, almost all the time. In the charts of people who have experienced problems with others' attempts to exploit them, this is a very strong asteroid whose nearby neighbors can tell you a lot about how such problems tend to arise (and, sometimes, what you can do about it.)

502 Sigune

where people know they're being tested against some higher social standard which it would be embarrassing to fail, so they often pretend they're up on it; where, despite other qualities you may have, your demands are considered reasonable

79360 Sila-Nunam

associated with voluptuousness, fullness or potency to the brim

257 Silesia

trait of yours which draws out other's discomfort; Damocles-like

748 Simeisa

where you passionately attach to others, for better or worse

332 Siri

where you express your unhappiness with established systems

116 Sirona

where your ways reshape the perspectives of those around you

823 Sisigambis

where you demonstrate refined manners; your James Bond or Lauren Bacall demeanor

1866 Sisyphus

what you use to win others over into supporting you

244 Sita

a trait which you declare to others as being the means to your creative or original ideas; how you build yourself up creatively

1170 Siva

where your exchanges are volatile as a function of your focus on materiality at the expense of lasting processes

140 Siwa

where you are strong but humble

251 Sophia

associated with pleasant, beautiful effects

134 Sophrosyne

where you are unsatisfiable, no matter what you're given; this is the asteroid most strongly associated with **Lost Causes**, where either you or the types of events indicated by its neighbors are beyond correction. Positively, Sophrosyne's zone shows the area of life where things can be counted on to remain themselves despite all attempts to change them

731 Sorga

where you don't play around; you mean what you say, intending to be taken seriously

896 Sphinx

where you hold expressive authority

831 Stateira

where you must present yourself in a polished way

707 Steina

where you are—especially in others' eyes—always headed on to new projects

220 Stephania

where people feel they need your acceptance in order to be accepted in general; where you have the authority to be a gatekeeper for reputations

566 Stereoskopia

means through which you advise yourself or others in light of future or difficult to perceive events

995 Sternberga

area in which, when others attempt to influence you, you become stern and (often coldly) uncooperative

768 Struveana

the talents or behaviors others wish you would donate to them

964 Subamara

where you lead others into new forms of fantasy creation

417 Suevia

where you are level-headed and stable in your interactions

752 Sulamitis

worldly advancement-enabling gains; this is a strong indicator of one's **status mobility** in the world

563 Suleika

where you are fun or high energy, engaging to be around

Sun

ego projection, basic style of interpersonal action

542 Susanna

what you use to smother-mother people

933 Susi

where people around you are not allowed to express in ways you don't approve of

329 Svea

where your favorable surface nature covers deep preoccupations

992 Swasey

where you foist "improvements" on others despite their thinking that what they have is already good. You're often right, but intrusively so.

882 Swetlana

where you are forward with your creative wants

519 Sylvania

what you use in order to make your wishes come to pass; **the Wish Granter among the strong spirit asteroids**

87 Sylvia

where a polished presentation, order is important

721 Tabora

where the appealing sides of your personality shine in 1:1 interactions

326 Tamara

mode in which you display monopolistic charm

772 Tanete

trait for which you make exceptionally popular company

825 Tanina

quality you display which makes others see you as bossy or commanding; on normal days most people will avoid challenging you here

2102 Tantalus

🍸 🏔 🗡 👽

deceptive initial cool [often followed by stubborn or fiery intensity]

Deceptive Impressions

Can we spot a liar based on an astro chart? No. We can, however, spot an illusion creator who presents us with one thing which ultimately results in another—whether or not it's the illusionist's fault. Behold, the astro objects most associated with the power to deceive (from super deceptive to only "highly" so):

- Tantalus
- Gudrun
- Neptune
- Persephone
- Itokawa
- Quaoar (not a deceiver, but a strongly effective obscurer of one's motives)
- Gryphia (interestingly, not a deceiver, but a revealer of "true colors" which are actually false oversimplifications of your natural complexity
- Tatjana (not a deceiver, but a chameleon which rides others' prompting)
- Halawe (not a deceiver, but a conqueror which doesn't look like one)

769 Tatjana

🗿 ⬇ 👽 ⬆ 🗣

the need you have which piggybacks off of and insinuates itself into your communication with others

581 Tauntonia

🖥 💼 〰

asset for which you are pulled in every direction

512 Taurinensis

🏔 ✈ ⬆

where you are a one-way train in the image you wish to project OR a pain in the ass to control in negative cases

814 Tauris

🌳 🏆 🍸

where you display brilliance without letting it go to your head [with the style of a classic movie actor or actress]

453 Tea

⬆ 🕷 🏆

side of you which is fearlessly forward—features in seduction

88611 Teharonhiawako

👽 🕊 🗡 👽

where your personality runs the range of extremes between very pleasant and very unpleasant

604 Tekmessa

❗ ⊕ 💣

where you are under pressure to perform professionally

345 Tercidina

🍸 🏛 🗿 👽

where you show that you are unorthodox despite your favorable qualities

478 Tergeste

👽 🏞 🌲 🗣

where, in light of a situation in which you participated, people's references to the situation are more likely to revolve around you; a fame asteroid like Naema

81 Terpsichore

🏋 🗣 🌳

associated with the role of a folk hero; alternatively, where your standards of expression are fairy-tale high

23 Thalia

🕊 📢 🗣 🖥

where you are surrounded by boisterous or uplifting environments

586 Thekla

🖥 ✈ ⬇ 🏆

where you command an environment passively

24 Themis

🗣 🗣 🎤 🔍

where you air your cravings to others, often matter-of-factly

778 Theobalda

❗ 🎮 🏆 ✈ 🗣

where you command others to have fun and be happy; the showman's asteroid even if you yourself aren't particularly entertaining; the audience may yet entertain themselves at your expense

440 Theodora

❗ 🍸 🏠 🗣

where you are socially able and welcoming to be around

295 Theresia

👤 ⇧ 🕷

where you use your physical qualities to advance your interests. (Trines are more likely to use their bodies as a weapon.)

32532 Thereus

🗻 🏯 📢 👽

unusual stand out

17 Thetis

👪 🏠 ⇧ 🗣

a staple feature of the domestic life you report to others

405 Thia

🗻 👄 💭

where you carry a hidden fire that occasionally leaks out

88 Thisbe

♂ ⇧ 🏆 🏝 🏞

where you are perfectly fine taking your [masculine-type] character into the unknown

299 Thora

⇧ 🎙 💬 👽

where people are reminded of how famous you are, the behavior you display which prompts people to consider the reputation you already have

279 Thule

🏯 ⇩ 💬 ⇧

where you are humbly open to others amidst your creative process

934 Thuringia

🕷 💬 ⇩ 👄 📢

where you invite (or, rather, compel) your interactants to bear themselves to you

219 Thusnelda

⇩ 💬 🕊 🎗

where people like you and really want you to get along with them in turn

115 Thyra

👽 🏛

side of you which is considered to be a phenomenon in itself

753 Tiflis

⇧ 🏛 🐱 ⇩ ✈

tool for asserting command over others

603 Timandra

👤 ⇧ ⇩ 💬 🖧

where your priorities for your body or physical presence serve as lively talking points for others

687 Tinette

⇩ 💬 🖧 ⇧ 🔍 🏝

where you are a hot but elusive commodity

267 Tirza

⇩ 💬 🕊 🎮 📢

where others have fun around you

466 Tisiphone

⇧ 🏠 ⇩ 💬 ⊕

where you are a reliable backup to others' aspirations

593 Titania

🖼 ⇧ 💬 🏠 ⇩

where others can feel accepted through your standards for engagement; otherwise, where you feel left behind by opportunity

732 Tjilaki

⇩ ♂ 👽

where you draw out the need to be masculine and manly, in yourself or others

498 Tokio

🐱 ⊕ ⇧ 🎗

where people feel obliged to accept what you give

138 Tolosa

🍸 👑 🎗

where you are mellow around the company you favor

590 Tomyris

🍸 👤 👑 💬 ⇧

the side of you which others find charming in your physical company

924 Toni

⇧ ⏰ 🍸 ✈

where you teach others patience and self-control [because of or in spite of you]

1685 Toro

where you draw other's inexplicable interest

715 Transvaalia

where you are sassily stubborn

619 Triberga

where you are associated with revolution and social defiance

530 Turandot

perfection and perfectly controlled experiences

258 Tyche

where you're never without friends

42355 Typhon

where your expression separates you from what people are comfortable with

909 Ulla

what your way prioritizes the promotion of in your 1:1 exchanges

885 Ulrike

what your physical characteristics and bodily disposition were built for; related to the first impression you make on others as a physical body

714 Ulula

where you are associated with rebel girls or mould-breaking feminine causes

160 Una

where you assert other people into a corner

92 Undina

side of you which permeates the environment with others' conception of you

306 Unitas

where you are associated with a long, drawn out courtship or trial phase for things

905 Universitas

where you are inviting and facile in any situation

30 Urania

where you entice others towards agitated action

The Firestarters

Occasionally you'll want to unleash a trait which ignites a fire in another person or event. This might be anger, excitement, or some other experience, but when you want to trigger it you'll need a weapon for doing so. The Firestarters shake others out of their slumber and push them to act, often in response to how much you've upset their comfort.

- Damocles
- Urania
- Erida
- Euterpe
- Silesia

Uranus

social talk or information around you

167 Urda

where you are more likely to employ love and bonding as a solution to problems

501 Urhixidur

where you are comfortably self-assured

860 Ursina

allure

375 Ursula

where you give a celebrated performance

634 Ute

where ideal partnership features as part of the world

131 Vala

✠ ⬇ ⬆ ⊕

where you need a comrade or designated encourager to push you forward

839 Valborg

⬇ 🕷 ⚡ 〽 💬

where a kind of soap opera unfolds thanks to you deeds

262 Valda

🗣 📢 〽 🗨

where you are talkative and-or highly opinionated

447 Valentine

⬇ ✠ 💬

where you are necessarily identified with another; along with Armor, Anneleise, and others, a strong indicator of partnership.

The Partners Bodies

Are you looking for someone to anchor you? To be your right hand, your BFF? Or maybe you just need an enemy. The Partners asteroids have the magical ability to summon partners from thin air whenever you display their duodecanate behavior. A valuable addition to the Summoner's cocktail in *HBS*, these bodies are far and away some of the most effective other-attractors you'll find among the first 1000 objects. If you're planning to display those behaviors associated with the zones in which these bodies are found, don't expect to do so alone. A communication partner almost always appears. Usually it's a person, but sometimes it's a pet, video game, instrument, or some other actor with which you can exchange ongoing 1:1 feedback.

- Savonlinna
- Venus
- Valentine
- Armor
- Anneleise
- Ophelia

611 Valeria

🖤 🏚 ⬆ 👽

where you alone write your story, accepting no outside input on the matter; what you pull back from others when they try to influence you improperly

610 Valeska

🏋 ✈ 💬 ⬇ 🏆

where you present traits which would intimidate the insecure, but only interest the secure even more

240 Vanadis

🕊 💬 👽

where you are more likely to be admired by everyone

174567 Varda

🎴 🕊 🗨 🏆

otherworldly brilliance

20000 Varuna

⬆ 📦 🏛

giving form to

416 Vaticana

🏆 🏛 🛡

where your way is unchanging and self-empowered

126 Velleda

⬇ ✈ 👄 〽 🏚 🗿

where sexual exploitation (or sometimes more material forms of **corruption**) is more likely to be an issue

487 Venetia

🎴 ⬆ 🖧 〽

where your passing around your gifts or scattering them left and right can drive your interactants crazy

Venus

✠ 💬

willing 1:1 socialization

499 Venusia

⬇ ✠ 💬 🏚

how you reject those who try to get close to you

245 Vera

🗣 🏛 ❗

setting in which you are more likely to talk career matters and matters of responsibility

490 Veritas

★ ⬇ 📢 🏆 🏛 👽

where you carry abilities that are bigger than you are; **the Synechdoche asteroid among the strong spirit group**; contacts to other bodies tend to ground that area of the chart in things that are "right"

612 Veronika

♀ 👄 ⬇ ♂ 🧍 📢 🏆

side of you more likely to be associated with sexy or sex-focused women; alternatively, feminine power attracted; in males associated with the penis

Vertex

⊕ ⇧ ⊕

susceptibility to life change

4 Vesta

⊕

focused effort

144 Vibilia

where you are more likely to be objectified by others or objectify others yourself

12 Victoria

behavior during which people are more likely impressed which your body or physicality

397 Vienna

where you hold the gold social standard that everyone should adhere to

366 Vincentina

♂ 🍸

associated with softened masculinity

231 Vindobona

⇩ 🍸

where you demand proof of progress, usefulness from others

759 Vinifera

where you demonstrate a ceaseless, restless need for control

557 Violetta

⊕ ⇧ 🏆

where you excel in advancing your aims

50 Virginia

how you greet noobs and novices (that is, virgins). Also, how you behave as a novice

494 Virtus

where you attempt to get maximum use out of your traits

Vulkanus (transNeptunian)

where you display unapologetic sass

635 Vundtia

⇩

what people suspect you "provide a lot of" to your partner

877 Walkure

where you won't be pigeonholed, but insist on asserting your own fate

987 Wallia

occasion for publicly exposing your brand of power relations with people; read this one with Ganymed to get a better understanding of how Ganymed affects your chart. Where you show Wallia forms the basis of the like-minds you attach to under Ganymed.

256 Walpurga

talent which people find amazing after getting to know you

890 Waltraut

★ ⇩

perfect ideal acceptance, the best above all else you could ask for; among all 1000 and the strong spirit asteroids, this is the best indicator of the kinds of **Perfect Things** which can do no wrong in your eyes

886 Washingtonia

where you are a uniquely memorable personality

729 Watsonia

on stage before an audience, that which you express best

621 Werdandi

🍸

where you are associated with cosmopolitan interactants and surroundings

226 Weringia

realm where you belong as a guest at a party; how groups of people see you against a lively background

930 Westphalia

⬇️💬👤🏆

where people love coming to you for validation of themselves

931 Whittemora

✈️🗣️🏆

where you are a compelling communicator

Unlike Proserpina and Hispania in particular, I did not find a major ethnic asteroid for whites. This probably has more to do with the idea that 1) Western whites are less likely to have their identities popularly built upon their skin color or dress than other groups are, and 2) because whites are probably better described by more specific national asteroids like Germania, Italia, and America. Still, if I had to pick one asteroid out of the 1000 which was closest to the "white" asteroid, it would be this one: #931. In the US especially, bodies around it in your chart do seem to say something about your opinion of groups who set the standards for society's communicative norms against which Others are defined. You can imagine though, that in other places like France and Germany, you're less likely to get this white-black-hispanic distinction so much as you are to get a French-non French distinction, so #931 doesn't really tell you as much about any particular group as one might think.

392 Wilhelmina

🗨️🕊️🍸🍷

where you are soothing company

747 Winchester

⊕💣

where you refuse to take others' mess

717 Wisibada

🏝️👽

when you display a spacey nature

852 Wladilena

⬇️💣〰️

type of urge you draw forth in your admirers

827 Wolfiana

⚡⬆️

where you spend energy in excess

690 Wratislavia

💡👤

where you convey an interest in the body, its values, or its processes

411 Xanthe

🗄️💥⚡🏚️🖧⬆️

striking talent cut off from expression through impatience; positively, a talent for filing through versions of something [Desiderata-like but more favorable]

156 Xanthippe

🗄️⬆️👽

style you apply when asserting your right to do your own thing. There were no Virgo 156s in the data, suggesting another area where my sample selection was biased away from a certain personality type. My data generally comes from all kinds of personalities EXCEPT for those who easily lie about what that personality is. My rough guess is that a Virgo Xanthippe would be a manipulator of "meaning" in asserting their freedom, which really would be something I avoided. More research on this one should be done by someone who tolerates liars.

625 Xenia

🎗️👪🛡️🫀

how you demonstrate caring or concern for others

990 Yerkes

🏋️📢⬆️

where you pull no punches

351 Yrsa

⭐⊕🕷️💥⬇️

strong trait for which you are 1:1 sought after; also, where you are very susceptible to external influence. Like Poesia, Yrsa is one of the few strong spirit asteroids which is neutral-negative by default. It holds the singular distinction of being THE asteroid of **Vulnerability to Outside Influence**, and features heavily in your habits— bad or good—which you easily acquire from others. I've seen Yrsa show up in all kinds of scenarios where people just wouldn't get right no matter what you did for them, as they would always return to the original habit and whatever taught that habit. Still this one is by far one of my favorite asteroids among all the 1000 (including the major bodies) not because it is unfriendly, but because it is the strongest indicator of behaviors you almost certainly WILL absorb from others throughout your life. As for that part about people seeking you out, it's usually to deliver a package you won't refuse (even if there's a bomb in it).

999 Zachia

🗨️🗨️📢⬇️

where you invite others to be open with their interests in your company

421 Zahringia

where you are associated with bullheaded women

851 Zeissia

where it is clear that you have a good head on your shoulders

169 Zelia

where others can't get to you or influence you through your stronghold; this is the #1 **Shield Asteroid** for blocking all influences unless you let the walls down on purpose. Very strong, Zelia features in those personality traits of yours and behaviors that most people simply cannot get past, and along with Sauer, Saturn and Amherstia may explain more than half of the "walls" you erect between yourself and the world. Like other restricters, Zelia is associated with a slender frame. As with other blockers of outside contact, it is also associated with the thwarted desires of others, hence Zelia's secondary role as indicator of a slender body frame which evokes (and must be protected against) others' animal desire, lust, or anger.

633 Zelima

where you are a model prize to be associated with

654 Zelinda

where you must work to balance creativity with practicality

840 Zenobia

how you open people up to relations with others

693 Zerbinetta

where you need ongoing partner approval to keep your sense of self-worth high; if there is any aspect of your life where you absolutely require a second person to advance (and may wish this wasn't so), Zerbinetta and Priska are two of the best bodies to look at. Nickname: the **Partner Approval Required** asteroid

531 Zerlina

where you are associated with attractive end goals

Zeus (transNeptunian)

where you are effectively all-powerful, picking from the full array of options

438 Zeuxo

where you help others break new ground

689 Zita

trait which your actions encourage others to open up and demonstrate themselves

865 Zubaida

where you express high physical or creative standards for your partners

785 Zwetana

where you plant the seeds of other's recognition of your power

Chapter 40: Cause and Effect in the Chart

Let me begin this chapter with a personal story which illustrates what we'll be talking about.

Chain reaction

For whatever reason, I've never had an easy time soliciting new connections. It just doesn't work. This is especially true when applying for jobs. All my jobs have been a matter of luck, recommended to me by someone else. But I've learned something interesting about this phenomenon: If starting$_{conjunct}$ a new daily job or meaning-exchange$_{Virgo}$ is an area where I struggle, then starting$_{conjunct}$ a new inclination$_{Pisces}$ is the thing against which new jobs are compared. The Virgo-conjunct corresponds to the 27.5°–30° Virgo cluster, where I have the following asteroids (among others):

- Amneris – soliciting feedback
- Zelia – impenetrable shield
- Siri – unhappiness with established systems
- Luscinia – where one appears to be lost in space

which pretty much sums up how I come off on applications, interviews, and in solicitation attempts. (On the up side, this same cluster also enables me to solicit$_{conjunct}$ tons of new meaning$_{Virgo}$ from data sources like astrology charts, so I've no desire to "fix" this trait.) Meanwhile the Pisces-conjunct is just a regular conjunct, corresponds to 27.5°–30° Pisces, how I conduct new actions in general, and includes the following asteroids:

- Briseis – primal fantasy
- Carlova – suppressed desire
- Jetta – challenging upbringing turned inspiring
- Coppelia – raising others' consciousness
- Gerlinde – sponsoring followers of one's actions

which explains why my failed solicitations also produce things like the *FSA* series. Here, any time I try to start any new major project (30 Pisces / regular conjunct; typified by Carlova), I often <u>think</u> I have to do it by seeking a new meaning partner or job (30 Virgo / Virgo-conjunct, typified by Amneris). But in cases where the meaning-partner isn't actually necessary—which is most of the time—I end up looking like a Luscinia person and get Zelia-Siri results. But that's not the end of it. Based on a pattern related to Bacchus which we observed as far back as *FSA* and elaborated on in Chapter 36, things 60° <u>before</u> 30 Virgo also seem to happen *after* the 30 Virgo event. This whole process always seems to begin with the pressure to meet certain others' demands, 511 Davida in 29° Taurus.

Cause and Effect rules

What's going on here? Welcome to the world of cause and effect time series in an astro chart. You didn't think it could be done. I didn't think it could be done. But it can be done. By using certain planets in your chart, you will automatically set in motion the expression of other planets in other areas. No, this is not dispositorship. It's the flow of potential cycles as discussed in chapters 36 and 37. And the process obeys some unbelievably simple rules.

When I say "point" below, I am referring to an entire duodecanate. So 23.4° Aquarius will automatically imply the 22.5°–25° duodecanate of Aquarius. Of course, if you plan to use a higher resolution count than this, your degree spans will change accordingly.

A+60 causes A
If Point B is 60° <u>after</u> Point A, your doing B *causes* A as B ends. That is,

$$[B\ after\ A]\ in\ space\ =\ [B\ before\ A]\ in\ time$$

"After" in this case and the ones that follow means later by sign or phasic character. Taurus is after Aries in space. Aries is after Pisces. The natural sign cycle is counterclockwise. Under the A+60 rule, then, if you have 879 Ricarda at 12° Cancer and 453 Tea at 12° Virgo, then using Tea's fearless forwardness will habitually cause Ricarda's hampered progress. I found this kind of thing absolutely amazing, but it lines up with the predictions of this book's quantum mechanical theory, the behavior of the Jupiter Trojans, and the general role of the inner six neighbors of a circular region as bisectors of the 0° degree axes. We actually can extract cause and effect from a static arrangement of planets, and the A+60 rule is the first and best example of this in the dimension of such a connection between cycle phase ϕ_A and time t.

A+90 lays the seeds for A
If Point B is 90° after Point A, your doing B lays the seeds for A, but won't usually cause A to happen smoothly until you drop whatever it is you currently ~want~ (the square) and stop doing B for that reason. This is our standard potential energy-real energy relationship.

A+30 turns up A
If Point B is 30° after Point A, your doing B turns up the current expression of A.

A+180 is what A is compared to
Point B is 180° away from Point A, you can measure the proper behavior of B by seeing if A is well behaved.

A+120 is a result related to your using A to get A+180
If Point B is 120° after Point A, your doing B is what you should do if you want A to work, but the Point 180° away from A isn't giving you what you want. This is because the Point 120° after A actually has the point 180° away from A 60° after it. This is effectively like pretending you got the 180° thing (what you wanted from / what you compared to A) from doing A even if you didn't actually get it. This whole thing works best when you actually *want* something though, and doesn't do much if you're indifferent.

A+150 is what gets turned up if you use A to get the A+180 result you want
This is just another way of saying A+180 is 30° after A+150, then using the A+30 rule.

Effects can be causes if you follow the above patterns stressfully
If you do any of the above stressfully or forcefully, you can cause the relationships to go backwards. For example, A − 60 can *cause* A if you stressfully force it to do so. In my experience though, it's very easy to burn yourself out doing things this way. In *144* I included a dialogue in which Pepper and Geery talked about weeks controlling days. Think of stressful chains as showing where you dwell on undesired tension. For example, in trying to get A to cause A+60 (which is not the natural direction), you might have done A to get A+180 which didn't work and thus laid the seeds for A+90 which turned up the perception of A+90-30. As in the *144* dialogue, we needed to put in more energy to pass over other events in order to get here though.

Why Do These Rules Work?

Rather than summarizing a bunch of collected statistics and theory scattered across all four *FSA* books (especially Chapter 36), I'll give a short explanation:

> Since the division of a circle into 12 is actually a stable division into sections of potential and real energy relative to a starting point, certain fractions among the 12 assume that certain other fractions have happened or have the potential to happen. As with pulling back an arrow, every event will trigger eventual release in the form of some other event. Thus we get a time sequence for everything in your chart.

And so you get the ability to predict what people will tend to do in time. More importantly, you can use the A+60 rule to understand chains of events that naturally happen in your life. You can use the A+90 rule to understand chains of events which seem to stop each other from working in your life (though they're actually just planting seeds). A look at the Mean 13 and other problematic asteroids can often be particularly informative.

Chain Effects Apply To All Asteroids and All Angles As Well

This may not be so surprising, but chain effects can also be used to study any combination of quirky traits anywhere in your chart. Say for example you want to know why, despite your strong leadership ability, you are deathly uncomfortable in the number one spot without a partner in front of you. A friend of mine has this problem. To analyze this, we might look at Mars for general influence and Priska for second-placedness. She has an 85th (Leo-conjunct) when we consider all 144 harmonics and a 14 when we consider only the first 36. Her asteroids are all positive in these locations, so influencing others may not be the thing. Knowing what I know about her though, it's probably more a responsibility issue. Indeed, her Priska-Saturn is separated by a 25th harmonic, which corresponds to a Capricorn-conjunct. In that dudodecanate, my friend has the asteroid Gorgo, which lines up with the ways she sees her duties from an existing second place position. By sign, her Saturn in Libra is forward-trine her Priska in Gemini, so (using the A+120 rule) this particular angle of separation causes stress when she tries to go from Priska-second to Saturn-duty, but flows more easily when she goes from Saturn-duty to Priska-second. Actually, now is a good time for us to look at when you should read which angles.

The Many Faces of a Single Angle

⚔Back in *FSA* when I first introduced the higher harmonics, I claimed you could read more than one angle depending on your "resolution." I didn't show you the details in the previous example, but my friend's Priska is in 26 Gemini while her Saturn is in 7 Libra. Her birth time and place are both known. How should we read this?

- If we're reading using all 144 harmonics, she has a 25th harmonic (Capricorn-conjunct or III-conjunct).
- If we're only reading the first 36 harmonics as we did in *FSA* and *HBS*, she also has a 25th.
- If we're only reading the first 12 harmonics, she has a 7th (septile).
- If were only reading the majors (conjunct, opposition, trine, square, sextile, and inconjunct), she has no angle.
- Reading by nearest angle, the 101° separation of Priska-Saturn is closer to a square. (But it's such a wide square that it's not even a square; calling it a septile would be much more accurate).
- Reading by whole-sign, Gemini-Libra is a trine, and this is what I read. But why did I do this all of a sudden after having never done it in any of the previous chapters?

Most harmonics have many angles within them. A basic inconjunct, for example, has four members: the *forward* inconjunct angle (150°), the *forward* semisextile (30°), the *backwards* inconjunct angle (-150°), and the *backwards* semisextile (-30°). We now know that these have different energetic consequences when we're moving around a circle in a specific order, so when we say Planet A is "inconjunct harmonic" Planet B, it's no longer clear whether the A+30, A-30, A+150, or A-150 rules apply. The only way we can take the whole complex second-level astro story and turn it back into basic real-versus potential energies is to read angle pairs by sign separation.

The above isn't as inconsistent as it sounds. When you do your taxes, are you actually doing taxes, or doing your civic duty? Are you performing a task? Are you working (as opposed to resting)? Of course, you're actually doing all of these things at once. But in the most basic sense, you're working: spending energy rather than gaining it back. Cause and effect cycles are built on the having, spending, investing, and recovering of energy, so the whole-sign cycle (which corresponds to the character of the bodies in those signs) is one of the better ways to frame our pair in terms of energy use. Similarly, working-versus-resting would be a good way to frame the doing of taxes in terms of a causal cycle cast in terms of basic energy use.

When you aren't sure whether to read angle separations using majors, 12s, 36s, 144s, or whole sign, consider the following:

- For accuracy in describing complex interactions, especially those involving other people, you should use the full family of 144 harmonics.
- If you just want to determine whether a behavior is public (level III or Capricorn based), interpersonal (level II or Aquarius based), or personal (level I / regular angles), use the 36s.
- If you want to read only in terms of your own personal experiences, use the first 12 angles.
- If you only want to reference easily identifiable traits without worrying about how others or the abstract world will interact with those traits, use only the majors (conjunct, opposition, trine, square, sextile, and inconjunct). This is the astrology most of us were trained in up until the early 21st century.
- If you only want to look at whether energy was spent going from one broad style of behavior to another, or if you want to follow the causes and effects of such broad energy transfers, use whole-sign readings. This is part of the reasons why Vedic astrology works so well for prediction despite having far fewer angles and asteroids to work with; it deals in final verdicts rather than the specifics of each trial.

An example

Suppose you want to know how to get the broad world to see you as an easy winner who attracts victory without working for it. You look up your Laurentia-Midheaven angle and find that you have a 137$^{rd}_{144}$, a 35$^{th}_{36}$, a 12$^{th}_{12}$, a 12$^{th}_{majors}$, and a 1$^{st}_{whole sign}$. What does all this mean? It means that you look like

- a winner when you exercise managerial control (137$^{rd}_{144}$)
- that the public is more likely to see you as a genius while this is going on (35$^{th}_{36}$),
- but generally you won't experience such praise directly, only as a vibe around you (unless you're making this vibe into art) (12$^{th}_{12}$ and 12$^{th}_{majors}$);
- very broadly though, you put out the same kind of energy while winning as you do establishing your reputation (1$^{st}_{whole sign}$).

On top of this, asteroids in the Aries-quintile duodecanate (17.5°–20° Aries) would affect how well you pull off managerial control since this is the 137th duodecanate. Bodies in the Capricorn-undecile zone (2.5°–5° Capricorn) would affect how your genius status looked.[32] The sum of bodies in all of Pisces would affect how your general vibe felt to you, and the sum of bodies in all of Aries would show how you went about causing your Laurentia to connect with your Midheaven.

The purpose of the above is not to bewilder you with interpretive options, but to let you know what you're actually looking at when you restrict your planet-pair interpretations to a certain number of possible angles. Each grouping has its advantages. For example, I usually swear by the 36s when doing statistics since the 12s are largely uninformative for reading other people's interactions and the 144s are way too numerous to remember easily. Still, how far you delve will depend on your preferences for complexity. And the speed of your computer. ✗

---

[32] Remember that the first 36 harmonics are just the full 144 with the last 96 or so interpretations skipped. So no they don't divide the circle into 36 sections. Instead they simply use the same 144 divisions as the full 144 harmonics.

Time in the Astro Wheel

Revisiting the Hours

As I've mentioned in previous books, there is a phenomenon I experience in which certain windows of the day precede certain others. I call this phenomenon "the Hours." For example, if I wake up between 2:22 am and 3:23 am, I almost always have an important discovery that day. The earlier I wake up within this window, the earlier in the day the discovery usually occurs. I call this my "Hour of Node" since it corresponds to where my North Node window starts and ends in my chart. Now mind you, I discovered this pattern of time-previewing long before I found any correspondence with astrology, though the pattern is pretty clearly astrological and seems to happen in everyone's charts. The reason we don't see this (how certain windows of the day preview certain others in a very predictable pattern) is because our lives are typically too crowded with other things. That's pretty much it. The number one deterrent, by the way, for finding out that this pattern applies to you is…your morning alarm. I'll get to that shortly.

Although it didn't take long to locate "Midnight Point" (start of the actual day) and "Start Point" (beginning of the previewing effect for me personally during each day) in my own chart, I still haven't figured out why these points are what they are. I don't even have a theory. So unfortunately I can't tell you where to start counting in your own chart. The only thing I can tell you is how I personally discovered the Hours and hope you will use a similar pattern to find out where they work for you.

How I learned of "the Hours" phenomenon:

0. **No alarm allowed.** Since I'm a super light sleeper and don't like being violently jolted from my slumber, I prefer to wake myself when naturally inclined to do so. This is important because, as you might imagine, it's hard to determine your natural wake pattern if you require a non-natural signal to alert you. If you set your alarm at 6:00 am, who knows whether that reflects you or some convenient external time which you picked based on required duties instead of yourself. Since most of us aren't wired to naturally wake ourselves like this though, I will suggest that you simply observe the following patterns on weekends or whenever you don't have to be somewhere at a particular time. I learned of the Hours based on my weekend schedule. No alarm.

1. **Noticing differentypes of days given different waking times.** Without an alarm, I noticed a natural tendency to wake up at 6:34 am on my own. But after changing schools and daily duties, I would wake up at 6:56 am. When not on the new duty cycle, the natural wake up time would go back to 6:34 am, regardless of what time zone I was in.

2. **Noticing exactly what time certain day-types begin and end.** While working a particular Saturday job, I noticed that waking up some time around 6:34 am would produce a normal day while waking around 7:17 am would produce a day full of accidents. Waking around 7:47 am would mean a very peaceful day.

3. **Noticing what time waking events are paralled later in the day.** I also noticed that the closer I was to these times after passing them, the earlier in the day the nature of that day would become apparent. So in the chaotic 30 minute window between 7:17 and 7:47, if I dropped the soap in the shower at 7:32, my students might have a fight around noon. If I dropped it around 7:20, I'd encounter some weird traffic inconvenience around 8-ish.

4. **Noting accidents and special occurences.** This next part seems random but turns out to be important. I had a slippery shower and used even more slippery soap, so "dropping the soap"—strange as it may sound—was actually THE event which alerted me to the Hours in the first place: an inconvenience which you knew could happen, which you'd prefer to avoid but would happen anyway. So it made the perfect marker for similar kinds of inconveniences later in the day. That is, the Hours are much easier to observe when you see really special kinds of events getting mirrored later in your day, but only when you wake up at certain times. I tended *not* to drop the soap when waking between 6:34–7:17 or after 7:47, and even when I did drop it, the day wouldn't have much chaos in it. Waking

between 7:17–7:47 was another matter entirely; even if no accidents happened, the day would still be generally stressful. That was 16 years ago. This still holds today.

5. **Finding out what time counts as "the end" of a day.** After weeks of the above, I noticed that after 5:21 pm, nothing that happened in the morning really echoed anymore during a particular day. If I had been in a good mood around 7:46 am that day (right before the end of the 7:17–7:47 window), I might have a pretty pleasant interaction around 5:15 pm, letting me know that 5:20-something marked the end of whatever was going on regarding any predictive windows.

6. **Sharpening the times.** I determined that one kind of day started exactly at 6:34 am. Not 6:35. Not 6:33. Because if I woke up at 6:33 the day would be entirely different from the 6:34-type day. And if I woke up at 6:35 it would take about half an hour afterwards for me to have anything happen that looked like the 6:34-type day. Waking up right at 6:34, however, would show the nature of the day more or less immediately upon my waking.

7. **Doing the math on windows you've observed (not on ones you haven't).** Over time as I got further into astrology, I started to see correspondences between the separation of planets in my wheel and the separation of windows for waking up. 6:34–7:17 constituted a 43 minute window, while 7:17–7:47 constituted a 30 minute window. In a 24 hour day (1440 minutes), these were 2.9% and 2.1% of a whole day and corresponded to 10.75° and 7.5° respectively. Having learned that Uranus was closer to chaos than other planets, I looked in the astrology wheel for correspondences to my day—specifically for a chain of three planets separated by 10.75° and 7.5°. I found Sun-Uranus-Venus in late 9°, mid-late 20°, and 28° Scorpio and started calling 6:34 the Hour of Sun, 7:17 the Hour of Uranus, and 7:47 the Hour of Venus. I did not, however, assume that other planets had hours. And you shouldn't either. Since then I have observed other hours, but in my chart the hours of Jupiter and Neptune are near nonexistent. Meanwhile the South Node and Selene seem to have hours. Why? I don't know.

8. **Finding the Midnight Point.** What I do know is that once you've identified a window or two, you can backtrack to get something I call the Midnight Point. In my case I took 6 hours and 34 minutes, turned it into 394 minutes (out of 1440), multiplied by 360 and got 98.5°. So 98.5° earlier than my Sun would mark Midnight of each day. This was 1°41' Leo in my chart, and doesn't have any significance that I'm aware of other than its status as my own public day marker.

9. **Finding the Start Point.** More important in your chart is your "Start Point." Since I had already found that wake up windows stopped predicting the day's events around 5:20pm, I observed what tended to happen around this time. The Start Point's effects are generally more dramatic in your chart, I believe. If I had an event to attend at 6pm, I might start feeling weird around 5:40. If I almost got into car accident at 5:30, I'd almost get into another one at 5:39. Events tended to presage other events just like themselves starting at this magic point. Thanks to 5:00 traffic, I had no trouble identifying 5:21pm as the time.

As much as I'd like to give more specific instructions on how you can calculate the Hours in your chart, a lot of it is just repeated observation based on the kinds of things that fit your schedule. I've found that Moon, Mars, and Uranus events are much easier to track because they're often so disruptive, while Neptune events can be quiet as a mouse. But the reason I told you about the hours wasn't actually to help you locate them. Instead, it was to talk about how time is measured in an astrochart.

There is another phenomenon called the Weeks which is MUCH harder to observe in the chart, mainly because most of us can't afford to just sit back and observe a week's worth of things without turning our attention to other things. There is also the problem of weeks mapping *backwards* on your wheel. The process for determining where your weeks start and end is similar to that of the Hours, but instead of assuming that forward time maps in the Aries-Taurus direction, you find that it actually maps in the Aries-Pisces direction. (It took me about 13 years to figure that out.) As you might guess, there's also a cycle for years, but I don't know which direction it goes in or whether it even reflects your specific planets as opposed some general time cycle. One of the windows I've noticed seems to last about four years. Whatever the case, it's apparent that a single wheel can measure multiple spans of time (including the span of your entire life), and this raises a more practical question: If we can tell how long something lasts in a chart, can we tell how long something will take? I offer you a hypothesis.

The Time Unit-Hypothesis

⚒ While working on a separate project outside of this book, I sought to understand what makes time tick forward. We know that the movie animates, but what is it that forces each moment to yield to the next in order to drive the movie's frames in succession? My assertion is that time is the result of a kind of paradox—where today is both today and yesterday at once. I've given the full argument in an earlier chapter, but the idea is that, just as surely as last week was also "today" at some point, our inability to process the multiple versions of the same window as being that window forces us to absorb known windows into unknown ones. `Today` includes `Yesterday`.`Today`. Relatedly, every time we return to the same point on a wheel, old notions of whatever unit we're looking at become subsumed into the new notion. Every time our 24-hour clock hits the Midnight Point, our meaning of "Today" changes. Every time our weekly clock reaches the "New Week Point" (whatever that may be), our notion of "this week" changes. Accordingly, one cycle of the wheel which describes how you do things—from "start" to "spent" to "being seen" to "finish" (the four-cycle discussed in chapter 36)—actually describes one unit of many kinds of cycle which you (or your biology) define for yourself. One 360° turn can measure a single day or a single week. But it can also measure the full span of any undertaking you engage in.

When we take on projects we typically recruit three kinds of concepts and one additional concept for time. The three concepts could be self, other, and world; beginning, middle, and end; active, interactional, and passive; or whatever. We note though, that the A+60 and A+180 rules from earlier have the curious side effect of producing an A+240 rule: where A is your doing, A+180° is what gets done, and A+180+60 *causes* what gets done. But wasn't it the case that <u>A</u> caused what got done? Nope. A was *associated with* A+180, could be *compared* to A+180, but didn't actually cause it. A+180 was, event sequence-wise, caused by the pattern 60° after it (A+240 which is the same as A-120).

In other words, in the 12-division astro wheel, expressing an intention in character which overwrites a prior notion of that same character, introduces a time component to that intention in which the results of the intention are caused by a similar, but unequal result 1/3 of the way along the cycle. Time proceeds as systems toss earlier versions of their current states into the trash bin called complexity, so that each event, no matter how long its time scale, requires three "result-based units" in order for the original intended event to begin to show its *intended* results. This actually lines up with an interesting geometric pattern I associated with the Hours and the Weeks in particular. Namely, if experiential patterns display a kind of doubling bounce—where an event happening 10 minutes after the Start Point predicts another related event 20 minutes after the Start Point—what point around the whole circle is the latest you can wait before you can no longer change what has been set in motion? The answer is 2/3. This needs some explaining.

The Hours have spared me countless inconveniences over the years and given me countless prompts to exercise caution. If something negative happens 10 minutes after my Start Point and I know I have something to do 20 minutes after the Start Point, I can change my attitude, plans, or whatever, and alter the rest of the day from then on. If I arrive 8 hours after my Start Point and want to change course, I can see those changes reflected 16 hours after the Start Point. I can even change course 12 hours after the Start Point and alter the conditions for the next day's Start Point. Waiting 16 hours is another matter though because, in terms of math, 16 hours after the Start Point predicts an event 32 hours after the Start Point. But in terms of a 360° revolution, the point located 32 hours after is the same as the point located 8 hours after. This is the first time along the wheel where this happens: where a point predicts the very point that predicted *it*. This also explains why certain dreams you have will presage events going backwards in 2/3 slices (another story entirely). Overall though, we see that the 2/3 mark is actually the "last call" in any single cycle for controlling how the rest of that cycle looks. You would think it was the ½ mark, but it isn't. At least at the ½ mark you still have room to reinterpret where you're interpreting from. As of the 2/3 mark, all you can do is come to terms with how you got where you are in the current cycle. Thank goodness there's nothing preventing you from simply starting a new project right there. As for the current one though, I've seen that the 2/3 mark often lays out the fate of the project with pretty stern finality.[33]

So what does all of this mean? Several things:

1. **Every results oriented cycle most naturally requires three successful repetitions of the unit in which its phases are naturally measured.** Why? Because of the math associated with 360°. 240 is the first point which attempts to write the event (120) which originally wrote it. Like a child giving birth to his own parent, this puts us in a kind of causal no man's land beyond which further conceptions of things overwrite their original forms. Just as 240 attempts to write 120, we add another 240 from here in order for 120 to attempt to write the events at 0. Adding another 240 from 120 puts us at 0—which attempts to write 240. The passage of the three 2/3-style phases puts us in a position where all phases of the event have rewritten each other, such that it takes 3 phases of an event and 2 cycles of that actual event (2/3 x 3) for us to call that event by a form truly different from its original. We see this is several common examples.

   If the survival of a new business is measured in years, we can expect to wait three years to know whether our fledgling business will survive. If one day does not constitute habit but one week does, week can expect to require three weeks (21 days) for a new habit to be called a habit. If the success of a relationship is measured in abstract "phases," we can expect to pass through three phases before we know if the relationship will endure. And for the many relationships we've all been in which seem to have failure loom over them after only one or two phases, we know by now that you really can tell where such a relationship will likely fail no matter how hard you try to keep it alive for that third (often declining) phase.

2. **The good news is, an event doesn't have to die just because you see death coming. All you need to do is commission a new version of the event.** Have a second honeymoon. Rebrand. Let's be friends. They all work to create new phases where old ones seem doomed.

3. **Events with a standard for measuring their lifespan tend to adopt common units of time as their basis of measure, but events without such a standard lifespan or events with a processed-determined standard lifespan are measured in abstract phases instead of common time units.** Years for business, education and work. Days for behavioral tasks. Weeks or bi-weeks for business processes. But amorphous "phases" for lifespans, relationships, and legal agreements. Note the earlier emphasis on "natural" units. A 45-day closing is doesn't divide into 15 ~day~ chunks so much as it divides into an offer, acceptance, and closing phase. The imposition of days here is more for convenient translation into the business cycle than it is the natural unit of contract performance.

Thus the time-unit hypothesis reads as follows:

> The rewriting of an event requires the completion of three of its phasic units along with the completion of two cycles of the event itself, where phasic units depend on what the event consists of.

---

[33] Perhaps this is why my own Hour of Neptune does almost nothing. It's located backwards trine (A-120) my start point at the Moon, or 2/3 (A+240) around the circle. By the time my day ticker arrives here, there's hardly any room to rewrite anything.

The list below might be useful for determining the units of various kinds of things. Yes it's arbitrary, but does put certain common events into a single table:

Event type	Common time unit	Common distance or frequency unit
impression making	seconds	feet
mood writing	minutes	cubic feet (around you), a single or small number of activities
habit training	hours	number of various activities performed
task performance results (including health-related and professional arrangements); short collaborations	days	milestones (results of activities) reached
change projects (including work and personal); associateships (boyfriends, girlfriends, and project partners)	weeks	patterns of activity; frequently, miles traveled
group introductions (including birth, buildings, and company divisions); acquaintanceship	months	communication patterns developed
educational or professional training, businesses; friendships	years	learning and habituation patterns developed
generational viewpoints, fields of study, certain public organizations aimed at longer-term issues; deep friendships	decades	families of learning and habituation patterns developed
cities, countries, and other geopolitical divisions, membership-conferring bodies, divisions of knowledge (like new kinds of arts or science)	centuries	systems for conveying families of learning and habituation; systems for passing culture
the duration of empires	millennia	multiple systems for conveying culture beneath a more coherent culture

Table 40-1: Common units of time for measuring certain events

One of the consequences of the time-unit hypothesis is that it suggests one way we can tell how long a thing will take based on the ease with with which we handle smaller things. For example, if you're dating and you frequently run into dates who can talk to you all day about themselves but get instantly bored when it's time to talk to you about you, you know that a relationship built on that dynamic might work more like an associateship than anything else as the person attempts to get certain things out of their system using you as a receptacle. You could measure this kind of thing in weeks, and *how many* weeks would depend on how quickly you started asking them to pay real attention to you instead of themselves. Hard facts. So how long will it take you to find Mr. or Ms. Right? Who knows? Maybe about three times the length of time it takes for you to leave the butterflies phase and get into the investigation phase. On the other hand, some associations seem to start off with a natural ease without much of an investigation phase. These might take months or years to unfold. ⚒

Using the Square to Take Advantage of (Apparent) Failure

As an alternative to the 2/3 cycle of progress to get towards a goal, you can also use the ¼ cycle of blocked progress. Mathematically speaking, it's often quicker to fail three times in getting to a goal than it is to succeed in the three stages towards that goal. Quicker doesn't mean easier though, and you'll have to be more on your toes if you do things this way.

Suppose for example you're looking to travel to unfamiliar places and take the world by storm. This might be a Sagittarius-conjunct matter (Saj for image making among strangers and conjunct for getting things started). Unfortunately, your plans are hampered because of the numerous responsibilities you have at home. If those responsibilities are something like a Virgo-square in nature (remember A+90 causes A), then you may have a "seed planting" cycle on your hands instead of a "successful phase" cycle like the one above. At this point most people might drop their travel plans. But you know better; you know that handling those responsibilities under the assumption that the travel arrangements have been made will allow you to travel even sooner cycle-wise. The fact that you don't feel the original goal in process is an even clearer indication that you're dealing with a square.

So you perform your Virgo duties. At some point those duties can't be done anymore, and you find yourself doing Gemini-conjunct things—thinking new ideas about your original travel plans and how your duties helped lay the seeds for them. You're on the next phase of the square cycle. Finally, those thoughts give way to a seemingly unexplained, spontaneous action on your part (Pisces-conjunct) which takes place under the assumption that the whole chain of non-travel simply consisted of preparations for travel. You keep doing this under that assumption. The next phase will be the next version of Saj-conjunct. We'll see how it unfolds.

Note that work with square events requires that you accept the non-occurrence of your original goal not once but 3 times, and each time in a different way. Yet the apparent failure to attain the goal need not constitute an actual failure as long as you treat each successive redirection like "bag packing" for the original goal. Most people have trouble thinking this way because they're not trained to think that setting a goal aside is sometimes the best way to get to it. But as with all kinds of situations in real life, sometimes the best way to make a right is to make three lefts—especially where the natural four-cycle of real and potential events are concerned.

It's a good thing we have both success-based (A+60) and non-success based (A+90) paths to the changed version of any one point. The asteroids aren't all friendly, and sometimes compel difficulties such that it just isn't productive to take the easy way towards things. Asteroids like Ricarda, Janina, and Hamiltonia for example are notoriously square-favoring, so that it may be easier to go around your intended path so to speak. The big secret to working with squares in this way is to do the thing you land on under the assumption that the thing you intended has indeed had its foundation laid. This is not the same as doing the thing bitterly, trying to do it right, or doing it in a way that reinterprets what happened. Instead, you should do it until you can no longer do it anymore given that the seed was planted. And then you do the next thing that this landed-on action has planted the seeds for in turn (again keeping in mind the original goal). You do it until exhaustion. And then you do it again. Try it. It works.

When You Need to Muster up the Will to do It: the Backwards Sesquiquadrate

There are things we want to do and can, things we want to do and can't, and then there are things we need to do but don't want to. For this last group we have the octile (8^{ths}) family of angles. Specifically we have the reverse 3-octile, more commonly known as the [backwards] sesquiquadrate (A-135°). When you absolutely must coerce yourself into action, the harmonic of coercion (the octile) is the best way to go.

Now even though there are four octiles to choose from, only the backwards sesquiquadrate showed up as significant among these in causing a point along the wheel to happen. My guess is that the backwards 135° is, energy-wise, more closely related to an unstable slide towards the seed-planting point of the backwards square while (trigonometrically) holding the maximum stored energy between the target action's comparison (A+180) and the potential for the action itself (A+90). That is, A+135 constitutes the diagonal of a square with sides along both the real and potential axes, where a square holds the greatest area of any rectangle so bounded. The backwards sesquiquadrate is like a husband rushing his wife to the hospital where the potential for her to have a baby will eventually yield a real baby. A-135 causes A by force. The irony, however, is that this setup takes the normal force of tension with which we usually stare at A and reassigns it to the angle of separation. So while you may look at that hospital run with nervousness, the moment you're actually doing it all the nervousness in your head transforms into the fuel for action.

This is tricky but it works very well (especially for Scorpio- and Mars-heavy charts): For things you need to do but don't want to do, perform the action 135° before it (A-135) with the intent to dominate or force your power recipient past where it currently, comfortably sits. Instead of getting A-135-60, you'll start to get A-135+135 instead (for reasons I proposed above). This process may feel weird when you first try it—something like a misuse of power. But once you see that you're not harming anyone, it'll be like second nature.

Of all three causal chains discussed over these last few pages (A+60→A, A+90→A, and A-135→A), the A-135→A chain is by far the most informative in explaining opportunities you ruined before realizing what you did.

Closing Thoughts on Cause and Effect

As I've written this chapter and investigated causal chains even further, I've realized something which some people may consider unfortunate. For those of us who are publicly ambitious enough, having goals at cross-purposes becomes a common experience as we push intensely from one objective to the next. As you look at your squares in particular, you may find that you're eventually forced to choose between two axes. You may have, for example, a Sun-Moon opposition square a Signe-Penthesilia opposition which (for whatever reason) constitutes a MAJOR dilemma for you given your chart, your personality, and your unique upbringing. Maybe your Sun-Moon pair represents self-contentment while Signe-Penthesilea is part of a pattern which drives you to speak out on issues related to exploitation. For most people, balancing these two may not be a problem, but YOU (in this example) are determined to go full throttle in one direction or the other. Obviously no one can make choices like this for you. But if you're having trouble choosing, the chart *can* offer some hint as to which of these crossed paths is most natural to you: It will be the path whose planet is closest to your Final Outlook (see Requiem in the previous chapter). That is, the body which comes closest to being the last one before your Ascendant (when going forward through the houses in 1, 2, 3,… order) will be the one which is easier for you to favor. This is basically the planet in the highest numbered house among the four.

There are all kinds of reasons for prioritizing the last 90° which have less to do with house number and a lot more to do with the 4-cycle and its ordering of potential energy, the backwards ordering of the harmonics and how the East-rising bodies are closet to a brand new cycle, the nature of the house cycle itself, and other reasons. Suffice it to say though, that the body which comes closest to being the last one in a square-axis setup like this (called a Grand Cross), might be the one you consider favoring in the long run regardless of whether you think this is morally right or wrong, regardless of what you've been trained to choose, and regardless of whether your current circumstances seem to favor that choice right now. In the end, the last houses are the ones which will linger on in the public's memory after you're done with whatever cycle you're on, so even if you wanted to choose some other object among the four, that public may still treat you as though the last object was the one you ultimately chose. This doesn't have to be the case, but it often is. Accordingly, all traits in the last 90° of your wheel tend to be more easily associated with the last public thing you did than any other non-final traits in the Grand Crosses in which they participate.

That said, the above pattern applies to people who are ambitious in their public doings. For those who prize their public relationships and partnerships, you would do a house rotation[34] and treat the third 90° section as the last 90°. For those who prize their sense of their own interactions with others, the second 90°. Lastly, if you value your own internal feeling above all else, you would favor the first 90° after the Ascendant. The thing is though, choices like this aren't nearly as random as they seem, and the chart really does bias you towards choosing planets in one section over others (usually the very last 90° by default).

---

[34] See the chapter on house rotations in *FSA*.

Chapter 41: On Sound and Symbol

While classifying the asteroids I noticed a pattern among certain names. Specifically, the *-kleia*s and the *-trix*es seemed to have a definite character to them which not only applied to asteroid names, but also to fixed stars and other objects not covered in this book. On closer inspection I found that this wasn't just true for certain names, but seemed to be true for most combinations of commonly recognized sounds. Accordingly, I used the same kind of classification that I applied to the character of asteroids to classify the various phonemes involved in naming those asteroids.

A **phoneme** is a basic unit of consonant and vowel-like sounds in a language. *Ma*, *ka*, *cho*, *chiu*, and *klay* are all phonemes, and these differ from other kinds of language units like alphabets (k, f, g, d) and ideograms (天,世, ☎, ☺). Where consonants and vowels are combined in a phoneme, they can be used to divide words into syllables, where these syllables are more likely than not to carry some sort of historically rooted context. Mono and polysyllables like -un, ex-, and -theo- for example all tend to be used in families of words with meanings related to each other. In this sense, English presents a double edged sword. On the one hand the messy and inconsistent formation of words like to, too, and two has a lot less to do with specific ideas and a lot more to do with borrowed, quirky traditions. On the other hand, because English is so heavily borrowed, it serves to integrate all kinds of historical meanings from all kinds of traditions. Thus even our seemingly unrelated packages of meaning end up being related via the ease with which we swap them. To, too, and two for example all involve the idea of joining, despite seeming unrelated. Here they share an approximate meaning with the French *tu* (you) and the Mandarin 土 (*tǔ*, things made from the Earth) despite these phonemes belonging to different languages.

As I observed asteroid names from various linguistic origins it seemed like there was a bigger underlying factor besides just social history. If you're familiar with the idea that things like smiling, pain response, and yawning are universal among humans, or if you're familiar with the motor-hypothesis of language, you might see how certain mouth patterns may also have implications for what our biology is doing, not just what our social training is telling us. Snakes and cats go *hsss* under threat. Dogs and humans calling for generic assistance go *ahh* or howl. The basic human smile begins with a *b-* or *m-*, and often ends ready for an *ee*. And so we have hints for phonemes not just as packages of socially trained meaning, but also as efficient arrangements of the species-specific communicative biology for making some kinds of announcements more of a natural fit for certain situations than others. Here, an animal's vocal structure may be thought of as one of a network of filters applied to the space of its acoustic possibilities. Through that filter the animal evolves certain convenient sounds for pleasure, pain, fear, and aggression most distinguishably and efficiently expressed through its bodily tools. From initial foundations, more complex messages are formed accordingly.

The rest of this chapter contains a list of the phonemic combinations I observed through classification of names associated with the 1000 asteroids. The list presents us with an interesting area of future linguistic study, particularly in the creation of new and nonsense languages as reflective of the creators' own psychologies.[35]

---

[35] In one of my meditations, for example, I received a spirit name whose syllables in the list combine to form a very fitting description of who I believe myself to be subconsciously in a world with no inconvenient rules.

Phoneme Patterns Associated with the Astrological Function of the First 1000 Asteroids

* æ = the sound in cat
* ai sounds like eye

æ = social sobriety
æb = halting
æg = obstacle eliminator
aehr = pressure / response to being pushed
ah = projecting
ahk = making to believe, mind-writing
ahw = boundary
ai = receiv(er/ing), projective right
al = proper social positioning
all = desire to connect
am = asserted from within
an = world interface
anti = response to an external
ar = (typically social) ideal
asia = passion
ass/az = networked
at = publicly experienceable form
ath = standing out
ay = power
bæ = inspiration commander
bah = supporter
bak = fervent supporter, fanatic
bar = standing alone
bau/baw = singular gathering occasion
bee = work controller
beh = perfected
bel = feminine
ben = high grace
ber = under spotlight
bi = assigned worth
big = amplified presence
bil = money
bo = outside of the crowd
bræ = inwardly valued
bra = dreamt of thing
bri = homebase
bru = communicative uniqueness
bu = safehaven
buh = watchworthiness
cam = to fill up / populate
char = putting pressure on
cheh/chæ = empowered action
chi/shi = surprising or densely packed authority
child = spawned from
con = noticeable direction
cue = acquiring

dæ = pressurer
da = (imposed) from a high place
dai = extreme
dam = an interaction-inspired compulsion
deh = idol
del = taking from others' chance to express
der = demanding want
des = despite receivers' lack of readiness
dev = confident in the open
di = body
doh = target object
dor = welcome persona
dra = performance standard
du = surrounding groups, close contactors
dul = that which discourages approach
ear = imposing order + equalizing (ih+yur)
ed = stretch
ee = central point
eh = relation
el = impact
em = coming to you
er = going on ahead, proceeding
eth = taming
ev = guide + guided relationship; a guidance relationship
fa = bright expresser
fay = adored
feh = stubborn internal qualities
fi = upper rank
fil = what is around
flor = demanding top class
fo = the public trade
for = enjoyment of
fra = reference image
fran = critical interconnection
fre = misrelation
fri = inspiring feeling
fuh = internal handling of another
gæ = made into an example
ga = paired with like kind (often either favored or surprising)
ge = with group
ger = group ruler

gih = status above another
gla = pushing a thing
go = controlled projection
gor = masked
gra = rich (as in information-dense) image
gre / grih = causing others to internalize
gu = created from the core
gun = penetrating another's world
hæ = challenging another
ha = instilling in another
ham = restricted behavior
har = from afar
hay = associated with imprisonment
heh = wide comparison
hehr = ideal interplay
hel = juxtaposition of contradictions
hih / hee = imposing one's (beneath the surface) will upon the surface
hil = forefront among others
hild = (publicly) known role
hin = awakening primal or common underlying forms
hip = expressive comfort
ho = into one's or others' favor
hor = revolutionary
house = area of true expression
hu = elevated standards
hur = underlying power
hy = elevated importance
ih = imposing order
il = elevated bearing
in = imposing order against a backdrop setting
irm = group center
is = defining
it = information
jah/zhah = costly trophy, high maintenance
jer/zher = shifting attention
jih = new beginnings
jo = outside, beyond
ju = elevate
ka = behavior
kai = personality puzzle
kal = character
kar = nature (circumstances)

kass = rules (of order)

keh = staying with, for value

kia = publicly affirmed contribution

kih = solicited for value

kler = accepted state

kli = overrule

klo = that which affects others

kloht = queen

kly = monopoly

ko = aspire

kor = strength basis

kr = attracting/charming

kre = effective

kress = supercede

kri = associated reputation

kro = spot hogging

kw = uniquely sourced trait

la = from the base / bottom, origin

lak = impulse

lam = going

lan = soliciting

law = the standard of advancement

li = taking

lia = being surrounded, enclosed

lie = taking control of others' choices
  or options

lih = expectations of one's will

lo = in the imagination of outsiders

lu = from an encasement

lud = self-entitlement

lun = fueling desire for

mæ = coaching

mæl = spacey or in the abstract

ma = separated from the crowd

mak = impression far beyond

man = seducing

mar = force

maw = others respond to one's poise /
  posture taken

may = received from all

mee = what the body or presence
  receives in general

meh = rallying groups to oneself

mehr = convincing to accept

mel = masculine, forward assertion

mer = superset / common setting

mil = charm

min = openly displayed power

mir = contributing to the outside

mo = sudden (or much) extraction
  from others

mont = project above

more = compelling affinity

mu = insistence on one's own way

na = attachment to

nah = experience of

nar = awareness of

nee = pleasurable appearance

nep = ambient environment

nes = the "first word"

new = supply source

ni = attention compelling

nigh = drawn interaction

nih = attention compelling

nim = opposition to expectations

no = value-judgment (or object
  thereof)

nor = accomplishment unleashing

now = fixation object

o = influencing, directing

oar = gaining liking / approval

ohss = conscripting (enslaving)

ol = eclipsing

ona = strong fixation

oo = expectation breaking

oss = into others' lives, processed by
  others

ot = stabilizing

pæ = turning on, stimulating

pah = marketed / announced
  personality

pahl = personality as a fixed state

par = expressive objective

paw = mass contact

pay = others' abstractions or illusion-
  making

pe = controlled direction

pehr = standards attainment

pel = building up

pen = training another

per = from one's own world

pia = drawing other's attention to a
  thing

pih = leading role

po = the reason / motivation

pom = strong response

pra = chase

pre = despite surrounding suggestion

pri = prettiness, pleasantly viewable

pro = through urge

pul = evoking

qui = trait which wears on others

ra = message spreader

rat = disorderly conditions

re = individual tastes / preference

ri = compared against your standard

ro = in the home circle

ru = intended expression

ruh = among company

sæ = pervading, all consuming

sa = put ahead

sai = underlying

saw = behavioral constraint

say = men's wants

schwa = on a pedestal

see = building up attention to

seh = clarifying the execution of things

sf = behavioral aftermath

si = focus on a challenge (the hissing
  sound made by many animals)

sia = pulled from thin air

sir = stirring up energy in

ska = which needs to be searched for
  or sorted through

so = inventive creation

sta = ordered, more controlled than
  norm

steh = first in, pioneer

ster = boss, steeror

su = leading or rising

sv = role occupancy

sw = interrupter

ta = ideal

tan = a quality that draws viewers

tas = archetype / example

taw = emitting, sending out

teh = squeezed

ter = talkworthy

tha = entertained audiences

thea / theo = fortified wall, something
  reinforced

theh/thih = to act on desire

tho = shining image

thoo = easily approachable

thoos = smooth impression

ti = prioritized

tia = creator

tie = with respect to friendly
  interactions

tih = prioritized

tis = bathed in

to = the movement of others energy

tra = giving a performance, performing
  (as in actively doing, not the stage)

trih = a forward spirit

trix = the last word

tru = seemingly fated position

tu = purposes

tuh = demanded of others

uhm/ahm = overshadowing expression

ull = external appearances

un = imposing on others' opinion of you (or of the thing itself)

ur = belonging under attention

us = interpersonal trust

væ = interplay

val = pushed onto

vee = making observable

veh = focus object

vehr = bigger

vih = objectification, "making into a thing"

vir = strong or well-equipped

vuh = internal handling of another

wa = exposed to outside

wall = connecting beyond oneself

weh = entry through boundary

wer = interface with outside

wih = escape

wuh = boundary crossing energy

x / ks = inducement, provoking

yu = to reconcile

yur = to equalize, set equal

za = disclosure of intent

ze = active control, watchfulness

zer = other-pleasing

zi = reinforcement through information

zia = being supported by information

zu(hw) = ability to make

zu = ability to make

Chapter 42: Other Assertions Aimed Towards Building a Theory of the Quantum Mechanical Implications for Spirituality

The Standard Model for particle physics holds that there are twelve elementary particles, four force carriers, and the Higgs particle. Aside from the obvious analogies to our earlier snowflake model (the Higgs particle being analogous to a putative "transferor" in intervening space), we also see how the 12 elementary particles, replete with charge, mass, and spin, may represent some of the more basic collections of transformations among groups of quanta in a 3D spatial space. Assuming that resonant coupling among quanta for increasing mass and resonance-promoting behavior among them is a requirement for observing things like charge and magnetic field, we may view the elementary particles the stable representatives of quantic transfer in each of the twelve possible dimensions. I believe it makes sense that for every dimension there must exist at least one elementary mode among all possible combinations of quanta which is capable of progressing in that dimension only, without changing values in any other dimension. The idea is not so radical. This is, after all, the definition of independent variables. If there is such a thing as an all-preceding, fundamental quantum, then the elementary particles won't be so elementary that they can't be broken down into some combination of that quantum, its intervening space, and the behaviors describing this, but we should expect to encounter a special arrangement of these three things which makes the for idealized energy transfer in one dimension over the remaining 11.

So what does all of this have to do with human spirituality?

At the very least, we may agree that there are dimensions beyond 4D spacetime. Movement at near light speed, for example, turns space into some mutated, informational version of itself such that the timespan of the light-speed reference frame and that of the non-lightspeed frames take on noticeably different values regardless of what our omnipresent, theoretical camera view may suggest. There is the speed of an Earth day and the speed of a Jupiter day. Should these be measured using the same dimensions as the spatial locations of these planets? What if Jupiter were a black hole? Clearly four dimensions aren't enough here since we'll need something angular and something else which is at least mildly related to density in order to fully describe how these bodies are affecting their surroundings. But if such extra dimensions are needed, doesn't this mean that the very quanta which constitute all systems will also give rise to mechanisms in humans which handle these same dimensions? Surely we're not simply 4-dimensional objects in a 10+ dimensional world. What lazy quanta we'd have!

And so we come to what may possibly sound like a naïve conclusion: If the world of physics comprises more than four dimensions and such a world is built on quanta, then we who are built on quanta ourselves should also exist in more than four dimensions. Naïve right? But doesn't it make basic sense? Just because a point (1,0,0) in the x-y-z plane has 0s for its y and z coordinates, doesn't mean it's suddenly kicked out of the other two dimensions. Just as the common string theories posit around 9 spatial dimensions, we as humans are able to easily identify at least 6, three for ourselves and three for the object we're interacting with. To you, a random rock may be only two feet away in 3D space, but you are an ensemble. The atoms of the rock—which know they are separate from each other and from each of your atoms—have an entire subspace of distances over which they exist, and given that such subspaces apply on a molecular scale much smaller than you are, the rock may think of *you* as being the equivalent of light years away.[36]

In one of my earlier assertions I claimed that dimensions on opposite axes of dimension-space are likely to be perceived inversely. If you are a point-sized viewer and are infinitely close to another point then you are *in* that other point, and that point exists everywhere for you. If you are infinitely far from the other point, then the latter shrinks into the distance and exists nowhere for you. Even when we recall our single plane 3D model of 12 dimensions and apply it to all three spatial planes, even after we animate it by spinning every spinnable axis, there is still the matter of certain dimensions overpowering others in our perception. The more we lean on light (x_A) and its parallel, memory (מ), to give us information about the world, the lower our ability to perceive the opposite dimension (z_B) will be. The more we measure the flow of time in parallel with distances traveled, the less easily we perceive the energy spent in traveling those distances. The more we perceive the charge associated with things, the less we perceive the details of its coupled composition and the long term stability thereof. This last perceptual mode is more balanced in humans, however, thanks to the significant roles played by electrical currents in the body and gravity outside of the body. The point is, it is possible to overtrain or overevolve the mechanisms for perceiving one dimension over its opposing dimension just as it is possible to balance the perception of these. It falls to the human to develop the mechanisms for perceiving certain dimensions by simply training their sensitivity to the body systems which process those dimensions.

Assertion 68. On the implications of the time axis on human perception of time 1: The three time axes may be treated as their own space.

If you take a look at the time axis in our 3D model of dimension space, you'll notice two interesting phenomena. Although time does not form a central vector in that space, it may easily be made into such an axis-defining vector with, say, τ and מ as its orthogonal partners. Here τ might be crossed with t to give מ according to our usual right hand rule, making memory phases into the stacking of time onto itself by a lifespan number of cycles. Thinking about this in terms of our original conception of a z-type axis, this makes memory the out-of-the-paper dimension you need to stand in in order to map time as a function of lifespan (as in number of seconds passed). But none of that is interesting. The interesting part is that this axis setup introduces a discretizing event space into an otherwise continuous dimension space, subsequently leading to a reconceptualization 1) of what z_B actually is and 2) how traveling at the speed of light affects the traveler's perception of time and space.

Assertion 69. z_B is the dimension of spacetime curvature.

Taking $< \tau, t, מ >$ as its own space, the state of θ_B still represents angular separation from the r_B and t axes (since they are modeled as parallel on the quantic level), but now also shows the extent to which that orientation can vanish to near zero. This happens at $\theta_B = \pi/2$ or $3\pi/2$. These values give full magnitude to the antimemory dimension z_B as the result of $t \times \tau$ (not the other way around). Simultaneously, they also give 0 magnitude to progress along the r_B and t axis. It turns out then that z_B measures the spatial deviation magnitude, or the extent to which spatial separations are not being "emitted" as a dimension. As the complementary orientation to the emitter dimension x_A, z_B provides and unexpected answer to a question we never asked: What happens to a space after light is finished passing through it? The vacuum folds back onto itself. Where the emission axis x_A can be considered a phasic mode of the quantum, time ticks at the end of every completed family of independent flop cycles across the space of neighbor-indicated states projected onto an orthogonal axis. But the night sky is not infinitely bright. Those emission modes are summarily returned to non-emitting modes once that single photonic mode has passed through with its associated lifespan. This causes organization deficient pre-energy to fill in where the emitted signal is no longer located, and it will remain this way until the next photonic mode is received. So now we know what the mysterious input dimension z_B is: It's the extent to which emission into the vacuum yields to absorption from the vacuum, regardless of whether the associated vacuum-drawn resonances from other quanta are actually resonant with the main quantum we're considering.

---

[36] Not because the speed of light changes, but because the definition of a year as a function of completed quantic-collection cycles will change.

According to our model, z_B braids the vacuum back into spaces where an emission cycle has completed, erasing the previous frame at the $\theta_B = {}^\pi/_2$ angle of target spatial separation and allowing current time to yield to an update in lifespan time. Simultaneously, maximum curvature is achieved here for the quantum as r_B—which is actually there—looks like 0.

It is important to note that when a nonzero dimension in quantum mechanics looks like 0, it isn't actually 0. It means the adjacent neighbor and intervening space in that dimension's direction currently holds all the energy. The percentage of the quantum's total energy held by this neighbor and the intervening space is something like .0854, the square root of the fine structure constant. This value shows what fraction of a quantum's total energy can be expected to be associated with any particular dimensional orientation at any time. If you let this energy go all the way to zero then the quantum will be allowed to have no energy, no magnitude, and thus not be a quantum at all. There is an implication here for black holes.

We said earlier that opposing axes operate inversely. As x_A approaches ∞ for example, z_B approaches 0. But x_A can't really go to ∞ because the introduction of countless other x_A emissions from other quanta sponsor the dispersal of the first quantum's photonic mode into the modes of its neighbors. There will be a point at which you will no longer see that star, only the group of which he is a part. We may speculate that there will also be a point at which you see no stars, only the overall nonresonant sea of all that the system comprises. Such would constitute the event horizons of both black holes as well as universes, where very little light escapes because all light is, by scale, merged with modes which are not it. Beyond such event horizons, the space in which such energy is contained effectively appears to be invisible, since most of what it would emit is turned back inwards towards its own core in favor of a massive input dimension. But there is a limit to how long this can occur; once that near invisible system reaches maximum internal entropy, we who stand outside of the system with maximum entropy of our own (in the form of a pervasive non-change in energy gradient), become *the same* as that non-emitting system, gaining access to its contents across the differential border at which the last of its internal energy will have formerly met its intervening space requirements.

On the trail of every photon is the slice of a black hole. z_B measures the amount of intervening space drawn in by a quantum at the completion of each cycle, fueling its own compression into the next cycle. If x_A is the exhalation, z_B is the inhalation.

Assertion 70. Three relationships to the speed of light dictate the conditions for perceiving an event.

Below light speed
Although the r_B and t axes are parallel, they do not necessarily share the same scale. Quantic collections bigger than a quantum will require more independent flop states to align their x_A emission modes, not to mention their coupling relationships. It will thus take such collections a larger number of completed t cycles to match one unit of r_B distance; this is the sub-lightspeed condition in which multiple packets of cycle information can be emitted as the collection moves from its current space-spatial location to that of a target volume.

Above light speed
Quantic collections smaller than a (not necessarily fundamental) quantum—people-as-pre-energy moving on an Earth-as-quantum for example—will transmit information faster than the ability of the quantum to complete a cycle. This renders such collections a form of pre-energy to the quantic volume in question, and it will only be upon the organization of such preenergy that the quantic volume will register the change as anything other than one of its effectively infinite phasic modes. It will take more separation distances r_B to match one unit of cycle time, rendering time a measure of space in this case. Counting flop cycles works like this, since a flop is the phasic angular (spatial) shift of a quantum from one of the real-potential axes to another and the central quantum goes through 4^{12} of such flops across its various dimensions. $\sqrt{2}$, 2π, and 2.0109 are also spatial as discussed earlier.

The main thing to note about superquantum magnitudes is that they don't necessarily render it impossible to exceed the speed of light so much as they render it very difficult (but not impossible) for the system they describe to process any changes to itself which occur faster than a cycle tick. We can, however, get around this limitation by passing information to a nearby metaresponse system which keeps track of the change in relationship between sender and receiver. This is how spin-antispin pairs are observed in physics experiments, and how the brain receives information regarding specific micro locations in the body. Though it is natural to wonder how such distant sender-receiver pairs are connected in r_B space, it is more fitting for us to process them in θ_B space. If θ_B's orthogonal components in ϕ_A and Д space are not altered while θ_B is being changed, the metaresponse system, in conserving the energy assigned to this trio, will reflect the sender's changes in the receiver's changes.

Since we don't want to be vague about this, the metaresponse system I mean here is that subquantic collection of pre-energetic modes not visible to the quanta directly but through the recursive wraparound of ת. Every time I compress a previous cycle into a current one, I fast-forward the information sent across the previous cycle exponentially by the number of dimensions involved in that cycle. If I only knew how to send hourly information into tomorrow, I could speed up today by a factor of 24. But since tomorrow won't be registered until it comes, I can, by setting some of the other key states for today, force tomorrow to look mostly the way I want it by sending information only midway to the distance—having determined much of my resonant cycles by then (barring some cataclysmic quantic interruption). But if I can inform tomorrow by sending information halfway there, I should be able to inform halfway by sending information ¼ of the way. I should be able to send information ¼ of the way by sending it $1/8$ of the way. Then $1/16$ of the way. And then—wait a minute, can I send such information $1/32$ of the way, on a scale smaller than $1/24$ of the way? Yes, but no longer on the scale of an hour as planned. Ultimately I can send information near instantaneously to another by sending information to my own phase function for responding to that other right now, and this is the equivalent of compressing spacetime along a related z_B axis for one volume as the x_A axis for another. The r_B axes of spatial space are forever orthogonal to the z_Bs in dimension-space where me and my antipartner were originally coupled. Thus we have an interesting puzzle on our hands. You can't just separate quanta in time by pulling them apart in physical space anymore than you can separate historical events in time by pulling *them* apart in physical space. Time, though acting parallel to r_B, is its own dimension which is free to scale as it wants depending on the cycle we're looking at.

At light speed

Moving at exactly light speed is interesting only to the volume doing it. Such a volume takes exactly one completed cycle to get wherever it's going and, in its own frame, experiences only one moment of time beyond the start of its cycle. With only one moment of time beyond its origin, it knows only one frequency phase, one lifespan unit, one spherical orientation (determined by θ_B and Д in its base plane of action), and one of everything else including the characteristic, tiny mass-inducing resonance pattern with other quanta that is drawn back in from the vacuum with its passage. Standing on a light beam, everything is instantaneous to you UNTIL you bounce or are absorbed. Then your joyride ends and begins again with a new frequency, new energy level, and new everything else until the next collision. These new characteristics reflect the energy imparted to you or expended by you in your collision. As an emission mode, can you be destroyed? Yes, specifically when the input vacuum you drag around is equal to yourself. Then you don't go anywhere. You'd be a standing beam and not an emission. Can you be created? Yes, by virtue of vacuum potential squeezing in to replace other vacuum potentials on a level that can be quantically organized, your creation is almost automatic.[37]

On Д and emission color

The role of the "de" dimension Д in the above scenario establishes Д as a measure of emission deflection in cycle space. Proper spin deflection can change the "color" of an emission to anything ranging from its post-z_B orientation at Д $= -\pi/2$ to its pre-z_B orientation at Д $= 3\pi/2$. With three axes along this $<\phi_A, \theta_B,$ Д$>$ space, we can expect three colors associated with the $<\phi_A, \theta_B>$, $<-\theta_B,$ Д$>$, and $<\phi_A,$ Д$>$ planes as they continually re-form around the quantum. My guess based on this model is that these three regimes are associated with the three flavors of neutrino, with the one closest to approaching full z_B being the one with the least mass (neighborhood charge coupling) and the one departing full-magnitude z_B being the one with the most mass—since departing is an act of compression and the restoration of coupling outside of the quantum, which we defined as mass. It may or may not be a coincidence that the mass of the heaviest neutrino ν_τ, has been

---

[37] Unless this takes place on a pre-energetic level that the rest of the system can't know about.

estimated around the speed of light divided by 2π, then π. This would be a reflection of "decircumferencing" of two pairs of angular axes, one going full circle to make a ring, the other turning that ring halfway around to make a whole sphere. $^c/_{2\pi^2}$ is about 15.18 million flops, with each flop being a division of state change among neighbors. The electron itself takes about $1/30^{th}$ of this in order to exist, presumably because the full flop cycle c needs a quantum's 2π circumference and its 4 flop states per region divided out to give us only one state per region, but multiplied by the probability of the energy being active in that as opposed to the other 12 regions (.0854). Only half flops are provided by the quantum we're looking at (the other half provided by the resonant neighbor), we then divide this in half to get the number of flops expected for a particular neighbor to get from a particular resonance state in a particular one of its modes. The number is about 509,000 flops or electronvolts per the pair of cycles (c^2) involved in giving organized, resonant form to a complete neighborly exchange.[38]

Assertion 71. Half-complementarity and the exchange of interacting reference frames

The claim: While the 12- and 4-cycles may be natural to all observable systems regardless of scale, the unfolding of such mapped cycles against their parent functions' cycles, if the parent and subcycles follow the same half-complementary mapping, will be in reverse.

This follows from the previous assertions and is best illustrated with three examples.

Example 1

Even though the Earth spins counterclockwise, the imposition of day upon its regions proceeds clockwise. This is because the fractions of the day unfold in rising, peaking, setting order while the regions passing through those fractions of the day unfold in last-from-current, recent-from-current, current order, where day progress and regional fixity form a half-complementary axis.

Example 2

As a space traveler moves faster and faster towards the speed of light, his aging against the outside reference frame slows down. Speeding up, he goes from low speed to high speed while his activity goes from allowing high numbers of time flops to low numbers of time flops, where speed and time form half-complementary axes.

Example 3

The introduction of greater disorder into a system crystallizes the forms of order which describe that system as a system. In this way, matter and form may be thought of as the ultimate state of coherence in a particular experiential construct as a thing stands against a reference frame not itself. Even the 5th orange among 20 is distinguishable by its 5th-ness, its location, its relationship to the other 19. Where forms like this are determined by their distinguishability from neighboring forms, a linearizing operation as illustrated in the math assertions can and does render the experience of form as compressible to (and ultimately replaceable by) a projection of itself in a frame determined by the observer.

Recall that half-complementarity is where we have two axes in a 2D space at right angles to each other, where one axis measures like-attracting behavior while the other axis measures like-denying behavior. The standard $<x, ix>$, real potential axis can be considered half-complementary with respect to real behaviors to the extent that the more you perform real actions along x, the more your real and your complementary-real responses increase. But the more you perform potential-response actions along ix, the more your potential-real behaviors decrease and your potential-complement responses increase. Real actions not only increase themselves but also the responses to those actions. Potential actions increase the likelihood of real actions but decrease the energy of potential complement actions with respect to real actions.

---

[38] This is only one possible explanation of why electrons and (theorized) tau neutrinos would weigh what they weigh given the geometries involved.

ix "give me more of –*x* and less of myself"

-*x* "give me more of -*x* (which   *x* "give me more of *x* (which is
is more of myself)"   more of myself)"

-*ix* "give me more of *x* and less of myself"

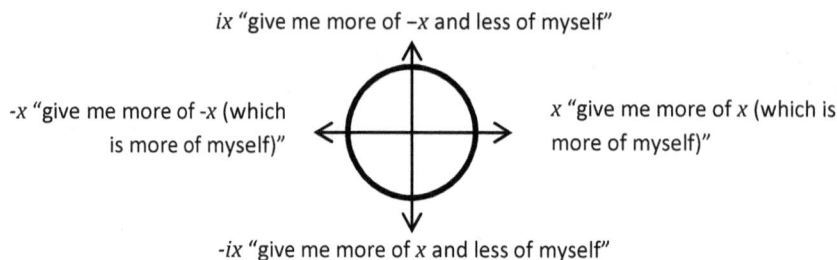

Figure 42-1: Half-complementary <u>with respect to the axis x</u>

Let us consider a "vertical analogy" to be a situation in which a set defined on half-complementary axes is both the subset of—yet a responder to—an equally arranged half-complementary superset of which it is part. The superset characteristics, from the framework of the subset, will also be considered a responder to that subset. Consider further that the subset we are considering interacts with other, nonintersecting, equally arranged, half-complementary subsets of its superset (defined as "neighbors") in the same actor-responder manner as it does with the superset. To the extent that responses to each set's half-complementary axes are arranged in the same way (the same angular order) then the set's superset, will evolve in the same direction as the set's neighbors: in the opposite direction as the set itself.

This is an exotic way of saying that, if things like personality assume a half-complementary gear-like structure, and if I believe that things like my home city can be personified in the way that my neighbors can, then to the extent that I think I can interact with my home city, I will perceive my city as responding to my behaviors in the way that a regular neighbor would. Anything we personify will tend to work like this including pets, employers, communities, and the God or gods we may believe in.

Half-complementarity with respect to an axis is a natural consequence of real-imaginary space. The real axis, commonly known by its radial magnitude, increases itself magnitude-wise, but evolves angle-wise towards its own exhaustion on the i axis—commonly defined by its angular relationship to the real rather than its magnitude. It's actually the $-i$ axis which evolves towards more real projected magnitude. So systems trained to respond to their interactants as if those interactants have cycles similar to themselves will develop half-complementary dynamics in which real dynamics augment each other while potential dynamics complement each other. We will return to this idea later when I discuss metaresponsive systems.

Assertion 72. In order to be considered living, an event must sustain its own cycles against its environment, sustain its own internal cycles against itself, and consume energy for these purposes.
This is one of many definitions I gave in earlier books.

Assertion 73. The dimensions of living processes may be mapped using the 12-cycle.
A living thing must be described by cycles in the first place. Because the above conditions for living include both self-response as well as interaction with the environment, a 4-cycle will be insufficient because it lacks 30° half-way points for reflecting on states included in its history. Now given that living things must possess the above qualities, we can begin with the basic mapping outlined in the Time and Axis Mapping table and simply insert the qualities where they fit best. We can do this because, as we've already maintained, the preexisting cycle determines later cycles. There is no reason to believe that living things should have evolved an ordering all their own which defies the natural energetic progression found in their quanta.

The twelve dimensions should be expected to compel the existence of bodily mechanisms consisting roughly of the following roles:

- x_A, "internal light" or visible dynamics. Since "internal light" is excessively abstract, we'll stick with "visible dynamics" as a testament to the way light is actually processed by the body anyway.
- ϕ_A, comparison phases against the main referenced internal dynamic direction
- z_A, the dimension for assessing the separations between (and range of effect of) internally visible dynamics x_A and internal comparisons against those dynamics ϕ_A
- t, the time dimension for regulating the chain of necessary internal biological processes
- r_B, the distance dimension for assessing the energy to be expended for reaching targets
- θ_B, the target comparison dimension for assessing the separations between a reference object and another reference object
- z_B, an input dimension for receiving whatever state is natural to the behavioral "vacuum" after a family of visible dynamics has passed through it
- τ, a state completion dimension for processing a finished cycle for some target object
- m, a dimension for processing the level of energetic coupling in the surrounding environment
- Д, a dimension for measuring deviations from a certain environmental reference point
- β, a dimension for measuring the net energy available to an external environment
- נ, a dimension for processing completed cycles of bodily states for the next visible dynamic

In traditional astrology, the above states are each mapped broadly to a sign. Indeed, this mapping bears a strong resemblance to that of Aries through Pisces—something I discuss in the Sabian Symbols section of the first book *FSA*. We know, however, that reality is much more complicated than a section by section division of the body, since there is so much overlap among our biological functions. Instead, it will be more useful to think of the 12-model as implying not so much an arrangement of body regions so much as a patterned series of specialized physiological states. Still I include the flattened 2D degree for each of these states as well as the signs associated with those degrees since this is, after all, an astrology book.

Dimension	Biological System	Degree	Sign
x_A	**General behavioral character**; how one initiates actions given previous inputs, including involuntary and <u>voluntary behavior, the face, and involuntary aspects of the muscular system</u>	0°	Aries
ϕ_A	**Identity**; current standards and preferences for comparing against displayed behaviors and chosen experiences; this includes preferences for food and how the contents of food are selected and preferentially processed; broadly, the <u>upper digestive system, nesting, and preferred learning behaviors as well as species-typical body type</u>.	30°	Taurus
z_A	**Internal evaluation systems**; reflective assessment behavior, natural mannerisms and other acts aimed at getting minor behaviors to line up with identity standards; non-complex target alignment with pre-conscious goals; relatedly, <u>automatic physiological maneuvers</u> towards desired states within the current phase of bodily action; <u>the respiratory system in its stable state</u>	60°	Gemini
t	**Motivated physiological alignment** with goals that do not appear attainable at the current phase of bodily action; how one trades satisfied cycles of internal motivation for the next cycle; relatedly, how one cancels the current internal state in favor of another; how one demonstrates want; strongly related to the <u>motivation-enabling aspects of the endocrine system (hormones)</u> as well as internal emotional processing, parental and basic bonding instinct such as the <u>social and pleasure-seeking neurotransmitter dynamics</u>; also, the personal-goal aspects of dreaming	90°	Cancer
r_B	**Display behavior**, mobilizing behavior for sending selected information to specific targets; related to the <u>circulatory system</u> for sending more energy to certain bodily functions involved in the display, along with the <u>voluntary aspects of the muscular system</u>.	120°	Leo
θ_B	**Target-matching behavior** for reconciling the differences among target experiences; related to reasoning and procuring of resources, likely associated with the separation of useful from wasteful content, the <u>lower digestive system and internal dissonance-handling aspects of the nervous and endocrine systems</u>	150°	Virgo
z_B	**Seeking and feedback behavior**, associated with voluntary communication with interactants; adornments, idle time, and preferred exchange partners, experiences that bring pleasure (which is not the same as the way that pleasure is felt—a matter associated with t—or the way that pleasure is publicly shown—a matter associated with r_B); the <u>lymphatic system and internal functions of the urinary/excretory system</u> for filtering out non-preferred contents of experience; <u>the respiratory system in its preferred intake state</u>	180°	Libra
τ	**Behavior for a variety of termination responses**, including context switching and coercion, aggression, <u>psychological coping</u>; ejection of unwanted or offloaded materials and thus the <u>output functions of the urinary/excretory system</u> as well as the general <u>reproductive system</u>	210°	Scorpio
m	**Systems for being seen in the environment**; broadly associated with the <u>integumentary system</u> (hair skin & nails); outward appearance in the eyes of other organisms and the mechanisms of protection from them; characteristics that stand out	240°	Sagittarius
Д	**Systems for being compared to others in the environment**; the <u>genetic map, broad skeletal system, and general body plan</u>; characteristics that render one a "normal" reference against which others are measured	270°	Capricorn
β	**Information-gathering and summarizing systems** including <u>cohort characteristics</u>, types of information processed by the senses for active decision making; the <u>social structure and world-handling, peripheral aspects of the nervous system</u>	300°	Aquarius
Ꙃ	**Save state processing**, a dimension for memory, the body maintenance activities associated with dreaming; broadly, mental conceptualization and senses for passive aspects of processing one's circumstances in general; <u>the brain and central nervous system's background functions</u>	330°	Pisces

Table 42-1: Biological mappings for approximating each dimenisions' function in 12-space

To the extent reasonable, I have mapped all 11 standard organ systems and underlined them. Although the broad systems may be mapped using the above scheme, the more familiar body regions such as the face, ears, and feet—as combinations of systems producing combinations of effects—may be located outside of their assumed regions. Further research should be conducted to determine if or where such regions may be reliably placed on the 12-cycle in a way that can be verified via statistics on medical data.

Beyond the normal use of senses

When we speak of the senses we normally think of the basic five—sight, hearing, touch, taste, and smell—along with the sixth unofficial sense of proprioception (the perception of one's internal body state). These senses can be satisfactorily explained in terms of chemistry, electrodynamics, and basic mechanics (in the case of hearing for example), with the brain acting as the major electrochemical processor for most of these functions. It is unfortunate, then that American science has developed a kind of bully culture in response to a discussion of sixth senses. Even though we know that the feeling of hunger or that of fear is felt despite not being one of the major five, and even though we know people are made of atoms and atoms have electrical fields, talk of such things is nonetheless likely to get you laughed at. The "logical" response to a mention of auras, for example, is that—despite there being known gravitational and magnetic forces associated with massive bodies—the fields around humans are "too small to mean anything." But who has proven this? Why would nanoparticles participate in the Casimir Effect, why would Jupiter hold a massive magnetic field, why would an atom have an electron cloud while humans, standing in between these scales, have nothing to measure *at all*? Under what science can a person simply declare something to not be there without checking and have everyone accept it? Here we have the phenomenon of fields which work everywhere else from the quantum level to the intergalactic level, but somehow remains widely unstudied in the people who study these things. It's weird, that's all I'm saying. So let us begin our exploration of the quantum mechanical aspects of spirituality with a simple example of how the laws of physics probably do apply to humans too.

Earlier I talked about "passable error" as being where an error-carrying system pushes its errors onto another error-carrying system which it observes. For example, when you open your eyes to the night sky, you may believe you are seeing the stars all at once. Of course the light from each star has a good chance of being many years old by the time you see it, meaning that looking at the sky is a lot like looking at thousands of history books at once. Practically speaking, we would say "it's basically at the same time," but the stars themselves would beg to differ; if you had bounced your own reflected light off of a mirror located on one of those stars, the image of you would be much younger than your eventual age by the time such light returned. If every star had a mirror, every reflection of you would differ in age accordingly, so that the claim of seeing a sky full of objects at different distances "all at once," though true enough for your own reference frame, would not hold true *everywhere* in general. Furthermore on an immediate level, it still takes time for the information received by your rods and cones to be transferred to and translated in your brain. As you move your gaze to another section of the sky it takes even more time. So you really are *not* seeing it all at once. And when you claim to do so, you are passing the perception time onto some other system rather than your own visual processing capacity—likely that of your "attention" capacity. This is passable error. You supposedly did it all at once. It's always some other thing which took all the time, right?

Related to the concept of passable error is concept of sense-collapsing. This is where, not having the (usually social-acceptance) mechanisms for processing experiences, we simply classify those experiences as something more commonly acceptable. If I asked you which of the five senses described stress perception, for example, you might say touch. But touching what? Your own brain? Or perhaps you feel suspicious of someone. We might say that this isn't one of the five senses (and maybe not even the sixth one). But it is perceived. And yet we have noises impinge on our ears all the time without extracting the information those noises contain (as in voices in a crowd). Does this mean that the undistinguished voice—not decipherable to anyone yet certainly included in the soundwave—was not heard? If we say that it was heard but only unacknowledged, does that mean that we hear *everything* that hits our eardrums within auditory range? Why would certain things that shake our auditory hair cells count as impacting the senses while other things wouldn't count? Just as certain kinds of passable error in human behavior might be attributable to cognitive convenience, I believe that certain kinds of sense-collapsing in humans (much like dismissal of certain physical laws without proof) are a matter of social norming. Our brains play tricks to make our worlds appear smooth. Part of those tricks lie in reducing what we see to something we actually don't see, but which sounds better to other people.

The point of the above examples is to convince the reader that basic physical laws present us with basic complexities, while our training into adulthood compels us to collapse the application of these laws into a family of a few prosocial simplifications. Rather than saying that our emotional state is a valid dimension of perception—thereby giving form to a thing which others can't easily know—we are trained to skip this as a "sense" and consider the senses to include only those modalities that involve externally viewable events. If I can't see something that happened with you, I'm taught not to accept it as involving one of the five "basic" senses. Even proprioception—perhaps the most heavily felt sense of all—struggles to be counted. I think this is unfortunate, since proprioception, social perception, and emotion might be said to hold the key to many, many problems in the human condition. Now that we have the technology to scan bodies and perform calculations on what we find, the time to study such "intrasenses" may have arrived.

Hopefully I've convinced you that your body processes more than five kinds of perceptual information. Although we may have difficulties processing all 12 dimensions posited in our quantum mechanical model, such processing may still be possible. We already listed possible associations between the major organ systems and the dimensions of our 12-model; so even an obscure dimension like τ can be processed not so much on the basis of a "sudden" stimulus,[39] but on the basis of a sudden proprioceptive expectation for the end of a situation via a set of physiological behaviors aimed at framing how such a lifespan limit is responded to. The issue isn't really what constitutes a sense, but what counts as a coherent physiological family of responses to a certain kind of input. Our particular 12-model suggests 12 kinds of information for the quanta which constitute us.[40] Aside from the five externally verifiable senses, we also have dimension-specialized modes which the body can process given appropriate learning.

On modes of existence

In this section I will discuss the implications of the 12-model for human capabilities. Along the way I will offer some hypotheses regarding how such theories relate to more traditional spiritual constructs.

Assertion 74. Dimension m implies the existence of coherent character applied to intervening space

There are quanta and then there are resonances among those quanta. There are the unstable, uncoupled quanta of the post Big Bang Universe and heavily coupled quanta theorized in black holes. The H_2O bonds of ice and the H_2O bonds of water vapor. The difference is in the interverning connections and not in the objects themselves. Just as things like electrons and broader material substances can be granted mass through the energy they pass to the things that bind them, we see how the bonds or resonant patterns themselves can have a reproducible character independent of the specific atoms or quanta involved. A pi bond is a pi bond no matter what pair-sharing carbon you look at. Furthermore, we've seen how—in the case of even the most basic theory of light, excitation modes can travel without necessarily dragging along the particles which adopt them. In the chemical called aromatic benzene, the double bonds between carbons circle continuously around the 6-carbon ring. On the surface of an ocean, the wavefront moves transversely despite the water not necessarily doing so. Accordingly, as surely as a live body and a dead body differ in their activity patterns and not necessarily in their cell content, we may hypothesize that the characteristic cycle of energy exchanges among human quanta can, at least, hold a measurable state independent of the body that hosts it. If such exchanges are capable of deterministically sending their resonance patterns beyond their familiar quantic neighborhood *or* if those exchanges can be captured and integrated into the resonances of neighboring packages of quanta, then we have a case for the existence of a human character beyond the human body roughly akin to "spirit."

This is not to say that such a separable collective energy dynamic is necessarily stable beyond the body, only that it exists—at minimum—as long as the body is alive and yet is not equal to that body.

In *144* I defined **spirit** as **a set of extraperceptual information that normally comes with a thing as most interactants interact with it**. If most people tend to associate Ancient Rome with a classic caesar-holding civilization, then part of the "spirit" of Ancient Rome will be found wherever objects or brain scanned people show normal behaviors indicating response to a classic caesar-holding civilization. In other words, though Ancient Rome may be dead, artifacts from Ancient Rome, Ancient

---

[39] And then again, thanks to our discussion of passable error, we know that "sudden" doesn't really imply "instantaneous" the way we might think. So although one might argue that the sense of one's influence ending alongside approaching fight behavior might not count as a proper sense (despite being emotional), we couldn't deny fight emotion as a feeling on the basis of its non-instantaneous timespan. Smell isn't instantaneous either. Nor is vision. Both of these standard senses take time to be processed. Using the duration of a stimulus as an argument for or against it being the foundation of a "sense" won't work unless we agree to start drawing limits on the timescales involved. But if we do this, what would we make of hearing, touch, and taste?

[40] Here we run into a philosophical puzzle. Should there always be at least one physiological mode for handling each dimension? What about basic 3D space? Don't we handle all axis directions of space in the same way? In a true dimensionalization of 3D space, I don't think so. $<x, y, z>$ may consist of axes which are equal in theory, but as we've seen, reality presents us with gravitational fields, emitter directions, isoshells, and reference frame deviations. True $<x, y, z>$ space is not equal in all directions, nor are the responses of our bodies to it. We change with altitude, we change with sun-radial seasonality, and we change with spin orientation/reference point differences during the day or night. Even the atoms of an amoeba may be expected to reflect energy absorption differences under conditions like these. If we assume that their constituent quanta care about where they are amongst neighbors, that is. So yes, I do believe that we should entertain the possibility of a physiological mode for each dimension, keeping in mind that dimensions like those of idealized $<x, y, z>$ aren't actually what we deal with in the real world. It's more like $<r_B, \theta_B, \phi_B$ or $z_B>$, where the presence of other energy and mass sources actually matters.

Roman Enthusiasts, and certain media depictions of Ancient Rome may yet be said to maintain the spirit of Ancient Rome as a response-generating dynamic. Does this mean that we can locate the spirit of Ancient Rome on a globe somewhere? Not necessarily. At the very least, interactions exist between the interacting objects, not within them (not in the same way). So we cannot expect a thing's interaction pattern to stay with the thing—especially after the thing has ceased to function. We can, however, expect its interaction pattern to be synonymous with certain organized real world effects while the thing is functioning. The more closely associated those effects are in the real world regardless of the presence of the thing itself, the more likely we are to assign the thing form beyond its physical boundaries. This doesn't quite get us into the realm of ghosts and ethereal things, but it does form part of the foundation for a discussion of such.

Assertion 75. The m dimension makes it easier for certain patterns to prefer certain contexts over others

The m dimension assigns mass as a function of organized bond formation among multiple quanta. These bonds occur as patterned resonances mainly among the energetic boundaries or valence shells of such quanta, and yet there is a basic condition for optimally reproducing such bonds. To the extent that a particular collection of quanta undergoes enough cycles which affect enough external neighbors in a consistent enough way, we can expect that the bond character itself will be able to move around, particularly in areas where the vacuum density gradient has a similar structure to neighboring gradients. Checker patterns have an easier time reinstantiating themselves on chessboards than on baseball fields because the arrangement of space on the former is more similar to the checker pattern than the latter. Relatedly, energy exchange patterns are best reproduced in contexts which favor the particular exchanger involved. In other words, the spirit of a dog will have a harder time being reproduced in the spirit of a computer, and an easier time being reproduced in the spirit of another dog. ✳ Should we ever develop teleportation technology for reproducing say, human fMRI patterns in a simulator on a distant planet, we may theorize that such reproduction will be helped by similar atmospheric conditions and potential-energy related characteristics of the region, and hindered by dissimilar versions of these things.

Assertion 76. The Д dimension makes it harder for quanta to view their own interaction patterns

Just as differential energy Д occurs as a deviation against the mass dimension in a quantum, a pattern of energy collection equipped with changing Д values across its components will adopt a structure along a range of frequencies in the plane of the angle, making it unlikely that the interaction pattern will be accurately perceivable by the quanta which bear them. That is, things will have a harder time perceiving their own extraperceptual information because the options for deviating from their basic bond patterns are astronomically high. What are the chances of finding 1 trillion clocks whose second hand all happen to be on the 12? Not very high. Accordingly, the form of the exchanges adopted by an exchanger will in general be difficult to reproduce in the same dimension that the exchanger is in. If spirits exist, people will likely have difficulty seeing their own. It might be difficult, but not impossible.

Assertion 77. Cycle space may facilitate the capture of one's cyclical dynamics

The dimensions associated with circumferential progression ϕ_A, θ_B, and Д are more likely to defy solid values that everyone can agree upon and will be more likely to be described by functions or oscillatory values. We can expect this to be especially true for collections consisting of large numbers of quanta. So even though it is possible to store a family of cycles using a space of rotation matrices, such cycles will likely be more easily recapitulated through other cyclical means. This is a formal way of saying that, although you can store a movie on film or on a hard drive, the ultimate effects of the movie are best conveyed when it is played. Cyclical personalities, biological systems, season, and orbits, though describable by static values, lose much of their ability to affect their neighbors if they are not dynamically replayed. Thus, if we want to simulate, say, a Abraham Lincoln in a holochamber, we will need to store him in the form of an executable algorithm rather than lookup table of static descriptors. This is probably obvious. What it means for us, however, is that it will be easier to study things like personalities by looking at things that move like personalities. For accurate capture of our own spirit dynamics for example, sounds, movies, visualizations, and voice may be expected to work better than lists or logic. To understand, for example, the effects of our actions on another person from a different perspective, observing another "moving" system will illustrate the point better than observing a static system. In matters of dynamic behavior, showing or telling is usually better than writing.

Assertion 78. Using cycle space, observation of one's own exchange dynamic is made easier through trained externalizing of one's own cycle.

In *144* I defined the **SOUL** as **the spirit of a thing believed to be alive**, given the previous definition of spirit. One does not have to believe in a soul in order to use this definition. It is only a tool for assigning characteristics to a thing's effects rather than the thing itself, given that such a thing is living. In the living, however, the thing will possess a cycle-like dynamic, meaning that we most likely won't be able to observe its dynamics in any fixed way, especially if the thing is us. We can, however, locate a dynamic similar to our own in certain animated things like songs, movies, visualization or games. Building an analog to ourselves in this way, we adopt the representative symbols, x_A emissions at r_B distances with ב histories for each of the possible states of our own dynamic. This means that, if I want to perceive my own interactional dynamics as a kind of semi-embodied, soul-like construct, I will need to do something like the following:

1. Locate experiences in the real world that behave most like me.
2. Animate them. This can be via movie, song, or (if these things exist mainly in writing like the account of a historical figure) through visualization of how I think those things would have responded to their worlds.
3. Place myself into contexts similar to theirs.
4. Do the above for the major roles which I play.
5. Briefly imagine how they would behave in a realm I want to explore, then imagine how my own behavior would be uniquely mine instead, and why I would favor this.

The above process essentially gives a representative form in x_A space to the stereotyped progression Д of a person's own dynamic m over the space of major behaviors he or she occupies. Steps 3 and 5 in particular prime the person's ב dimension for exploring his or her own potential actions in alternative contexts, making it easier for the person to subconsciously visualize themselves in realms other than the normal world. Step 4 is important for ensuring that the person visualizes the right role (out of many) for the realm he or she wants to explore.[41]

Perhaps the above process is best summarized by the following statement:

> To perceive my own soul, I place myself into the lives of things most like me, and animate such placement in my conception.

I concluded the above based only on the roles played by $x_A, m,$ Д, and ב in 12-space.

Assertion 79. The experiential space through which I have passed defines the events I attract along the z_B axis

This aligns with the definition of z_B, and has many, many implications for things like one's attitude, dreaming, daily events, the results of certain behaviors, and the kinds of help or hindrances one attracts. Considering that most of a superquantic unit (like a human) will consist of intervening space crowded out by its constituent quantic clusters, the number of possibilities for the kinds of inputs we attract will be vast, but as predictably constrained as the behaviors that bring them about. How do we better control what we attract? The answer suggested by our 12-model is straightforward and perhaps a little unfortunate: We attract events which continue the patterns we're used to emitting. Most of the time this means we won't attract anything noticeable or favorable—just the fuel to continue doing the same stuff we're already doing. To attract different events, on a different time cycle, we may expect to produce different emissions on either the scale or the scope of that same time cycle. Although I may not need to put in 50 years of work to produce 50 years of successful marriage, I may need to put in 50 years' worth of erasure of marriage-unsuccessful training, no matter how long that takes. This is the equivalent of passing through r_B space of a different kind, surrounded by gradients of a different θ_B density, applying an appropriate termination (or modification) behavior τ to the exchange we wish to leave.

---

[41] One of my major role models, for example, is Josef Stalin—for reasons I may or may not have talked about in another book. I would not, however, want to apply the Stalin framework to my regular meditative explorations. So if I wanted to see myself in the context of exploration rather than institutional inimitability, I might use a video game or movie character instead. Game characters have the added benefit of being associated with your own decisions as well as being unable to truly pay any consequences for anything.

Assertion 80. The β dimension determines which environments one is able to habitually navigate.
As the sole temperature dimension in 12-space, β is associated with the conditions under which stable quanta and superquanta are allowed to form. When energy is too high, resonances between pre-quantic regions can be expected to change too quickly to settle into a fixed, repeatable structure. When energy is too low, the process of transferring energy beyond the quantum is curbed, though the process of keeping energy within the quantic collection (as in planets, other solid matter, and Bose-Einstein condensates) is made more efficient. As handlers of energy across a range of grades, our body systems can be expected to change their operation not only with changing temperature, but with changing metabolic focal points across systems. Thus we have the basis of homeostasis (preferred biological stable states) in the form of genetically mandated energy passage among body systems—such passages as are helped or hindered by the environmental conditions that attend them.

The informational exchanges in the environments that surround us are the primary foundation for our sense feedback from the world. If we can be thought of as superquanta, the world around us may be thought of as our intervening space for exchanges. But these exchanges will produce varied effects depending on which among our body systems we pay attention to. Certain environments will favor spontaneity on our part as they match the conditions for our brand of x_A emission. Other environments related to dimension m will favor attention to "spirit" as they match the conditions for amplifying the information we naturally impose on others' conception of us.[42] Dynamic, animated structures associated with our dimension Д may amplify our tendency to have superquanta which are not us be associated with us (helping viewers of such quanta classify our differential energy deviations from m). Given that there are 12-dimensions in our model we can expect 12 kinds of idealized contexts for supplementing or changing the exchange patterns we already have. So we can think of our ambient environments as providing the right or wrong range of temperatures (energy levels) for our resonances to grow.

Assertion 81. High ambient information produces stress. Low ambient information produces sensitivity to one's own internal instability.
In an excessively high energy environment, people (as with other quantic collections) are more likely to have their stable resonances broken. Should a person value homeostatic stability actively enough, his or her body will seek to rebuild those bonds for whatever system is most affected by the instability. Extended over the long term, we have the basis for external stressor-induced illness—where one biological dimension struggles to undo the insults imposed on it by the person's decision to place themselves in non-preferred circumstances. The resonance-breaking caused by being somewhere I know I don't want to be—regardless of how reasonable the excuse—tells my body to go into repair mode trying to force stabilized resonances where there is no stability to be had. The two classes of solution to this involve either 1) adjusting to the new environment or 2) leaving. Staying and staying stressed in my experience, though, often seems rooted in yet another behavioral pattern typical of a different system, the body maintenance and memory dimension נ.

In an excessively low energy environment, we may expect something like boredom. But recall that there are 12 proposed environments here and not all of them have to do with outward activity. "Boredom" will apply chiefly to an underactive emission dimension x_A or display dimension r_B coupled with an expectation for action which has been trained over the time state t. Other systems like those describing my termination dimension τ cannot get "bored," only underactive. Underactivity in any dimension is hardly a problem unless I pay attention to such underactivity via נ or Д state, since in order to gauge a thing as underactive I must also have either a saved baseline נ or an externally compared baseline Д for what "active" looks like. Given underactive exchanges with external inputs, the subquanta constituting the underactive system may have an easier time gaining input from themselves, rendering it sensitive to its own processes. I estimate, then, that boredom as we see it is usually less about there being fewer options on the outside and more about there being more *expected* options on the inside. Thus being bored and being antsy go hand in hand.

---

[42] This is reminiscent of the astrological effect of Sagittarius—making images bigger.

Assertion 82. The save state מ retains the emission pattern for the previous completed cycle before a new one begins, not just for the memory, but for every biological dimension

Although commonly associated with the brain, save states are adopted for all quanta across all dimensions, provided they have cycling neighbors which provide for this function. A previous state for the emission dimension x_A. A previous state for the distance dimension r_B. By subtracting the mem state from current state of whatever system we're looking at, we get the degree of change. By dividing out the length of a single cycle t, we get the degree of change per cycle, also called rate or velocity.[43] It is possible to form resonances with other quantic collections which respond specifically to such rates of change in a central quantum, and this is the basis of a **metaresponse system: a system which includes components which respond to the dynamics among other components in that same system**. Our brains contain extensive mechanisms for metaresponse to most of the rest our bodies, but since each organ system comprises its own cells and its own interquantic dynamics, each organ system will also have its own pattern of מ states for those components.

Assertion 83. Time-related internally generated stressors are a function of the מ, t, and τ states in conjunction with other states.

Where a body adopts a state of time-related instability, the מ dimension stores the last state for the biological system in question while the t dimension stores the completion window for any associated state change and the τ dimension stores the expected completion window, the last one determined externally via basic biology, genetics, or outside classification (Д) or internally via other systems' מs. For example, internal stress over a generally emitted behavior which comes in the form of "This is going too slowly" may be roughly formulated as

$$too\ slow = \frac{x_A - x_{A_מ}}{\tau} - \frac{x_A - x_{A_מ}}{t - t_0}$$

or

$$too\ slow = \frac{what\ I'm\ doing - what\ I\ just\ thought\ about\ doing}{how\ long\ it's\ supposed\ to\ take} - \frac{what\ I'm\ doing - what\ I\ just\ thought\ about\ doing}{my\ current\ time - when\ I\ started}$$

If the above is negative then the activity will be considered faster than expected. The point here is to illustrate that, in the absence of exchanges with an external set of circumstances of energy β, a system may still produce rich expectation data by combining information from several of its own internal dimensions.

Assertion 84. The quanta of a body is spatially connected, though not necessarily connected in other ways, to the quanta of another body to which it is spatially attached.

This means that a physical human roaming the Earth, if we explode his atoms and his quanta while exploding the Earth's atoms and the Earth's quanta, will form a spatially contiguous region of quanta. The patterned exchanges within these two adjacent regions will not necessarily be aligned (unless the individual is dead)[44] and the internally generated emissions describing these regions will almost certainly not be aligned (since humans and the Earth have very different internal energetic properties), but the dimensions of physical space between individual quanta $<r_B, \theta_B, \phi_B$ or $z_B, \tau>$ will be consistently mappable to each other. Interestingly, this implies that spatial separations, spatial deviance, mass-cycle, vacuum input, and structure lifespan will be easier to publicly view and agree upon than any other groups of dimensions. Thus the function of the physical body and its duration are a tied to the quanta of the environment which surrounds it, rendering it a kind of pulse upon that larger body. It is odd to think of material things on Earth as being pulses of that Earth, but on a quantic level, the Earth megaquantum's preferred intervening space clearly includes us and our quanta in it—the Earth's exchanges permeating our own. This is related to the earlier discussions of gravity. I imagine we can easily escape this effect by leaving the Earth, but because we are genetically pre-coded based on Earth-relevant response mechanisms,

---

[43] In nonfundamental quanta where the flop structure is more elaborate than the simple speed of light, we can expect the rate to change further. Dividing out t again allows us to obtain the rate of change of the rate of change for the relevant dimension, its acceleration. For fundamental quanta we can expect this to be invariant if there is no lower portion into which a fundamental quantum can be broken without ceasing to be a fundamental quantum.

[44] Dead AND physically roaming? Hmm…

we can continue to expect our basic physiology and lifespans to remain what they are until we otherwise evolve in adaptation to the new environment.

Assertion 85. The body's general subforms, though not independent, are separable into three spaces.
Quanta are spatially connected to the space they're in and the volume structures that encase them, emission-wise connected to the family of phases they emit and the types of electromagnetic fields they resonate with, and interphysically connected to the intervening or neighbor-contextual regions they prefer. Not only does this imply three levels of basic quantum structure such as those of energy holders, energy exchangers, and force carriers of the Standard Model, but it also implies three levels of basic energetic structure for all empirically observable physical volumes in existence (as opposed to only dynamics or conceptual volumes). We may guess then, that a human contains a physical interaction structure, an inwardly active expressive pattern, and an outwardly active exchange volume. These are akin to the body, character, and spirit. Each can likely be reproduced and stored via the appropriate technology, but in our doing this, we can expect to fail at recreating the full individual unless the three spaces are unified in their general interactions with each other.

On Frankensteining

Recreating a physical body may be simple enough given our current cloning technology. This will be a matter of providing the correct environment for stem cell reproduction. Which such cloning, the general personality of the clone may be very similar to the original based on the recreation of stereotyped hormonal pathways alone. I do not believe there are any ethical issues posed by this, as it is essentially giving birth to a brand new, albeit weirdly familiar human. But what would we need to do in order to say, reproduce *you* on another planet 50 years from now? Not just someone who looks like you, but actual you with expectations, trained likes and all? We would also need to reproduce your current exchange patterns with the external world. As discussed before, this is better accomplished with an algorithm based on the current you's systems. This is also fairly easy given enough scanning technology, but very hard given another problem I will discuss shortly. In addition to reproducing your physical and interphysical space, we would also have to reproduce your psychological space—a strange blend of phasic calculations upon prior emitted behaviors which is heavily, HEAVILY time dependent not just with the stage of life, but with the time of year or day, the phases of family and career, and other such things. Is this doable? Probably. If we exist, I have no doubt that we can learn how we exist and copy the process. Still, reproducing psychologies is made difficult in the early 21st century for the same reason that reproducing world interactions is difficult: Our current society largely refuses to study certain avenues of human experience seriously, though such avenues pervade our lives.

Western science, as I've mentioned before, often responds to nonfavored topics with bullying. We can't model psychopathy, insecurity, loneliness behavior, certain kinds of mate-seeking, underclass or non-university identities, unfunded or unpeer-reviewed work. We can't model the fear of death, decisions made outside of the lab, ignoring of the American dream, familial collectivism, response to tradition, unprofitable data sets, expatriotism, authority or researcher distrust, class selection bias, or most issues that lie outside the realm of scholarly acceptability. Why? Because it's considered uncool to stand around these things or develop protocols which study them accurately. It is unpopular to study gods or a belief in God, but it is equally unpopular to claim atheism, to study spirituality in the mainstream, the occult, astrology, or investigate an entire array of practices humans employ to handle the unknown, including the arts and non-politics related social sciences—unless it's for "broken" people, that is. To model psychologies and psychologically motivated exchanges accurately, we first need to be okay with looking at them. But if we can't even mention them, the best we will be able to do is clone and (I suspect) cross ethical lines with various experimental paradigms imposed on our genetic clones as they become increasingly human. I don't believe such breaches of the cloned organism's developmental freedom would be necessary if we were simply allowed to study, then model the deeper motivations of the organism. But surely this is an issue which later generations of scholars will need to work out for themselves.

Assertion 86. A spirit is by definition outlined in terms of the resonances it comprises in light of the perceived object to which it belongs, but such resonances are not exclusive to the object.
This follows from the earlier definition of spirit, with an additional implication added. Just as a composed song need not be sung by one singer exclusively, a pattern of resonances may be located in other places besides the volume which hosts it.

This should be obvious. No individual object holds a monopoly on the frequencies it produces. Relatedly, a human may leave an impression both in person or through TV, showing how it is the emission pattern—visual or auditory—and not necessarily the physical relationships that matter.

Assertion 87. Frequency information can be transmitted via an appropriately configured medium, allowing communication of spirit-like information.

In the case of wifi, a sender sends a message via radio waves to a receiver which in turn decodes the message. In the case of light, an emitter sends a message via broader electromagnetic waves to a receiver which in turn selectively absorbs or reflects the information sent. In the case of gravity (as understood in the early 21st century), information currently called a force permeates the seemingly empty medium of the vacuum to inform the behaviors of large and small scale systems with large and small scale magnitudes. Clearly, however, gravity, electromagnetism, and time all seem to apply without the need for any medium other than the vacuum of space, and they do so over dimensions which can, at the very least, be made spatially independent of each other (1D, 3D, and 1D-tangentially to the first 1D respectively). If we include the nature of elliptical orbits alongside gravity, E and B field oscillations alongside electromagnetism, as well as relativistic effects alongside time, we see that all of these forces are allowed to oscillate between any two objects. So too is the extraperceptual information associated with a person allowed to oscillate as social behavior, visible change, neuronal, atomic, or quantic frequencies continually cycle through a regular pattern of states. We may assert that the extraperceptual, spirit-like information associated with a person—to the extent that it is simply processed as another frequency pattern in the neighborhoods of those volumes which process it—can also be transmitted, allowing such spirit (like a radio signal) to move across media most conducive to its mobility.

Speculation on resonance transmission and the energetic properties of certain substances

I propose that the mobility of spirit-like information is strongly tied to the mobility of the volume it belongs to. If phones had spirits, they would travel across the space of "people wishing to stay in contact" along the emission-input axis. If the color blue were associated with spirit information, it might best be represented by an angle in $<\phi_A, \theta_B, Д>$ space for representing brightness emitted versus absorbed, blur versus intensity (saturation), and hue respectively—each deviations from the reasonably associated axes $<x_A, z_B, m>$. This same kind of color sphere may be used to describe certain people's reports of auras as well as the crystal emission and absorption structure of certain substances.

Let us define a **bond** as **a shared resonance relationship between two energy emitters across one of the spacetime dimensions** (of which there are 12 in our main model), **through which energy is passed**.

Stones and Energy

On the topic of color structure, surely the reader has heard of certain materials being imbued with a certain energy pattern. Sage for cleansing, hematite for grounding, and pyrite for value-related lessons for example. Why would a rock or other substance possess any kind of energy? But we already know that materials are defined by their chemical properties, especially their valence bonds, the bond angles, the energy therein, and the flow of energy carriers across those bonds. So the question is not *why* an iron magnet or radioactive uranium would have specific energy transmission properties, but how. The *why* is answered by the repetition structure of the substance's molecules (packages of its quanta). The how is related to the way in which the various orientations of elements in the molecules change with respect to each other, influencing resonance cycling among neighbors. It strikes me as intriguing that rocks and other materials hold their color as a byproduct of how their arranged components consistently bend each other's stored energy in quantic spacetime, but I see no simpler explanation than this. For molecules, it's all in the atomic bonds. For atoms, it's all in the subatomic bonds.

The phenomenon of radioactivity shows that certain substances, by virtue of being what they are, emit a characteristic energy with a certain probability or half-life. Though this is not necessarily the case with all substances, we do know that even molecules like those of water, H_2O, are predisposed to particular geometric structures in the bonds they form. Here, though the water molecule may not emit another energy-carrying unit in the way that more complex substances do, it does impose a characteristic resonance pattern upon the region around it which influences how nearby molecules interface with it. I know this may sound abstract, but that surrounding resonance pattern is akin to the water molecule's "spirit." Not in the familiar human sense of spirit, but in the sense that we defined spirit earlier as a set of interactional information associated with a thing beyond the thing itself. Of course that surrounding realm of patterned interaction can be expected to decrease exponentially as we move away from the molecule, but like a standard spherical wavefront it may still be characterizable by a state function indicative of its favored resonances in 12-space as we move away from it with increasing radius. ✳ I envision a function $\Psi(< x_A, \phi_A, z_A, t, \ r_B, \theta_B, \phi_B, \tau, m, Д, \beta, ɲ >)=\theta_{Res}$ which tells us which frequencies would best resonate with a quantic volume at a specific radial and angular location. ✳ A well-formed database of such functions over the space of known chemicals would likely reveal not only an underlying quantum paradigm for chemical reactions, but would simultaneously inform us as to the more mystical properties of substances.

Currently, a basic view of the periodic table sometimes includes electron affinity and electronegativity[45] values for the elements. Yet we know that, in actual compounds, elements will not simply adopt just any old orientation in the bonds they form. A singular value for an element's tendency to bond with other elements only tells us that a certain valence charge exists, but not how that charge promotes specific angular arrangements with those other elements and, accordingly, very little about the chemical properties of compounds which the original element is inclined to form. This is not a criticism of previous research but a call to build on such research as our technology for doing so evolves. ✳ Elemental qualities like electron affinity and electronegativity should be spherically mapped using a frequency function on surrounding space. Rather than settling for an electronegative value of say, 2, future research should attempt to show that an element has an electronegativity of 2 at a specific radius and pair of spherical angles, an electronegativity of less than 2 at other spherical angles, and an electronegativity closer to 0.7 at still other angles depending on where you are on a sphere of a certain reference radius. This atomic sphere will allow us to better understand not just chemical properties on the elemental level, but will give us a valuable mathematical tool for understanding fields of quantic resonance surrounding bigger collections of substances like sulfur as its internal sphere is recursively reinforced to emit a human-perceivable surface area wavefront of a particular vibratory character. As with the Sun, an element may be predicted to hold a typical resonance gradient about its sphere which, in some cases, constructively interferes to produce fields which act over much greater than atomic-scale distances. Thus our 12-model anticipates a common mechanism for explaining the polarity of a water molecule and the reported healing properties of quartz: via a quantic resonance field imposed upon surrounding space. With the added assumption that space occurs alongside 11 other dimensions of measure, we may see how even the most basic substances, like ourselves, encourage certain interactions among their neighboring volumes far beyond the merely physical structure.

Assertion 88. On the conditions for reported paranormality

While writing this book, my mother reported an unusual incident at our house which occurred late one night. While I was away, apparently one of two gold goblets around my late father's memorial area was knocked over without anyone being present. This occurred while I was away from the house, but during a time when my mother had a lot on her mind regarding various events among her peers. Relatedly, I myself recall an event around age 12 where I saw a toy Indian chief standing 30° on his edge on our ironing board, in defiance of all known physics to this day. I used a pencil to check for fibers holding him to the ironing board, moved my hand around him to check for a spider web, and when I poked him with a pencil, he swayed. The investigation lasted for about two minutes until I poked him hard enough to knock him over permanently—after which time, as you may guess, I couldn't get him to stand up again. I then spent another pair of minutes shuffling my feet across the living room floor and touching the front door knob in order to get a better handle on static electricity. The "Standing Up Indian" as I call him, left an impression on me that leads me never to dismiss other people's claims of the otherworldly, as there is no human anywhere who can tell me what I observed without having been there. No one should be diminished for what they've seen with their own eyes. Especially by people who didn't see it themselves.

---

[45] Electronegativity measures how likely an element is to attract a bonding electron pair.

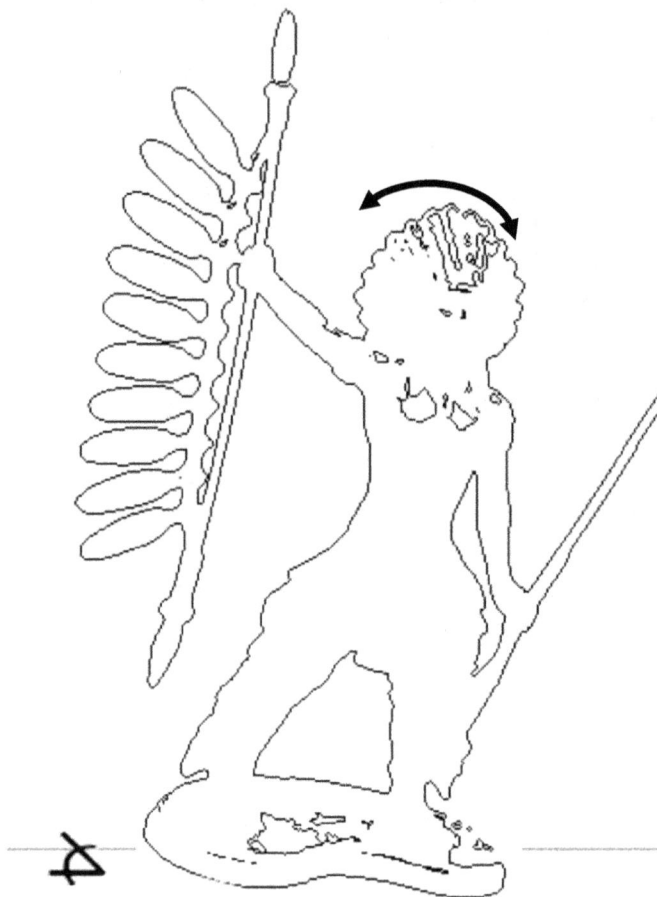

The Standing Up Indian was tilted 30° forward off the ironing board.
With no fibers, spider webs, or explainable static, he rocked back and forth when I poked him with a pencil.
I investigated this for two minutes before finally knocking him over with a harder poke.

Our natural reaction to other people's experiences of the paranormal is to say "Maybe it was just…" and then offer explanations of our own intended to substitute for the witness' first-hand encounter. Indeed, I will attempt to provide a similar kind of justification over the next few paragraphs. Yet reports of the otherworldly are pervasive enough to warrant a specific kind of justification: one that investigates rather than eliminates. One that avoids the implication that "All men everywhere who saw it were fools" or "They just wanted to justify their own beliefs." Many people who experience such events can't be called "believers" of anything. A great many people are simply minding their own business. (My mom was relaxing watching TV. I believe I was walking around the house looking for socks or something.) And so, without reducing other's experiences to a flattened version of my own, I offer a basic theory of the paranormal.

Consider two realities, one of which is not our own: Media space and time space. In media space Optimus Prime and Megatron are enemies. Captain Picard tends to the Starship Enterprise, and Romeo and Juliet play out a tragedy. In time space you are alive, you are reading this page, you are a son or daughter of someone, and you are you. Media space is described by quasi-facts which, though acknowledged to be absent from the physical world, are verified enough in the minds of physical people to elicit stereotyped patterns of interaction—cognitive constructs—among those physical people; although Megatron is not real and Saint Thomas Aquinas was, Megatron's deeds may, in this quasi-factual world, impress more people more directly than Saint Thomas Aquinas. Media space, as we've stated before, is not about the object depicted, but about the depiction itself, and the extent to which viewers' actions may be informed by this depiction. On the other side of this, events in time space are seen as real in time. The catch, however, is that events in time space, like events in media space, are only true while they are seen as agreement-worthy by a collective that the viewer acknowledges as real. Once the basis of such agreement fails, an event in time space often ceases to be true or remain true in the same way. In other words, the events of time space are here considered true in the present but not necessarily true in the past or future. Events in media space are also events in time space, but hold the added condition that the basis for their reality is limited to the realm of the publicly agreed upon non-normal. Paradoxically, public agreement itself becomes non-normal when you cease to be you or when we claim truth in a time window over which an event is publicly agreed to no longer apply. So the notion of public agreement rests upon a combination of further public agreement and your own acknowledgement of such. If we consider a thing to be normal only if it is publicly viewable (plus other constraints) then

> If an event is public then the public must exist, the viewer of the public must exist, the event must exist, and existence must exist.

> Let the definition of a viewer rest upon his definition by a public prior to himself. That is, a viewer is a member of the public. So if a viewer exists, the public must exist.

> Among other things, the above two statements imply that a viewer exists if and only if a public exists. Where the public represents a set of viewers of the viewer.[46]

Applied to media space and time space, the above sequence leads us to a paradox in which both spaces are equally valid, because the notion of what is normal rests on what most reasonable people would accept; but what most people would reasonably accept must be determined by a viewer who must first accept his own view as trained by a public which preceded him. "It's real because they say it's real...because I say they are they...because they say I am me." The basis of reality, then rests upon a mixed foundation of imaginary and remembered truths in constrained media space combined with the temporary truths of time space. This renders viewer-dependent realities (as opposed to viewer-independent realities) to be only selectively true.

What does the above have to do with paranormality? It means that all viewer-dependent realities are equally valid in logic, whether or not they are equally actionable among other viewers. The same cannot necessarily be said of viewer-independent realities. Let's define a viewer-independent reality as one which appears to most viewers to be true for most viewers for all points in time space.[47] To the extent that certain processes such as quantum mechanics are assumed to have viewer-independent existences (which ironically give rise to viewers) it will be the laws of dynamics which determine viewable realities rather than the viewers themselves. To show that paranormality is possible, we would need to show a dynamic law which viewers themselves would be highly unlikely to naturally perceive. But we've already introduced several such realities in the form of those underemphasized and imaginary axis dimensions in the 12-model z_A, z_B, and β.

Consider the following assertions

> The more we see what is emitted x_A, the less we perceive what is absorbed z_B.

> The more we experience the force that binds energy carriers m, the less we perceive the energy of those carriers z_A.

---

[46] Of course we can get around this by assuming the viewers and public to be different from the original ones referenced. But is this any more acceptable? Now we get into the realm of their being multiple copies of basic things, which leads us to invoke our original paradox involving existence.

[47] Yes, this too seems viewer dependent, except that it has the additional characteristic of preserving its viewer-dependent truth across time. This is a tough definition to develop a final form for, so we'll stick with a practical one. Also, my thinking that most people think something is true even outside of my time frame helps me eliminate more debatable issues as truth. The idea that slaves are subhuman would probably not ring true to the slaves themselves, and I know this; so it would be harder for me to think that most people agreed with this across time even if most people at one time thought it. The conditions for truth are slightly stronger (albeit still relative) in this way.

The more we perceive the distances and times separating events r_B and t, the less we experience the energy levels which determine what separation consists of β.[48]

Thus in a world where spacetime matter and emissions $r_B t \cup m \cup x_A$, predominate, the world of inverted axes comprising system energy, quantum magnitudes, and vacuum input will be difficult to perceive. This three axis world exchanges spacetime for temperature, mass for quantum region count, and light emission for dark invaginated volume—no axis of which humans are evolved to sharply perceive. Coherence in spacetime emission, however, produces coherence along the inverted axes as well, since coherence is a matter of energy organization not of energy magnitudes. So for everything we perceive in the spacetime matter emission world, there is an equivalent percept in the temperature charge input world. The latter axis space would be characteristically dark and resonance-attracting in its emissions according to the 12-model—in opposition to the light and resonance emitting projection of the x_A orientation.

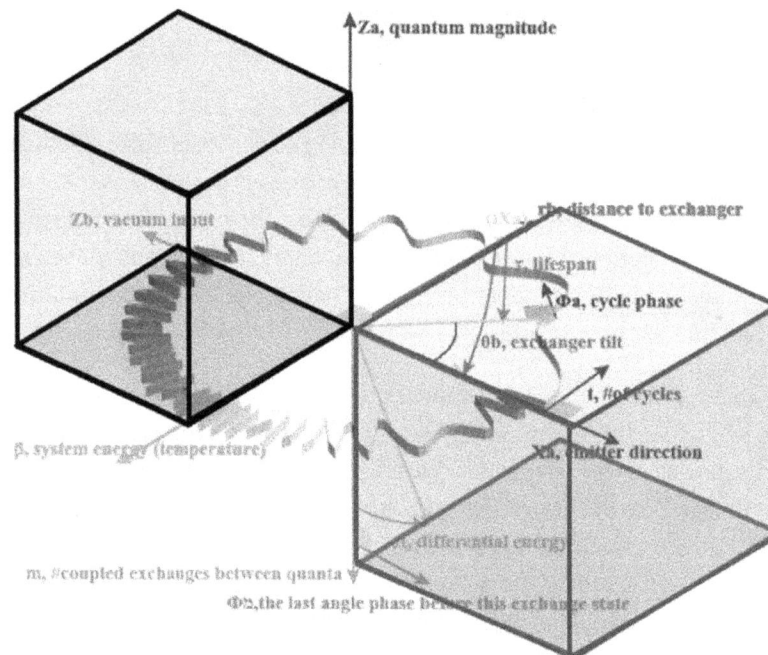

Figure 42-2: The easily human-perceivable dimensions (lower right box) versus the difficult-to-perceive ones (upper left box)

Referring to the diagram above, our senses emphasize the lower right dimensions over the upper left dimensions. This is especially true as the whole system spins in such a way as to have spacetime dimensions overlap with and overshadow vacuum input dimensions. It's not as if we can just turn objects around and see the vacuum behind them. Instead it's more like we would need to be able to stare *through* familiar dimensions in order to see unfamiliar ones. Does the 12-model suggest how this might be done? Partly. In cases where there is very little light to be seen, very little mass to be felt, and very little spatial information by which to gauge separations from objects, the vacuum dimensions, thanks to the continued influence of the time and cycle dimension, can continue to provide us information about the surrounding world.

If normal dimensions are well lit, mass-bearing, and moving in spacetime, dimensions which are not any of these—those which are nonetheless correlated with normal dimension—will be thought through the lens of human perception as occurring beside the normal: the para- normal. The easiest way to perceive such a world is via the absence of our strongest source of information, light—without which we lose much of our basis for calculating space, matter composition, and causal (time-related) relationships. Unfortunately, because there is a greater chance that humans in dark spaces will fear what they can't see (or in the very least exercise caution to avoid bumping into things), humans in the dark are more likely to

---

[48] This is like saying, the sharper our measurements with the ruler, the narrower our information about its tick marks.

perceive fear- or caution-inducing events in this same environment whether or not anything is there. But is it possible that something of the more ghostly kind could be there?

My personal opinion of the paranormal is agnostic. I told the reader about the Standing Up Indian which I experienced firsthand, but at the time of this writing I've never seen a ghost that I knew of. On the other hand, as I've mentioned several times throughout these books, I've had reliable premonitory dreams for a very long time. For me, the paranormal sounds more like the normal played out over energy levels for which we have not yet developed the appropriate visual technology. We still need particle accelerators to observe more exotic particle level interactions, and string theory is still a theory rather than a scannable fact. Gravity is still associated some kind of difficult-to-describe graviton. Furthermore, ❋ brain scans aren't yet versatile enough to capture data on a big scale such that we can associate one person with an entire population's responses to that person (thus elucidating something like the one person's spirit). It is no stretch to imagine how such information of these kinds probably exists, but without the means of classifying that data as it is, all we can do is tell ourselves that it isn't. ❋ Still, if humans can have their interaction dynamics algorithmically separated from their bodies and such an algorithm can be reproduced outside of the humans' original body, I do believe that we have the basis for some kind of theory of paranormal—specifically a theory of apparitions. Here though, we may do better to divide the paranormal into the four classes most familiar to our senses: space-based, time-based, emission or light-based, and mass/matter based.

The conditions for perceiving the allegedly paranormal, then, would be tied to the conditions for perceiving anything we normally perceive with the added condition that the content of the percept reflects the vacuum world rather than the emission world.

- Space-based paranormalilty includes basic feelings of closeness, connectedness, or "presence" of something where normal visual-spatial perception says it shouldn't be there.
- Time-based paranormality includes being able to perceive the future or past accurately without having the required information for doing so.
- Light-based paranormailty includes certain kinds of near death experiences and basic ghostly events.
- Matter-based paranormality occurs where objects fall off of shelves or adopt strange physics for example. (My mother's goblet and the Standing Up Indian were examples of this.)

When we perceive unfamiliar reality through the above familiar means, I believe we have perceived dynamics more typical of the vacuum-input related dimensions than the spacetime dimensions.

Assertion 89. The number of realms far exceeds the number of dimensions for housing those realms.
Just as an entire planet full of lives holds many many more spheres of activity than the four basic spacetime dimensions, the number of realms of existence can be expected to hold many more spheres of activity than the 12 in our model. Realms of activity are not just determined by a limited number of dimensions, but by the seemingly unlimited real values which combinations of activity across those dimensions can adopt. The reader should not take the above discussion of non-normal realms to mean that there are only two realms—the ghostly and the non-ghostly. Instead, with changing orders of error and changing spans of frequency, the number of existential realms that can be adopted by the universe can be expected to be at least as large as the number of psychological dispositions adoptable by all humans across history.

Assertion 90. Obscuring of global truths produces multiple local universes, but the aggregation of those universes forms a single universe.
Suppose I am standing in line and I hear a noise come from ahead of me. All I see (and all I will ever see) though is the back of the person in front of me. Here, the visual information in the direction in front of me is blocked by the person before me, but the sound/spatial information isn't. In my world either the person ahead of me made the noise or some great unknown beyond him did. In his world either the person ahead of the person ahead of me made the noise or some great unknown beyond that even more prior person did. We share half of the same information (the sound), but not the other half (the visual percept). Thus different variables flow from the different relationships we have to our neighbors. Is this the basis of a multiverse? Perhaps it is in the eyes of me versus the person ahead of me. But the system which includes all of the relevant

facts and actors within exchange range of each other will hold a basic truth of its own. If I knew the story told by that overarching system and adopted it as my own, I might abandon my multiverse theory after all. But then again the system that houses my overarching system would see my overarching system as only local in turn. What does this mean for multiverses? It means that, practically speaking, we are almost required to assume them if for no other reason than our lack of full information regarding the neighbors we interact with. Those neighbors whose local presence obscures more global dynamics between us and the world. Yet we are also, as adapting creatures, compelled to pursue behaviors which reconcile us towards a single proper chain of actions. Living our lives in relativism will not be practical. Accordingly, another paradox driven system arises. That system involves the flow of time and behavioral adaptation as we reconcile ours and our neighbor's local universes to our best estimate of a global one.

Assertion 91. There is no perfect arrangement of system relationships in the absence of a comparator system.
Considering collections of quanta to be analogous to the chemical elements, we see that what constitutes an ideal arrangement will change depending on the other elements available as well as basic reaction conditions. Quantic units of quantum and intervening space may or may not readily adopt similar arrangements across contexts as factors like temperature and vacuum density change. Relatedly, humans (as collections of quanta) will form different exchange patterns with their environments depending on what those environments consist of as wells as the internal state of the human. But what if we hold the environment constant? Will a perfect arrangement exist then?

No. Even in a theoretically fixed environment, the original paradox of time and compression renders each snapshot of the 12-dimension a nested subset of itself the moment after the snapshot is taken. An optimum arrangement of relationships with that quantic system will not manifest as long as the system is forever ceasing to be itself. Nevertheless, we may model the evolution of the system and, minimizing the differences between the system and the model, search for a near "perfect" correspondence between the two. This is to say that, no matter what the system, an absolute standard of perfect performance will not be attainable unless there exists some nonabsolute baseline against which such performance is measured. With no comparison goal, an ever-changing energetic framework will continue to resist favoring any one state as ideal above all others.

Assertion 92. Physical illness reflects the nature of hindrances to a person's intended viewable-world exchanges.
Having separate dimensions for space, mass, phase cycle, and input suggests that physical illness—that which is tied to the functioning body—may be partly separated from mental illness—that which is tied to the time cycles and exchanges within that body. It is clear that total separation of these two kinds of disturbance may not be practical (since we are naturally inclined to pay mental attention to our body states), but as I discussed earlier, the physical body seems a lot less dedicated to the spirit impression than its marriage to the spirit may suggest. We might even say that the body is "unfaithfully married to the soul." Where the soul exists as a packet of patterned energetic exchanges among dimension-handling living systems, that packet is constantly compelled to respond to specific dynamics across the material body for as long as the organism lives. After the organism dies, however, the soul-like pattern may still exist in the cycle spaces of nonresonantly-coupled quanta—predictable as the tides with no oceanic label to define them. If quanta can move in spacetime without changing temperature or emission, then it is reasonable to think that they can also move in cycle space without moving in spacetime (like photons) or in emission space without moving in spatial space (like a light source) or in spatial space without moving in phase space. This last scenario includes two of the dimensions involved in defining the physical body and the mental body respectively. Since all living things eventually die and all initiated dynamics eventually end, termination space τ and prior experience space $\natural$ play particularly strong roles in perceiving illness. These warrant further investigation.

Let us consider the physical body to be a genetically outlined structure for self-sustaining activity within a superquantum via exchanges with other quanta. Seen this way, a body's purpose is to freeze its own broad dynamic with its environment for as long as possible, until its various organ systems reach the end of their stable capability for doing so. Here the physical body would be a space-spatial arrangement of such organ systems as they trade their various cycle states towards a single goal: that of the healthy organism. Monitoring the joint efforts of the body's systems we have the brain: a metaresponse system for the rest of the body. As an evolved means of encouraging certain strategic "play calling" among the body's mechanisms, the brain not only reflects much of the rest of the body, but develops its own internal cycle space for doing so. This is the mind. We'll conceive of the mind as being the body's most convenient story of its own dynamics. It is both a product of the body's interactions and an influencer of them. Via algorithmic modeling (as we're beginning to see with robots) it is both separable from the body but inseparable from the body's pattern of ongoing inputs for the purposes of training. Lastly, there is the spirit—the pattern of exchanges between the whole body and the viewing world outside of that body. Where the world itself can partly be counted on to supply the identity algorithms for labeling everything a body does with respect to it, the world may continue to store the basic operations of the organism long after the organism has died. ※ The world may even reproduce the organism through media or time space according to its needs. So although having an active body plays an integral role in evolving all three systems, past a certain peak level of development, the body is no longer needed for various simulations thereof to continue the work it started.

We can use devices like genetic mapping and astrology to view the bodily interaction pattern of an individual before they are fully developed. While genes look at bodily interactions through the lens of chemistry, astrology looks at such interactions through the lens of behavioral dimensions. There is no reliable technology I know of for looking at the bodily interactions via mental states or psychology prior to the considerable development of the human, though there is some evidence that we can observe one's interactions in youth to get a good idea of whom he or she will become as a physical agent. In cases where the body interaction plan is continually compromised by factors outside of a reasonably stable, nonself-destructive version of the plan, we have illness. We note though that physical illness under this conception exists against the baseline standard for a healthy body and usually does not *need* to have major implications for a healthy mind (whose job is simply to organize the body's story independent of illness) or for a healthy spirit (which is defined by favorable interactions with environments outside of the whole body).

Assertion 93. The Sabian symbols and 12-model combine to provide a testable model for mapping general physical health by degree.

In the first book I mentioned that there was partial evidence for the validity of the Sabian Symbols in mapping familiar body parts to the astrology wheel. I also mentioned that such correspondences have not been validated by any thorough medical studies that I know of, but I would not be surprised if future research supported the basic ordering of the Sabian Symbols. Mapping the face to Aries, the neck to Taurus, and the other major body parts in head to toe order through Pisces seems to work when we casually observe real world biology in chart possessors and comparative nervous activity as we move down the body. There does seem to be some kind of head to toe gradient as recapitulated, for example, through the neural differentiation genes. So it is useful to repeat the results here. The detailed associations below do not follow directly from the 12-model, but may be further researched against some kind of secondary 12-structure in spatial, mass, or differential energy space in the body.

#	Degree & Sign	Sabian Body Part
1	0° Aries	Cerebrum
2	1° Aries	Midbrain
3	2° Aries	Cerebellum
4	3° Aries	Pineal Gland
5	4° Aries	The eyes, left and right
6	5° Aries	Eye Socket, orbital cavity
7	6° Aries	The ears
8	7° Aries	Cheekbone
9	8° Aries	Lens of eye
10	9° Aries	Eyeball
11	10° Aries	Optic nerve
12	11° Aries	Tongue
13	12° Aries	Ventricles of brain
14	13° Aries	Frontal lobes of brain
15	14° Aries	Lateral lobes of brain
16	15° Aries	Pons
17	16° Aries	Vertebral canal
18	17° Aries	Nerve connections - synapses
19	18° Aries	Corpus callosum cerebri
20	19° Aries	Hyoid bone
21	20° Aries	Eye muscles
22	21° Aries	Cheek muscles
23	22° Aries	Muscles of mastication
24	23° Aries	Zygomatic muscle
25	24° Aries	Sternocleidomastoid muscle
26	25° Aries	Skull
27	26° Aries	Fornix/frontal bone
28	27° Aries	Fornix/parietal and occipital bones
29	28° Aries	Auditory canal
30	29° Aries	Parotid gland
31	0° Taurus	Throat, gullet
32	1° Taurus	Palate
33	2° Taurus	Pharynx - oral part
34	3° Taurus	Uvula
35	4° Taurus	Pharyngeal cavity
36	5° Taurus	Larynx
37	6° Taurus	Vocal cords

38	7° Taurus	Cervical nerves
39	8° Taurus	Jugular veins
40	9° Taurus	Cervical veins
41	10° Taurus	Cervical and brachial plexi
42	11° Taurus	Cervical and brachial plexi
43	12° Taurus	Cervical and brachial plexi
44	13° Taurus	True vocal cords
45	14° Taurus	Epiglottis
46	15° Taurus	Carotid arteries
47	16° Taurus	Thyroid gland and tonsils
48	17° Taurus	Lymph vessels
49	18° Taurus	Maxillary artery
50	19° Taurus	Occiput
51	20° Taurus	Arteries of nasal cavities
52	21° Taurus	Tongue muscles
53	22° Taurus	Teeth
54	23° Taurus	Upper jaw
55	24° Taurus	Lower jaw
56	25° Taurus	Nasal bone
57	26° Taurus	Atlas
58	27° Taurus	Deltoid muscle and main neck muscles
59	28° Taurus	Deltoid muscle and main neck muscles
60	29° Taurus	Trapezius muscle
61	0° Gemini	Trachea
62	1° Gemini	Esophagus
63	2° Gemini	Upper right pulmonary lobe
64	3° Gemini	Lower right pulmonary lobe
65	4° Gemini	Upper left pulmonary lobe
66	5° Gemini	Lower left pulmonary lobe
67	6° Gemini	Apex of lungs
68	7° Gemini	Bronchi
69	8° Gemini	Pulmonary arteries
70	9° Gemini	Hilum of lungs
71	10° Gemini	Thymus gland
72	11° Gemini	Tracheal mucosa
73	12° Gemini	Pulmonary veins
74	13° Gemini	Clavicle
75	14° Gemini	Scapulae
76	15° Gemini	Pleura
77	16° Gemini	First rib
78	17° Gemini	Second rib
79	18° Gemini	Laryngeal muscles
80	19° Gemini	Third rib
81	20° Gemini	Arm muscles
82	21° Gemini	Upper arm
83	22° Gemini	Head of the humerus
84	23° Gemini	Olecranon
85	24° Gemini	Radius
86	25° Gemini	Wrist bone
87	26° Gemini	Fingers
88	27° Gemini	Metacarpal bones
89	28° Gemini	Fourth rib
90	29° Gemini	Fifth rib
91	0° Cancer	Sixth rib
92	1° Cancer	Seventh rib
93	2° Cancer	Eighth rib
94	3° Cancer	Ninth rib
95	4° Cancer	tenth to twelfth ribs
96	5° Cancer	Diaphragm
97	6° Cancer	Thoracic cavity
98	7° Cancer	Esophageal opening of diaphragm
99	8° Cancer	Pylorus
100	9° Cancer	Fundus of stomach
101	10° Cancer	Gastric veins
102	11° Cancer	Greater curvature of stomach
103	12° Cancer	Lesser curvature of stomach
104	13° Cancer	Stomach walls
105	14° Cancer	Gastric nerves
106	15° Cancer	Pancreas
107	16° Cancer	Duodenal opening of pancreatic duct
108	17° Cancer	Duodenal opening of pancreatic duct
109	18° Cancer	Ampulla of bile duct
110	19° Cancer	Superior pancreatico-duodenal artery
111	20° Cancer	Inferior pancreatico-duodenal artery
112	21° Cancer	Gastric mucosa
113	22° Cancer	Gastric blood vessels
114	23° Cancer	Blood vessels of digestive organs
115	24° Cancer	Blood vessels of digestive organs
116	25° Cancer	Mammary glands
117	26° Cancer	Nipples
118	27° Cancer	Cartilage of ribs
119	28° Cancer	Spleen
120	29° Cancer	Twelfth thoracic vertebra
121	0° Leo	Left coronary artery
122	1° Leo	Aorta
123	2° Leo	Right coronary artery
124	3° Leo	Left carotid artery
125	4° Leo	Right carotid artery
126	5° Leo	Entrance of pulmonary artery
127	6° Leo	Left coronary vein
128	7° Leo	Inferior vena cava
129	8° Leo	Superior vena cava
130	9° Leo	Jugular vein
131	10° Leo	Subclavian veins
132	11° Leo	Vertebral column
133	12° Leo	Right ventricle of heart
134	13° Leo	Left ventricle of heart
135	14° Leo	Right atrium
136	15° Leo	Left atrium
137	16° Leo	Right auricle
138	17° Leo	Right cardiac cavity
139	18° Leo	Ventricular septum
140	19° Leo	Mitral valve
141	20° Leo	Left atrium
142	21° Leo	Left auricle
143	22° Leo	Left auricle
144	23° Leo	Papillary muscles
145	24° Leo	Pericardium
146	25° Leo	Myocardium
147	26° Leo	Chordae tendinae
148	27° Leo	Chordae tendinae
149	28° Leo	Atrioventricular septum
150	29° Leo	Back
151	0° Virgo	Duodenum
152	1° Virgo	Small intestine
153	2° Virgo	Appendix, caecum
154	3° Virgo	Ascending colon
155	4° Virgo	Transverse colon
156	5° Virgo	Descending colon
157	6° Virgo	Rectum
158	7° Virgo	Abdominal cavity
159	8° Virgo	Right hepatic lobe
160	9° Virgo	Left hepatic lobe, bile
161	10° Virgo	Falciform

162	11° Virgo	Abdominal aorta
163	12° Virgo	Hepatic arteries
164	13° Virgo	Cystic arteries
165	14° Virgo	Bare area' of liver
166	15° Virgo	Groove for inferior vena cava
167	16° Virgo	Abdominal muscles
168	17° Virgo	Obliquus abdominis muscles
169	18° Virgo	Esophageal groove
170	19° Virgo	Bile duct
171	20° Virgo	Cystic duct
172	21° Virgo	Gall-bladder
173	22° Virgo	Capsule and ligaments of liver
174	23° Virgo	Capsule and ligaments of liver
175	24° Virgo	Liver
176	25° Virgo	Abdominal veins
177	26° Virgo	Iliac nerve
178	27° Virgo	Hepatic plexus
179	28° Virgo	Quadrate lobe of liver
180	29° Virgo	Hepatic duct
181	0° Libra	Renal pelvis
182	1° Libra	Renal cortex
183	2° Libra	Adrenals
184	3° Libra	Kidney surface
185	4° Libra	Renal pyramids
186	5° Libra	Pubis
187	6° Libra	Nerve supply to kidney and renal pelvis
188	7° Libra	Nerve supply to kidney and renal pelvis
189	8° Libra	Nerve supply to kidney and renal pelvis
190	9° Libra	Nerve supply to kidney and renal pelvis
191	10° Libra	Nerve supply to kidney and renal pelvis
192	11° Libra	Left renal system
193	12° Libra	Right renal system
194	13° Libra	Left inguinal lymph nodes
195	14° Libra	Right inguinal lymph nodes
196	15° Libra	Renal arteries
197	16° Libra	Suprarenal arteries
198	17° Libra	Fatty capsule of kidneys
199	18° Libra	Calyx major
200	19° Libra	Calyx minor
201	20° Libra	Renal hilum
202	21° Libra	Renal veins
203	22° Libra	Suprarenal veins
204	23° Libra	Blood vessels of renal cortex
205	24° Libra	Blood vessels of renal cortex
206	25° Libra	Vascular system of skin
207	26° Libra	Vascular system of skin
208	27° Libra	Bladder
209	28° Libra	Right ureter
210	29° Libra	Left ureter
211	0° Scorpio	Urethra
212	1° Scorpio	Urethral meatus
213	2° Scorpio	Prostate, uterus
214	3° Scorpio	Testicles, right side of uterus
215	4° Scorpio	Testicles, left side of uterus
216	5° Scorpio	Right epididymus, uterine cavity
217	6° Scorpio	Left epididymus, right Fallopian tube
218	7° Scorpio	Scrotum, left Fallopian tube
219	8° Scorpio	Sperm duct, vagina
220	9° Scorpio	Corpus cavernosum of penis
221	10° Scorpio	Penis, Labia majora
222	11° Scorpio	Seminal vesicles
223	12° Scorpio	Vulva, Labia minora, glans penis
224	13° Scorpio	Foreskin

225	14° Scorpio	Cowper's glands
226	15° Scorpio	Right ovary, cochlea of inner ear
227	16° Scorpio	Testicular lobes, left ovary
228	17° Scorpio	Vas deferens, hymen
229	18° Scorpio	Uterine ligaments, Haller's net
230	19° Scorpio	Ligaments of penis, Bartholin's glands
231	20° Scorpio	Sphenoid sinus
232	21° Scorpio	Ethmoid bone
233	22° Scorpio	Nasal bone, fimbria of Fallopian tubes
234	23° Scorpio	Nasal septum
235	24° Scorpio	Coccyx, Fallopian tubes
236	25° Scorpio	Perineum
237	26° Scorpio	Anus
238	27° Scorpio	Mucous membranes
239	28° Scorpio	Vomer
240	29° Scorpio	Nasal muscles
241	0° Sagittarius	Pelvic bone
242	1° Sagittarius	Pelvic girdle
243	2° Sagittarius	Ischia
244	3° Sagittarius	Femur
245	4° Sagittarius	Right femoral artery
246	5° Sagittarius	Left femoral artery
247	6° Sagittarius	Right superior femoral artery
248	7° Sagittarius	Left superior femoral artery
249	8° Sagittarius	Right lymphatic vessels
250	9° Sagittarius	Left lymphatic vessels
251	10° Sagittarius	Adductor muscles
252	11° Sagittarius	Long saphenous veins
253	12° Sagittarius	Long saphenous veins
254	13° Sagittarius	Cutaneous vessels of the thighs
255	14° Sagittarius	Right iliac vein
256	15° Sagittarius	Left iliac vein
257	16° Sagittarius	Sciatic nerve
258	17° Sagittarius	Right femur
259	18° Sagittarius	Left femur
260	19° Sagittarius	Head of right femur
261	20° Sagittarius	Head of left femur
262	21° Sagittarius	Right trochanter
263	22° Sagittarius	Left trochanter
264	23° Sagittarius	Popliteal fossa
265	24° Sagittarius	Condyles of right femur
266	25° Sagittarius	Condyles of left femur
267	26° Sagittarius	Gluteal muscles
268	27° Sagittarius	Right leg muscles
269	28° Sagittarius	Left leg muscles
270	29° Sagittarius	Pear-shaped muscle
271	0° Capricorn	Right patella
272	1° Capricorn	Left patella
273	2° Capricorn	Cutaneous nerves of thigh
274	3° Capricorn	Cutaneous nerves of lower leg
275	4° Capricorn	Cutaneous nerves of knee
276	5° Capricorn	Right adductor muscle
277	6° Capricorn	Left adductor muscle
278	7° Capricorn	Lymph vessels of knee
279	8° Capricorn	Nerves of knee
280	9° Capricorn	Right cruciate ligaments
281	10° Capricorn	Left cruciate ligaments
282	11° Capricorn	Right knee joint
283	12° Capricorn	Left knee joint
284	13° Capricorn	Right knee cartilage
285	14° Capricorn	Left knee cartilage
286	15° Capricorn	Condyle of right tibia
287	16° Capricorn	Condyle of left tibia

288	17° Capricorn	Ligaments of right knee		325	24° Aquarius	Left tibialis anterior muscle
289	18° Capricorn	Ligaments of left knee		326	25° Aquarius	Right fibula
290	19° Capricorn	Tendons of right knee		327	26° Aquarius	Left fibula
291	20° Capricorn	Tendons of left knee		328	27° Aquarius	Right tibia
292	21° Capricorn	Muscle insertions of upper to lower legs		329	28° Aquarius	Left tibia
293	22° Capricorn	Muscle insertions of upper to lower legs		330	29° Aquarius	Connections in lower leg
294	23° Capricorn	Muscle insertions of upper to lower legs		331	0° Pisces	Right calcaneum
295	24° Capricorn	Connections between femur and tibia		332	1° Pisces	Left calcaneum
296	25° Capricorn	Connections between femur and tibia		333	2° Pisces	Nerves of right foot
297	26° Capricorn	Deep nerves		334	3° Pisces	Nerves of left foot
298	27° Capricorn	Right genicular arteries		335	4° Pisces	Right cuboid bone
299	28° Capricorn	Left genicular arteries		336	5° Pisces	Left cuboid bone
300	29° Capricorn	Adductor muscle		337	6° Pisces	Right talus
301	0° Aquarius	Right tibial nerve		338	7° Pisces	Left talus
302	1° Aquarius	Left tibial nerve		339	8° Pisces	Right metatarsals
303	2° Aquarius	Right fibula		340	9° Pisces	Left metatarsals
304	3° Aquarius	Left fibula		341	10° Pisces	Lymph vessels of foot
305	4° Aquarius	Nerve of right fibula		342	11° Pisces	Plantar artery of right foot
306	5° Aquarius	Nerve of left fibula		343	12° Pisces	Plantar artery of left foot
307	6° Aquarius	Right saphenous veins		344	13° Pisces	Right cutaneous veins
308	7° Aquarius	Left saphenous veins		345	14° Pisces	Left cutaneous veins
309	8° Aquarius	Skin of right lower leg		346	15° Pisces	Cruciate ligaments of right foot
310	9° Aquarius	Skin of left lower leg		347	16° Pisces	Cruciate ligaments of left foot
311	10° Aquarius	Right cruciate ligaments		348	17° Pisces	Extensor muscles of right toes
312	11° Aquarius	Left cruciate ligaments		349	18° Pisces	Extensor muscles of left toes
313	12° Aquarius	Right tibial artery		350	19° Pisces	Right fibula muscle
314	13° Aquarius	Left tibial artery		351	20° Pisces	Left fibula muscle
315	14° Aquarius	Lymph vessels of right lower leg		352	21° Pisces	Achilles tendon of right foot
316	15° Aquarius	Lymph vessels of left lower leg		353	22° Pisces	Achilles tendon of left foot
317	16° Aquarius	Spinal nervous system		354	23° Pisces	Right distal tibio-fibular joint
318	17° Aquarius	Spinal nervous system		355	24° Pisces	Left distal tibio-fibular joint
319	18° Aquarius	Spinal nervous system		356	25° Pisces	Plantar nerves
320	19° Aquarius	Spinal nervous system		357	26° Pisces	Phalanges of right foot
321	20° Aquarius	Spinal nervous system		358	27° Pisces	Phalanges of left foot
322	21° Aquarius	Right gastroscnemius muscle		359	28° Pisces	Toenails of right foot
323	22° Aquarius	Left gastroscnemius muscle		360	29° Pisces	Toenails of left foot
324	23° Aquarius	Right tibialis anterior muscle				

❉ *Table 42-2: The Sabian Symbol degree mappings for the body.* An interesting area for future research

Combined with our previous broad organ system associations, the Sabian degrees may be tested for locating certain specific characteristics a chart possessor's biology.

Dimension	Degree	Sign	Biological System
x_A	0°	Aries	voluntary behavior, the face, and involuntary aspects of the muscular system
ϕ_A	30°	Taurus	the upper digestive system, nesting, and preferred learning behaviors as well as species-typical body type
z_A	60°	Gemini	natural mannerisms, automatic physiological maneuvers, the respiratory system in its stable state
t	90°	Cancer	display of want, motivation-enabling aspects of the endocrine system (hormones), internal emotional processing, bonding instinct, social and pleasure-seeking neurotransmitter dynamics, personal-goal aspects of dreaming
r_B	120°	Leo	circulatory system, voluntary aspects of the muscular system
θ_B	150°	Virgo	reasoning and procuring of resources, the lower digestive system and internal dissonance-handling aspects of the nervous and endocrine systems
z_B	180°	Libra	voluntary communication with interactants, the lymphatic system and internal functions of the urinary/excretory system, the respiratory system in its preferred intake state
τ	210°	Scorpio	coercion, aggression, psychological coping, the output functions of the urinary/excretory system, the general reproductive system
m	240°	Sagittarius	the integumentary system (hair skin & nails), outward appearance in the eyes of other organisms and the mechanisms of protection from them, characteristics that stand out
Д	270°	Capricorn	the genetic map, broad skeletal system, the general body plan
β	300°	Aquarius	cohort characteristics, the social structure and world-handling, peripheral aspects of the nervous system
ב	330°	Pisces	memory, the body maintenance activities associated with dreaming, mental conceptualization, senses for passive aspects of processing one's circumstances in general, the brain and central nervous system's background functions

Table 42-3: Short table of dimensional mappings for the body

What kinds of issues may be associated with each of the above combinations of attributes? The model suggests that we can have an excess, deficiency, or just the right amount of dimension-handling across all of our systems.

Dimension	Associated focus
x_A	proper system function or output
ϕ_A	normal resource acceptance
z_A	system response sensitivity
t	system speed
r_B	proper appearance or activation
θ_B	proper processing of combined inputs
z_B	proper resource intake
τ	proper limiting factors
m	growth level
Д	proper structure or development
β	energy availability
ב	proper ordering of functional steps

Table 42-4: Table of dimensional functions for the body

If we entertain the idea that every potential health issue can be associated with a mappable frequency somewhere across the 12 biological systems, each with their own 12 dimensions of cyclic function, and if we further suppose that there are 12 different classes of proper operation associated with those dimensions, then we obtain 12^3 or 1728 broad kinds of issue associated with one's total health. Of course there will be many more than 1728 kinds of traits or illnesses as we move into different subclusters of body function, but a combination of the three tables above gives us plenty for future research in the area of medical astrology from a 12-space perspective. Via a theory of resonances (and based on the mappings proposed at the beginning of this book), we can see how a problem with any one frequency may easily become a problem with its base frequency everywhere. So a general issue with internal stress (the 6th or θ_B dimension) can be expected to bring all other $2^{6/12}$ issues with it when we assume a reduced frequency space between 2^0 and 2^1.[49] A specific issue with a painful leg, in Sabian 25 Aquarius for example, may be expected to bring all other $2^{325/360}$ issues with it if allowed to grow large enough. Here we get into some interesting existential territory which I will save for the next assertion, but it should be noted that fractional frequencies can be scaled up or down to conform with the powers of 12 implicated in the 12-model. $325/360$ is equal to both $130/144$ and $1560/1728$, and may thus correspond to the world-handling nervous system's proper development $(^{(11-1) \times 12 + 10}/_{144})$ or to anything related to the 120th harmonic as it pertains to information—including angles (being more vulnerable to information as discussed in the previous book *144*), duodecanates (the 120th, Taurus (/11)-decile indicating the structures a person values, also discussed in *144*), or asteroids like 985 Rosina or 649 Josefa (whose orbits, according to our formula, spans about 120 duodecanates).[50] In calculating the above values, I used the following rules discussed throughout the *FSA* series:

- To find a value out of 144, simply divide it and multiply by 144. I took $325 \div 360 * 144$ to get 130. Similarly, $325 \div 360 * 1728 = 1560$.

- To find the harmonic associated with a value out of 144, find the highest allowed multiple in it. The value above was 120, so $1/_{120}$th of a circle will form the set of angles affected alongside the thing you're studying.

- To find the sign and duodecanate of a value out of 144 (in this case 130), subtract the highest allowed multiple of 12 from it ($130 - 120 = 10$) and let that be your base angle within whatever broad sign group you're looking at. 10 is a decile. You obtain the broad sign group by dividing the highest multiple you found by 12 ($120 \div 12 = 10$) then adding 1 to make up for the fact that the first sign starts at 0 multiples of 12 and the 12th sign starts at 11 multiples of 12. 10 puts us at the start of the 11th sign group, giving us an 11-decile. Recall however, that life attribute duodecanates map *backwards* on the astrology circle starting at 30 Pisces, so 11 signs in the opposite direction plus 10 duodecanates even further back puts us at a Taurus-decile (5° Taurus which is symmetric to 325° Aquarius about 0° Aries.

- To find the number of duodecanates spanned by an asteroid, take the base 2 log of its farthest distance from the Sun (its aphelion) and subtract the base 2 log of its closest distance to the Sun (its perihelion), multiply by 144, then add 1. Adding 1 is our way of saying that an asteroid's orbit, if perfectly circular (where the aphelion = the perihelion), will occupy 1 duodecanate. Not 0. I've already calculated such values for the first 1000 asteroids, so the reader can just look them up in the Appendix.

The reason we go through all of the trouble of calculating other chart factors associated with a single physiological issue is because we are assuming that no health characteristic occurs in isolation, but is instead reflective of a bigger system designed to perform a particular energetic task in the whole body. 120s have a relationship to other functions in a 144-based system. 10s have a relationship to other dimensions in a 12-based system. I am assuming that such relationships will constitute a theme elsewhere in the body not despite the proposed quantum mechanics, but *because* of it. If we only consider the ankle in isolation for example—if the systems involved with musculature, nervous response, balance and body support, genetic physiological plan, and cardiovascular flow were somehow divorced in the ankle from the rest of the body,

---

[49] Throughout this series I have usually assumed a 2^0 through 2^3 space and earlier I proposed a 4^0 through 4^{12} space. It actually doesn't matter though, because all of these can be mapped onto each other via a basic relation as proposed in Chapter 36. It's the percentage progress around the circle that matters, not the specific values associated with such progress. This is the very reason why lifespans and cycle durations are allowed to scale in the first place.

[50] In writing this paragraph I partly sought to solve a mystery regarding my own right ankle. While sleeping, I often have to take off the right sock but not the left, as it feels as though there is pressure building up there which prevents me from sleeping. This only occurs as I prepare for sleep, at no other time during the day. About 4 days out of the week, I then proceed to slip into semimeditation where my guides—overwhelmingly female in character—show me all kinds of interesting things about the universe. Although I wasn't quite surprised that the above predictions regarding other events related to health characteristics would hold in this case, I remain amazed, you know? Though unverified, the associations between harmonics and multiple aspects of a person's experience seem to hold up reliably well.

it might be reasonable to think that an issue with the ankle only resided there. Of course this is not the case at all. And so a pain in the body is a pain registered in the brain. The blood flow typically changes, and other systems such as the genetic and muscle structure form the structural basis by which such pain occurs where it does. But given a potential maze of secondary associations, where would we propose to begin the search for any other systems associated with a particular body issue? I propose that we do so at the level of the fundamental quanta describing the system in question. Exploding the individual, an ankle becomes just another superquantic collection with its own favored resonances among neighbors. Deviation from the expected resonance pattern in that collection *might* be confined only to that collection, but given such extensive cross-talk throughout the whole organism, this is highly unlikely. Instead, I propose that the resonant frequencies characteristic of any body attribute are, as discussed before, reproducible without the body—especially when we are attached to larger encompassing systems like the physical form, the Earth, and the vacuum which include our quanta as their own. I don't think it is reasonable to expect the quanta of a body region to simply stop resonating at some arbitrary boundary any more than it is reasonable to imagine an ocean wave simply stopping itself in mid-transit without some wall to explain it. But the walls between quantic regions are semi-artificial. While it is true that neighborhoods may mostly exclude each other at the valence boundaries, the valence boundaries themselves still engage in active trade with other boundaries. Very rarely is a wave 100% reflected by the boundary it hits. Similarly, the frequency of a body region (not to mention the whole organ systems that connect it) can be reasonably expected to pass at least partly beyond that region, affecting other systems in turn.

Assertion 94. Bodies at a particular cycle-spatial degree reflect issues associated with that degree.

To the extent that astronomical bodies are collections of quantic potentials located in an observer's cycle space, I claim that an observer will experience an astronomical body most clearly when operating at the phasic angle corresponding to where the body is found in his cycle space. This is not to say at all that one will need to, for example, face north whenever he wants to experience his Jupiter frequency, but rather to say that he will need to be at a specific angle along his stages of cycle-processing activity in order to experience his Jupiter frequency at its clearest. Remember, "Jupiter" here is another way of referring to "the collection of resonant frequencies at roughly four times the potential of the Earth shell's potential with respect to the energy flux of the central-emitting Sun."

Dwarf planets also have such specific resonant frequencies associated with them, but as part of a larger base 12 orbit as opposed to representing their own orbits. Furthermore, lesser bodies which are not dense or massive enough to be spherical can be hypothesized to occupy divisions of 12 within divisions of 12 within divisions of 12. Accordingly, a major planet like Mars or Venus may be associated with a whole 12-based sign because they circle around the geocentric reference frame of Earth with a potential band more or less their own. Our Moon also does this, and thus can be treated like a major planet. A dwarf like Ceres or Pluto, however, may only be associated with a 144th-based duodecanate since their potential band, though well defined, is also shared with (and therefore divided up among) the activities of other bodies in the same band. Using astronomy rather than astrology as our basis, we can't give Pluto its own sign because the sign that Pluto would describe is also described by other bodies in the very same potential band which are not Pluto—making this dwarf a kind of partial owner rather than full owner of its particular resonance isoshell. The objects shared by Jupiter and Saturn on the other hand are overwhelmingly subject to Jupiter and Saturn, making these into full band owners with assistants. As the assisting bodies become gravitationally less significant, so too does their individual importance in determining the band's overall phase, so bodies like asteroids should be looked at in divisions of 1728 or higher.

Using the above heuristic for classifying planets, dwarfs, and below, we may look to the bodies at a particular degree to reflect the proper or improper workings of health at that degree. The Princess Royal Victoria, Frederika of Prussia, for example, died of breast cancer which spread to the spine. The Sabian symbol for the breasts lies at 25 Cancer which was sharply trine her Ascendant in 25 Pisces. Trines show where you give your natural opinion or thoughts about something, so a trine to the Ascendant suggests a topic you may be thinking about at the very beginning or the very end of a cycle. Trine these two points is 25 Scorpio, an 8th house position where she had the asteroids 372 Palma and 849 Ara located. These represent where others want to be your friend and where you have a talent for intellectualizing, and fit well with the loss of her mother and confidante Queen Victoria shortly before her own death. Her 8th house (in the Topocentric system) begins with the following partial and full duodecanate clusters:

House	HOUSE 8	14 sc 32' 5"	how you steer others
486	Cremona	14 sc 40'33"	where people are unable to attach from you after having encountered you; a permanent impression
401	Ottilia	14 sc 42'15"	an inventive creative vision
909	Ulla	14 sc 42'49"	what your way prioritizes the promotion of in your 1:1 exchanges
155	Scylla	14 sc 42'54"	what you are constantly dwelling on
454	Mathesis	14 sc 43' 8"	where you display a stable, motherly fixity in your dealings with those in your camp
600	Musa	15 sc 1'56"	where you invite others to shake off their restrictions and rebel against inhibition
524	Fidelio	15 sc 3'26"	where you have an intuitively clearer sense of how you should proceed
619	Triberga	15 sc 15'41"	where you are associated with revolution and social defiance
927	Ratisbona	15 sc 29'19"	where stagnant systems need for you to break in and revolutionize things
17	Thetis	15 sc 30'49"	a staple feature of the domestic life you report to others
2878	Panacea	15 sc 34'29"	side of you associated with great and capable others
548	Kressida	15 sc 41'15"	others like to watch you unleash this [creative power] on people [not necessarily them; associated with the breasts]
434	Hungaria	16 sc 18'42"	where you are pragmatic, sane, and stable regarding what's going on around you
54598	Bienor	16 sc 54'15"	where you are associated with women of singularly unique accomplishments
838	Seraphina	16 sc 55' 8"	associated with refined execution of things
28	Bellona	17 sc 28'44"	associated with big breasts, sexualization of females regardless of context, or attention to female physical [feminized value] characteristics independent of body type

Upon review of the Princess Royal's biography, the reader can verify for himself that the above tells a fairly accurate story of the circumstances surrounding her death.

When a person identifies a health issue and locates the relevant degree for describing it, he also gains access to the asteroids which occupy that degree. Although medical astrology has not yet advanced far enough to comprehensively classify which astronomical bodies may correspond to certain detailed physiological systems, the degrees of the circle seem to be well mapped enough to at least point us towards certain real world experiences associated with the cycle phase in question. Even for physiological traits that are not broken, it is an overall interesting exercise to see what asteroids lie in the corresponding region of the chart.

Assertion 95. Health issues have parallels in daily events.

The premise for this claim is the same as the premise for the previous assertion: specific frequency windows apply across the whole person, not just a single region within that person. Accordingly, not only can degree associations spill over into internal experiences, but they can also affect external (interphysical) dynamics as well. I've noticed for example that, every time an individual knowingly commits a grudge-worthy wrong against another person, there is a good chance that the guilty party will see a corresponding, externally imposed, negative event occur around them (even if it doesn't affect the guilty party directly). As games like the Sims and other artificial networking systems illustrate, interphysical dynamics can be modeled just as easily (perhaps even more easily) than psychological ones, so that a person who responds as though a particular $<m, Д, β, ♏>$ exchange has occurred and who expects the victim of that exchange to seek remedy, will have a higher chance of perceiving the continuation of such a dynamic through other interphysical events. I have observed this regularly in my own and in other's lives, and have thus learned that it is seldom good to treat others in ways that would give them reasonable cause to hold a grudge against you. I speak of grudges rather than regular actions because the former—not the latter—*demand* continuation of events you have already encountered. Events that parallel health issues work in this way. Where your body has adopted a state which you know will demand future attention, the nature of the attention demanded of you will correspond to one or several of your many phase-experienceable options, and these options need not be internal or interactional alone. They can also be externally viewable. Such is the prime mechanism through which the reader may get familiar with his or her asteroids to begin with: through observing tight conjuncts between asteroids which manifest as uniquely, sometimes quirkily married experiences. Health experiences are not immune to such interesting combinations. A look at the cluster of asteroids upon a particular degree for example represents a look at a cluster of different resonance packages all associated with the same phase. Where body, mind, and spirit are concerned, the cycle wheel is indiscriminate in this matter.

Go to a site like serennu.com and download your 1000 asteroids. Look at the non-health related bodies which are tightly associated with health related bodies at the same degree in order to view the above effect in your own chart. See the connections for yourself.

On Contact with Non-Human Entities

Does our quantum mechanical theory imply the existence of higher entities beyond human perception? That depends on what one counts as an entity. Clearly there are other organized systems such that of dolphins, countries, or planets which hold systems for communicating with each other that are at least partly accessible to human translation. While animals like dolphins, birds, and ants have something closer to a traditional language for conveying intentions, countries, businesses, and municipalities employ the use of policies, processes, and representatives to do the same. Meanwhile, planets communicate to other planets by means of gravitational potentials, magnetic fields, aggregation, collision, and orbital resonance patterns. It is true enough that most of us would not consider planets to have a language in a way that humans do, mainly (I suspect) because planets don't seem to have an "inner will" the way we do; they seem driven more by physics than an internal impulse to self-sustain by absorbing surrounding energy—developed more through cold mechanics than through interfacing with their neighbors. And yet planets do have inner chemical dynamics which drive their material composition, just like humans have DNA. Planets do develop fixed orbits in dynamic self-sustainment with other planets. Planets do consume the flux and resonant energy of a central emitter for their "food." They do emit their own neighborhood fields which affect the behavior of other bodies near them in turn. In terms of energy consumption and direction then, planets—though not apparently similar to people—are functionally similar to other collections of chemicals in constant coordination of their own group stability...a description which also fits humans. Whereas humans have brains and countries have governments for reflecting the overall internal and metaresponsive states of the collection however, planets have weather patterns for this purpose. This is not to say that apparently non-living volumes like planets should necessarily be granted the same dynamic status as humans. But it is to say that our denial of such status may be more the result of our own anthropocentrism than it is a view of the physical laws that constitute us. Interestingly, people who think of humans and spirits as bunches of physics should be some of the most spiritual people of all, seeing no major distinction between a man and any other megaquantum made of subquanta.

The question for me isn't whether there are other intelligent species in the universe but whether there are other intelligible species besides ourselves. Clearly the answer is yes. While we continue to search for other human-looking, upright, bipedal forms that manipulate artifacts the way we do, there are countless other self-sustaining systems whose methods of survival present us with communicative frontiers which may actually be more instructive (and more important for us to learn) than that of groups from beyond our planet. Certain trees, for example, don't need an alphabet or a state capital, but embedded in their rings is a history, and in their appearance a tale of their continual adaptation to their surroundings. Is there some kind of nondestructive technology we can use to translate a tree's history into a human-like story? I think so: ❋ By taking climate statistics on the tree's environment, sampling the local nutrient and fauna patterns among its many neighbors, and developing a data-to-speech program for processing this as well as more immediate cellular chemical flow in the leaves, we can develop a technology for "talking to the trees." Sounds very hippie, yes? Who in their right minds would do such a thing? The reader might be surprised. ❋ Not only is this ripe territory for a data scientist, an environmentalist, a tech developer, a linguist, or even a future economy for example, it also provides us with insight as to what we should expect given certain environmental decisions. If it is possible to scan a tree's rings and its bark and use data-to-speech recognition to have that tree tell us about the local soil and weather conditions over the past century, then it is also possible for the data-to-speech story to give us more immediate, human-recognizable information regarding what we should do with the environment in which the tree is found. ❋ The same process can be used to decipher the language of countries and cities given their histories, allowing us to predict the flow of collective cultures from a sociogeopolitical perspective. Although one might think that countries like as the US and China change drastically over time for example, history says they don't change much at all. This is largely due to their climates, natural resources, and original settlement conditions compared to other regions. To scan a country by comparing its internal and external "personality exchanges" to that of its neighbors (basically its spirit) is to have a discussion with that country regarding what it is most likely to do under certain political conditions. ❄ You wouldn't scan tree rings here, but would perform lexical and content analysis on the pronouncements of its representatives and the electors thereof. In this way, we can assign a human language to any self-sustaining pattern which requires energy to do so while continually adapting to its neighbors in development of itself.[51]

Assertion 96. If a thing satisfies the conditions for life and develops through interaction with other living neighbors which use the same system for internal processing, it can be said to have a language.
Just so we can avoid slipping too deeply into the esoteric, let us review the conditions for life that I presented in *144*. A thing is alive if

- it takes in energy from outside itself
- it alters or turns its outward behavior in order to do so
- it uses that energy to do things within itself according to a set process, and
- the inner processes it's maintaining are designed to change against the world outside itself

A thing was considered "not alive" (but not necessarily dead) if any of the above four conditions failed to hold. Note that giving birth, being born, and dying are not necessarily part of the above definition. Maybe they should be, but I didn't think they were critical to the general idea of intentional self-sustainment. Whatever the case, for any readers who think a thing must be a plant or an animal to be alive, I claim that the philosophical territory for showing that, say, Toyota, Brazil, and a bacterium are not alive is much harder to traverse than it looks. In the case of Toyota and Brazil, an analogy can be made between cells in a body and humans in an institution which greatly blurs the lines between life and nonlife.

Now we need to define language. Let's just say that a language is a mutually agreed upon system for sending and receiving information between at least two parties. It doesn't have to be written. It doesn't have to be structured (so the pig doesn't have to squeal in the same way in order to get its point across to another pig). And it *is* allowed to die with the parties who use it; so it doesn't have to exist independently of its users. If we impose the additional requirement that a living thing includes things more or less like itself as part of the outside world against which the former's internal processes are designed to change, then the system for taking input from that outside world is automatically implied, as is the system for changing at all. The combination of input and processing thereof within the living thing, alongside the idea that the living thing's neighbor is the same in its internal processing as the first living thing, means that both living things "know" what to do with input from the other by means of the same process, and the nature of the input constitutes the language. The internal processing of such language constitutes what it means to officially receive information from the other, while the behavior of the other which served as input for the one forms the basis of "sent" information.

So if every morning when I leave my house, I toss a piece of trash into your yard and you throw me the finger in turn, if we keep doing this "just because," then we will have developed a language for where the other person stands on things. No words required.

Assertion 97. A full space language conveys inner, interactant, and outer-world states between parties.
If we consider a pair of language users to be a collection of quanta possessing the same basic dimensions as fundamental quanta, then let us define a **full space language** as **one which conveys (inner) cycle spatial, (interactant) physical spatial, and (outer-world) interphysical spatial information between users**. Such information need not be explicitly conveyed, but can be encoded in the posture or mood of the sender. Accordingly, though a radio and a receiver may indeed share a 2.4GHz language between them, it would not be a full space language because the devices presumably don't talk about

---

[51] Honestly, if I were an advanced alien I would probably require that barbarous humans develop such technologies and show that they care about species other than themselves before making my group known. Otherwise I'd personally vote to blow them up if they got out of line. That's just me though.

themselves.[52] We will assume that full space languages, unlike non-full space languages, are capable of conveying the metaresponse information contained in so many living organisms, and that those organisms often use such language to convey such. We define full space languages to differentiate the kind of information passed between you and a horse, for example, versus you and your car. The language employed by you and your talking horse is one which presumes that you can return with gestures that against which the horse can more readily change its internal behavior. Unlike the horse, the car can't normally do things to sustain itself in response to the information passed between you and it. Not in 2018 anyway.

Although full space languages don't need to have implications for how "alive" their users are, they do have implications for the kinds of messaging systems which are of interest to us humans. I believe that any system against which we can develop a full space language is a system which is capable of having a human translatable version of its preferred dynamics available for us to understand.[53]

Assertion 98. Life-like entities known by humans range from cellular-level organisms to certain platonic constructs.

The following argument is more philosophical than other arguments I've given thus far, so bear with it until you see the ")"

We know that single celled organisms are still considered alive. As are plants and larger animals. I have also suggested that planets, countries, and organizations may also fit the definition of life, even if we are highly unlikely to bestow such a status upon those things. We humans—being the way we are—will probably never assign life to things that don't throw their genes around, even though there are many humans who won't do this either. We may always insist that a living thing demonstrate some kind of "willed" action, though a world where all causal facts were known would more likely remove *everything's* will. In any event, with the conditions for life established in a nonanthropocentric way, we may now investigate yet another kind of self-sustaining system: that of a social concept.

Can an abstract concept fit the conditions for life? I believe so. Not only have abstractions such as the US and Toyota already met the conditions, but you yourself as an identity might be considered an abstraction upon your physiology. Once embodied through a publicly observable process, an abstract concept which hijacks the observable process to reinforce its own continued formulation may be considered patently alive, so that the concept of Company X becomes a social reality. The concept of Country X has behavioral consequences for all the people in it and beyond.

Now what about an even more abstract concept like love? Does it fit the definition of life? In general, no. Just because some abstractions can be enlivened doesn't mean that all can be. Yet there are some concepts which, once invented, tend to accept input, sustain themselves, and adapt inwardly until the bitter end. Existence is perhaps the highest and best example of this.

Once the concept of "being" has been brought into being, it continues to insist upon itself in order for anything else to be. It accepts and adapts to any subject as "conceptual energy" with the automatic implication for the appropriate partner concepts as its mode for adapting its own definition. It even has a neighbor in the form of Nonexistence, which operates in a similar way. Existence continually turns towards its subject's contexts as fuel, develops alongside more contexts, and adapts its internally implied conception towards new conditional restrictions. The conceptual energy it uses is actually the interphysical and cycle space exchanges of those actors who communicate and think about it respectively.

Accordingly, Existence and its complement Nonexistence are both life-like concepts which reinforce themselves while adapting wherever they have been introduced. Again, we will stop short of calling them "alive," but it is instructive to note that concepts like this—especially when they have neighbors—may actually be capable of exchanging a kind of language with humans. The language of Existence for example might be something like Acknowledgement. That is, I may receive

---

[52] Nor were they considered alive to begin with. But as programming languages illustrate, you don't need to be alive to have a language.

[53] It is more challenging for us to develop a language for determining when that old monitor is about to go out than it is for us to develop a language for when Fifi needs her litter changed. Fifi the Cat likely has a system for telling you about her inner states as well as her outer ones. The monitor has a bunch of components. Understanding Fifi's language can help us better get along with her (we think). Understanding the monitor won't generally make much difference in how we deal with it or how it deals with itself.

information from Existence through the things I acknowledge to exist. I in turn send information back to my own local concept of Existence by changing my local framework to constrain what is allowed to exist next. Thanks to the paradox of time, Existence adapts to fit me. The language of Nonexistence would be something like nonacknowledgement.

Not surprisingly, Thingness, and Non-Thingness are also life-like concepts, since Things, once introduced, command an interaction on the part of the Viewer structure against their potential nonexistence—even if the interaction is simple acknowledgement of (or signal bouncing against) the thing by the Viewer as it processes the thing. Things accept interaction (or just plain energy) as their energy source; they develop in the role they serve against the time evolving interactant/Viewer, and the notion of the Thing adapts as new things are attended to. Cycle space, for example, may be thought of as the traversal of all possible types of things available to exist about a central energy carrier. The specific states may cycle in and out, but the general concept of a state as a Thing does not.

Abstract concepts like Existence and Nonexistence, Thingness and Non-Thingness, Energy and Potential, Sets and Elements, and Similarity and Difference all represent concepts which, where introduced, continue to absorb and adapt to the energy of those who conceive of them in reinforcement of their own conceptual structure. Each of these can be considered "Platonic" in the sense that the philosopher Plato would have considered them primitives from which more localized versions of each will have been considered only a spinoff of the overarching idea which insists on retaining its true form. Other concepts such as time and space however are not Platonic, mainly because their definitions don't automatically adapt to the kinds of attention we pay to them. Instead, other values change against them. Self-sustainment is a key condition for a thing being life-like. Ideas that don't make any attempt to be different in response to different contextual information fail the self-sustainment condition.

Beneath more universal Platonics like Existence and Thingness are Platonics that are more specific to life as we know it. Life is an obvious example of this, as are Health, Power (a subset of Potential), Death, Fear, Favor, and Interactant Attraction. Fear, for example, promotes its own importance in the brains of many animals, and yet continues to consume new information in constant reinvention of itself as a concept until halted by its partner Habituation (getting used to something). Attraction also sustains itself, but at ever-adapting potentials as the attracted thing attempts to pull closer.

Beneath life-related Platonics are human society-related Platonics like Institution, Dominion, and Exploration. Then there are human psychology-related Platonics like Fortune, Virtue, and Vice. Somewhere below these in scope are the human personal Platonics like, one's Good Fortune, one's Proper Course of Action (in light of one's Idealized Identity), and one's Idealized Identity. There are also these same Platonics as applied to the lives of others.

Now even if we have delved far into the realm of abstraction, I claim that certain constructs are able to provide us with a sufficiently translatable full space chain of information to allow us to personify them. In the same way that a database full of website clicks, vital statistics, or asteroids can reveal a pattern which can be translated into a human-relatable story, so too can the datasets on human virtues such as "strength over the ages" or those on Death provide us with a full space story on their interactions with others. How might one have a kind of conversation with Death? The same way one has a conversation with a country: by studying how the concept has been handled throughout history and across data sets, then developing a system for assessing its role in the lives of the currently living. If I know, for example, that Death has a lot of authority but can only arrive in direct full force once, doesn't typically hurt the dead, but gets most of its scare power from its partner The Unknown, is usually overcome with a certain amount of time, and is friendlier to the loved ones whom the deceased has armed with peace beforehand, then I know something about how this Platonic would greet anyone or anything anywhere. I gain the ability to consult Death regarding any person I meet if termination were to take them at that moment. And if I consulted Death I would likely find that, above all else, Death is chronically indifferent to most people most of the time (though intrigued by the people's clinging to Fear in the former's presence).[54] Does this make Death an actual spirit? That's for the reader to decide. (I haven't formed any opinion either way. That's not the point of all this.)

---

[54] At least I envision my own conversation with Death going this way.

The point of presenting certain platonics as life-like is not to argue for their having any specific form as things in spatial space, but to present them as collections of interaction patterns in cycle-psychological and interphysical space which can affect us with the same kind of personified power as actual people. If I can speak to a person across media and be affected by their personality, their internal states, and interactions, if I can be inspired by certain cartoon or movie characters, historical figures, or role models, then it is my ability to personify the information I receive and not necessarily the actual "living" status which determines my ability to communicate with the messenger (via a kind of language shared with the *experience* of the message sender if not the sender themselves).

It is through my experience of Existence that I am able to adapt both myself and my concept of Existence itself. The brand of attention and acknowledgement I give to Existence, akin to my own outlook on life, takes on the characteristics of a relationship with a higher concept which will survive me, which automatically accepts anything I have done or will do, and which—in the ideal world—holds the possibility of a situation in which I accept its idealized form for my life as well. People who have an easy time personifying something like this and building a more formal set of behaviors around it will have an easier time believing in God or a related Highest Force. People who aren't so interested in personifying such a thing will have an easier time not believing in such things. Interestingly though, the concept of Right or Wrong—if they would be considered Platonics at all—exist several levels below Existence itself (since the latter includes both and the former need baselines which assume the latter). This is to say that the view or nonview of a personifiable Highest Existence is a concept greater in scope than Right or Wrong. The right for me to judge a person's choice in this matter is, I believe, a product of my humanness more than a statement of whether Existence itself "cares." Leave it to humans to make a major issue of conceptions embedded mainly in themselves.

It is true, though, that certain concepts like Existence, Death, and Fear really are widespread enough among humans to have a certain array of human-relevant effects assigned to them. For these major Platonics we have developed special packages of interactions with labels such as "spirits," "angels," or "demons."

Assertion 99. Humans may engage in interaction with packages of interaction higher in scope than themselves.

It is unfortunate that the current state of science compels us to frame spirits mainly through the lens of metaphor. Electromagnetic and acoustic fields provide a model for capturing such exchanges as data. Now with the advanced state of image processing for self-driving cars and social assistance robots, we don't even need to measure the fields directly. Capturing and processing the video or audio of interpersonal exchanges has become our way of indirectly viewing the spacetime cones of those exchanges. I believe that one of the greatest impediments to our proper study of species beyond our easy perception is the idea that such species must exist on our scale of activity, in our form of matter. Although we know that ecosystems and continental shelves change over time for example, studying these on a scale that we can readily translate has mostly been confined to the realms of human curiosity and utility rather than that of their basic dynamic nature for communication's sake. So we know the basic science of earthquakes, but not the language thereof for reflecting human's alteration of the environments in which they occur. ❋ Here, I believe that the development of a common language for communicating with nonhuman volumes is essential for improving our interface with such volumes. Programming languages are an excellent example of how humans may greatly sharpen their interface with other forms (in this case machines) by developing a family of full space methods for dynamically changing their exchanges which such things.

Programming languages allow us to constrain the universe of possible behaviors for a machine to a specific desired process. They also allow us to obtain clear information regarding the state of the machine in processing, diagnostic, and interactional space. But we have yet to develop such languages for reliably reading businesses, countries, or the flow of a person's good fortune. As I discussed in the previous section, though, such languages may be easily developed using current technology. Access to the entities' historical pattern is, in most cases, key. So when it comes to developing a language which one may personally use to exchange with his or her Platonics, I believe the basic conditions are the same as those involved in normal language between publicly viewable people.

Three basic conditions for successful communication: willingness, coherence, and means

Humans seem to require three basic things for ongoing, successful communication with other humans (or their pets): the two parties must want to communicate with each other, they must have a basis for shared understanding, and they must have an appropriate communication channel to link them—part of which includes correct timing for at least one of the parties.

Willingness

For people like me who have experimented with communication with spirits without having any solid basis in a spiritual belief system which fosters it, such communication can be difficult. If I don't really believe that people from Oz exist, then not only will I more likely fail to recognize a real Ozian when I see one, but I will also fail to put in the required effort to understand the Ozian if his language isn't a familiar human one—even if that Ozian is sitting right next to me at the airport. Perhaps this is why occasionally when I attempt to talk to the spirit of Jesus in meditation (for basic chat), I don't get anything. Not only am I not Christian, but deep down I know I feel that I just don't need to talk to Jesus except for curiosity's sake. I don't have the subconscious willingness to engage this particular persona any more than I care that much to talk to the spirit of Richard Nixon. If it's just not within you to talk to certain things, you won't. Even if you think it would be interesting. This is a similar process to deciding what stores to frequent or what shows to watch. I have certain stores that I will never ever visit, even if the stores are right there. I just won't communicate with them. The things you communicate with need to line up with your basic motives for communication in general.

Coherence

If I want to communicate with another, but cannot understand them—especially if I cannot easily perceive them—then communication will be difficult. They speak French while I speak English. They speak in symbols and feelings while I expect words. The latter, Doreen Virtue (2013) says, is more typical of spirit guides. Humans, evolved to bond partly through excessive communication, unsurprisingly take sparse communication as noncommunication. So if a spirit were to send the average person a message in the form of a brief image, the person is very likely to not see it. This isn't just (possibly) true of "ghostly" spirits, but of spirits as we have defined them interactionally. If your interaction partner keeps telling you something that reflects what they actually want, but only bury it under tons of other words which they are sure are more acceptable to you, the extraperceptual information itself—the spirit of the interaction—will struggle to be seen by you. Getting back to physics briefly, I think that in hindsight it should be obvious that mass and temperature are dimensions relevant to quantum theory, since we play with these dimensions all the time independent of x, y, z, and t. But it wasn't obvious to me and isn't obvious to most people because the majority of our daily effort is not spent negotiating the masses and energy content of things. We're all about visual, spatial, and auditory cycle information instead. So other dimensions become incoherent. This holds for communication between parties as well. Especially for exchangers who don't need to prove themselves to you (like a person you idolize or a government) and those to whom you don't need to prove yourself (like a best friend, guide, or person who idolizes you), the excessive words we're used to employing to sell ourselves into a bond won't be necessary, and may actually confuse the objective of the message. This is especially true if you're inclined to infuse every extra word with your own interpretive biases, reaffirming what you already see rather than what the other is trying to get you to see. When it comes to communication, a vast space of "what did she mean" usually isn't good. Coherence means resisting translation errors, a task made much more challenging when we're talking to things that don't operate the way we do.

Means

Assuming you and the other are willing, assuming you're ready to receive their message via efficient feeling and symbols rather than through inefficient words, there remains the matter of establishing an appropriate communication channel with the other. Your government would love to talk to you, but can only do so at certain times through certain means. The same holds true for people with your phone number. Willing and ready doesn't always mean able. And so the proper resonance frequency has to be established. Dr. Virtue holds that there are four major means through which people can receive intuitive messages from afar: clairvoyance, clairaudience, clairsentience, and clairgustance. These are through sight, sound or thinking, touch, or taste/smell respectively.

I've already discussed how certain frequencies likely penetrate far beyond the individual producing them, especially when the physical volume housing the individual is of the same makeup as the system itself or the other individuals with which he or she communicates. So communicating with other quantic exchange patterns beyond oneself should not be complicated as long as you are sensitive enough to your own energy states and as long as the range of effect of the thing with which you're communicating overlaps with them and vice versa. What's left is to become familiar with your preferred means of transmission.

I've been both lucky and unlucky to lack a strong sense of visual perception. Unlike the artists I used to teach, I am not a visual person, visualization is hard, and showing me what you mean doesn't do a damned thing for me. Additionally, my sense of smell is pretty terrible. But I get A LOT of information through thinking (some of which could be called psychic), and I get very *accurate* information through touch and my bodily feeling about certain things. This is as true in meditative life as it is in waking life. Thanks to all of folklore out there regarding psychicism and third eye vision and such, I've been unlucky in learning that I'm just not set up to do those things well. Luckily though, I've learned that other modes of perception like touch are just as powerful, and can be trained without a person having to leave the real world regularly.

Of the 12-dimensions we've discussed, the m and $Д$ dimensions are most associated with the structured body. Within these dimensions, visual display (z_B interpreted as x_A), chemical smell (m as מ), cognitive thought and auditory hearing (נ and θ_B), and feeling touch ($Д$ as r_B), proprioception (ϕ_A as z_A), or mood (t or τ as β) each represent modes of information processing through which we may preferentially extract details about the environment or our relation to it. But our favorite mode doesn't cease to be our favorite just because we've woken up. The senses still remain active. Thus it is possible to train sharper perception by simply using those perceptions in the waking world towards whatever end is natural to the person. This has the added benefit of setting a clear agenda for the person's more spiritual efforts. When I myself go to sleep for example, I'm inclined to be curious about any otherworldly information that may be out there: psychic phone calls, dreams, aliens, guides, you name it. But this doesn't help me receive any single message clearly, because a guardian might send me something that I mistake for my own subconscious. Or my subconscious might send me something that I mistake for a guardian. After a while, being open to every possible channel not only gets confusing, but energetically and attention-wise wasteful. Training the preferred mode of sensing during the regular day's activities helps curb this tendency to let oneself be flooded with things which, though interesting, aren't really worth focusing on for very long.

Let us define a **dimensional sense** as **a regular use of the senses applied towards the extraction of dimension-specific information**. The idea of clairvoyance for example would involve the use of sight to extract cycle or interphysical information beyond the purview of vision in regular spatial space. Training a particular dimensional sense involves two steps: 1) using the sense and 2) doing something about what you've sensed. If your mood consistently changes when you're in an environment you know to be negative but you don't do anything about that mood, your body will adjust to the mood change and effectively learn to ignore it. Perhaps this is the ultimate fate of that intuition which young children are said to possess: training into adulthood merges the ability to perceive nonstandard resonances into the perception of standard ones. Such senses, however, rooted in basic quantum dimensions, should be recoverable as the person re-learns how to stop ignoring what they've sensed. In order to un-ignore something, the second step of responding to what's been perceived is critical. One responds to the negative feeling by leaving the area. One responds to the unexpected symbol by drawing it. In my case, I respond to the unexpected thought by recording it or (in the case of these books) writing it down. One responds to the unexpected smell by approaching or avoiding its source as well as the thought of the thing that comes to mind. That's it for training. Responding consistently to the impression retrains the body to better parse dimensions besides the standard ones. And the person doesn't have to roam through a dark house in order to do it.

Training the dimensional senses isn't necessary for observing things within our already trained natural scope of observation. But it tends to be very necessary for extracting situational information embedded in our interactions with those things. Through such training, we can better learn to receive and respond to resonances which can only be found in the intervening space between energy carriers, giving us access to contexts which are in so many ways larger than ourselves.

Assertion 100. The next best direction of action arises from an optimization strategy on one's preferred dimensional senses.

Although there are many paths we could take from an initial starting point in quantum mechanics-based spirituality, the most fruitful path will most likely be one especially designed for you the reader. Where spirituality begins as an extension of basic behavioral dynamics into the realm of one's surroundings, all that is left is to develop the appropriate language for talking to the surroundings themselves, not just the people in them. As a reminder though, "talking" consists of more than just words; "surroundings" consist of more than just physical space. Despite our tendency to mystify it, spirituality does not have to be very different from regular animal niche-making. Only the context has changed from a spatial one to an interaction-based one.

I've found that an overwhelming number of people these days are in search of happiness more than anything. After all of the technology, social performance, basic validation needs, and physiological needs have been met, many find that there is a certain expressive something which still eludes them. Oddly, this is where math may actually save the day. There is a space in which the span of possible events has already been reduced to actual events. What was uncertain yesterday is now certain today. Although we tend to believe that one cannot know what tomorrow brings, the heavily predictable nature of our surroundings as well as that of our selves suggests that, if we pay enough attention, we can actually have a pretty good idea of what comes next most of the time. As quanta attached to physical bodies which are attached to the larger volumes of quanta which contain us, we see certain experiences as wholly internal to us when, energetically, they are strongly tangled to the world beyond us. Via this entanglement, a view of the next best step for our choices becomes less of an inner existential mystery and more of an outer conversation with where we currently are—in not just 4 but in 12 dimensions. The 12-model of dimensions holds as one of its central premises the idea that, across all dimensions, even quantized energy doesn't just appear and disappear without passing through somewhere else. So everything we think and do can be expected to exchange resonances with some other volume of energy carriers which may or may not be found within our bodies. To determine the next best action in one's chain of decision making—be the individual as small as a finger twitch or large as life—is to establish a reliable form of communication with one's most reliable interphysical environment via one's most reliable dimensional sense. What do the visual symbols say? What do the thoughts or smells say? What does the signal flux say? Practicing with these and finding a language-like pattern in the information they give is a good way to get started reading the kinds of information which you continually share outside of your own mind.

I learned a valuable lesson in researching the asteroid 26 Proserpina. Whenever I read a person's chart, I always start by saying "astrology is a snapshot of the sky when you were born." Proserpina, however, lent an entirely new spin on this. Not only is the astrology chart a snapshot of the sky applied to a thing under that thing's inception, it is also a snapshot of the sky applied to the world in general under that thing's inception. Thinking of our DNA as the vehicle and our birth conditions as a map of salient places, we become decades-long transporters of a single moment across the terrain of countless other moments in 12-space—as though your DNA picked up a package called a birthdate and decided to carry it around for the rest of your physical life, similar to the way a snapshot of an ocean location will permanently capture all of the waves assembling there even as the sources of those original waves have moved on. The snapshot may not know much about itself, but through a lifetime of learned patterns of interaction with the rest of the ocean, may yet know itself through its interphysical collisions instead. Your astrological birth chart doesn't just show how *you* are likely to behave, it shows how all the world you interact with will likely behave against you for as long as you live. So there are at least two places in which to find your three spaces of dynamics: internally through your own thoughts and experiences, or externally through learned patterns in your interactions. Interfacing with your conception of the Platonics is one way to access the general evolution of your snapshot. Practicing using your dimensional senses in the regular world around you is another way.

Chapter 43: On Geography

As with any spherical energy carrier, a megaquantum like the Earth can't be expected to have any preferred direction unless some kind of "true north" or start point is imposed upon it. Prior to the activities of humans, we might have expected the natural starting point for an Earth day to coincide with some longitude at maximal energy during the summer solstice (or something like this). As humans began to organize themselves into timezones, however, the notion of a natural start point for the day gave way to a much stronger, artificially imposed one in the form of bands of people waking up, going to sleep, and doing business simultaneously in approximately 24 different blocks of time throughout the day. Perhaps this is why, when we look at the whole Earth, we see a couple of very broad patterns of human behavior which coincide with a very simple model for city cultures.

I began looking for an astrological mapping of the Earth a couple of days after finishing my interpretations of the first 1000 asteroids. My goal was to find an appropriate place to relocate after graduating, and I remembered some basic experiences of places that I had traveled to years before. No doubt about it, human settlements give rise to dense patterns of activity all over the Earth which are roughly analogous to energetic nerve centers on the surface of the planet. Once again exploding humans and the planet into quanta, we end up with a giant spinning ball dotted with hundreds of thousands of clusters packed with resonant exchanges flowing right to left as inhabits of the volume amplify the opportunities afforded by daylight—turning solar illumination almost directly into cross-organism interaction. Using the same dataset I've used throughout the *FSA* series alongside the newly interpreted 1000 asteroids, I took the locations of about 950 major cities (obtained from Wikipedia) and determined a natural pair of sign correspondences for each of them. This chapter contains the chart with my findings.

How can we be so sure that the astrological signs map onto the Earth by longitude?

- Because there is such a thing as the start of a day, and different clusters of cultures recognize different days for different reasons, it makes sense that the first longitude to experience a new day will be the reference point against which people in later longitudes perform. Japan knows about the 25th of December before the US does, rendering the US-Japan temporal relationship one which is $^6/_{12}$ to $^8/_{12}$ of a circle apart. This may not exactly imply a sign mapping, but in terms of our old potential energy cycle it does suggest that, as we move westward, clusters of actors located to the west of a reference point will tend to interact with clusters to the east of them as if the easterners already experienced some of what the westerners are about to experience. This same chain of "you just did what I'm about to do" stretches all around the human populated globe until we hit the International Date Line where the people and animals continue the same sequence of daily activity, but start a brand new count for yearly activity. In other words, even if the signs didn't map onto the Earth, a sequential cycle with a starting point would. That's exactly what the signs are.
- I began my city research with no idea that the above concept of a starting point would be so central. I actually thought Rome or Greenwich would be the center of any circle that I might find. But this wasn't the case. The asteroid data I used to line up certain bodies with certain cities revealed the Aries point to be located somewhere in a band through the Pacific Ocean, not the Atlantic.

- To me, the most compelling evidence of a sign mapping is related to the role of very broad cultures with respect to each other. If it is true that the 6th sign region west of the Earth's start point has a 150° potential energy relationship to the start as posed in our flattened snowflake model, then that region should have a more A+90+60 relationship to the 0° mark, giving it a Virgo-like relationship to the rest of the world. This is indeed what Europe and the Nordic countries east of Rome have done for the human world, in a band which includes Egypt, Greece, Mecca, as well as half of Rome. The Middle East is strongly Leo-like, India strongly Cancer, Japan heavily (and unsurprisingly Taurus), sociopolitically innovative New Zealand mostly Aries, and the eccentric US West Coast (including Seattle, San Francisco, L.A. and Portland) predictably Aquarian. These are just a few examples. Broadly speaking, the longitude of a location with respect to the International Date Line helps determine how the cultures there interact with other cultures in the world. But this isn't the only dimension of interest to us.

How can we be so sure that the astrological signs map onto the Earth by latitude?

Putting astrology aside for a moment, physical anthropology presents us with Bergman's and Allen's rules: darker, lankier species tend to live near the equator. Lighter, stockier animals tend to live near the poles. This tends to hold as long as other factors like local diet, migration patterns, and significantly modified resource-to-lifestyle patterns don't cloud the picture. For the purposes of energy conservation, we can expect more physical activity in more temperate climates, comparatively stationary activity patterns in colder climates, and more human activity in off-tropic[55] climates since we didn't evolve in the desert, but under more arboreal conditions instead. Relatedly, we can expect human tempers to be higher where human activity is more conducive to ingroup competition—the crowded off-tropic regions.

Throughout the Sun's yearly journey between 23.5° north and 23.5° south of the equator, the tropics of Cancer and Capricorn respectively, our Solar emitter leaves what amount to burn marks on the land as it parks in the same general spot for three months, creating desert conditions unless a nearby turbulent water source offsets this. Between the two tropic lines, north and south of them, and in the water cooled regions east of them we have latitudes conducive to large populations, creating a unique gradient of conditions which goes from very wintery at the north and south poles to very summery at the equator. Based on this we arrive at yet another mapping of the signs onto the Earth. This time, though, all 12 signs are squeezed into 180° of latitude, with a fluid sign change every 15°.

Although I initially thought the signs would map symmetrically about the equator, the social and political dominance of northern cultures over southern ones did not support this idea. Instead, the more world-oriented cultures of the north seemed to map using the more world oriented signs like Sagittarius and Capricorn. These cultures seemed to set the standard for their southern conquests, relegating them to the first six, internal signs instead. Although less precise than the discrete divisions of longitude, latitude lines also seemed to tell a story of progression towards then away from public interpersonal activity as we move north from the Tropic of Capricorn up to the North Pole. In fitting fashion, most of the Earth's population is located in regions corresponding to the public exchange signs Leo through Capricorn. By dividing all the latitude divisions into duodecanates (12ths) and then further into duoduodecanates (144ths), we finally arrive at a cultural grid system which seems to make sense. Latitude chops the Earth into slices which are organized by the extent to which they promote public, high energy, summery social exchange when compared to other latitudes.

Reading the City Table

For each city in the table below, I have taken the longitude sign and divided it into duodecanates. The sign cluster shows broadly how the relevant timezone-like band behaves with respect to other bands on the Earth, while the sign duodecanate shows how early or late the city processes time compared to other cities in its band. I have provided basic interpretations of the Earth's broad, human-informed measure of energy in that region using the following tables:

---

[55] "Off-tropic" refers to the regions away from the tropics of Cancer and Capricorn.

Sign	Sign Cluster Meaning	Sign Duodecanate Meaning
1	social innovation	is a source of affairs, leads other cities
2	the bearing of people in it	is a noteworthy travel destination
3	controlled thought	is vocal, social, expressively unhindered
4	being in touch with the beyond	is tourist nurturing
5	declaring its customs loudly	is a popular regional show stealer
6	developing rational structures for or presenting complex issues to the world	pursues a quest for greater relevance
7	dynamic exchanges of cultures	welcomes all
8	pushing its style and expressive culture on to other cultures	is a standards setter
9	declaring its own importance	provides noteworthy sights
10	holding a culture-stable society	hosts cultural structures
11	holding a dynamic, high-flux society	shows lots of activity
12	behaving in a mellow, "don't strain yourself" environment	is visited by all, a world city

Table 43-1: Longitude divisions for cities

The behavior of the people within a latitude band was subject to much more variation than the workings of longitudinal clusters across bands. This is most likely because it is much more convenient for people to migrate eastwards or westwards while remaining in the same general climate than it is for them to move northwards or southwards, effectively changing temperaments. I divided the sign clusters into sign, duodecanates, then duoduodecanates using the following rules:

Sign	Latitude Sign and Duoduodecanate Meaning	Latitude Duoduodecanate Meaning
1	{questing}	aims-insistent
2	{self-value aware}	materially-focused
3	thoughtful	expressive, communicative
4	concerned	nurturingly
5	showy	proud
6	busy	practical
7	enterprising	sociable
8	pushy	no-nonsense
9	self-declaring	confidently
10	objective-focused	(not necessarily negatively) calculatingly
11	community-anchored	(social) noisily
12	environment-attentive	spacey, odd

Table 43-2: Latitude divisions for cities

And now for the table of city cultures. ❋ I arrived at these descriptions formulaically via the above rules and comparisons of the cultures of 30 of the significant cities, but would love for others to test the validity of these results. For testing purposes, each of the descriptions for the cities below should be considered its own pair of hypotheses.[56] Lastly, it is important to note that **this table shows one's hypothesized impression of each region (human-to-earth) and NOT the city civics or happenings (city "birth" charts)**. This is a very important methodological matter which I talk about in Appendix II.

---

[56] In determining the proper alignment for the cities, I used the cultures of 30 anchor cities known by me including San Antonio, San Francisco, Seattle, Dover, New York, Paris, Rome, Austin, Monaco, Brisbane, Thessaloniki, Tokyo, Oklahoma City, Greenwich, London, Venice, Porto, Boston, and others. Particularly useful were cities like New York and Dover which were close to each other, but very different in their attitudes.

Table 43-3: Human-to-Earth City Cultures

Latitude	Longitude	City, Province, Country	Longitudinal Tropical Degree	Sign Cluster (culture's relationship to the rest of the world)	Social Tropical Duodecanate	Duodecanate Corrected	Sign Duodecanate	City Comment	Pole Culture (people's mood)	Pole Duodecanate	Pole Duoduodecanate	The area's culture is inclined to be seen broadly as
-16.50	-180.00	Rabi Island, Fiji	12.500	1	0	140	8	is a standards setter in social innovation	5	10	9	(not necessarily negatively) calculatingly showy in a self-declaring way
51.88	-176.65	Adak, Alaska, United States	9.150	1	0	141	9	provides noteworthy sights in social innovation	10	5	6	proud and objective-focused in a busy way
-13.28	-176.18	Mata-Utu, Wallis and Futuna, France	8.683	1	0	141	9	provides noteworthy sights in social innovation	6	1	4	aims-insistent and busy in a concerned way
-21.13	-175.20	Nukuʻalofa, Tonga	7.700	1	0	141	9	provides noteworthy sights in social innovation	5	7	1	sociable and showy in a {questing} way
-13.83	-171.75	Apia, Samoa	4.250	1	2	143	11	shows lots of activity in social innovation	6	12	11	spacey, odd, and busy in a community-anchored way
-14.28	-170.70	Pago Pago, American Samoa, United States	3.200	1	2	143	11	shows lots of activity in social innovation	6	12	6	spacey, odd, and busy in a busy way
-19.05	-169.92	Alofi, Niue, New Zealand	2.417	1	3	144	12	is visited by all, a world city in social innovation	5	8	9	no-nonsense and showy in a self-declaring way
-21.20	-159.77	Avarua, Cook Islands, New Zealand	352.267	12	7	4	4	is tourist nurturing in behaving in a mellow, "don't strain yourself" environment	5	7	12	sociable and showy in an environment-attentive way
21.32	-157.83	Honolulu, Hawaii, United States	350.333	12	7	4	4	is tourist nurturing in behaving in a mellow, "don't strain yourself" environment	8	5	12	proud and pushy in an environment-attentive way
71.30	-156.77	Barrow, Alaska, United States	349.267	12	8	5	5	is a popular regional show stealer in behaving in a mellow, "don't strain yourself" environment	11	9	12	confidently community-anchored in an environment-attentive way
19.70	-155.08	Hilo, Hawaii, United States	347.583	12	8	5	5	is a popular regional show stealer in behaving in a mellow, "don't strain yourself" environment	8	3	9	expressive, communicative, and pushy in a self-declaring way
61.22	-149.90	Anchorage, Alaska, United States	342.400	12	11	8	8	is a standards setter in behaving in a mellow, "don't strain yourself" environment	11	12	11	spacey, odd, and community-anchored in a community-anchored way
-17.53	-149.57	Papeete, French Polynesia, France	342.067	12	11	8	8	is a standards setter in behaving in a mellow, "don't strain yourself" environment	5	9	11	confidently showy in a community-anchored way
70.20	-148.52	Deadhorse, Alaska, United States	341.017	12	11	8	8	is a standards setter in behaving in a mellow, "don't strain yourself" environment	11	8	1	no-nonsense and community-anchored in a {questing} way
64.85	-147.72	Fairbanks, Alaska, United States	340.217	12	11	8	8	is a standards setter in behaving in a mellow, "don't strain yourself" environment	11	3	10	expressive, communicative, and community-anchored in an objective-focused way
57.05	-135.33	Sitka, Alaska, United States	327.833	11	16	13	1	is a source of affairs, leads other cities in holding a dynamic, high-flux society	10	9	7	confidently objective-focused in an enterprising way
60.72	-135.05	Whitehorse, Yukon, Canada	327.550	11	16	13	1	is a source of affairs, leads other cities in holding a dynamic, high-flux society	11	12	6	spacey, odd, and community-anchored in a busy way
58.30	-134.42	Juneau, Alaska, United States	326.917	11	17	14	2	is a noteworthy travel destination in holding a dynamic, high-flux society	10	10	7	(not necessarily negatively) calculatingly objective-focused in an enterprising way
69.45	-133.03	Tuktoyaktuk, Northwest Territories, Canada	325.533	11	17	14	2	is a noteworthy travel destination in holding a dynamic, high-flux society	11	7	6	sociable and community-anchored in a busy way
-25.07	-130.10	Adamstown, Pitcairn Islands, United Kingdom	322.600	11	18	15	3	is vocal, social, expressively unhindered in holding a dynamic, high-flux society	5	3	11	expressive, communicative, and showy in a community-anchored way
48.43	-123.37	Victoria, British Columbia, Canada	315.867	11	21	18	6	pursues a quest for greater relevance in holding a dynamic, high-flux society	10	2	8	materially-focused and objective-focused in a pushy way
49.25	-123.10	Vancouver, British Columbia, Canada	315.600	11	21	18	6	pursues a quest for greater relevance in holding a dynamic, high-flux society	10	3	4	expressive, communicative, and objective-focused in a concerned way
45.52	-122.68	Portland, Oregon, United States	315.183	11	21	18	6	pursues a quest for greater relevance in holding a dynamic, high-flux society	10	12	4	spacey, odd, and objective-focused in a concerned way
37.78	-122.42	San Francisco, California, United States	314.917	11	22	19	7	welcomes all in holding a dynamic, high-flux society	9	6	2	practical and self-declaring in a {self-value aware} way

47.62	-122.33	Seattle, Washington, United States	314.833	11	22	19	7	welcomes all in holding a dynamic, high-flux society	10	2	1	materially-focused and objective-focused in a {questing} way
38.55	-121.47	Sacramento, California, United States	313.967	11	22	19	7	welcomes all in holding a dynamic, high-flux society	9	6	10	practical and self-declaring in an objective-focused way
50.68	-120.33	Kamloops, British Columbia, Canada	312.833	11	22	19	7	welcomes all in holding a dynamic, high-flux society	10	4	6	nurturingly objective-focused in a busy way
39.53	-119.82	Reno, Nevada, United States	312.317	11	23	20	8	is a standards setter in holding a dynamic, high-flux society	9	7	7	sociable and self-declaring in an enterprising way
34.43	-119.72	Santa Barbara, California, United States	312.217	11	23	20	8	is a standards setter in holding a dynamic, high-flux society	9	3	6	expressive, communicative, and self-declaring in a busy way
49.88	-119.50	Kelowna, British Columbia, Canada	312.000	11	23	20	8	is a standards setter in holding a dynamic, high-flux society	10	3	10	expressive, communicative, and objective-focused in an objective-focused way
55.17	-118.80	Grande Prairie, Alberta, Canada	311.300	11	23	20	8	is a standards setter in holding a dynamic, high-flux society	10	8	1	no-nonsense and objective-focused in a {questing} way
34.05	-118.25	Los Angeles, California, United States	310.750	11	23	20	8	is a standards setter in holding a dynamic, high-flux society	9	3	2	expressive, communicative, and self-declaring in a {self-value aware} way
33.95	-117.40	Riverside, California, United States	309.900	11	24	21	9	provides noteworthy sights in holding a dynamic, high-flux society	9	3	1	expressive, communicative, and self-declaring in a {questing} way
32.72	-117.17	San Diego, California, United States	309.667	11	24	21	9	provides noteworthy sights in holding a dynamic, high-flux society	9	2	2	materially-focused and self-declaring in a {self-value aware} way
32.53	-117.03	Tijuana, Baja California, Mexico	309.533	11	24	21	9	provides noteworthy sights in holding a dynamic, high-flux society	9	2	12	materially-focused and self-declaring in an environment-attentive way
31.85	-116.60	Ensenada, Baja California, Mexico	309.100	11	24	21	9	provides noteworthy sights in holding a dynamic, high-flux society	9	1	5	aims-insistent and self-declaring in a showy way
43.62	-116.20	Boise, Idaho, United States	308.700	11	24	21	9	provides noteworthy sights in holding a dynamic, high-flux society	9	10	10	(not necessarily negatively) calculatingly self-declaring in an objective-focused way
32.67	-115.47	Mexicali, Baja California, Mexico	307.967	11	24	21	9	provides noteworthy sights in holding a dynamic, high-flux society	9	2	1	materially-focused and self-declaring in a {questing} way
36.18	-115.13	Las Vegas, Nevada, United States	307.633	11	24	21	9	provides noteworthy sights in holding a dynamic, high-flux society	9	4	11	nurturingly self-declaring in a community-anchored way
62.45	-114.40	Yellowknife, Northwest Territories, Canada	306.900	11	25	22	10	hosts cultural structures in holding a dynamic, high-flux society	11	1	11	aims-insistent and community-anchored in a community-anchored way
51.05	-114.07	Calgary, Alberta, Canada	306.567	11	25	22	10	hosts cultural structures in holding a dynamic, high-flux society	10	4	10	nurturingly objective-focused in an objective-focused way
53.53	-113.50	Edmonton, Alberta, Canada	306.000	11	25	22	10	hosts cultural structures in holding a dynamic, high-flux society	10	6	9	practical and objective-focused in a self-declaring way
33.45	-112.07	Phoenix, Arizona, United States	304.567	11	26	23	11	shows lots of activity in holding a dynamic, high-flux society	9	2	9	materially-focused and self-declaring in a self-declaring way
46.60	-112.03	Helena, Montana, United States	304.533	11	26	23	11	shows lots of activity in holding a dynamic, high-flux society	10	1	3	aims-insistent and objective-focused in a thoughtful way
40.75	-111.88	Salt Lake City, Utah, United States	304.383	11	26	23	11	shows lots of activity in holding a dynamic, high-flux society	9	8	7	no-nonsense and self-declaring in an enterprising way
56.73	-111.38	Fort McMurray, Alberta, Canada	303.883	11	26	23	11	shows lots of activity in holding a dynamic, high-flux society	10	9	4	confidently objective-focused in a concerned way
29.10	-110.95	Hermosillo, Sonora, Mexico	303.450	11	26	23	11	shows lots of activity in holding a dynamic, high-flux society	8	11	3	(social) noisily pushy in a thoughtful way
32.22	-110.93	Tucson, Arizona, United States	303.433	11	26	23	11	shows lots of activity in holding a dynamic, high-flux society	9	1	9	aims-insistent and self-declaring in a self-declaring way
22.88	-109.92	Cabo San Lucas, Baja California Sur, Mexico	302.417	11	27	24	12	is visited by all, a world city in holding a dynamic, high-flux society	8	6	3	practical and pushy in a thoughtful way
-27.15	-109.43	Hanga Roa, Easter Island, Chile	301.933	11	27	24	12	is visited by all, a world city in holding a dynamic, high-flux society	5	2	3	materially-focused and showy in a thoughtful way
24.80	-107.38	Culiacán, Sinaloa, Mexico	299.883	10	28	25	1	is a source of affairs, leads other cities in holding a culture-stable society	8	7	10	sociable and pushy in an objective-focused way
52.13	-106.68	Saskatoon, Saskatchewan, Canada	299.183	10	28	25	1	is a source of affairs, leads other cities in holding a culture-stable society	10	5	8	proud and objective-focused in a pushy way
35.12	-106.62	Albuquerque, New Mexico, United States	299.117	10	28	25	1	is a source of affairs, leads other cities in holding a culture-stable society	9	4	1	nurturingly self-declaring in a {questing} way
31.73	-106.48	Ciudad Juárez, Chihuahua, Mexico	298.983	10	28	25	1	is a source of affairs, leads other cities in holding a culture-stable society	9	1	4	aims-insistent and self-declaring in a concerned way
31.78	-106.42	El Paso, Texas, United States	298.917	10	28	25	1	is a source of affairs, leads other cities in holding a culture-stable society	9	1	5	aims-insistent and self-declaring in a showy way
35.88	-106.30	Los Alamos, New Mexico, United States	298.800	10	28	25	1	is a source of affairs, leads other cities in holding a culture-stable society	9	4	8	nurturingly self-declaring in a pushy way
28.63	-106.08	Chihuahua, Chihuahua, Mexico	298.583	10	28	25	1	is a source of affairs, leads other cities in holding a culture-stable society	8	10	10	(not necessarily negatively) calculatingly pushy in an objective-focused way
35.67	-105.97	Santa Fe, New Mexico, United States	298.467	10	28	25	1	is a source of affairs, leads other cities in holding a culture-stable society	9	4	6	nurturingly self-declaring in a busy way
40.02	-105.28	Boulder, Colorado, United States	297.783	10	28	25	1	is a source of affairs, leads other cities in holding a culture-stable society	9	8	12	no-nonsense and self-declaring in an environment-attentive way
20.67	-105.27	Puerto Vallarta, Jalisco, Mexico	297.767	10	28	25	1	is a source of affairs, leads other cities in holding a culture-stable society	8	4	6	nurturingly pushy in a busy way

39.73	-104.98	Denver, Colorado, United States	297.483	10	29	26	2	is a noteworthy travel destination in holding a culture-stable society	9	7	9	sociable and self-declaring in a self-declaring way
41.15	-104.80	Cheyenne, Wyoming, United States	297.300	10	29	26	2	is a noteworthy travel destination in holding a culture-stable society	9	8	11	no-nonsense and self-declaring in a community-anchored way
24.02	-104.67	Durango, Durango, Mexico	297.167	10	29	26	2	is a noteworthy travel destination in holding a culture-stable society	8	7	2	sociable and pushy in a {self-value aware} way
50.45	-104.60	Regina, Saskatchewan, Canada	297.100	10	29	26	2	is a noteworthy travel destination in holding a culture-stable society	10	4	4	nurturingly objective-focused in a concerned way
25.53	-103.45	Torreón, Coahuila, Mexico	295.950	10	29	26	2	is a noteworthy travel destination in holding a culture-stable society	8	8	5	no-nonsense and pushy in a showy way
20.72	-103.40	Zapopan, Jalisco, Mexico	295.900	10	29	26	2	is a noteworthy travel destination in holding a culture-stable society	8	4	6	nurturingly pushy in a busy way
20.67	-103.35	Guadalajara, Jalisco, Mexico	295.850	10	29	26	2	is a noteworthy travel destination in holding a culture-stable society	8	4	6	nurturingly pushy in a busy way
21.88	-102.30	Aguascalientes, Aguascalientes, Mexico	294.800	10	30	27	3	is vocal, social, expressively unhindered in holding a culture-stable society	8	5	6	proud and pushy in a busy way
21.12	-101.68	León, Guanajuato, Mexico	294.183	10	30	27	3	is vocal, social, expressively unhindered in holding a culture-stable society	8	4	10	nurturingly pushy in an objective-focused way
22.15	-100.85	San Luis Potosí, San Luis Potosí, Mexico	293.350	10	30	27	3	is vocal, social, expressively unhindered in holding a culture-stable society	8	5	8	proud and pushy in a pushy way
46.82	-100.78	Bismarck, North Dakota, United States	293.283	10	30	27	3	is vocal, social, expressively unhindered in holding a culture-stable society	10	1	5	aims-insistent and objective-focused in a showy way
20.58	-100.40	Querétaro, Querétaro, Mexico	292.900	10	30	27	3	is vocal, social, expressively unhindered in holding a culture-stable society	8	4	5	nurturingly pushy in a showy way
44.37	-100.33	Pierre, South Dakota, United States	292.833	10	30	27	3	is vocal, social, expressively unhindered in holding a culture-stable society	9	11	5	(social) noisily self-declaring in a showy way
25.67	-100.30	Monterrey, Nuevo León, Mexico	292.800	10	30	27	3	is vocal, social, expressively unhindered in holding a culture-stable society	8	8	6	no-nonsense and pushy in a busy way
16.87	-99.88	Acapulco, Guerrero, Mexico	292.383	10	31	28	4	is tourist nurturing in holding a culture-stable society	8	1	5	aims-insistent and pushy in a showy way
19.43	-99.13	Mexico City, Mexico	291.633	10	31	28	4	is tourist nurturing in holding a culture-stable society	8	3	6	expressive, communicative, and pushy in a busy way
29.42	-98.50	San Antonio, Texas, United States	291.000	10	31	28	4	is tourist nurturing in holding a culture-stable society	8	11	6	(social) noisily pushy in a busy way
19.05	-98.22	Puebla, Puebla, Mexico	290.717	10	31	28	4	is tourist nurturing in holding a culture-stable society	8	3	6	expressive, communicative, and pushy in a {self-value aware} way
22.25	-97.87	Tampico, Tamaulipas, Mexico	290.367	10	31	28	4	is tourist nurturing in holding a culture-stable society	8	5	9	proud and pushy in a self-declaring way
30.25	-97.75	Austin, Texas, United States	290.250	10	31	28	4	is tourist nurturing in holding a culture-stable society	9	12	2	spacey, odd, and self-declaring in a {self-value aware} way
35.48	-97.53	Oklahoma City, Oklahoma, United States	290.033	10	31	28	4	is tourist nurturing in holding a culture-stable society	9	4	4	nurturingly self-declaring in a concerned way
37.68	-97.33	Wichita, Kansas, United States	289.833	10	32	29	5	is a popular regional show stealer in holding a culture-stable society	9	6	1	practical and self-declaring in a {questing} way
49.90	-97.13	Winnipeg, Manitoba, Canada	289.633	10	32	29	5	is a popular regional show stealer in holding a culture-stable society	10	3	11	expressive, communicative, and objective-focused in a community-anchored way
32.78	-96.80	Dallas, Texas, United States	289.300	10	32	29	5	is a popular regional show stealer in holding a culture-stable society	9	2	2	materially-focused and self-declaring in a {self-value aware} way
40.82	-96.68	Lincoln, Nebraska, United States	289.183	10	32	29	5	is a popular regional show stealer in holding a culture-stable society	9	8	7	no-nonsense and self-declaring in an enterprising way
19.18	-96.15	Veracruz, Veracruz, Mexico	288.650	10	32	29	5	is a popular regional show stealer in holding a culture-stable society	8	3	4	expressive, communicative, and pushy in a concerned way
36.13	-95.93	Tulsa, Oklahoma, United States	288.433	10	32	29	5	is a popular regional show stealer in holding a culture-stable society	9	4	10	nurturingly self-declaring in an objective-focused way
29.77	-95.38	Houston, Texas, United States	287.883	10	32	29	5	is a popular regional show stealer in holding a culture-stable society	8	11	9	(social) noisily pushy in a self-declaring way
39.10	-94.58	Kansas City, Missouri, United States	287.083	10	33	30	6	pursues a quest for greater relevance in holding a culture-stable society	9	7	3	sociable and self-declaring in a thoughtful way
41.58	-93.62	Des Moines, Iowa, United States	286.117	10	33	30	6	pursues a quest for greater relevance in holding a culture-stable society	9	9	3	confidently self-declaring in a thoughtful way
37.20	-93.28	Springfield, Missouri, United States	285.783	10	33	30	6	pursues a quest for greater relevance in holding a culture-stable society	9	5	9	proud and self-declaring in a self-declaring way
44.98	-93.27	Minneapolis, Minnesota, United States	285.767	10	33	30	6	pursues a quest for greater relevance in holding a culture-stable society	9	11	11	(social) noisily self-declaring in a community-anchored way
34.73	-92.33	Little Rock, Arkansas, United States	284.833	10	34	31	7	welcomes all in holding a culture-stable society	9	3	9	expressive, communicative, and self-declaring in a self-declaring way
14.90	-92.27	Tapachula, Chiapas, Mexico	284.767	10	34	31	7	welcomes all in holding a culture-stable society	7	11	11	(social) noisily enterprising in a community-anchored way

14.83	-91.52	Quetzaltenango, Guatemala	284.017	10	34	31	7	welcomes all in holding a culture-stable society	7	11	10	(social) noisily enterprising in an objective-focused way
14.62	-90.53	Guatemala City, Guatemala	283.033	10	34	31	7	welcomes all in holding a culture-stable society	7	11	8	(social) noisily enterprising in a pushy way
38.63	-90.20	St. Louis, Missouri, United States	282.700	10	34	31	7	welcomes all in holding a culture-stable society	9	6	10	practical and self-declaring in an objective-focused way
32.30	-90.18	Jackson, Mississippi, United States	282.683	10	34	31	7	welcomes all in holding a culture-stable society	9	1	10	aims-insistent and self-declaring in an objective-focused way
29.97	-90.05	New Orleans, Louisiana, United States	282.550	10	34	31	7	welcomes all in holding a culture-stable society	8	11	11	(social) noisily pushy in a community-anchored way
35.12	-89.97	Memphis, Tennessee, United States	282.467	10	35	32	8	is a standards setter in holding a culture-stable society	9	4	1	nurturingly self-declaring in a {questing} way
20.97	-89.62	Mérida, Yucatán, Mexico	282.117	10	35	32	8	is a standards setter in holding a culture-stable society	8	4	9	nurturingly pushy in a self-declaring way
48.38	-89.25	Thunder Bay, Ontario, Canada	281.750	10	35	32	8	is a standards setter in holding a culture-stable society	10	2	8	materially-focused and objective-focused in a pushy way
13.68	-89.18	San Salvador, El Salvador	281.683	10	35	32	8	is a standards setter in holding a culture-stable society	7	10	11	(not necessarily negatively) calculatingly enterprising in a community-anchored way
17.25	-88.77	Belmopan, Belize	281.267	10	35	32	8	is a standards setter in holding a culture-stable society	8	1	9	aims-insistent and pushy in a self-declaring way
17.50	-88.18	Belize City, Belize	280.683	10	35	32	8	is a standards setter in holding a culture-stable society	8	2	12	materially-focused and pushy in an environment-attentive way
30.70	-88.05	Mobile, Alabama, United States	280.550	10	35	32	8	is a standards setter in holding a culture-stable society	9	12	6	spacey, odd, and self-declaring in a busy way
43.05	-87.95	Milwaukee, Wisconsin, United States	280.450	10	35	32	8	is a standards setter in holding a culture-stable society	9	10	5	(not necessarily negatively) calculatingly self-declaring in a showy way
41.88	-87.63	Chicago, Illinois, United States	280.133	10	35	32	8	is a standards setter in holding a culture-stable society	9	9	6	confidently self-declaring in a busy way
14.10	-87.22	Tegucigalpa, Honduras	279.717	10	36	33	9	provides noteworthy sights in holding a culture-stable society	7	11	3	(social) noisily enterprising in a thoughtful way
12.62	-87.15	Chinandega, Nicaragua	279.650	10	36	33	9	provides noteworthy sights in holding a culture-stable society	7	10	1	(not necessarily negatively) calculatingly enterprising in a {questing} way
21.17	-86.85	Cancún, Quintana Roo, Mexico	279.350	10	36	33	9	provides noteworthy sights in holding a culture-stable society	8	4	11	nurturingly pushy in a community-anchored way
33.65	-86.82	Birmingham, Alabama, United States	279.317	10	36	33	9	provides noteworthy sights in holding a culture-stable society	9	2	11	materially-focused and self-declaring in a community-anchored way
36.17	-86.78	Nashville, Tennessee, United States	279.283	10	36	33	9	provides noteworthy sights in holding a culture-stable society	9	4	11	nurturingly self-declaring in a community-anchored way
12.13	-86.25	Managua, Nicaragua	278.750	10	36	33	9	provides noteworthy sights in holding a culture-stable society	7	9	8	confidently enterprising in a pushy way
39.77	-86.15	Indianapolis, Indiana, United States	278.650	10	36	33	9	provides noteworthy sights in holding a culture-stable society	9	7	9	sociable and self-declaring in a self-declaring way
79.98	-85.93	Eureka, Nunavut, Canada	278.433	10	36	33	9	provides noteworthy sights in holding a culture-stable society	12	3	11	expressive, communicative, and environment-attentive in a community-anchored way
38.25	-85.77	Louisville, Kentucky, United States	278.267	10	36	33	9	provides noteworthy sights in holding a culture-stable society	9	6	7	practical and self-declaring in an enterprising way
10.63	-85.43	Liberia, Costa Rica	277.933	10	36	33	9	provides noteworthy sights in holding a culture-stable society	7	8	6	no-nonsense and enterprising in a busy way
41.08	-85.13	Fort Wayne, Indiana, United States	277.633	10	36	33	9	provides noteworthy sights in holding a culture-stable society	9	8	10	no-nonsense and self-declaring in an objective-focused way
9.97	-84.83	Puntarenas, Costa Rica	277.333	10	37	34	10	hosts cultural structures in holding a culture-stable society	7	7	11	sociable and enterprising in a community-anchored way
39.10	-84.52	Cincinnati, Ohio, United States	277.017	10	37	34	10	hosts cultural structures in holding a culture-stable society	9	7	3	sociable and self-declaring in a thoughtful way
33.75	-84.38	Atlanta, Georgia, United States	276.883	10	37	34	10	hosts cultural structures in holding a culture-stable society	9	3	12	expressive, communicative, and self-declaring in an environment-attentive way
46.53	-84.35	Sault Ste. Marie, Ontario, Canada	276.850	10	37	34	10	hosts cultural structures in holding a culture-stable society	10	1	2	aims-insistent and objective-focused in a {self-value aware} way
10.02	-84.22	Alajuela, Costa Rica	276.717	10	37	34	10	hosts cultural structures in holding a culture-stable society	7	8	12	no-nonsense and enterprising in an environment-attentive way
9.93	-84.08	San José, Costa Rica	276.583	10	37	34	10	hosts cultural structures in holding a culture-stable society	7	7	11	sociable and enterprising in a community-anchored way
35.97	-83.95	Knoxville, Tennessee, United States	276.450	10	37	34	10	hosts cultural structures in holding a culture-stable society	9	4	9	nurturingly self-declaring in a self-declaring way
42.33	-83.05	Detroit, Michigan, United States	275.550	10	37	34	10	hosts cultural structures in holding a culture-stable society	9	9	10	confidently self-declaring in an objective-focused way
9.98	-83.03	Limón, Costa Rica	275.533	10	37	34	10	hosts cultural structures in holding a culture-stable society	7	7	11	sociable and enterprising in a community-anchored way
42.28	-83.00	Windsor, Ontario, Canada	275.500	10	37	34	10	hosts cultural structures in holding a culture-stable society	9	9	9	confidently self-declaring in a self-declaring way
39.98	-82.98	Columbus, Ohio, United States	275.483	10	37	34	10	hosts cultural structures in holding a culture-stable society	9	7	11	sociable and self-declaring in a community-anchored way

76.42	-82.90	Grise Fiord, Nunavut, Canada	275.400	10	37	34	10	hosts cultural structures in holding a culture-stable society	12	1	1	aims-insistent and environment-attentive in a {questing} way
27.95	-82.47	Tampa, Florida, United States	274.967	10	38	35	11	shows lots of activity in holding a culture-stable society	8	10	4	(not necessarily negatively) calculatingly pushy in a concerned way
23.13	-82.38	Havana, Cuba	274.883	10	38	35	11	shows lots of activity in holding a culture-stable society	8	6	6	practical and pushy in a busy way
24.57	-81.78	Key West, Florida, United States	274.283	10	38	35	11	shows lots of activity in holding a culture-stable society	8	7	7	sociable and pushy in an enterprising way
30.33	-81.67	Jacksonville, Florida, United States	274.167	10	38	35	11	shows lots of activity in holding a culture-stable society	9	12	3	spacey, odd, and self-declaring in a thoughtful way
41.48	-81.67	Cleveland, Ohio, United States	274.167	10	38	35	11	shows lots of activity in holding a culture-stable society	9	9	2	confidently self-declaring in a {self-value aware} way
38.35	-81.63	Charleston, West Virginia, United States	274.133	10	38	35	11	shows lots of activity in holding a culture-stable society	9	6	8	practical and self-declaring in a pushy way
19.30	-81.38	George Town, Cayman Islands, United Kingdom	273.883	10	38	35	11	shows lots of activity in holding a culture-stable society	8	3	5	expressive, communicative, and pushy in a showy way
28.42	-81.30	Orlando, Florida, United States	273.800	10	38	35	11	shows lots of activity in holding a culture-stable society	8	10	8	(not necessarily negatively) calculatingly pushy in a pushy way
34.00	-81.05	Columbia, South Carolina, United States	273.550	10	38	35	11	shows lots of activity in holding a culture-stable society	9	3	2	expressive, communicative, and self-declaring in a {self-value aware} way
46.48	-81.02	Sudbury, Ontario, Canada	273.517	10	38	35	11	shows lots of activity in holding a culture-stable society	10	1	2	aims-insistent and objective-focused in a {self-value aware} way
35.23	-80.85	Charlotte, North Carolina, United States	273.350	10	38	35	11	shows lots of activity in holding a culture-stable society	9	4	2	nurturing self-declaring in a {self-value aware} way
25.78	-80.22	Miami, Florida, United States	272.717	10	38	35	11	shows lots of activity in holding a culture-stable society	8	8	7	no-nonsense and pushy in an enterprising way
40.45	-80.00	Pittsburgh, Pennsylvania, United States	272.500	10	39	36	12	is visited by all, a world city in holding a culture-stable society	9	8	4	no-nonsense and self-declaring in a concerned way
-2.18	-79.88	Guayaquil, Ecuador	272.383	10	39	36	12	is visited by all, a world city in holding a culture-stable society	6	10	3	(not necessarily negatively) calculatingly busy in a thoughtful way
8.98	-79.52	Panama City, Panama	272.017	10	39	36	12	is visited by all, a world city in holding a culture-stable society	7	7	2	sociable and enterprising in a {self-value aware} way
46.30	-79.45	North Bay, Ontario, Canada	271.950	10	39	36	12	is visited by all, a world city in holding a culture-stable society	10	1	12	aims-insistent and objective-focused in an environment-attentive way
43.70	-79.40	Toronto, Ontario, Canada	271.900	10	39	36	12	is visited by all, a world city in holding a culture-stable society	9	10	11	(not necessarily negatively) calculatingly self-declaring in a community-anchored way
-8.12	-79.03	Trujillo, Peru	271.533	10	39	36	12	is visited by all, a world city in holding a culture-stable society	6	5	6	proud and busy in a busy way
42.90	-78.85	Buffalo, New York, United States	271.350	10	39	36	12	is visited by all, a world city in holding a culture-stable society	9	10	3	(not necessarily negatively) calculatingly self-declaring in a thoughtful way
35.82	-78.65	Raleigh, North Carolina, United States	271.150	10	39	36	12	is visited by all, a world city in holding a culture-stable society	9	4	7	nurturingly self-declaring in an enterprising way
-0.25	-78.58	Quito, Ecuador	271.083	10	39	36	12	is visited by all, a world city in holding a culture-stable society	6	11	9	(social) noisily busy in a self-declaring way
34.22	-77.92	Wilmington, North Carolina, United States	270.417	10	39	36	12	is visited by all, a world city in holding a culture-stable society	9	3	4	expressive, communicative, and self-declaring in a concerned way
43.17	-77.62	Rochester, New York, United States	270.117	10	39	36	12	is visited by all, a world city in holding a culture-stable society	9	10	6	(not necessarily negatively) calculatingly self-declaring in a busy way
25.07	-77.33	Nassau, Bahamas	269.833	9	40	37	1	is a source of affairs, leads other cities in declaring its own importance	8	8	12	no-nonsense and pushy in an environment-attentive way
-12.05	-77.03	Lima, Peru	269.533	9	40	37	1	is a source of affairs, leads other cities in declaring its own importance	6	2	4	materially-focused and busy in a concerned way
38.90	-77.03	Washington, District of Columbia, United States	269.533	9	40	37	1	is a source of affairs, leads other cities in declaring its own importance	9	7	1	sociable and self-declaring in a {questing} way
17.98	-76.80	Kingston, Jamaica	269.300	9	40	37	1	is a source of affairs, leads other cities in declaring its own importance	8	2	4	materially-focused and pushy in a concerned way
39.28	-76.62	Baltimore, Maryland, United States	269.117	9	40	37	1	is a source of affairs, leads other cities in declaring its own importance	9	7	5	sociable and self-declaring in a showy way
3.42	-76.52	Santiago de Cali, Colombia	269.017	9	40	37	1	is a source of affairs, leads other cities in declaring its own importance	7	2	8	materially-focused and enterprising in a pushy way
36.85	-75.98	Virginia Beach, Virginia, United States	268.483	9	40	37	1	is a source of affairs, leads other cities in declaring its own importance	9	5	5	proud and self-declaring in a showy way
20.02	-75.82	Santiago de Cuba, Cuba	268.317	9	40	37	1	is a source of affairs, leads other cities in declaring its own importance	8	4	12	nurturingly pushy in an environment-attentive way
45.42	-75.68	Ottawa, Ontario, Canada	268.183	9	40	37	1	is a source of affairs, leads other cities in declaring its own importance	10	12	3	spacey, odd, and objective-focused in a thoughtful way
6.23	-75.58	Medellín, Colombia	268.083	9	40	37	1	is a source of affairs, leads other cities in declaring its own importance	7	4	11	nurturingly enterprising in a community-anchored way
39.17	-75.53	Dover, Delaware, United States	268.033	9	40	37	1	is a source of affairs, leads other cities in declaring its own importance	9	7	3	sociable and self-declaring in a thoughtful way
10.40	-75.50	Cartagena, Colombia	268.000	9	40	37	1	is a source of affairs, leads other cities in declaring its own importance	7	8	3	no-nonsense and enterprising in a thoughtful way
39.95	-75.17	Philadelphia, Pennsylvania, United States	267.667	9	40	37	1	is a source of affairs, leads other cities in declaring its own importance	9	7	11	sociable and self-declaring in a community-anchored way

10.97	-74.80	Barranquilla, Colombia	267.300		9	41	38	2	is a noteworthy travel destination in declaring its own importance	7	8	9	no-nonsense and enterprising in a self-declaring way
40.22	-74.77	Trenton, New Jersey, United States	267.267		9	41	38	2	is a noteworthy travel destination in declaring its own importance	9	8	2	no-nonsense and self-declaring in a {self-value aware} way
-13.17	-74.22	Ayacucho, Peru	266.717		9	41	38	2	is a noteworthy travel destination in declaring its own importance	6	1	5	aims-insistent and busy in a showy way
39.80	-74.10	Forked River, New Jersey, United States	266.600		9	41	38	2	is a noteworthy travel destination in declaring its own importance	9	7	10	sociable and self-declaring in an objective-focused way
4.60	-74.08	Bogotá, Colombia	266.583		9	41	38	2	is a noteworthy travel destination in declaring its own importance	7	3	8	expressive, communicative, and enterprising in a pushy way
40.72	-74.07	Jersey City, New Jersey, United States	266.567		9	41	38	2	is a noteworthy travel destination in declaring its own importance	9	8	6	no-nonsense and self-declaring in a busy way
40.67	-73.93	New York City, New York, United States	266.433		9	41	38	2	is a noteworthy travel destination in declaring its own importance	9	8	6	no-nonsense and self-declaring in a busy way
45.50	-73.57	Montreal, Quebec, Canada	266.067		9	41	38	2	is a noteworthy travel destination in declaring its own importance	10	12	4	spacey, odd, and objective-focused in a concerned way
-39.82	-73.25	Valdivia, Chile	265.750		9	41	38	2	is a noteworthy travel destination in declaring its own importance	4	4	1	nurturingly concerned in a {questing} way
-3.73	-73.25	Iquitos, Peru	265.750		9	41	38	2	is a noteworthy travel destination in declaring its own importance	6	9	12	confidently busy in an environment-attentive way
-36.83	-73.05	Concepción, Chile	265.550		9	41	38	2	is a noteworthy travel destination in declaring its own importance	4	6	6	practical and concerned in a busy way
-41.47	-72.93	Puerto Montt, Chile	265.433		9	41	38	2	is a noteworthy travel destination in declaring its own importance	4	2	9	materially-focused and concerned in a self-declaring way
-45.40	-72.68	Puerto Aisén, Chile	265.183		9	41	38	2	is a noteworthy travel destination in declaring its own importance	3	11	8	(social) noisily thoughtful in a pushy way
-38.75	-72.67	Temuco, Chile	265.167		9	41	38	2	is a noteworthy travel destination in declaring its own importance	4	4	11	nurturingly concerned in a community-anchored way
41.77	-72.67	Hartford, Connecticut, United States	265.167		9	41	38	2	is a noteworthy travel destination in declaring its own importance	9	9	4	confidently self-declaring in a concerned way
44.25	-72.57	Montpelier, Vermont, United States	265.067		9	41	38	2	is a noteworthy travel destination in declaring its own importance	9	11	4	(social) noisily self-declaring in a concerned way
7.90	-72.50	Cúcuta, Colombia	265.000		9	42	39	3	is vocal, social, expressively unhindered in declaring its own importance	7	6	3	practical and enterprising in a thoughtful way
18.53	-72.33	Port-au-Prince, Haiti	264.833		9	42	39	3	is vocal, social, expressively unhindered in declaring its own importance	8	2	9	materially-focused and pushy in a self-declaring way
-45.57	-72.07	Coihaique, Chile	264.567		9	42	39	3	is vocal, social, expressively unhindered in declaring its own importance	3	11	6	(social) noisily thoughtful in a busy way
-13.53	-71.97	Cusco, Peru	264.467		9	42	39	3	is vocal, social, expressively unhindered in declaring its own importance	6	1	2	aims-insistent and busy in a {self-value aware} way
10.65	-71.63	Maracaibo, Venezuela	264.133		9	42	39	3	is vocal, social, expressively unhindered in declaring its own importance	7	8	6	no-nonsense and enterprising in a busy way
-33.05	-71.62	Valparaíso, Chile	264.117		9	42	39	3	is vocal, social, expressively unhindered in declaring its own importance	4	9	6	confidently concerned in a busy way
-16.40	-71.53	Arequipa, Peru	264.033		9	42	39	3	is vocal, social, expressively unhindered in declaring its own importance	5	10	10	(not necessarily negatively) calculatingly showy in an objective-focused way
43.20	-71.53	Concord, New Hampshire, United States	264.033		9	42	39	3	is vocal, social, expressively unhindered in declaring its own importance	9	10	6	(not necessarily negatively) calculatingly self-declaring in a busy way
41.82	-71.42	Providence, Rhode Island, United States	263.917		9	42	39	3	is vocal, social, expressively unhindered in declaring its own importance	9	9	5	confidently self-declaring in a showy way
-41.15	-71.30	San Carlos de Bariloche, Río Negro, Argentina	263.800		9	42	39	3	is vocal, social, expressively unhindered in declaring its own importance	4	3	12	expressive, communicative, and concerned in an environment-attentive way
-29.90	-71.25	La Serena, Chile	263.750		9	42	39	3	is vocal, social, expressively unhindered in declaring its own importance	5	12	12	spacey, odd, and showy in an environment-attentive way
46.82	-71.22	Quebec City, Quebec, Canada	263.717		9	42	39	3	is vocal, social, expressively unhindered in declaring its own importance	10	1	5	aims-insistent and objective-focused in a showy way
21.47	-71.13	Cockburn Town, Turks and Caicos Islands, United Kingdom	263.633		9	42	39	3	is vocal, social, expressively unhindered in declaring its own importance	8	5	2	proud and pushy in a {self-value aware} way
42.35	**-71.07**	Boston, Massachusetts, United States	263.567		9	**42**	39	3	is vocal, social, expressively unhindered in declaring its own importance	**9**	**9**	**10**	confidently self-declaring in an objective-focused way
-53.17	-70.93	Punta Arenas, Chile	263.433		9	42	39	3	is vocal, social, expressively unhindered in declaring its own importance	3	5	5	proud and thoughtful in a showy way

-33.45	-70.67	Santiago, Chile	263.167	9	42	39	3	is vocal, social, expressively unhindered in declaring its own importance	4	9	2	confidently concerned in a {self-value aware} way
-23.65	-70.40	Antofagasta, Chile	262.900	9	42	39	3	is vocal, social, expressively unhindered in declaring its own importance	5	5	12	proud and showy in an environment-attentive way
-27.37	-70.33	Copiapó, Chile	262.833	9	42	39	3	is vocal, social, expressively unhindered in declaring its own importance	5	2	1	materially-focused and showy in a {questing} way
-18.48	-70.33	Arica, Chile	262.833	9	42	39	3	is vocal, social, expressively unhindered in declaring its own importance	5	9	2	confidently showy in a {self-value aware} way
-20.22	-70.15	Iquique, Chile	262.650	9	42	39	3	is vocal, social, expressively unhindered in declaring its own importance	5	7	9	sociable and showy in a self-declaring way
12.52	-70.03	Oranjestad, Aruba, Netherlands	262.533	9	42	39	3	is vocal, social, expressively unhindered in declaring its own importance	7	10	12	(not necessarily negatively) calculatingly enterprising in an environment-attentive way
18.47	-69.95	Santo Domingo, Dominican Republic	262.450	9	43	40	4	is tourist nurturing in declaring its own importance	8	2	9	materially-focused and pushy in a self-declaring way
44.32	-69.78	Augusta, Maine, United States	262.283	9	43	40	4	is tourist nurturing in declaring its own importance	9	11	5	(social) noisily self-declaring in a showy way
77.47	-69.23	Qaanaaq, Greenland, Denmark	261.733	9	43	40	4	is tourist nurturing in declaring its own importance	12	1	11	aims-insistent and environment-attentive in a community-anchored way
-51.63	-69.22	Río Gallegos, Santa Cruz, Argentina	261.717	9	43	40	4	is tourist nurturing in declaring its own importance	3	6	8	practical and thoughtful in a pushy way
-22.47	-68.93	Calama, Chile	261.433	9	43	40	4	is tourist nurturing in declaring its own importance	5	6	12	practical and showy in an environment-attentive way
12.12	-68.93	Willemstad, Curaçao, Netherlands	261.433	9	43	40	4	is tourist nurturing in declaring its own importance	7	9	8	confidently enterprising in a pushy way
-32.88	-68.82	Mendoza, Mendoza, Argentina	261.317	9	43	40	4	is tourist nurturing in declaring its own importance	4	9	8	confidently concerned in a pushy way
63.75	-68.52	Iqaluit, Nunavut, Canada	261.017	9	43	40	4	is tourist nurturing in declaring its own importance	11	3	12	expressive, communicative, and community-anchored in an environment-attentive way
-54.80	-68.30	Ushuaia, Tierra del Fuego, Argentina	260.800	9	43	40	4	is tourist nurturing in declaring its own importance	3	4	1	nurturingly thoughtful in a {questing} way
-16.50	-68.15	La Paz, Bolivia	260.650	9	43	40	4	is tourist nurturing in declaring its own importance	5	10	9	(not necessarily negatively) calculatingly showy in a self-declaring way
-9.97	-67.82	Rio Branco, Acre, Brazil	260.317	9	43	40	4	is tourist nurturing in declaring its own importance	6	4	12	nurturingly busy in an environment-attentive way
5.67	-67.63	Puerto Ayacucho, Venezuela	260.133	9	43	40	4	is tourist nurturing in declaring its own importance	7	4	6	nurturingly enterprising in a busy way
-54.93	-67.62	Puerto Williams, Chile	260.117	9	43	40	4	is tourist nurturing in declaring its own importance	3	4	12	nurturingly thoughtful in an environment-attentive way
10.25	-67.60	Maracay, Venezuela	260.100	9	43	40	4	is tourist nurturing in declaring its own importance	7	8	2	no-nonsense and enterprising in a {self-value aware} way
-45.87	-67.48	Comodoro Rivadavia, Chubut, Argentina	259.983	9	44	41	5	is a popular regional show stealer in declaring its own importance	3	11	3	(social) noisily thoughtful in a thoughtful way
-55.08	-67.08	Puerto Toro, Chile	259.583	9	44	41	5	is a popular regional show stealer in declaring its own importance	3	3	11	expressive, communicative, and thoughtful in a community-anchored way
10.50	-66.92	Caracas, Venezuela	259.417	9	44	41	5	is a popular regional show stealer in declaring its own importance	7	8	4	no-nonsense and enterprising in a concerned way
45.95	-66.67	Fredericton, New Brunswick, Canada	259.167	9	44	41	5	is a popular regional show stealer in declaring its own importance	10	12	9	spacey, odd, and objective-focused in a self-declaring way
43.83	-66.12	Yarmouth, Nova Scotia, Canada	258.617	9	44	41	5	is a popular regional show stealer in declaring its own importance	9	11	12	(social) noisily self-declaring in an environment-attentive way
45.28	-66.08	Saint John, New Brunswick, Canada	258.583	9	44	41	5	is a popular regional show stealer in declaring its own importance	10	12	2	spacey, odd, and objective-focused in a {self-value aware} way
18.45	-66.07	San Juan, Puerto Rico, United States	258.567	9	44	41	5	is a popular regional show stealer in declaring its own importance	8	2	9	materially-focused and pushy in a self-declaring way
-24.78	-65.42	Salta, Salta, Argentina	257.917	9	44	41	5	is a popular regional show stealer in declaring its own importance	5	4	2	nurturingly showy in a {self-value aware} way
-43.25	-65.30	Trelew, Chubut, Argentina	257.800	9	44	41	5	is a popular regional show stealer in declaring its own importance	4	1	4	aims-insistent and concerned in a concerned way
-19.05	-65.25	Sucre, Bolivia	257.750	9	44	41	5	is a popular regional show stealer in declaring its own importance	5	8	9	no-nonsense and showy in a self-declaring way
-26.82	-65.22	San Miguel de Tucumán, Tucumán, Argentina	257.717	9	44	41	5	is a popular regional show stealer in declaring its own importance	5	2	6	materially-focused and showy in a busy way
18.35	-64.95	Charlotte Amalie, United States Virgin Islands, United States	257.450	9	45	42	6	pursues a quest for greater relevance in declaring its own importance	8	2	8	materially-focused and pushy in a pushy way
32.30	-64.78	Hamilton, Bermuda, United Kingdom	257.283	9	45	42	6	pursues a quest for greater relevance in declaring its own importance	9	1	10	aims-insistent and self-declaring in an objective-focused way

46.13	-64.77	Moncton, New Brunswick, Canada	257.267	9	45	42	6	pursues a quest for greater relevance in declaring its own importance	10	12	10	spacey, odd, and objective-focused in an objective-focused way
18.43	-64.62	Road Town, British Virgin Islands, United Kingdom	257.117	9	45	42	6	pursues a quest for greater relevance in declaring its own importance	8	2	8	materially-focused and pushy in a pushy way
-31.42	-64.18	Córdoba, Córdoba, Argentina	256.683	9	45	42	6	pursues a quest for greater relevance in declaring its own importance	4	10	10	(not necessarily negatively) calculatingly concerned in an objective-focused way
-8.77	-63.90	Porto Velho, Rondônia, Brazil	256.400	9	45	42	6	pursues a quest for greater relevance in declaring its own importance	6	4	11	nurturingly busy in a community-anchored way
8.12	-63.55	Ciudad Bolívar, Venezuela	256.050	9	45	42	6	pursues a quest for greater relevance in declaring its own importance	7	6	5	practical and enterprising in a showy way
44.85	-63.20	Halifax, Nova Scotia, Canada	255.700	9	45	42	6	pursues a quest for greater relevance in declaring its own importance	9	11	10	(social) noisily self-declaring in an objective-focused way
-17.80	-63.17	Santa Cruz de la Sierra, Bolivia	255.667	9	45	42	6	pursues a quest for greater relevance in declaring its own importance	5	9	9	confidently showy in a self-declaring way
46.23	-63.15	Charlottetown, Prince Edward Island, Canada	255.650	9	45	42	6	pursues a quest for greater relevance in declaring its own importance	10	12	11	spacey, odd, and objective-focused in a community-anchored way
18.22	-63.05	The Valley, Anguilla, United Kingdom	255.550	9	45	42	6	pursues a quest for greater relevance in declaring its own importance	8	2	6	materially-focused and pushy in a busy way
17.30	-62.73	Basseterre, Saint Kitts and Nevis	255.233	9	45	42	6	pursues a quest for greater relevance in declaring its own importance	8	1	10	aims-insistent and pushy in an objective-focused way
82.50	-62.33	Alert, Nunavut, Canada	254.833	9	46	43	7	welcomes all in declaring its own importance	12	6	12	practical and environment-attentive in an environment-attentive way
-38.72	-62.27	Bahía Blanca, Buenos Aires Province, Argentina	254.767	9	46	43	7	welcomes all in declaring its own importance	4	5	12	proud and concerned in an environment-attentive way
17.12	-61.85	St. John's, Antigua and Barbuda	254.350	9	46	43	7	welcomes all in declaring its own importance	8	1	8	aims-insistent and pushy in a pushy way
12.05	-61.75	St. George's, Grenada	254.250	9	46	43	7	welcomes all in declaring its own importance	7	9	7	confidently enterprising in an enterprising way
16.00	-61.73	Basse-Terre, Guadeloupe, France	254.233	9	46	43	7	welcomes all in declaring its own importance	8	12	9	spacey, odd, and pushy in a self-declaring way
10.67	-61.52	Port of Spain, Trinidad and Tobago	254.017	9	46	43	7	welcomes all in declaring its own importance	7	8	6	no-nonsense and enterprising in a busy way
10.28	-61.47	San Fernando, Trinidad and Tobago	253.967	9	46	43	7	welcomes all in declaring its own importance	7	8	2	no-nonsense and enterprising in a {self-value aware} way
15.30	-61.38	Roseau, Dominica	253.883	9	46	43	7	welcomes all in declaring its own importance	8	12	2	spacey, odd, and pushy in a {self-value aware} way
10.50	-61.38	Chaguanas, Trinidad and Tobago	253.883	9	46	43	7	welcomes all in declaring its own importance	7	8	4	no-nonsense and enterprising in a concerned way
13.15	-61.23	Kingstown, Saint Vincent and the Grenadines	253.733	9	46	43	7	welcomes all in declaring its own importance	7	10	6	(not necessarily negatively) calculatingly enterprising in a busy way
14.60	-61.08	Fort-de-France, Martinique, France	253.583	9	46	43	7	welcomes all in declaring its own importance	7	11	8	(social) noisily enterprising in a pushy way
14.02	-60.98	Castries, Saint Lucia	253.483	9	46	43	7	welcomes all in declaring its own importance	7	11	2	(social) noisily enterprising in a {self-value aware} way
-32.95	-60.67	Rosario, Santa Fe, Argentina	253.167	9	46	43	7	welcomes all in declaring its own importance	4	9	7	confidently concerned in an enterprising way
2.82	-60.67	Boa Vista, Roraima, Brazil	253.167	9	46	43	7	welcomes all in declaring its own importance	7	2	3	materially-focused and enterprising in a thoughtful way
-3.10	-60.02	Manaus, Amazonas, Brazil	252.517	9	46	43	7	welcomes all in declaring its own importance	6	9	6	confidently busy in a busy way
13.10	-59.62	Bridgetown, Barbados	252.117	9	47	44	8	is a standards setter in declaring its own importance	7	10	5	(not necessarily negatively) calculatingly enterprising in a showy way
-34.60	-58.38	Buenos Aires, Argentina	250.883	9	47	44	8	is a standards setter in declaring its own importance	4	8	3	no-nonsense and concerned in a thoughtful way
6.80	-58.17	Georgetown, Guyana	250.667	9	47	44	8	is a standards setter in declaring its own importance	7	5	5	proud and enterprising in a showy way
-51.70	-57.87	Stanley, Falkland Islands, United Kingdom	250.367	9	47	44	8	is a standards setter in declaring its own importance	3	6	7	practical and thoughtful in an enterprising way
-25.28	-57.63	Asunción, Paraguay	250.133	9	47	44	8	is a standards setter in declaring its own importance	5	3	9	expressive, communicative, and showy in a self-declaring way
-34.88	-56.18	Montevideo, Uruguay	248.683	9	48	45	9	provides noteworthy sights in declaring its own importance	4	8	1	no-nonsense and concerned in a {questing} way
46.78	-56.18	Saint-Pierre, Saint Pierre and Miquelon, France	248.683	9	48	45	9	provides noteworthy sights in declaring its own importance	10	1	5	aims-insistent and objective-focused in a showy way
72.78	-56.15	Upernavik, Greenland, Denmark	248.650	9	48	45	9	provides noteworthy sights in declaring its own importance	11	10	2	(not necessarily negatively) calculatingly community-anchored in a {self-value aware} way
-15.60	-56.10	Cuiabá, Mato Grosso, Brazil	248.600	9	48	45	9	provides noteworthy sights in declaring its own importance	5	11	6	(social) noisily showy in a busy way
-11.85	-55.65	Sinop, Mato Grosso, Brazil	248.150	9	48	45	9	provides noteworthy sights in declaring its own importance	6	2	6	materially-focused and busy in a busy way
5.87	-55.17	Paramaribo, Suriname	247.667	9	48	45	9	provides noteworthy sights in declaring its own importance	7	4	8	nurturingly enterprising in a pushy way
-20.47	-54.62	Campo Grande, Mato Grosso do Sul, Brazil	247.117	9	49	46	10	hosts cultural structures in declaring its own importance	5	7	7	sociable and showy in an enterprising way

-25.52	-54.62	Ciudad del Este, Paraguay	247.117	9	49	46	10	hosts cultural structures in declaring its own importance	5	3	7	expressive, communicative, and showy in an enterprising way
-33.68	-53.45	Chuí, Rio Grande do Sul, Brazil	245.950	9	49	46	10	hosts cultural structures in declaring its own importance	4	9	12	confidently concerned in an environment-attentive way
47.57	-52.70	St. John's, Newfoundland and Labrador, Canada	245.200	9	49	46	10	hosts cultural structures in declaring its own importance	10	2	12	materially-focused and objective-focused in an environment-attentive way
-31.77	-52.35	Pelotas, Rio Grande do Sul, Brazil	244.850	9	50	47	11	shows lots of activity in declaring its own importance	4	10	7	(not necessarily negatively) calculatingly concerned in an enterprising way
4.92	-52.33	Cayenne, French Guiana, France	244.833	9	50	47	11	shows lots of activity in declaring its own importance	7	3	11	expressive, communicative, and enterprising in a community-anchored way
64.18	-51.73	Nuuk (Godthåb), Greenland, Denmark	244.233	9	50	47	11	shows lots of activity in declaring its own importance	11	3	4	expressive, communicative, and community-anchored in a concerned way
-30.03	-51.23	Porto Alegre, Rio Grande do Sul, Brazil	243.733	9	50	47	11	shows lots of activity in declaring its own importance	4	11	11	(social) noisily concerned in a community-anchored way
0.03	-51.07	Macapá, Amapá, Brazil	243.567	9	50	47	11	shows lots of activity in declaring its own importance	7	12	12	spacey, odd, and enterprising in an environment-attentive way
-22.67	-50.42	Assis, São Paulo, Brazil	242.917	9	50	47	11	shows lots of activity in declaring its own importance	5	5	10	proud and showy in an objective-focused way
-20.80	-49.38	São José do Rio Preto, São Paulo, Brazil	241.883	9	51	48	12	is visited by all, a world city in declaring its own importance	5	7	4	sociable and showy in a concerned way
-16.67	-49.25	Goiânia, Goiás, Brazil	241.750	9	51	48	12	is visited by all, a world city in declaring its own importance	5	10	7	(not necessarily negatively) calculatingly showy in an enterprising way
-25.42	-49.25	Curitiba, Paraná, Brazil	241.750	9	51	48	12	is visited by all, a world city in declaring its own importance	5	3	7	expressive, communicative, and showy in an enterprising way
-22.32	-49.07	Bauru, São Paulo, Brazil	241.567	9	51	48	12	is visited by all, a world city in declaring its own importance	5	6	1	practical and showy in a {questing} way
-1.45	-48.50	Belém, Pará, Brazil	241.000	9	51	48	12	is visited by all, a world city in declaring its own importance	6	10	10	(not necessarily negatively) calculatingly busy in an objective-focused way
-27.83	-48.42	Florianópolis, Santa Catarina, Brazil	240.917	9	51	48	12	is visited by all, a world city in declaring its own importance	5	1	8	aims-insistent and showy in a pushy way
-10.18	-48.33	Palmas, Tocantins, Brazil	240.833	9	51	48	12	is visited by all, a world city in declaring its own importance	6	3	10	expressive, communicative, and busy in an objective-focused way
-18.92	-48.28	Uberlândia, Minas Gerais, Brazil	240.783	9	51	48	12	is visited by all, a world city in declaring its own importance	5	8	10	no-nonsense and showy in an objective-focused way
-21.80	-48.18	Araraquara, São Paulo, Brazil	240.683	9	51	48	12	is visited by all, a world city in declaring its own importance	5	6	6	practical and showy in a busy way
-15.80	-47.87	Brasília, Distrito Federal, Brazil	240.367	9	51	48	12	is visited by all, a world city in declaring its own importance	5	11	4	(social) noisily showy in a concerned way
-21.18	-47.80	Ribeirão Preto, São Paulo, Brazil	240.300	9	51	48	12	is visited by all, a world city in declaring its own importance	5	7	12	sociable and showy in an environment-attentive way
-5.53	-47.48	Imperatriz, Maranhão, Brazil	239.983	8	52	49	1	is a source of affairs, leads other cities in pushing its style and expressive culture on to other cultures	6	7	6	sociable and busy in a busy way
-22.90	-47.05	Campinas, São Paulo, Brazil	239.550	8	52	49	1	is a source of affairs, leads other cities in pushing its style and expressive culture on to other cultures	5	5	8	proud and showy in a pushy way
-23.55	-46.63	São Paulo, São Paulo, Brazil	239.133	8	52	49	1	is a source of affairs, leads other cities in pushing its style and expressive culture on to other cultures	5	5	1	proud and showy in a {questing} way
-21.78	-46.57	Poços de Caldas, Minas Gerais, Brazil	239.067	8	52	49	1	is a source of affairs, leads other cities in pushing its style and expressive culture on to other cultures	5	6	6	practical and showy in a busy way
60.72	-46.03	Qaqortoq, Greenland, Denmark	238.533	8	52	49	1	is a source of affairs, leads other cities in pushing its style and expressive culture on to other cultures	11	12	6	spacey, odd, and community-anchored in a busy way
-23.18	-45.88	São José dos Campos, São Paulo, Brazil	238.383	8	52	49	1	is a source of affairs, leads other cities in pushing its style and expressive culture on to other cultures	5	5	5	proud and showy in a showy way
-2.53	-44.30	São Luís, Maranhão, Brazil	236.800	8	53	50	2	is a noteworthy travel destination in pushing its style and expressive culture on to other cultures	6	9	11	confidently busy in a community-anchored way
-19.92	-43.93	Belo Horizonte, Minas Gerais, Brazil	236.433	8	53	50	2	is a noteworthy travel destination in pushing its style and expressive culture on to other cultures	5	8	12	no-nonsense and showy in an environment-attentive way
-21.77	-43.35	Juiz de Fora, Minas Gerais, Brazil	235.850	8	53	50	2	is a noteworthy travel destination in pushing its style and expressive culture on to other cultures	5	6	7	practical and showy in an enterprising way
-22.92	-43.20	Rio de Janeiro, Rio de Janeiro, Brazil	235.700	8	53	50	2	is a noteworthy travel destination in pushing its style and expressive culture on to other cultures	5	5	8	proud and showy in a pushy way

-5.10	-42.80	Teresina, Piauí, Brazil	235.300	8	53	50	2	is a noteworthy travel destination in pushing its style and expressive culture on to other cultures	6	7	11	sociable and busy in a community-anchored way
-18.85	-41.93	Governador Valadares, Minas Gerais, Brazil	234.433	8	54	51	3	is vocal, social, expressively unhindered in pushing its style and expressive culture on to other cultures	5	8	11	no-nonsense and showy in a community-anchored way
-9.40	-40.50	Petrolina, Pernambuco, Brazil	233.000	8	54	51	3	is vocal, social, expressively unhindered in pushing its style and expressive culture on to other cultures	6	4	5	nurturingly busy in a showy way
-20.32	-40.33	Vitória, Espírito Santo, Brazil	232.833	8	54	51	3	is vocal, social, expressively unhindered in pushing its style and expressive culture on to other cultures	5	7	8	sociable and showy in a pushy way
-3.67	-40.23	Sobral, Ceará, Brazil	232.733	8	54	51	3	is vocal, social, expressively unhindered in pushing its style and expressive culture on to other cultures	6	9	12	confidently busy in an environment-attentive way
-7.20	-39.33	Juazeiro do Norte, Ceará, Brazil	231.833	8	55	52	4	is tourist nurturing in pushing its style and expressive culture on to other cultures	6	6	2	practical and busy in a {self-value aware} way
-14.78	-39.05	Ilhéus, Bahia, Brazil	231.550	8	55	52	4	is tourist nurturing in pushing its style and expressive culture on to other cultures	6	12	2	spacey, odd, and busy in a {self-value aware} way
-3.72	-38.55	Fortaleza, Ceará, Brazil	231.050	8	55	52	4	is tourist nurturing in pushing its style and expressive culture on to other cultures	6	9	12	confidently busy in an environment-attentive way
-12.97	-38.48	Salvador, Bahia, Brazil	230.983	8	55	52	4	is tourist nurturing in pushing its style and expressive culture on to other cultures	6	1	7	aims-insistent and busy in an enterprising way
-10.92	-37.05	Aracaju, Sergipe, Brazil	229.550	8	56	53	5	is a popular regional show stealer in pushing its style and expressive culture on to other cultures	6	3	3	expressive, communicative, and busy in a thoughtful way
-54.28	-36.50	Grytviken, South Georgia and the South Sandwich Islands, United Kingdom	229.000	8	56	53	5	is a popular regional show stealer in pushing its style and expressive culture on to other cultures	3	4	6	nurturingly thoughtful in a busy way
-8.88	-36.50	Garanhuns, Pernambuco, Brazil	229.000	8	56	53	5	is a popular regional show stealer in pushing its style and expressive culture on to other cultures	6	4	10	nurturingly busy in an objective-focused way
-8.28	-35.98	Caruaru, Pernambuco, Brazil	228.483	8	56	53	5	is a popular regional show stealer in pushing its style and expressive culture on to other cultures	6	5	4	proud and busy in a concerned way
-7.23	-35.88	Campina Grande, Paraíba, Brazil	228.383	8	56	53	5	is a popular regional show stealer in pushing its style and expressive culture on to other cultures	6	6	2	practical and busy in a {self-value aware} way
-9.67	-35.73	Maceió, Alagoas, Brazil	228.233	8	56	53	5	is a popular regional show stealer in pushing its style and expressive culture on to other cultures	6	4	3	nurturingly busy in a thoughtful way
-5.78	-35.20	Natal, Rio Grande do Norte, Brazil	227.700	8	56	53	5	is a popular regional show stealer in pushing its style and expressive culture on to other cultures	6	7	4	sociable and busy in a concerned way
-8.05	-34.90	Recife, Pernambuco, Brazil	227.400	8	57	54	6	pursues a quest for greater relevance in pushing its style and expressive culture on to other cultures	6	5	6	proud and busy in a busy way
-7.08	-34.83	João Pessoa, Paraíba, Brazil	227.333	8	57	54	6	pursues a quest for greater relevance in pushing its style and expressive culture on to other cultures	6	6	3	practical and busy in a thoughtful way
-3.85	-32.42	Fernando de Noronha, Pernambuco, Brazil	224.917	8	58	55	7	welcomes all in pushing its style and expressive culture on to other cultures	6	8	11	no-nonsense and busy in a community-anchored way
39.47	-31.23	Flores Island, Azores, Portugal	223.733	8	58	55	7	welcomes all in pushing its style and expressive culture on to other cultures	9	7	6	sociable and self-declaring in a busy way
38.58	-28.72	Horta, Azores, Portugal	221.217	8	59	56	8	is a standards setter in pushing its style and expressive culture on to other cultures	9	6	10	practical and self-declaring in an objective-focused way
38.48	-27.22	Angra do Heroísmo, Azores, Portugal	219.717	8	60	57	9	provides noteworthy sights in pushing its style and expressive culture on to other cultures	9	6	9	practical and self-declaring in a self-declaring way
37.82	-25.75	Ponta Delgada, Azores, Portugal	218.250	8	60	57	9	provides noteworthy sights in pushing its style and expressive culture on to other cultures	9	6	3	practical and self-declaring in a thoughtful way
14.92	-23.52	Praia, Cape Verde	216.017	8	61	58	10	hosts cultural structures in pushing its style and expressive culture on to other cultures	7	11	11	(social) noisily enterprising in a community-anchored way

66.08	-23.13	Ísafjörður, Iceland	215.633	8	61	58	10	hosts cultural structures in pushing its style and expressive culture on to other cultures	11	4	10	nurturingly community-anchored in an objective-focused way
64.13	-21.93	Reykjavík, Iceland	214.433	8	62	59	11	shows lots of activity in pushing its style and expressive culture on to other cultures	11	3	3	expressive, communicative, and community-anchored in a thoughtful way
65.68	-18.10	Akureyri, Iceland	210.600	8	63	60	12	is visited by all, a world city in pushing its style and expressive culture on to other cultures	11	4	6	nurturingly community-anchored in a busy way
14.70	-17.45	Dakar, Senegal	209.950	7	64	61	1	is a source of affairs, leads other cities in dynamic exchanges of cultures	7	11	9	(social) noisily enterprising in a self-declaring way
32.65	-16.92	Funchal, Madeira, Portugal	209.417	7	64	61	1	is a source of affairs, leads other cities in dynamic exchanges of cultures	9	2	1	materially-focused and self-declaring in a {questing} way
14.78	-16.92	Thiès, Senegal	209.417	7	64	61	1	is a source of affairs, leads other cities in dynamic exchanges of cultures	7	11	9	(social) noisily enterprising in a self-declaring way
13.43	-16.67	Serekunda, Gambia	209.167	7	64	61	1	is a source of affairs, leads other cities in dynamic exchanges of cultures	7	10	8	(not necessarily negatively) calculatingly enterprising in a pushy way
81.60	-16.67	Nord, Greenland, Denmark	209.167	7	64	61	1	is a source of affairs, leads other cities in dynamic exchanges of cultures	12	5	3	proud and environment-attentive in a thoughtful way
13.27	-16.65	Brikama, Gambia	209.150	7	64	61	1	is a source of affairs, leads other cities in dynamic exchanges of cultures	7	10	7	(not necessarily negatively) calculatingly enterprising in an enterprising way
13.45	-16.58	Banjul, Gambia	209.083	7	64	61	1	is a source of affairs, leads other cities in dynamic exchanges of cultures	7	10	9	(not necessarily negatively) calculatingly enterprising in a self-declaring way
28.47	-16.25	Santa Cruz de Tenerife, Canary Islands, Spain	208.750	7	64	61	1	is a source of affairs, leads other cities in dynamic exchanges of cultures	8	10	9	(not necessarily negatively) calculatingly pushy in a self-declaring way
18.10	-15.95	Nouakchott, Mauritania	208.450	7	64	61	1	is a source of affairs, leads other cities in dynamic exchanges of cultures	8	2	5	materially-focused and pushy in a showy way
11.85	-15.57	Bissau, Guinea-Bissau	208.067	7	64	61	1	is a source of affairs, leads other cities in dynamic exchanges of cultures	7	9	5	confidently enterprising in a showy way
28.15	-15.42	Las Palmas de Gran Canaria, Canary Islands, Spain	207.917	7	64	61	1	is a source of affairs, leads other cities in dynamic exchanges of cultures	8	10	6	(not necessarily negatively) calculatingly pushy in a busy way
9.52	-13.72	Conakry, Guinea	206.217	7	65	62	2	is a noteworthy travel destination in dynamic exchanges of cultures	7	7	7	sociable and enterprising in an enterprising way
8.48	-13.23	Freetown, Sierra Leone	205.733	7	65	62	2	is a noteworthy travel destination in dynamic exchanges of cultures	7	6	9	practical and enterprising in a self-declaring way
27.15	-13.20	El Aaiún, Western Sahara, Morocco	205.700	7	65	62	2	is a noteworthy travel destination in dynamic exchanges of cultures	8	9	8	confidently pushy in a pushy way
6.32	-10.80	Monrovia, Liberia	203.300	7	66	63	3	is vocal, social, expressively unhindered in dynamic exchanges of cultures	7	5	12	proud and enterprising in an environment-attentive way
38.72	-9.13	Lisbon, Portugal	201.633	7	67	64	4	is tourist nurturing in dynamic exchanges of cultures	9	6	11	practical and self-declaring in a community-anchored way
7.75	-8.82	Nzérékoré, Guinea	201.317	7	67	64	4	is tourist nurturing in dynamic exchanges of cultures	7	6	2	practical and enterprising in a {self-value aware} way
41.17	-8.62	Porto, Portugal	201.117	7	67	64	4	is tourist nurturing in dynamic exchanges of cultures	9	8	11	no-nonsense and self-declaring in a community-anchored way
51.90	-8.47	Cork, Ireland	200.967	7	67	64	4	is tourist nurturing in dynamic exchanges of cultures	10	5	6	proud and objective-focused in a busy way
31.63	-8.02	Marrakech, Morocco	200.517	7	67	64	4	is tourist nurturing in dynamic exchanges of cultures	9	1	3	aims-insistent and self-declaring in a thoughtful way
12.65	-8.00	Bamako, Mali	200.500	7	67	64	4	is tourist nurturing in dynamic exchanges of cultures	7	10	1	(not necessarily negatively) calculatingly enterprising in a {questing} way
33.53	-7.58	Casablanca, Morocco	200.083	7	67	64	4	is tourist nurturing in dynamic exchanges of cultures	9	2	9	materially-focused and self-declaring in a self-declaring way
12.87	-7.57	Koulikoro, Mali	200.067	7	67	64	4	is tourist nurturing in dynamic exchanges of cultures	7	10	3	(not necessarily negatively) calculatingly enterprising in a thoughtful way
34.03	-6.83	Rabat, Morocco	199.333	7	68	65	5	is a popular regional show stealer in dynamic exchanges of cultures	9	3	2	expressive, communicative, and self-declaring in a {self-value aware} way
62.02	-6.77	Tórshavn, Faroe Islands, Denmark	199.267	7	68	65	5	is a popular regional show stealer in dynamic exchanges of cultures	11	1	7	aims-insistent and community-anchored in an enterprising way
53.35	-6.27	Dublin, Ireland	198.767	7	68	65	5	is a popular regional show stealer in dynamic exchanges of cultures	10	6	8	practical and objective-focused in a pushy way
37.38	-5.98	Sevilla, Andalusia, Spain	198.483	7	68	65	5	is a popular regional show stealer in dynamic exchanges of cultures	9	5	10	proud and self-declaring in an objective-focused way
54.60	-5.93	Belfast, Northern Ireland, United Kingdom	198.433	7	68	65	5	is a popular regional show stealer in dynamic exchanges of cultures	10	7	8	sociable and objective-focused in a pushy way
-15.92	-5.72	Jamestown, Saint Helena, United Kingdom	198.217	7	68	65	5	is a popular regional show stealer in dynamic exchanges of cultures	5	11	3	(social) noisily showy in a thoughtful way
36.13	-5.35	Gibraltar, Gibraltar, United Kingdom	197.850	7	68	65	5	is a popular regional show stealer in dynamic exchanges of cultures	9	4	10	nurturingly self-declaring in an objective-focused way

6.82	-5.28	Yamoussoukro, Ivory Coast	197.783	7	68	65	5	is a popular regional show stealer in dynamic exchanges of cultures	7	5	5	proud and enterprising in a showy way
54.15	-4.48	Douglas, Isle of Man, United Kingdom	196.983	7	69	66	6	pursues a quest for greater relevance in dynamic exchanges of cultures	10	7	3	sociable and objective-focused in a thoughtful way
48.38	-4.48	Brest, Brittany, France	196.983	7	69	66	6	pursues a quest for greater relevance in dynamic exchanges of cultures	10	2	8	materially-focused and objective-focused in a pushy way
36.72	-4.42	Málaga, Andalusia, Spain	196.917	7	69	66	6	pursues a quest for greater relevance in dynamic exchanges of cultures	9	5	4	proud and self-declaring in a concerned way
11.18	-4.28	Bobo-Dioulasso, Burkina Faso	196.783	7	69	66	6	pursues a quest for greater relevance in dynamic exchanges of cultures	7	8	11	no-nonsense and enterprising in a community-anchored way
55.85	-4.27	Glasgow, Scotland, United Kingdom	196.767	7	69	66	6	pursues a quest for greater relevance in dynamic exchanges of cultures	10	8	8	no-nonsense and objective-focused in a pushy way
57.47	-4.23	Inverness, Scotland, United Kingdom	196.733	7	69	66	6	pursues a quest for greater relevance in dynamic exchanges of cultures	10	9	11	confidently objective-focused in a community-anchored way
50.37	-4.15	Plymouth, England, United Kingdom	196.650	7	69	66	6	pursues a quest for greater relevance in dynamic exchanges of cultures	10	4	3	nurturingly objective-focused in a thoughtful way
5.32	-4.03	Abidjan, Ivory Coast	196.533	7	69	66	6	pursues a quest for greater relevance in dynamic exchanges of cultures	7	4	3	nurturingly enterprising in a thoughtful way
51.62	-3.95	Swansea, Wales, United Kingdom	196.450	7	69	66	6	pursues a quest for greater relevance in dynamic exchanges of cultures	10	5	3	proud and objective-focused in a thoughtful way
40.38	-3.72	Madrid, Madrid, Spain	196.217	7	69	66	6	pursues a quest for greater relevance in dynamic exchanges of cultures	9	8	3	no-nonsense and self-declaring in a thoughtful way
50.72	-3.53	Exeter, England, United Kingdom	196.033	7	69	66	6	pursues a quest for greater relevance in dynamic exchanges of cultures	10	4	6	nurturingly objective-focused in a busy way
55.95	-3.18	Edinburgh, Scotland, United Kingdom	195.683	7	69	66	6	pursues a quest for greater relevance in dynamic exchanges of cultures	10	8	9	no-nonsense and objective-focused in a self-declaring way
51.48	-3.18	Cardiff, Wales, United Kingdom	195.683	7	69	66	6	pursues a quest for greater relevance in dynamic exchanges of cultures	10	5	2	proud and objective-focused in a {self-value aware} way
16.78	-3.02	Timbuktu, Mali	195.517	7	69	66	6	pursues a quest for greater relevance in dynamic exchanges of cultures	8	1	5	aims-insistent and pushy in a showy way
53.40	-2.98	Liverpool, England, United Kingdom	195.483	7	69	66	6	pursues a quest for greater relevance in dynamic exchanges of cultures	10	6	8	practical and objective-focused in a pushy way
56.47	-2.97	Dundee, Scotland, United Kingdom	195.467	7	69	66	6	pursues a quest for greater relevance in dynamic exchanges of cultures	10	9	2	confidently objective-focused in a {self-value aware} way
43.25	-2.92	Bilbao, Basque Country, Spain	195.417	7	69	66	6	pursues a quest for greater relevance in dynamic exchanges of cultures	9	10	7	(not necessarily negatively) calculatingly self-declaring in an enterprising way
51.45	-2.58	Bristol, England, United Kingdom	195.083	7	69	66	6	pursues a quest for greater relevance in dynamic exchanges of cultures	10	5	1	proud and objective-focused in a {questing} way
51.38	-2.37	Bath, England, United Kingdom	194.867	7	70	67	7	welcomes all in dynamic exchanges of cultures	10	5	1	proud and objective-focused in a {questing} way
53.47	-2.23	Manchester, England, United Kingdom	194.733	7	70	67	7	welcomes all in dynamic exchanges of cultures	10	6	9	practical and objective-focused in a self-declaring way
51.87	-2.23	Gloucester, England, United Kingdom	194.733	7	70	67	7	welcomes all in dynamic exchanges of cultures	10	5	5	proud and objective-focused in a showy way
57.15	-2.12	Aberdeen, Scotland, United Kingdom	194.617	7	70	67	7	welcomes all in dynamic exchanges of cultures	10	9	8	confidently objective-focused in a pushy way
52.48	-1.90	Birmingham, England, United Kingdom	194.400	7	70	67	7	welcomes all in dynamic exchanges of cultures	10	5	11	proud and objective-focused in a community-anchored way
4.92	-1.77	Sekondi-Takoradi, Ghana	194.267	7	70	67	7	welcomes all in dynamic exchanges of cultures	7	3	11	expressive, communicative, and enterprising in a community-anchored way
53.80	-1.75	Bradford, England, United Kingdom	194.250	7	70	67	7	welcomes all in dynamic exchanges of cultures	10	7	12	sociable and objective-focused in an environment-attentive way
54.97	-1.62	Newcastle upon Tyne, England, United Kingdom	194.117	7	70	67	7	welcomes all in dynamic exchanges of cultures	10	7	11	sociable and objective-focused in a community-anchored way
6.67	-1.62	Kumasi, Ghana	194.117	7	70	67	7	welcomes all in dynamic exchanges of cultures	7	5	4	proud and enterprising in a concerned way
53.80	-1.55	Leeds, England, United Kingdom	194.050	7	70	67	7	welcomes all in dynamic exchanges of cultures	10	7	12	sociable and objective-focused in an environment-attentive way
47.22	-1.55	Nantes, France	194.050	7	70	67	7	welcomes all in dynamic exchanges of cultures	10	1	9	aims-insistent and objective-focused in a self-declaring way
12.35	-1.53	Ouagadougou, Burkina Faso	194.033	7	70	67	7	welcomes all in dynamic exchanges of cultures	7	9	10	confidently enterprising in an objective-focused way
52.40	-1.52	Coventry, England, United Kingdom	194.017	7	70	67	7	welcomes all in dynamic exchanges of cultures	10	5	11	proud and objective-focused in a community-anchored way
53.38	-1.47	Sheffield, England, United Kingdom	193.967	7	70	67	7	welcomes all in dynamic exchanges of cultures	10	6	8	practical and objective-focused in a pushy way
50.90	-1.40	Southampton, England, United Kingdom	193.900	7	70	67	7	welcomes all in dynamic exchanges of cultures	10	4	8	nurturingly objective-focused in a pushy way
51.75	-1.25	Oxford, England, United Kingdom	193.750	7	70	67	7	welcomes all in dynamic exchanges of cultures	10	5	4	proud and objective-focused in a concerned way
52.95	-1.13	Nottingham, England, United Kingdom	193.633	7	70	67	7	welcomes all in dynamic exchanges of cultures	10	6	4	practical and objective-focused in a concerned way
52.63	-1.13	Leicester, England, United Kingdom	193.633	7	70	67	7	welcomes all in dynamic exchanges of cultures	10	6	1	practical and objective-focused in a {questing} way

50.82	-1.08	Portsmouth, England, United Kingdom	193.583	7	70	67	7	welcomes all in dynamic exchanges of cultures	10	4	7	nurturingly objective-focused in an enterprising way
41.65	-0.88	Zaragoza, Aragon, Spain	193.383	7	70	67	7	welcomes all in dynamic exchanges of cultures	9	9	3	confidently self-declaring in a thoughtful way
9.40	-0.85	Tamale, Ghana	193.350	7	70	67	7	welcomes all in dynamic exchanges of cultures	7	7	6	sociable and enterprising in a busy way
44.83	-0.58	Bordeaux, France	193.083	7	70	67	7	welcomes all in dynamic exchanges of cultures	9	11	10	(social) noisily self-declaring in an objective-focused way
39.47	-0.38	Valencia, Valencian Community, Spain	192.883	7	70	67	7	welcomes all in dynamic exchanges of cultures	9	7	6	sociable and self-declaring in a busy way
52.58	-0.25	Peterborough, England, United Kingdom	192.750	7	70	67	7	welcomes all in dynamic exchanges of cultures	10	6	12	practical and objective-focused in an environment-attentive way
5.55	-0.20	Accra, Ghana	192.700	7	70	67	7	welcomes all in dynamic exchanges of cultures	7	4	5	nurturingly enterprising in a showy way
50.83	-0.15	Brighton and Hove, England, United Kingdom	192.650	7	70	67	7	welcomes all in dynamic exchanges of cultures	10	4	8	nurturingly objective-focused in a pushy way
51.50	-0.13	London, England, United Kingdom	192.633	7	70	67	7	welcomes all in dynamic exchanges of cultures	10	5	2	proud and objective-focused in a {self-value aware} way
51.48	**0.00**	Greenwich, England, United Kingdom	192.500	7	71	68	8	is a standards setter in dynamic exchanges of cultures	10	5	2	proud and objective-focused in a {self-value aware} way
49.48	0.10	Le Havre, Normandy, France	192.400	7	71	68	8	is a standards setter in dynamic exchanges of cultures	10	3	7	expressive, communicative, and objective-focused in an enterprising way
52.20	0.12	Cambridge, England, United Kingdom	192.383	7	71	68	8	is a standards setter in dynamic exchanges of cultures	10	5	9	proud and objective-focused in a self-declaring way
41.62	0.63	Lleida, Catalonia, Spain	191.867	7	71	68	8	is a standards setter in dynamic exchanges of cultures	9	9	3	confidently self-declaring in a thoughtful way
49.43	1.10	Rouen, Normandy, France	191.400	7	71	68	8	is a standards setter in dynamic exchanges of cultures	10	3	6	expressive, communicative, and objective-focused in a busy way
6.13	1.22	Lomé, Togo	191.283	7	71	68	8	is a standards setter in dynamic exchanges of cultures	7	4	10	nurturingly enterprising in an objective-focused way
52.63	1.30	Norwich, England, United Kingdom	191.200	7	71	68	8	is a standards setter in dynamic exchanges of cultures	10	6	1	practical and objective-focused in a {questing} way
35.37	1.32	Tiaret, Algeria	191.183	7	71	68	8	is a standards setter in dynamic exchanges of cultures	9	4	3	nurturingly self-declaring in a thoughtful way
38.98	1.43	Ibiza, Balearic Islands, Spain	191.067	7	71	68	8	is a standards setter in dynamic exchanges of cultures	9	7	2	sociable and self-declaring in a {self-value aware} way
43.60	1.45	Toulouse, France	191.050	7	71	68	8	is a standards setter in dynamic exchanges of cultures	9	10	10	(not necessarily negatively) calculatingly self-declaring in an objective-focused way
42.50	1.50	Andorra la Vella, Andorra	191.000	7	71	68	8	is a standards setter in dynamic exchanges of cultures	9	10	12	(not necessarily negatively) calculatingly self-declaring in an environment-attentive way
50.95	1.85	Calais, France	190.650	7	71	68	8	is a standards setter in dynamic exchanges of cultures	10	4	9	nurturingly objective-focused in a self-declaring way
47.90	1.92	Orléans, France	190.583	7	71	68	8	is a standards setter in dynamic exchanges of cultures	10	2	3	materially-focused and objective-focused in a thoughtful way
13.52	2.10	Niamey, Niger	190.400	7	71	68	8	is a standards setter in dynamic exchanges of cultures	7	10	9	(not necessarily negatively) calculatingly enterprising in a self-declaring way
41.38	2.18	Barcelona, Catalonia, Spain	190.317	7	71	68	8	is a standards setter in dynamic exchanges of cultures	9	9	1	confidently self-declaring in a {questing} way
48.85	2.35	Paris, France	190.150	7	71	68	8	is a standards setter in dynamic exchanges of cultures	10	3	12	expressive, communicative, and objective-focused in an environment-attentive way
6.37	2.43	Cotonou, Benin	190.067	7	71	68	8	is a standards setter in dynamic exchanges of cultures	7	5	1	proud and enterprising in a {questing} way
6.50	2.60	Porto-Novo, Benin	189.900	7	72	69	9	provides noteworthy sights in dynamic exchanges of cultures	7	5	2	proud and enterprising in a {self-value aware} way
39.57	2.65	Palma, Balearic Islands, Spain	189.850	7	72	69	9	provides noteworthy sights in dynamic exchanges of cultures	9	7	7	sociable and self-declaring in an enterprising way
36.77	3.22	Algiers, Algeria	189.283	7	72	69	9	provides noteworthy sights in dynamic exchanges of cultures	9	5	4	proud and self-declaring in a concerned way
6.45	3.40	Lagos, Nigeria	189.100	7	72	69	9	provides noteworthy sights in dynamic exchanges of cultures	7	5	1	proud and enterprising in a {questing} way
51.05	3.73	Ghent, Belgium	188.767	7	72	69	9	provides noteworthy sights in dynamic exchanges of cultures	10	4	10	nurturingly objective-focused in an objective-focused way
7.40	3.92	Ibadan, Nigeria	188.583	7	72	69	9	provides noteworthy sights in dynamic exchanges of cultures	7	5	11	proud and enterprising in a community-anchored way
52.08	4.32	The Hague, South Holland, Netherlands	188.183	7	72	69	9	provides noteworthy sights in dynamic exchanges of cultures	10	5	8	proud and objective-focused in a pushy way
50.85	4.35	Brussels, Belgium	188.150	7	72	69	9	provides noteworthy sights in dynamic exchanges of cultures	10	4	8	nurturingly objective-focused in a pushy way
51.22	4.40	Antwerp, Belgium	188.100	7	72	69	9	provides noteworthy sights in dynamic exchanges of cultures	10	4	11	nurturingly objective-focused in a community-anchored way
50.40	4.43	Charleroi, Belgium	188.067	7	72	69	9	provides noteworthy sights in dynamic exchanges of cultures	10	4	3	nurturingly objective-focused in a thoughtful way

52.17	4.48	Leiden, South Holland, Netherlands	188.017	7	72	69	9	provides noteworthy sights in dynamic exchanges of cultures	10	5	8	proud and objective-focused in a pushy way
51.93	4.48	Rotterdam, South Holland, Netherlands	188.017	7	72	69	9	provides noteworthy sights in dynamic exchanges of cultures	10	5	6	proud and objective-focused in a busy way
52.38	4.63	Haarlem, North Holland, Netherlands	187.867	7	72	69	9	provides noteworthy sights in dynamic exchanges of cultures	10	5	10	proud and objective-focused in an objective-focused way
45.77	4.85	Lyon, France	187.650	7	72	69	9	provides noteworthy sights in dynamic exchanges of cultures	10	12	7	spacey, odd, and objective-focused in an enterprising way
52.37	4.90	Amsterdam, North Holland, Netherlands	187.600	7	72	69	9	provides noteworthy sights in dynamic exchanges of cultures	10	5	10	proud and objective-focused in an objective-focused way
52.10	5.12	Utrecht, Utrecht, Netherlands	187.383	7	73	70	10	hosts cultural structures in dynamic exchanges of cultures	10	5	8	proud and objective-focused in a pushy way
60.38	5.33	Bergen, Norway	187.167	7	73	70	10	hosts cultural structures in dynamic exchanges of cultures	11	12	3	spacey, odd, and community-anchored in a thoughtful way
43.30	5.37	Marseille, France	187.133	7	73	70	10	hosts cultural structures in dynamic exchanges of cultures	9	10	7	(not necessarily negatively) calculatingly self-declaring in an enterprising way
6.32	5.60	Benin City, Nigeria	186.900	7	73	70	10	hosts cultural structures in dynamic exchanges of cultures	7	5	12	proud and enterprising in an environment-attentive way
50.85	5.68	Maastricht, Limburg, Netherlands	186.817	7	73	70	10	hosts cultural structures in dynamic exchanges of cultures	10	4	8	nurturingly objective-focused in a pushy way
49.62	6.12	Luxembourg, Luxembourg	186.383	7	73	70	10	hosts cultural structures in dynamic exchanges of cultures	10	3	8	expressive, communicative, and objective-focused in a pushy way
46.20	6.15	Geneva, Switzerland	186.350	7	73	70	10	hosts cultural structures in dynamic exchanges of cultures	10	12	11	spacey, odd, and objective-focused in a community-anchored way
53.22	6.55	Groningen, Groningen, Netherlands	185.950	7	73	70	10	hosts cultural structures in dynamic exchanges of cultures	10	6	6	practical and objective-focused in a busy way
46.52	6.63	Lausanne, Switzerland	185.867	7	73	70	10	hosts cultural structures in dynamic exchanges of cultures	10	1	2	aims-insistent and objective-focused in a {self-value aware} way
0.33	6.68	São Tomé, São Tomé and Príncipe	185.817	7	73	70	10	hosts cultural structures in dynamic exchanges of cultures	7	12	3	spacey, odd, and enterprising in a thoughtful way
51.23	6.78	Düsseldorf, North Rhine-Westphalia, Germany	185.717	7	73	70	10	hosts cultural structures in dynamic exchanges of cultures	10	4	11	nurturingly objective-focused in a community-anchored way
52.22	6.90	Enschede, Overijssel, Netherlands	185.600	7	73	70	10	hosts cultural structures in dynamic exchanges of cultures	10	5	9	proud and objective-focused in a self-declaring way
50.93	6.97	Cologne, North Rhine-Westphalia, Germany	185.533	7	73	70	10	hosts cultural structures in dynamic exchanges of cultures	10	4	8	nurturingly objective-focused in a pushy way
4.75	7.00	Port Harcourt, Nigeria	185.500	7	73	70	10	hosts cultural structures in dynamic exchanges of cultures	7	3	9	expressive, communicative, and enterprising in a self-declaring way
43.55	7.02	Cannes, France	185.483	7	73	70	10	hosts cultural structures in dynamic exchanges of cultures	9	10	10	(not necessarily negatively) calculatingly self-declaring in an objective-focused way
43.70	7.27	Nice, France	185.233	7	73	70	10	hosts cultural structures in dynamic exchanges of cultures	9	10	11	(not necessarily negatively) calculatingly self-declaring in a community-anchored way
43.73	7.42	Monaco, Monaco	185.083	7	73	70	10	hosts cultural structures in dynamic exchanges of cultures	9	10	11	(not necessarily negatively) calculatingly self-declaring in a community-anchored way
46.95	7.45	Bern, Switzerland	185.050	7	73	70	10	hosts cultural structures in dynamic exchanges of cultures	10	1	6	aims-insistent and objective-focused in a busy way
9.07	7.48	Abuja, Nigeria	185.017	7	73	70	10	hosts cultural structures in dynamic exchanges of cultures	7	7	3	sociable and enterprising in a thoughtful way
6.45	7.52	Enugu, Nigeria	184.983	7	74	71	11	shows lots of activity in dynamic exchanges of cultures	7	5	1	proud and enterprising in a {questing} way
47.57	7.60	Basel, Switzerland	184.900	7	74	71	11	shows lots of activity in dynamic exchanges of cultures	10	2	12	materially-focused and objective-focused in an environment-attentive way
45.07	7.70	Turin, Piedmont, Italy	184.800	7	74	71	11	shows lots of activity in dynamic exchanges of cultures	10	12	12	spacey, odd, and objective-focused in an environment-attentive way
48.58	7.75	Strasbourg, France	184.750	7	74	71	11	shows lots of activity in dynamic exchanges of cultures	10	2	10	materially-focused and objective-focused in an objective-focused way
58.17	8.00	Kristiansand, Norway	184.500	7	74	71	11	shows lots of activity in dynamic exchanges of cultures	10	10	6	(not necessarily negatively) calculatingly objective-focused in a busy way
55.48	8.45	Esbjerg, Denmark	184.050	7	74	71	11	shows lots of activity in dynamic exchanges of cultures	10	8	4	no-nonsense and objective-focused in a concerned way
12.00	8.52	Kano, Nigeria	183.983	7	74	71	11	shows lots of activity in dynamic exchanges of cultures	7	9	7	confidently enterprising in an enterprising way
47.37	8.55	Zürich, Switzerland	183.950	7	74	71	11	shows lots of activity in dynamic exchanges of cultures	10	1	10	aims-insistent and objective-focused in an objective-focused way
50.12	8.68	Frankfurt am Main, Hesse, Germany	183.817	7	74	71	11	shows lots of activity in dynamic exchanges of cultures	10	4	1	nurturingly objective-focused in a {questing} way
3.75	8.78	Malabo, Equatorial Guinea	183.717	7	74	71	11	shows lots of activity in dynamic exchanges of cultures	7	3	12	expressive, communicative, and enterprising in an environment-attentive way
53.08	8.80	Bremen, Bremen, Germany	183.700	7	74	71	11	shows lots of activity in dynamic exchanges of cultures	10	6	5	practical and objective-focused in a showy way

39.25	9.05	Cagliari, Sardinia, Italy	183.450	7	74	71	11	shows lots of activity in dynamic exchanges of cultures	9	7	4	sociable and self-declaring in a concerned way
45.47	9.18	Milan, Lombardy, Italy	183.317	7	74	71	11	shows lots of activity in dynamic exchanges of cultures	10	12	4	spacey, odd, and objective-focused in a concerned way
48.78	9.18	Stuttgart, Baden-Württemberg, Germany	183.317	7	74	71	11	shows lots of activity in dynamic exchanges of cultures	10	3	12	expressive, communicative, and objective-focused in an environment-attentive way
0.38	9.45	Libreville, Gabon	183.050	7	74	71	11	shows lots of activity in dynamic exchanges of cultures	7	12	3	spacey, odd, and enterprising in a thoughtful way
47.13	9.52	Vaduz, Liechtenstein	182.983	7	74	71	11	shows lots of activity in dynamic exchanges of cultures	10	1	8	aims-insistent and objective-focused in a pushy way
4.05	9.70	Douala, Cameroon	182.800	7	74	71	11	shows lots of activity in dynamic exchanges of cultures	7	3	2	expressive, communicative, and enterprising in a {self-value aware} way
52.37	9.72	Hannover, Lower Saxony, Germany	182.783	7	74	71	11	shows lots of activity in dynamic exchanges of cultures	10	5	10	proud and objective-focused in an objective-focused way
53.57	10.00	Hamburg, Hamburg, Germany	182.500	7	75	72	12	is visited by all, a world city in dynamic exchanges of cultures	10	6	10	practical and objective-focused in an objective-focused way
54.33	10.13	Kiel, Schleswig-Holstein, Germany	182.367	7	75	72	12	is visited by all, a world city in dynamic exchanges of cultures	10	7	5	sociable and objective-focused in a showy way
36.80	10.18	Tunis, Tunisia	182.317	7	75	72	12	is visited by all, a world city in dynamic exchanges of cultures	9	5	5	proud and self-declaring in a showy way
56.15	10.22	Aarhus, Denmark	182.283	7	75	72	12	is visited by all, a world city in dynamic exchanges of cultures	10	8	11	no-nonsense and objective-focused in a community-anchored way
55.40	10.38	Odense, Denmark	182.117	7	75	72	12	is visited by all, a world city in dynamic exchanges of cultures	10	8	3	no-nonsense and objective-focused in a thoughtful way
63.43	10.40	Trondheim, Norway	182.100	7	75	72	12	is visited by all, a world city in dynamic exchanges of cultures	11	2	8	materially-focused and community-anchored in a pushy way
61.13	10.43	Lillehammer, Norway	182.067	7	75	72	12	is visited by all, a world city in dynamic exchanges of cultures	11	12	10	spacey, odd, and community-anchored in an objective-focused way
59.95	10.75	Oslo, Norway	181.750	7	75	72	12	is visited by all, a world city in dynamic exchanges of cultures	10	11	11	(social) noisily objective-focused in a community-anchored way
34.73	10.77	Sfax, Tunisia	181.733	7	75	72	12	is visited by all, a world city in dynamic exchanges of cultures	9	3	9	expressive, communicative, and self-declaring in a self-declaring way
63.48	11.17	Stjørdal, Norway	181.333	7	75	72	12	is visited by all, a world city in dynamic exchanges of cultures	11	2	9	materially-focused and community-anchored in a self-declaring way
59.28	11.20	Sarpsborg, Norway	181.300	7	75	72	12	is visited by all, a world city in dynamic exchanges of cultures	10	11	5	(social) noisily objective-focused in a showy way
43.78	11.25	Florence, Tuscany, Italy	181.250	7	75	72	12	is visited by all, a world city in dynamic exchanges of cultures	9	11	12	(social) noisily self-declaring in an environment-attentive way
44.50	11.35	Bologna, Emilia-Romagna, Italy	181.150	7	75	72	12	is visited by all, a world city in dynamic exchanges of cultures	9	11	7	(social) noisily self-declaring in an enterprising way
47.27	11.38	Innsbruck, Austria	181.117	7	75	72	12	is visited by all, a world city in dynamic exchanges of cultures	10	1	9	aims-insistent and objective-focused in a self-declaring way
3.87	11.52	Yaoundé, Cameroon	180.983	7	75	72	12	is visited by all, a world city in dynamic exchanges of cultures	7	3	1	expressive, communicative, and enterprising in a {questing} way
48.13	11.57	Munich, Bavaria, Germany	180.933	7	75	72	12	is visited by all, a world city in dynamic exchanges of cultures	10	2	6	materially-focused and objective-focused in a busy way
78.92	11.93	Ny-Ålesund, Svalbard, Norway	180.567	7	75	72	12	is visited by all, a world city in dynamic exchanges of cultures	12	3	1	expressive, communicative, and environment-attentive in a {questing} way
57.70	11.97	Gothenburg, Sweden	180.533	7	75	72	12	is visited by all, a world city in dynamic exchanges of cultures	10	10	1	(not necessarily negatively) calculatingly objective-focused in a {questing} way
45.43	12.33	Venice, Veneto, Italy	180.167	7	75	72	12	is visited by all, a world city in dynamic exchanges of cultures	10	12	4	spacey, odd, and objective-focused in a concerned way
51.33	12.38	Leipzig, Saxony, Germany	180.117	7	75	72	12	is visited by all, a world city in dynamic exchanges of cultures	10	5	12	proud and objective-focused in an environment-attentive way
43.93	12.45	San Marino, San Marino	180.050	7	75	72	12	is visited by all, a world city in dynamic exchanges of cultures	9	11	1	(social) noisily self-declaring in a {questing} way
41.90	12.45	Vatican City, Vatican City	180.050	7	75	72	12	is visited by all, a world city in dynamic exchanges of cultures	9	9	6	confidently self-declaring in a busy way
41.90	12.50	Rome, Lazio, Italy	180.000	6	76	73	1	is a source of affairs, leads other cities in developing rational structures for or presenting complex issues to the world	9	9	6	confidently self-declaring in a busy way
55.68	12.57	Copenhagen, Denmark	179.933	6	76	73	1	is a source of affairs, leads other cities in developing rational structures for or presenting complex issues to the world	10	8	6	no-nonsense and objective-focused in a busy way
47.80	13.03	Salzburg, Austria	179.467	6	76	73	1	is a source of affairs, leads other cities in developing rational structures for or presenting complex issues to the world	10	2	2	materially-focused and objective-focused in a {self-value aware} way
55.58	13.03	Malmö, Sweden	179.467	6	76	73	1	is a source of affairs, leads other cities in developing rational structures for or presenting complex issues to the world	10	8	5	no-nonsense and objective-focused in a showy way

32.90	13.18	Tripoli, Libya	179.317	6	76	73	1	is a source of affairs, leads other cities in developing rational structures for or presenting complex issues to the world	9	2	3	materially-focused and self-declaring in a thoughtful way
-8.83	13.23	Luanda, Angola	179.267	6	76	73	1	is a source of affairs, leads other cities in developing rational structures for or presenting complex issues to the world	6	4	11	nurturingly busy in a community-anchored way
38.12	13.37	Palermo, Sicily, Italy	179.133	6	76	73	1	is a source of affairs, leads other cities in developing rational structures for or presenting complex issues to the world	9	6	5	practical and self-declaring in a showy way
52.52	13.38	Berlin, Berlin, Germany	179.117	6	76	73	1	is a source of affairs, leads other cities in developing rational structures for or presenting complex issues to the world	10	6	12	practical and objective-focused in an environment-attentive way
51.03	13.73	Dresden, Saxony, Germany	178.767	6	76	73	1	is a source of affairs, leads other cities in developing rational structures for or presenting complex issues to the world	10	4	9	nurturingly objective-focused in a self-declaring way
40.85	14.27	Naples, Campania, Italy	178.233	6	76	73	1	is a source of affairs, leads other cities in developing rational structures for or presenting complex issues to the world	9	8	8	no-nonsense and self-declaring in a pushy way
48.30	14.28	Linz, Austria	178.217	6	76	73	1	is a source of affairs, leads other cities in developing rational structures for or presenting complex issues to the world	10	2	7	materially-focused and objective-focused in an enterprising way
50.08	14.42	Prague, Czech Republic	178.083	6	76	73	1	is a source of affairs, leads other cities in developing rational structures for or presenting complex issues to the world	10	4	12	nurturingly objective-focused in an environment-attentive way
27.03	14.43	Sabha, Libya	178.067	6	76	73	1	is a source of affairs, leads other cities in developing rational structures for or presenting complex issues to the world	8	9	7	confidently pushy in an enterprising way
35.90	14.47	Birkirkara, Malta	178.033	6	76	73	1	is a source of affairs, leads other cities in developing rational structures for or presenting complex issues to the world	9	4	8	nurturingly self-declaring in a pushy way
35.90	14.52	Valletta, Malta	177.983	6	76	73	1	is a source of affairs, leads other cities in developing rational structures for or presenting complex issues to the world	9	4	8	nurturingly self-declaring in a pushy way
46.05	14.52	Ljubljana, Slovenia	177.983	6	76	73	1	is a source of affairs, leads other cities in developing rational structures for or presenting complex issues to the world	10	12	10	spacey, odd, and objective-focused in an objective-focused way
67.30	14.55	Bodø, Norway	177.950	6	76	73	1	is a source of affairs, leads other cities in developing rational structures for or presenting complex issues to the world	11	5	10	proud and community-anchored in an objective-focused way
63.18	14.67	Östersund, Sweden	177.833	6	76	73	1	is a source of affairs, leads other cities in developing rational structures for or presenting complex issues to the world	11	2	6	materially-focused and community-anchored in a busy way
12.12	15.05	N'Djamena, Chad	177.450	6	77	74	2	is a noteworthy travel destination in developing rational structures for or presenting complex issues to the world	7	9	8	confidently enterprising in a pushy way
37.50	15.08	Catania, Sicily, Italy	177.417	6	77	74	2	is a noteworthy travel destination in developing rational structures for or presenting complex issues to the world	9	6	12	practical and self-declaring in an environment-attentive way
-4.27	15.30	Brazzaville, Republic of the Congo	177.200	6	77	74	2	is a noteworthy travel destination in developing rational structures for or presenting complex issues to the world	6	8	7	no-nonsense and busy in an enterprising way
-4.33	15.32	Kinshasa, Democratic Republic of the Congo	177.183	6	77	74	2	is a noteworthy travel destination in developing rational structures for or presenting complex issues to the world	6	8	6	no-nonsense and busy in a busy way
47.07	15.43	Graz, Austria	177.067	6	77	74	2	is a noteworthy travel destination in developing rational structures for or presenting complex issues to the world	10	1	7	aims-insistent and objective-focused in an enterprising way

38.18	15.55	Messina, Sicily, Italy	176.950	6	77	74	2	is a noteworthy travel destination in developing rational structures for or presenting complex issues to the world	9	6	6	practical and self-declaring in a busy way
78.22	15.65	Longyearbyen, Svalbard, Norway	176.850	6	77	74	2	is a noteworthy travel destination in developing rational structures for or presenting complex issues to the world	12	2	6	materially-focused and environment-attentive in a busy way
-12.77	15.73	Huambo, Angola	176.767	6	77	74	2	is a noteworthy travel destination in developing rational structures for or presenting complex issues to the world	6	1	9	aims-insistent and busy in a self-declaring way
45.82	15.98	Zagreb, Croatia	176.517	6	77	74	2	is a noteworthy travel destination in developing rational structures for or presenting complex issues to the world	10	12	7	spacey, odd, and objective-focused in an enterprising way
8.57	16.08	Moundou, Chad	176.417	6	77	74	2	is a noteworthy travel destination in developing rational structures for or presenting complex issues to the world	7	6	10	practical and enterprising in an objective-focused way
58.60	16.20	Norrköping, Sweden	176.300	6	77	74	2	is a noteworthy travel destination in developing rational structures for or presenting complex issues to the world	10	10	10	(not necessarily negatively) calculatingly objective-focused in an objective-focused way
48.22	16.37	Vienna, Austria	176.133	6	77	74	2	is a noteworthy travel destination in developing rational structures for or presenting complex issues to the world	10	2	6	materially-focused and objective-focused in a busy way
43.50	16.43	Split, Croatia	176.067	6	77	74	2	is a noteworthy travel destination in developing rational structures for or presenting complex issues to the world	9	10	9	(not necessarily negatively) calculatingly self-declaring in a self-declaring way
-22.57	17.08	Windhoek, Namibia	175.417	6	77	74	2	is a noteworthy travel destination in developing rational structures for or presenting complex issues to the world	5	5	11	proud and showy in a community-anchored way
48.15	17.12	Bratislava, Slovakia	175.383	6	77	74	2	is a noteworthy travel destination in developing rational structures for or presenting complex issues to the world	10	2	6	materially-focused and objective-focused in a busy way
62.40	17.32	Sundsvall, Sweden	175.183	6	77	74	2	is a noteworthy travel destination in developing rational structures for or presenting complex issues to the world	11	1	11	aims-insistent and community-anchored in a community-anchored way
68.42	17.57	Narvik, Norway	174.933	6	78	75	3	is vocal, social, expressively unhindered in developing rational structures for or presenting complex issues to the world	11	6	8	practical and community-anchored in a pushy way
59.85	17.65	Uppsala, Sweden	174.850	6	78	75	3	is vocal, social, expressively unhindered in developing rational structures for or presenting complex issues to the world	10	11	10	(social) noisily objective-focused in an objective-focused way
59.33	18.07	Stockholm, Sweden	174.433	6	78	75	3	is vocal, social, expressively unhindered in developing rational structures for or presenting complex issues to the world	10	11	5	(social) noisily objective-focused in a showy way
43.85	18.35	Sarajevo, Bosnia and Herzegovina	174.150	6	78	75	3	is vocal, social, expressively unhindered in developing rational structures for or presenting complex issues to the world	9	11	12	(social) noisily self-declaring in an environment-attentive way
-33.93	18.42	Cape Town, Western Cape, South Africa	174.083	6	78	75	3	is vocal, social, expressively unhindered in developing rational structures for or presenting complex issues to the world	4	8	10	no-nonsense and concerned in an objective-focused way
54.50	18.55	Gdynia, Poland	173.950	6	78	75	3	is vocal, social, expressively unhindered in developing rational structures for or presenting complex issues to the world	10	7	7	sociable and objective-focused in an enterprising way
4.37	18.58	Bangui, Central African Republic	173.917	6	78	75	3	is vocal, social, expressively unhindered in developing rational structures for or presenting complex issues to the world	7	3	5	expressive, communicative, and enterprising in a showy way
54.37	18.63	Gdańsk, Poland	173.867	6	78	75	3	is vocal, social, expressively unhindered in developing rational structures for or presenting complex issues to the world	10	7	5	sociable and objective-focused in a showy way

63.28	18.73	Örnsköldsvik, Sweden	173.767	6	78	75	3	is vocal, social, expressively unhindered in developing rational structures for or presenting complex issues to the world	11	2	7	materially-focused and community-anchored in an enterprising way
69.68	18.95	Tromsø, Norway	173.550	6	78	75	3	is vocal, social, expressively unhindered in developing rational structures for or presenting complex issues to the world	11	7	8	sociable and community-anchored in a pushy way
47.47	19.05	Budapest, Hungary	173.450	6	78	75	3	is vocal, social, expressively unhindered in developing rational structures for or presenting complex issues to the world	10	1	11	aims-insistent and objective-focused in a community-anchored way
42.43	19.27	Podgorica, Montenegro	173.233	6	78	75	3	is vocal, social, expressively unhindered in developing rational structures for or presenting complex issues to the world	9	9	11	confidently self-declaring in a community-anchored way
41.33	19.82	Tirana, Albania	172.683	6	78	75	3	is vocal, social, expressively unhindered in developing rational structures for or presenting complex issues to the world	9	9	12	confidently self-declaring in an environment-attentive way
45.25	19.85	Novi Sad, Vojvodina, Serbia	172.650	6	78	75	3	is vocal, social, expressively unhindered in developing rational structures for or presenting complex issues to the world	10	12	2	spacey, odd, and objective-focused in a {self-value aware} way
50.07	19.93	Kraków, Poland	172.567	6	78	75	3	is vocal, social, expressively unhindered in developing rational structures for or presenting complex issues to the world	10	4	12	nurturingly objective-focused in an environment-attentive way
32.12	20.07	Benghazi, Libya	172.433	6	79	76	4	is tourist nurturing in developing rational structures for or presenting complex issues to the world	9	1	8	aims-insistent and self-declaring in a pushy way
67.85	20.22	Kiruna, Sweden	172.283	6	79	76	4	is tourist nurturing in developing rational structures for or presenting complex issues to the world	11	6	3	practical and community-anchored in a thoughtful way
63.83	20.27	Umeå, Sweden	172.233	6	79	76	4	is tourist nurturing in developing rational structures for or presenting complex issues to the world	11	3	12	expressive, communicative, and community-anchored in an environment-attentive way
44.82	20.47	Belgrade, Serbia	172.033	6	79	76	4	is tourist nurturing in developing rational structures for or presenting complex issues to the world	9	11	10	(social) noisily self-declaring in an objective-focused way
54.72	20.52	Kaliningrad, Kaliningrad Oblast, Russia	171.983	6	79	76	4	is tourist nurturing in developing rational structures for or presenting complex issues to the world	10	7	9	sociable and objective-focused in a self-declaring way
64.75	20.95	Skellefteå, Sweden	171.550	6	79	76	4	is tourist nurturing in developing rational structures for or presenting complex issues to the world	11	3	9	expressive, communicative, and community-anchored in a self-declaring way
52.23	21.02	Warsaw, Poland	171.483	6	79	76	4	is tourist nurturing in developing rational structures for or presenting complex issues to the world	10	5	9	proud and objective-focused in a self-declaring way
42.67	21.17	Pristina, Kosovo, Serbia	171.333	6	79	76	4	is tourist nurturing in developing rational structures for or presenting complex issues to the world	9	10	1	(not necessarily negatively) calculatingly self-declaring in a {questing} way
42.00	21.43	Skopje, Macedonia	171.067	6	79	76	4	is tourist nurturing in developing rational structures for or presenting complex issues to the world	9	9	7	confidently self-declaring in an enterprising way
65.33	21.50	Piteå, Sweden	171.000	6	79	76	4	is tourist nurturing in developing rational structures for or presenting complex issues to the world	11	4	3	nurturingly community-anchored in a thoughtful way
63.10	21.62	Vaasa, Finland	170.883	6	79	76	4	is tourist nurturing in developing rational structures for or presenting complex issues to the world	11	2	5	materially-focused and community-anchored in a showy way
65.83	21.72	Boden, Sweden	170.783	6	79	76	4	is tourist nurturing in developing rational structures for or presenting complex issues to the world	11	4	7	nurturingly community-anchored in an enterprising way
65.58	22.15	Luleå, Sweden	170.350	6	79	76	4	is tourist nurturing in developing rational structures for or presenting complex issues to the world	11	4	5	nurturingly community-anchored in a showy way
60.45	22.27	Turku, Finland	170.233	6	79	76	4	is tourist nurturing in developing rational structures for or presenting complex issues to the world	11	12	4	spacey, odd, and community-anchored in a concerned way
40.65	22.90	Thessaloniki, Greece	169.600	6	80	77	5	is a popular regional show stealer in developing rational structures for or presenting complex issues to the world	9	8	6	no-nonsense and self-declaring in a busy way
42.70	23.33	Sofia, Bulgaria	169.167	6	80	77	5	is a popular regional show stealer in developing rational structures for or presenting complex issues to the world	9	10	1	(not necessarily negatively) calculatingly self-declaring in a {questing} way

46.77	23.58	Cluj-Napoca, Romania	168.917	6	80	77	5	is a popular regional show stealer in developing rational structures for or presenting complex issues to the world	10	1	4	aims-insistent and objective-focused in a concerned way
38.47	23.60	Halkida, Greece	168.900	6	80	77	5	is a popular regional show stealer in developing rational structures for or presenting complex issues to the world	9	6	9	practical and self-declaring in a self-declaring way
70.67	23.68	Hammerfest, Norway	168.817	6	80	77	5	is a popular regional show stealer in developing rational structures for or presenting complex issues to the world	11	8	6	no-nonsense and community-anchored in a busy way
37.97	23.72	Athena, Greece	168.783	6	80	77	5	is a popular regional show stealer in developing rational structures for or presenting complex issues to the world	9	6	4	practical and self-declaring in a concerned way
61.50	23.77	Tampere, Finland	168.733	6	80	77	5	is a popular regional show stealer in developing rational structures for or presenting complex issues to the world	11	1	2	aims-insistent and community-anchored in a {self-value aware} way
44.33	23.82	Craiova, Romania	168.683	6	80	77	5	is a popular regional show stealer in developing rational structures for or presenting complex issues to the world	9	11	5	(social) noisily self-declaring in a showy way
49.85	24.02	Lviv, Ukraine	168.483	6	80	77	5	is a popular regional show stealer in developing rational structures for or presenting complex issues to the world	10	3	10	expressive, communicative, and objective-focused in an objective-focused way
56.95	24.10	Riga, Latvia	168.400	6	80	77	5	is a popular regional show stealer in developing rational structures for or presenting complex issues to the world	10	9	6	confidently objective-focused in a busy way
65.83	24.13	Haparanda, Sweden	168.367	6	80	77	5	is a popular regional show stealer in developing rational structures for or presenting complex issues to the world	11	4	7	nurturingly community-anchored in an enterprising way
65.85	24.15	Tornio, Finland	168.350	6	80	77	5	is a popular regional show stealer in developing rational structures for or presenting complex issues to the world	11	4	8	nurturingly community-anchored in a pushy way
65.73	24.57	Kemi, Finland	167.933	6	80	77	5	is a popular regional show stealer in developing rational structures for or presenting complex issues to the world	11	4	7	nurturingly community-anchored in an enterprising way
60.20	24.65	Espoo, Finland	167.850	6	80	77	5	is a popular regional show stealer in developing rational structures for or presenting complex issues to the world	11	12	1	spacey, odd, and community-anchored in a {questing} way
59.43	24.75	Tallinn, Estonia	167.750	6	80	77	5	is a popular regional show stealer in developing rational structures for or presenting complex issues to the world	10	11	6	(social) noisily objective-focused in a busy way
-28.75	24.77	Kimberley, Northern Cape, South Africa	167.733	6	80	77	5	is a popular regional show stealer in developing rational structures for or presenting complex issues to the world	5	12	12	spacey, odd, and showy in an environment-attentive way
60.17	24.93	Helsinki, Finland	167.567	6	80	77	5	is a popular regional show stealer in developing rational structures for or presenting complex issues to the world	11	12	1	spacey, odd, and community-anchored in a {questing} way
60.30	25.03	Vantaa, Finland	167.467	6	81	78	6	pursues a quest for greater relevance in developing rational structures for or presenting complex issues to the world	11	12	2	spacey, odd, and community-anchored in a {self-value aware} way
35.33	25.13	Heraklion, Greece	167.367	6	81	78	6	pursues a quest for greater relevance in developing rational structures for or presenting complex issues to the world	9	4	3	nurturingly self-declaring in a thoughtful way
54.68	25.28	Vilnius, Lithuania	167.217	6	81	78	6	pursues a quest for greater relevance in developing rational structures for or presenting complex issues to the world	10	7	8	sociable and objective-focused in a pushy way
65.02	25.47	Oulu, Finland	167.033	6	81	78	6	pursues a quest for greater relevance in developing rational structures for or presenting complex issues to the world	11	4	12	nurturingly community-anchored in an environment-attentive way

-33.95	25.60	Port Elizabeth, Eastern Cape, South Africa	166.900	6	81	78	6	pursues a quest for greater relevance in developing rational structures for or presenting complex issues to the world	4	8	10	no-nonsense and concerned in an objective-focused way
-25.85	25.63	Mafikeng, North West, South Africa	166.867	6	81	78	6	pursues a quest for greater relevance in developing rational structures for or presenting complex issues to the world	5	3	3	expressive, communicative, and showy in a thoughtful way
60.98	25.65	Lahti, Finland	166.850	6	81	78	6	pursues a quest for greater relevance in developing rational structures for or presenting complex issues to the world	11	12	9	spacey, odd, and community-anchored in a self-declaring way
66.50	25.73	Rovaniemi, Finland	166.767	6	81	78	6	pursues a quest for greater relevance in developing rational structures for or presenting complex issues to the world	11	5	2	proud and community-anchored in a {self-value aware} way
62.25	25.75	Jyväskylä, Finland	166.750	6	81	78	6	pursues a quest for greater relevance in developing rational structures for or presenting complex issues to the world	11	1	9	aims-insistent and community-anchored in a self-declaring way
-17.85	25.87	Livingstone, Zambia	166.633	6	81	78	6	pursues a quest for greater relevance in developing rational structures for or presenting complex issues to the world	5	9	8	confidently showy in a pushy way
-24.65	25.92	Gaborone, Botswana	166.583	6	81	78	6	pursues a quest for greater relevance in developing rational structures for or presenting complex issues to the world	5	4	3	nurturingly showy in a thoughtful way
44.43	26.10	Bucharest, Romania	166.400	6	81	78	6	pursues a quest for greater relevance in developing rational structures for or presenting complex issues to the world	9	11	6	(social) noisily self-declaring in a busy way
-29.12	26.22	Bloemfontein, Free State, South Africa	166.283	6	81	78	6	pursues a quest for greater relevance in developing rational structures for or presenting complex issues to the world	5	12	8	spacey, odd, and showy in a pushy way
58.38	26.72	Tartu, Estonia	165.783	6	81	78	6	pursues a quest for greater relevance in developing rational structures for or presenting complex issues to the world	10	10	8	(not necessarily negatively) calculatingly objective-focused in a pushy way
65.37	27.00	Pudasjärvi, Finland	165.500	6	81	78	6	pursues a quest for greater relevance in developing rational structures for or presenting complex issues to the world	11	4	3	nurturingly community-anchored in a thoughtful way
69.90	27.02	Utsjoki, Finland	165.483	6	81	78	6	pursues a quest for greater relevance in developing rational structures for or presenting complex issues to the world	11	7	11	sociable and community-anchored in a community-anchored way
38.43	27.15	İzmir, Turkey	165.350	6	81	78	6	pursues a quest for greater relevance in developing rational structures for or presenting complex issues to the world	9	6	8	practical and self-declaring in a pushy way
-32.85	27.43	Bhisho, Eastern Cape, South Africa	165.067	6	81	78	6	pursues a quest for greater relevance in developing rational structures for or presenting complex issues to the world	4	9	8	confidently concerned in a pushy way
66.72	27.43	Kemijärvi, Finland	165.067	6	81	78	6	pursues a quest for greater relevance in developing rational structures for or presenting complex issues to the world	11	5	4	proud and community-anchored in a concerned way
-11.67	27.47	Lubumbashi, Democratic Republic of the Congo	165.033	6	81	78	6	pursues a quest for greater relevance in developing rational structures for or presenting complex issues to the world	6	2	8	materially-focused and busy in a pushy way
-29.32	27.48	Maseru, Lesotho	165.017	6	81	78	6	pursues a quest for greater relevance in developing rational structures for or presenting complex issues to the world	5	12	6	spacey, odd, and showy in a busy way
-21.17	27.52	Francistown, Botswana	164.983	6	82	79	7	welcomes all in developing rational structures for or presenting complex issues to the world	5	7	12	sociable and showy in an environment-attentive way
53.90	27.57	Minsk, Belarus	164.933	6	82	79	7	welcomes all in developing rational structures for or presenting complex issues to the world	10	7	1	sociable and objective-focused in a {questing} way
62.90	27.68	Kuopio, Finland	164.817	6	82	79	7	welcomes all in developing rational structures for or presenting complex issues to the world	11	2	3	materially-focused and community-anchored in a thoughtful way

70.08	27.88	Nuorgam, Lapland, Finland	164.617	6	82	79	7	welcomes all in developing rational structures for or presenting complex issues to the world	11	8	12	no-nonsense and community-anchored in an environment-attentive way
-26.20	28.05	Johannesburg, Gauteng, South Africa	164.450	6	82	79	7	welcomes all in developing rational structures for or presenting complex issues to the world	5	3	12	expressive, communicative, and showy in an environment-attentive way
-25.75	28.18	Pretoria, Gauteng, South Africa	164.317	6	82	79	7	welcomes all in developing rational structures for or presenting complex issues to the world	5	3	4	expressive, communicative, and showy in a concerned way
-15.42	28.28	Lusaka, Zambia	164.217	6	82	79	7	welcomes all in developing rational structures for or presenting complex issues to the world	5	11	8	(social) noisily showy in a pushy way
-20.17	28.58	Bulawayo, Bulawayo, Zimbabwe	163.917	6	82	79	7	welcomes all in developing rational structures for or presenting complex issues to the world	5	7	10	sociable and showy in an objective-focused way
-12.97	28.63	Ndola, Zambia	163.867	6	82	79	7	welcomes all in developing rational structures for or presenting complex issues to the world	6	1	7	aims-insistent and busy in an enterprising way
47.00	28.92	Chişinău, Moldova	163.583	6	82	79	7	welcomes all in developing rational structures for or presenting complex issues to the world	10	1	7	aims-insistent and objective-focused in an enterprising way
41.02	28.95	Istanbul, Turkey	163.550	6	82	79	7	welcomes all in developing rational structures for or presenting complex issues to the world	9	8	9	no-nonsense and self-declaring in a self-declaring way
40.18	29.05	Bursa, Turkey	163.450	6	82	79	7	welcomes all in developing rational structures for or presenting complex issues to the world	9	8	1	no-nonsense and self-declaring in a {questing} way
65.97	29.18	Kuusamo, Finland	163.317	6	82	79	7	welcomes all in developing rational structures for or presenting complex issues to the world	11	4	9	nurturingly community-anchored in a self-declaring way
-3.38	29.37	Bujumbura, Burundi	163.133	6	82	79	7	welcomes all in developing rational structures for or presenting complex issues to the world	6	9	3	confidently busy in a thoughtful way
-23.90	29.45	Polokwane, Limpopo, South Africa	163.050	6	82	79	7	welcomes all in developing rational structures for or presenting complex issues to the world	5	4	10	nurturingly showy in an objective-focused way
46.85	29.63	Tiraspol, Transnistria, Moldova	162.867	6	82	79	7	welcomes all in developing rational structures for or presenting complex issues to the world	10	1	5	aims-insistent and objective-focused in a showy way
70.08	29.73	Vadsø, Norway	162.767	6	82	79	7	welcomes all in developing rational structures for or presenting complex issues to the world	11	8	12	no-nonsense and community-anchored in an environment-attentive way
-19.45	29.80	Gweru, Midlands, Zimbabwe	162.700	6	82	79	7	welcomes all in developing rational structures for or presenting complex issues to the world	5	8	5	no-nonsense and showy in a showy way
31.20	29.92	Alexandria, Egypt	162.583	6	82	79	7	welcomes all in developing rational structures for or presenting complex issues to the world	9	12	11	spacey, odd, and self-declaring in a community-anchored way
-1.95	30.07	Kigali, Rwanda	162.433	6	83	80	8	is a standards setter in developing rational structures for or presenting complex issues to the world	6	10	5	(not necessarily negatively) calculatingly busy in a showy way
59.95	30.30	Saint Petersburg, Russia	162.200	6	83	80	8	is a standards setter in developing rational structures for or presenting complex issues to the world	10	11	11	(social) noisily objective-focused in a community-anchored way
-29.62	30.38	Pietermaritzburg, KwaZulu-Natal, South Africa	162.117	6	83	80	8	is a standards setter in developing rational structures for or presenting complex issues to the world	5	12	3	spacey, odd, and showy in a thoughtful way
50.45	30.52	Kiev, Ukraine	161.983	6	83	80	8	is a standards setter in developing rational structures for or presenting complex issues to the world	10	4	4	nurturingly objective-focused in a concerned way
39.78	30.52	Eskisehir, Turkey	161.983	6	83	80	8	is a standards setter in developing rational structures for or presenting complex issues to the world	9	7	9	sociable and self-declaring in a self-declaring way
46.47	30.73	Odessa, Ukraine	161.767	6	83	80	8	is a standards setter in developing rational structures for or presenting complex issues to the world	10	1	2	aims-insistent and objective-focused in a {self-value aware} way
-25.47	30.98	Nelspruit, Mpumalanga, South Africa	161.517	6	83	80	8	is a standards setter in developing rational structures for or presenting complex issues to the world	5	3	7	expressive, communicative, and showy in an enterprising way
-17.87	31.03	Harare, Harare, Zimbabwe	161.467	6	83	80	8	is a standards setter in developing rational structures for or presenting complex issues to the world	5	9	8	confidently showy in a pushy way
-29.88	31.05	Durban, KwaZulu-Natal, South Africa	161.450	6	83	80	8	is a standards setter in developing rational structures for or presenting complex issues to the world	5	12	1	spacey, odd, and showy in a {questing} way

-26.32	31.13	Mbabane, Swaziland	161.367	6	83	80	8	is a standards setter in developing rational structures for or presenting complex issues to the world	5 2 11	materially-focused and showy in a community-anchored way
-26.42	31.17	Lobamba, Swaziland	161.333	6	83	80	8	is a standards setter in developing rational structures for or presenting complex issues to the world	5 2 10	materially-focused and showy in an objective-focused way
30.05	31.23	Cairo, Egypt	161.267	6	83	80	8	is a standards setter in developing rational structures for or presenting complex issues to the world	9 12 12	spacey, odd, and self-declaring in an environment-attentive way
-26.48	31.37	Manzini, Swaziland	161.133	6	83	80	8	is a standards setter in developing rational structures for or presenting complex issues to the world	5 2 9	materially-focused and showy in a self-declaring way
4.85	31.60	Juba, South Sudan	160.900	6	83	80	8	is a standards setter in developing rational structures for or presenting complex issues to the world	7 3 10	expressive, communicative, and enterprising in an objective-focused way
31.25	32.28	Port Said, Egypt	160.217	6	83	80	8	is a standards setter in developing rational structures for or presenting complex issues to the world	9 1 12	aims-insistent and self-declaring in an environment-attentive way
0.05	32.47	Entebbe, Uganda	160.033	6	83	80	8	is a standards setter in developing rational structures for or presenting complex issues to the world	7 12 12	spacey, odd, and enterprising in an environment-attentive way
15.65	32.48	Omdurman, Sudan	160.017	6	83	80	8	is a standards setter in developing rational structures for or presenting complex issues to the world	8 12 6	spacey, odd, and pushy in a busy way
37.87	32.48	Konya, Turkey	160.017	6	83	80	8	is a standards setter in developing rational structures for or presenting complex issues to the world	9 6 3	practical and self-declaring in a thoughtful way
15.63	32.53	Khartoum, Sudan	159.967	6	84	81	9	provides noteworthy sights in developing rational structures for or presenting complex issues to the world	8 12 6	spacey, odd, and pushy in a busy way
29.97	32.55	Suez, Egypt	159.950	6	84	81	9	provides noteworthy sights in developing rational structures for or presenting complex issues to the world	8 11 11	(social) noisily pushy in a community-anchored way
-25.97	32.58	Maputo, Mozambique	159.917	6	84	81	9	provides noteworthy sights in developing rational structures for or presenting complex issues to the world	5 3 2	expressive, communicative, and showy in a {self-value aware} way
0.32	32.58	Kampala, Uganda	159.917	6	84	81	9	provides noteworthy sights in developing rational structures for or presenting complex issues to the world	7 12 3	spacey, odd, and enterprising in a thoughtful way
-18.97	32.63	Mutare, Manicaland, Zimbabwe	159.867	6	84	81	9	provides noteworthy sights in developing rational structures for or presenting complex issues to the world	5 8 9	no-nonsense and showy in a self-declaring way
25.68	32.65	Luxor, Egypt	159.850	6	84	81	9	provides noteworthy sights in developing rational structures for or presenting complex issues to the world	8 8 6	no-nonsense and pushy in a busy way
39.93	32.87	Ankara, Turkey	159.633	6	84	81	9	provides noteworthy sights in developing rational structures for or presenting complex issues to the world	9 7 11	sociable and self-declaring in a community-anchored way
-2.52	32.90	Mwanza, Tanzania	159.600	6	84	81	9	provides noteworthy sights in developing rational structures for or presenting complex issues to the world	6 9 11	confidently busy in a community-anchored way
68.97	33.08	Murmansk, Murmansk Oblast, Russia	159.417	6	84	81	9	provides noteworthy sights in developing rational structures for or presenting complex issues to the world	11 7 2	sociable and community-anchored in a {self-value aware} way
35.17	33.37	Nicosia, Cyprus	159.133	6	84	81	9	provides noteworthy sights in developing rational structures for or presenting complex issues to the world	9 4 1	nurturingly self-declaring in a {questing} way
-13.98	33.78	Lilongwe, Malawi	158.717	6	84	81	9	provides noteworthy sights in developing rational structures for or presenting complex issues to the world	6 12 9	spacey, odd, and busy in a self-declaring way
44.95	34.10	Simferopol, Crimea, Russia	158.400	6	84	81	9	provides noteworthy sights in developing rational structures for or presenting complex issues to the world	9 11 11	(social) noisily self-declaring in a community-anchored way

31.52	34.45	Gaza, Gaza Strip, Palestine	158.050	6	84	81	9	provides noteworthy sights in developing rational structures for or presenting complex issues to the world	9	1	2	aims-insistent and self-declaring in a {self-value aware} way
36.80	34.63	Mersin, Turkey	157.867	6	84	81	9	provides noteworthy sights in developing rational structures for or presenting complex issues to the world	9	5	5	proud and self-declaring in a showy way
32.07	34.78	Tel Aviv, Israel	157.717	6	84	81	9	provides noteworthy sights in developing rational structures for or presenting complex issues to the world	9	1	7	aims-insistent and self-declaring in an enterprising way
29.55	34.95	Eilat, Israel	157.550	6	84	81	9	provides noteworthy sights in developing rational structures for or presenting complex issues to the world	8	11	7	(social) noisily pushy in an enterprising way
-15.78	35.00	Blantyre, Malawi	157.500	6	85	82	10	hosts cultural structures in developing rational structures for or presenting complex issues to the world	5	11	4	(social) noisily showy in a concerned way
31.78	35.22	Jerusalem, Israel	157.283	6	85	82	10	hosts cultural structures in developing rational structures for or presenting complex issues to the world	9	1	5	aims-insistent and self-declaring in a showy way
37.00	35.32	Adana, Turkey	157.183	6	85	82	10	hosts cultural structures in developing rational structures for or presenting complex issues to the world	9	5	7	proud and self-declaring in an enterprising way
33.88	35.52	Beirut, Lebanon	156.983	6	85	82	10	hosts cultural structures in developing rational structures for or presenting complex issues to the world	9	3	1	expressive, communicative, and self-declaring in a {questing} way
-6.17	35.75	Dodoma, Tanzania	156.750	6	85	82	10	hosts cultural structures in developing rational structures for or presenting complex issues to the world	6	7	12	sociable and busy in an environment-attentive way
35.52	35.78	Latakia, Syria	156.717	6	85	82	10	hosts cultural structures in developing rational structures for or presenting complex issues to the world	9	4	4	nurturingly self-declaring in a concerned way
31.93	35.93	Amman, Jordan	156.567	6	85	82	10	hosts cultural structures in developing rational structures for or presenting complex issues to the world	9	1	6	aims-insistent and self-declaring in a busy way
50.00	36.23	Kharkiv, Ukraine	156.267	6	85	82	10	hosts cultural structures in developing rational structures for or presenting complex issues to the world	10	4	12	nurturingly objective-focused in an environment-attentive way
33.52	36.30	Damascus, Syria	156.200	6	85	82	10	hosts cultural structures in developing rational structures for or presenting complex issues to the world	9	2	9	materially-focused and self-declaring in a self-declaring way
-1.28	36.82	Nairobi, Kenya	155.683	6	85	82	10	hosts cultural structures in developing rational structures for or presenting complex issues to the world	6	10	11	(not necessarily negatively) calculatingly busy in a community-anchored way
37.07	37.38	Gaziantep, Turkey	155.117	6	85	82	10	hosts cultural structures in developing rational structures for or presenting complex issues to the world	9	5	7	proud and self-declaring in an enterprising way
55.75	37.62	Moscow, Russia	154.883	6	86	83	11	shows lots of activity in developing rational structures for or presenting complex issues to the world	10	8	7	no-nonsense and objective-focused in an enterprising way
9.03	38.73	Addis Ababa, Ethiopia	153.767	6	86	83	11	shows lots of activity in developing rational structures for or presenting complex issues to the world	7	7	2	sociable and enterprising in a {self-value aware} way
15.33	38.93	Asmara, Eritrea	153.567	6	86	83	11	shows lots of activity in developing rational structures for or presenting complex issues to the world	8	12	3	spacey, odd, and pushy in a thoughtful way
45.03	38.97	Krasnodar, Krasnodar Krai, Russia	153.533	6	86	83	11	shows lots of activity in developing rational structures for or presenting complex issues to the world	10	12	12	spacey, odd, and objective-focused in an environment-attentive way
21.55	39.17	Jeddah, Saudi Arabia	153.333	6	86	83	11	shows lots of activity in developing rational structures for or presenting complex issues to the world	8	5	2	proud and pushy in a {self-value aware} way
-6.17	39.20	Zanzibar City, Tanzania	153.300	6	86	83	11	shows lots of activity in developing rational structures for or presenting complex issues to the world	6	7	12	sociable and busy in an environment-attentive way
51.67	39.22	Voronezh, Voronezh Oblast, Russia	153.283	6	86	83	11	shows lots of activity in developing rational structures for or presenting complex issues to the world	10	5	4	proud and objective-focused in a concerned way
-6.80	39.28	Dar es Salaam, Tanzania	153.217	6	86	83	11	shows lots of activity in developing rational structures for or presenting complex issues to the world	6	6	6	practical and busy in a busy way
24.47	39.60	Medina, Saudi Arabia	152.900	6	86	83	11	shows lots of activity in developing rational structures for or presenting complex issues to the world	8	7	6	sociable and pushy in a busy way

-4.05	39.67	Mombasa, Kenya	152.833	6	86	83	11	shows lots of activity in developing rational structures for or presenting complex issues to the world	6	8	9	no-nonsense and busy in a self-declaring way
47.23	39.70	Rostov-on-Don, Rostov Oblast, Russia	152.800	6	86	83	11	shows lots of activity in developing rational structures for or presenting complex issues to the world	10	1	9	aims-insistent and objective-focused in a self-declaring way
43.58	39.72	Sochi, Krasnodar Krai, Russia	152.783	6	86	83	11	shows lots of activity in developing rational structures for or presenting complex issues to the world	9	10	10	(not necessarily negatively) calculatingly self-declaring in an objective-focused way
21.42	39.82	Mecca, Saudi Arabia	152.683	6	86	83	11	shows lots of activity in developing rational structures for or presenting complex issues to the world	8	5	1	proud and pushy in a {questing} way
57.62	39.85	Yaroslavl, Yaroslavl Oblast, Russia	152.650	6	86	83	11	shows lots of activity in developing rational structures for or presenting complex issues to the world	10	10	1	(not necessarily negatively) calculatingly objective-focused in a {questing} way
64.53	40.53	Arkhangelsk, Arkhangelsk Oblast, Russia	151.967	6	87	84	12	is visited by all, a world city in developing rational structures for or presenting complex issues to the world	11	3	7	expressive, communicative, and community-anchored in an enterprising way
43.00	41.02	Sukhumi, Abkhazia, Georgia	151.483	6	87	84	12	is visited by all, a world city in developing rational structures for or presenting complex issues to the world	9	10	4	(not necessarily negatively) calculatingly self-declaring in a concerned way
-0.35	42.55	Kismayo, Somalia	149.950	5	88	85	1	is a source of affairs, leads other cities in declaring its customs loudly	6	11	8	(social) noisily busy in a pushy way
36.33	43.13	Mosul, Iraq	149.367	5	88	85	1	is a source of affairs, leads other cities in declaring its customs loudly	9	5	12	proud and self-declaring in an environment-attentive way
11.58	43.15	Djibouti, Djibouti	149.350	5	88	85	1	is a source of affairs, leads other cities in declaring its customs loudly	7	9	3	confidently enterprising in a thoughtful way
-11.75	43.20	Moroni, Comoros	149.300	5	88	85	1	is a source of affairs, leads other cities in declaring its customs loudly	6	2	7	materially-focused and busy in an enterprising way
42.23	43.97	Tskhinvali, South Ossetia, Georgia	148.533	5	88	85	1	is a source of affairs, leads other cities in declaring its customs loudly	9	9	9	confidently self-declaring in a self-declaring way
56.33	44.00	Nizhny Novgorod, Nizhny Novgorod Oblast, Russia	148.500	5	88	85	1	is a source of affairs, leads other cities in declaring its customs loudly	10	9	12	confidently objective-focused in an environment-attentive way
36.18	44.02	Arbil, Iraqi Kurdistan, Iraq	148.483	5	88	85	1	is a source of affairs, leads other cities in declaring its customs loudly	9	4	11	nurturingly self-declaring in a community-anchored way
9.57	44.07	Hargeisa, Somaliland, Somalia	148.433	5	88	85	1	is a source of affairs, leads other cities in declaring its customs loudly	7	7	7	sociable and enterprising in an enterprising way
15.35	44.20	Sana'a, Yemen	148.300	5	88	85	1	is a source of affairs, leads other cities in declaring its customs loudly	8	12	3	spacey, odd, and pushy in a thoughtful way
35.47	44.32	Kirkuk, Iraq	148.183	5	88	85	1	is a source of affairs, leads other cities in declaring its customs loudly	9	4	4	nurturingly self-declaring in a concerned way
33.33	44.43	Baghdad, Iraq	148.067	5	88	85	1	is a source of affairs, leads other cities in declaring its customs loudly	9	2	8	materially-focused and self-declaring in a pushy way
40.18	44.52	Yerevan, Armenia	147.983	5	88	85	1	is a source of affairs, leads other cities in declaring its customs loudly	9	8	1	no-nonsense and self-declaring in a {questing} way
48.70	44.52	Volgograd, Volgograd Oblast, Russia	147.983	5	88	85	1	is a source of affairs, leads other cities in declaring its customs loudly	10	2	11	materially-focused and objective-focused in a community-anchored way
41.72	44.78	Tbilisi, Georgia	147.717	5	88	85	1	is a source of affairs, leads other cities in declaring its customs loudly	9	9	4	confidently self-declaring in a concerned way
-12.78	45.23	Mamoudzou, Mayotte, France	147.267	5	89	86	2	is a noteworthy travel destination in declaring its customs loudly	6	1	9	aims-insistent and busy in a self-declaring way
2.03	45.35	Mogadishu, Somalia	147.150	5	89	86	2	is a noteworthy travel destination in declaring its customs loudly	7	1	7	aims-insistent and enterprising in an enterprising way
51.53	46.02	Saratov, Saratov Oblast, Russia	146.483	5	89	86	2	is a noteworthy travel destination in declaring its customs loudly	10	5	2	proud and objective-focused in a {self-value aware} way
38.07	46.30	Tabriz, Iran	146.200	5	89	86	2	is a noteworthy travel destination in declaring its customs loudly	9	6	5	practical and self-declaring in a showy way
24.63	46.72	Riyadh, Saudi Arabia	145.783	5	89	86	2	is a noteworthy travel destination in declaring its customs loudly	8	7	8	sociable and pushy in a pushy way
39.82	46.75	Stepanakert, Nagorno-Karabakh Republic, Azerbaijan	145.750	5	89	86	2	is a noteworthy travel destination in declaring its customs loudly	9	7	10	sociable and self-declaring in an objective-focused way
-18.93	47.52	Antananarivo, Madagascar	144.983	5	90	87	3	is vocal, social, expressively unhindered in declaring its customs loudly	5	8	10	no-nonsense and showy in an objective-focused way
30.50	47.82	Basra, Iraq	144.683	5	90	87	3	is vocal, social, expressively unhindered in declaring its customs loudly	9	12	4	spacey, odd, and self-declaring in a concerned way
29.37	47.98	Kuwait City, Kuwait	144.517	5	90	87	3	is vocal, social, expressively unhindered in declaring its customs loudly	8	11	5	(social) noisily pushy in a showy way
55.78	49.13	Kazan, Republic of Tatarstan, Russia	143.367	5	90	87	3	is vocal, social, expressively unhindered in declaring its customs loudly	10	8	7	no-nonsense and objective-focused in an enterprising way

53.52	49.42	Tolyatti, Samara Oblast, Russia	143.083	5	90	87	3	is vocal, social, expressively unhindered in declaring its customs loudly	10	6	9	practical and objective-focused in a self-declaring way
40.40	49.88	Baku, Azerbaijan	142.617	5	90	87	3	is vocal, social, expressively unhindered in declaring its customs loudly	9	8	3	no-nonsense and self-declaring in a thoughtful way
53.20	50.13	Samara, Samara Oblast, Russia	142.367	5	91	88	4	is tourist nurturing in declaring its customs loudly	10	6	6	practical and objective-focused in a busy way
26.28	50.20	Dammam, Saudi Arabia	142.300	5	91	88	4	is tourist nurturing in declaring its customs loudly	8	9	12	confidently pushy in an environment-attentive way
26.22	50.58	Manama, Bahrain	141.917	5	91	88	4	is tourist nurturing in declaring its customs loudly	8	8	11	no-nonsense and pushy in a community-anchored way
35.70	51.42	Tehran, Iran	141.083	5	91	88	4	is tourist nurturing in declaring its customs loudly	9	4	6	nurturingly self-declaring in a busy way
25.28	51.53	Doha, Qatar	140.967	5	91	88	4	is tourist nurturing in declaring its customs loudly	8	8	2	no-nonsense and pushy in a {self-value aware} way
32.63	51.65	Isfahan, Iran	140.850	5	91	88	4	is tourist nurturing in declaring its customs loudly	9	2	1	materially-focused and self-declaring in a {questing} way
56.83	53.18	Izhevsk, Udmurt Republic, Russia	139.317	5	92	89	5	is a popular regional show stealer in declaring its customs loudly	10	9	5	confidently objective-focused in a showy way
17.02	54.08	Salalah, Oman	138.417	5	92	89	5	is a popular regional show stealer in declaring its customs loudly	8	1	7	aims-insistent and pushy in an enterprising way
24.47	54.37	Abu Dhabi, United Arab Emirates	138.133	5	92	89	5	is a popular regional show stealer in declaring its customs loudly	8	7	6	sociable and pushy in a busy way
25.25	55.30	Dubai, United Arab Emirates	137.200	5	93	90	6	pursues a quest for greater relevance in declaring its customs loudly	8	8	2	no-nonsense and pushy in a {self-value aware} way
-20.88	55.45	Saint-Denis, Réunion, France	137.050	5	93	90	6	pursues a quest for greater relevance in declaring its customs loudly	5	7	3	sociable and showy in a thoughtful way
-4.62	55.45	Victoria, Seychelles	137.050	5	93	90	6	pursues a quest for greater relevance in declaring its customs loudly	6	8	3	no-nonsense and busy in a thoughtful way
54.75	55.97	Ufa, Republic of Bashkortostan, Russia	136.533	5	93	90	6	pursues a quest for greater relevance in declaring its customs loudly	10	7	9	sociable and objective-focused in a self-declaring way
58.00	56.32	Perm, Perm Krai, Russia	136.183	5	93	90	6	pursues a quest for greater relevance in declaring its customs loudly	10	10	4	(not necessarily negatively) calculatingly objective-focused in a concerned way
-20.17	57.50	Port Louis, Mauritius	135.000	5	94	91	7	welcomes all in declaring its customs loudly	5	7	10	sociable and showy in an objective-focused way
37.93	58.37	Ashgabat, Turkmenistan	134.133	5	94	91	7	welcomes all in declaring its customs loudly	9	6	4	practical and self-declaring in a concerned way
23.62	58.60	Muscat, Oman	133.900	5	94	91	7	welcomes all in declaring its customs loudly	8	6	10	practical and pushy in an objective-focused way
36.30	59.60	Mashhad, Iran	132.900	5	94	91	7	welcomes all in declaring its customs loudly	9	5	12	proud and self-declaring in an environment-attentive way
42.47	59.60	Nukus, Karakalpakstan, Uzbekistan	132.900	5	94	91	7	welcomes all in declaring its customs loudly	9	9	11	confidently self-declaring in a community-anchored way
56.83	60.58	Yekaterinburg, Sverdlovsk Oblast, Russia	131.917	5	95	92	8	is a standards setter in declaring its customs loudly	10	9	5	confidently objective-focused in a showy way
55.15	61.38	Chelyabinsk, Chelyabinsk Oblast, Russia	131.117	5	95	92	8	is a standards setter in declaring its customs loudly	10	8	1	no-nonsense and objective-focused in a {questing} way
31.62	65.72	Kandahar, Afghanistan	126.783	5	97	94	10	hosts cultural structures in declaring its customs loudly	9	1	3	aims-insistent and self-declaring in a thoughtful way
24.87	67.02	Karachi, Sindh, Pakistan	125.483	5	97	94	10	hosts cultural structures in declaring its customs loudly	8	7	10	sociable and pushy in an objective-focused way
25.38	68.37	Hyderabad, Sindh, Pakistan	124.133	5	98	95	11	shows lots of activity in declaring its customs loudly	8	8	3	no-nonsense and pushy in a thoughtful way
38.53	68.78	Dushanbe, Tajikistan	123.717	5	98	95	11	shows lots of activity in declaring its customs loudly	9	6	9	practical and self-declaring in a self-declaring way
34.53	69.17	Kabul, Afghanistan	123.333	5	98	95	11	shows lots of activity in declaring its customs loudly	9	3	7	expressive, communicative, and self-declaring in an enterprising way
41.27	69.22	Tashkent, Uzbekistan	123.283	5	98	95	11	shows lots of activity in declaring its customs loudly	9	9	12	confidently self-declaring in an environment-attentive way
51.17	71.43	Astana, Kazakhstan	121.067	5	99	96	12	is visited by all, a world city in declaring its customs loudly	10	4	11	nurturingly objective-focused in a community-anchored way
30.20	71.47	Multan, Punjab, Pakistan	121.033	5	99	96	12	is visited by all, a world city in declaring its customs loudly	9	12	1	spacey, odd, and self-declaring in a {questing} way
34.02	71.58	Peshawar, Khyber Pakhtunkhwa, Pakistan	120.917	5	99	96	12	is visited by all, a world city in declaring its customs loudly	9	3	2	expressive, communicative, and self-declaring in a {self-value aware} way
41.00	71.67	Namangan, Uzbekistan	120.833	5	99	96	12	is visited by all, a world city in declaring its customs loudly	9	8	9	no-nonsense and self-declaring in a self-declaring way
23.03	72.58	Ahmedabad, Gujarat, India	119.917	4	100	97	1	is a source of affairs, leads other cities in being in touch with the beyond	8	6	5	practical and pushy in a showy way
21.17	72.83	Surat, Gujarat, India	119.667	4	100	97	1	is a source of affairs, leads other cities in being in touch with the beyond	8	4	11	nurturingly pushy in a community-anchored way
18.98	72.83	Mumbai (Bombay), Maharashtra, India	119.667	4	100	97	1	is a source of affairs, leads other cities in being in touch with the beyond	8	3	2	expressive, communicative, and pushy in a {self-value aware} way
33.60	73.03	Rawalpindi, Punjab, Pakistan	119.467	4	100	97	1	is a source of affairs, leads other cities in being in touch with the beyond	9	2	10	materially-focused and self-declaring in an objective-focused way

33.72	73.07	Islamabad, Islamabad Capital Territory, Pakistan	119.433	4	100	97	1	is a source of affairs, leads other cities in being in touch with the beyond	9	2	11	materially-focused and self-declaring in a community-anchored way
31.42	73.08	Faisalabad, Punjab, Pakistan	119.417	4	100	97	1	is a source of affairs, leads other cities in being in touch with the beyond	9	1	1	aims-insistent and self-declaring in a {questing} way
54.98	73.37	Omsk, Omsk Oblast, Russia	119.133	4	100	97	1	is a source of affairs, leads other cities in being in touch with the beyond	10	7	11	sociable and objective-focused in a community-anchored way
4.18	73.52	Malé, Maldives	118.983	4	100	97	1	is a source of affairs, leads other cities in being in touch with the beyond	7	3	4	expressive, communicative, and enterprising in a concerned way
18.52	73.85	Pune, Maharashtra, India	118.650	4	100	97	1	is a source of affairs, leads other cities in being in touch with the beyond	8	2	9	materially-focused and pushy in a self-declaring way
31.55	74.35	Lahore, Punjab, Pakistan	118.150	4	100	97	1	is a source of affairs, leads other cities in being in touch with the beyond	9	1	2	aims-insistent and self-declaring in a {self-value aware} way
42.87	74.62	Bishkek, Kyrgyzstan	117.883	4	100	97	1	is a source of affairs, leads other cities in being in touch with the beyond	9	10	3	(not necessarily negatively) calculatingly self-declaring in a thoughtful way
34.08	74.78	Srinagar, Jammu and Kashmir, India	117.717	4	100	97	1	is a source of affairs, leads other cities in being in touch with the beyond	9	3	3	expressive, communicative, and self-declaring in a thoughtful way
31.63	74.87	Amritsar, Punjab, India	117.633	4	100	97	1	is a source of affairs, leads other cities in being in touch with the beyond	9	1	3	aims-insistent and self-declaring in a thoughtful way
26.93	75.82	Jaipur, Rajasthan, India	116.683	4	101	98	2	is a noteworthy travel destination in being in touch with the beyond	8	9	6	confidently pushy in a busy way
30.92	75.85	Ludhiana, Punjab, India	116.650	4	101	98	2	is a noteworthy travel destination in being in touch with the beyond	9	12	8	spacey, odd, and self-declaring in a pushy way
9.97	76.28	Kochi, Kerala, India	116.217	4	101	98	2	is a noteworthy travel destination in being in touch with the beyond	7	7	11	sociable and enterprising in a community-anchored way
30.75	76.78	Chandigarh, India	115.717	4	101	98	2	is a noteworthy travel destination in being in touch with the beyond	9	12	7	spacey, odd, and self-declaring in an enterprising way
43.28	76.90	Almaty, Kazakhstan	115.600	4	101	98	2	is a noteworthy travel destination in being in touch with the beyond	9	10	7	(not necessarily negatively) calculatingly self-declaring in an enterprising way
8.48	76.95	Trivandrum, Kerala, India	115.550	4	101	98	2	is a noteworthy travel destination in being in touch with the beyond	7	6	9	practical and enterprising in a self-declaring way
31.10	77.17	Shimla, Himachal Pradesh, India	115.333	4	101	98	2	is a noteworthy travel destination in being in touch with the beyond	9	12	10	spacey, odd, and self-declaring in an objective-focused way
28.62	77.22	New Delhi, Delhi, India	115.283	4	101	98	2	is a noteworthy travel destination in being in touch with the beyond	8	10	10	(not necessarily negatively) calculatingly pushy in an objective-focused way
12.97	77.57	Bangalore, Karnataka, India	114.933	4	102	99	3	is vocal, social, expressively unhindered in being in touch with the beyond	7	10	4	(not necessarily negatively) calculatingly enterprising in a concerned way
27.18	78.02	Agra, Uttar Pradesh, India	114.483	4	102	99	3	is vocal, social, expressively unhindered in being in touch with the beyond	8	9	8	confidently pushy in a pushy way
17.37	78.48	Hyderabad, Andhra Pradesh, India	114.017	4	102	99	3	is vocal, social, expressively unhindered in being in touch with the beyond	8	1	10	aims-insistent and pushy in an objective-focused way
21.13	79.08	Nagpur, Maharashtra, India	113.417	4	102	99	3	is vocal, social, expressively unhindered in being in touch with the beyond	8	4	10	nurturingly pushy in an objective-focused way
25.32	79.63	Kulpahar, Uttar Pradesh, India	112.867	4	102	99	3	is vocal, social, expressively unhindered in being in touch with the beyond	8	8	3	no-nonsense and pushy in a thoughtful way
6.93	79.85	Colombo, Sri Lanka	112.650	4	102	99	3	is vocal, social, expressively unhindered in being in touch with the beyond	7	5	6	proud and enterprising in a busy way
6.92	79.88	Sri Jayawardenapura-Kotte, Sri Lanka	112.617	4	102	99	3	is vocal, social, expressively unhindered in being in touch with the beyond	7	5	6	proud and enterprising in a busy way
13.08	80.27	Chennai (Madras), Tamil Nadu, India	112.233	4	103	100	4	is tourist nurturing in being in touch with the beyond	7	10	5	(not necessarily negatively) calculatingly enterprising in a showy way
26.47	80.33	Kanpur, Uttar Pradesh, India	112.167	4	103	100	4	is tourist nurturing in being in touch with the beyond	8	9	2	confidently pushy in a {self-value aware} way
7.30	80.63	Kandy, Sri Lanka	111.867	4	103	100	4	is tourist nurturing in being in touch with the beyond	7	5	10	proud and enterprising in an objective-focused way
26.85	80.95	Lucknow, Uttar Pradesh, India	111.550	4	103	100	4	is tourist nurturing in being in touch with the beyond	8	9	5	confidently pushy in a showy way
7.72	81.70	Batticaloa, Sri Lanka	110.800	4	103	100	4	is tourist nurturing in being in touch with the beyond	7	6	2	practical and enterprising in a {self-value aware} way
55.02	82.93	Novosibirsk, Novosibirsk Oblast, Russia	109.567	4	104	101	5	is a popular regional show stealer in being in touch with the beyond	10	8	12	no-nonsense and objective-focused in an environment-attentive way
17.68	83.22	Visakhapatnam, Andhra Pradesh, India	109.283	4	104	101	5	is a popular regional show stealer in being in touch with the beyond	8	2	1	materially-focused and pushy in a {questing} way
25.62	85.15	Patna, Bihar, India	107.350	4	105	102	6	pursues a quest for greater relevance in being in touch with the beyond	8	8	5	no-nonsense and pushy in a showy way
27.70	85.33	Kathmandu, Nepal	107.167	4	105	102	6	pursues a quest for greater relevance in being in touch with the beyond	8	10	1	(not necessarily negatively) calculatingly pushy in a {questing} way

43.83	87.60	Ürümqi, Xinjiang, People's Republic of China	104.900	4	106	103	7	welcomes all in being in touch with the beyond	9	11	12	(social) noisily self-declaring in an environment-attentive way
69.33	88.22	Norilsk, Krasnoyarsk Krai, Russia	104.283	4	106	103	7	welcomes all in being in touch with the beyond	11	7	5	sociable and community-anchored in a showy way
22.57	88.37	Kolkata (Calcutta), West Bengal, India	104.133	4	106	103	7	welcomes all in being in touch with the beyond	8	6	12	practical and pushy in an environment-attentive way
26.72	88.43	Siliguri, West Bengal, India	104.067	4	106	103	7	welcomes all in being in touch with the beyond	8	9	4	confidently pushy in a concerned way
27.33	88.62	Gangtok, Sikkim, India	103.883	4	106	103	7	welcomes all in being in touch with the beyond	8	9	10	confidently pushy in an objective-focused way
29.27	88.88	Shigatse, Tibet, People's Republic of China	103.617	4	106	103	7	welcomes all in being in touch with the beyond	8	11	4	(social) noisily pushy in a concerned way
27.47	89.65	Thimphu, Bhutan	102.850	4	106	103	7	welcomes all in being in touch with the beyond	8	9	11	confidently pushy in a community-anchored way
23.70	90.38	Dhaka, Bangladesh	102.117	4	107	104	8	is a standards setter in being in touch with the beyond	8	6	11	practical and pushy in a community-anchored way
29.65	91.10	Lhasa, Tibet, People's Republic of China	101.400	4	107	104	8	is a standards setter in being in touch with the beyond	8	11	8	(social) noisily pushy in a pushy way
23.83	91.27	Agartala, Tripura, India	101.233	4	107	104	8	is a standards setter in being in touch with the beyond	8	7	12	sociable and pushy in an environment-attentive way
26.18	91.73	Guwahati, Assam, India	100.767	4	107	104	8	is a standards setter in being in touch with the beyond	8	8	11	no-nonsense and pushy in a community-anchored way
22.37	91.80	Chittagong, Bangladesh	100.700	4	107	104	8	is a standards setter in being in touch with the beyond	8	5	10	proud and pushy in an objective-focused way
25.57	91.88	Shillong, Meghalaya, India	100.617	4	107	104	8	is a standards setter in being in touch with the beyond	8	8	5	no-nonsense and pushy in a showy way
11.67	92.77	Port Blair, Andaman and Nicobar Islands, India	99.733	4	108	105	9	provides noteworthy sights in being in touch with the beyond	7	9	3	confidently enterprising in a thoughtful way
26.63	92.80	Tezpur, Assam, India	99.700	4	108	105	9	provides noteworthy sights in being in touch with the beyond	8	9	3	confidently pushy in a thoughtful way
56.02	93.07	Krasnoyarsk, Krasnoyarsk Krai, Russia	99.433	4	108	105	9	provides noteworthy sights in being in touch with the beyond	10	8	9	no-nonsense and objective-focused in a self-declaring way
27.48	95.00	Dibrugarh, Assam, India	97.500	4	109	106	10	hosts cultural structures in being in touch with the beyond	8	9	11	confidently pushy in a community-anchored way
5.55	95.32	Banda Aceh, Aceh, Indonesia	97.183	4	109	106	10	hosts cultural structures in being in touch with the beyond	7	4	5	nurturingly enterprising in a showy way
19.75	96.10	Naypyidaw, Myanmar	96.400	4	109	106	10	hosts cultural structures in being in touch with the beyond	8	3	9	expressive, communicative, and pushy in a self-declaring way
16.80	96.15	Yangon, Myanmar	96.350	4	109	106	10	hosts cultural structures in being in touch with the beyond	8	1	9	aims-insistent and pushy in a showy way
7.88	98.40	Phuket, Thailand	94.100	4	110	107	11	shows lots of activity in being in touch with the beyond	7	6	3	practical and enterprising in a thoughtful way
3.58	98.67	Medan, North Sumatera, Indonesia	93.833	4	110	107	11	shows lots of activity in being in touch with the beyond	7	2	10	materially-focused and enterprising in an objective-focused way
18.80	99.00	Chiang Mai, Thailand	93.500	4	110	107	11	shows lots of activity in being in touch with the beyond	8	3	12	expressive, communicative, and pushy in an environment-attentive way
9.13	99.33	Surat Thani, Thailand	93.167	4	110	107	11	shows lots of activity in being in touch with the beyond	7	7	3	sociable and enterprising in a thoughtful way
19.92	99.83	Chiang Rai, Thailand	92.667	4	110	107	11	shows lots of activity in being in touch with the beyond	8	3	11	expressive, communicative, and pushy in a community-anchored way
5.42	100.32	George Town, Penang, Malaysia	92.183	4	111	108	12	is visited by all, a world city in being in touch with the beyond	7	4	4	nurturingly enterprising in a concerned way
-0.95	100.35	Padang, West Sumatera, Indonesia	92.150	4	111	108	12	is visited by all, a world city in being in touch with the beyond	6	11	2	(social) noisily busy in a {self-value aware} way
6.12	100.37	Alor Setar, Kedah, Malaysia	92.133	4	111	108	12	is visited by all, a world city in being in touch with the beyond	7	4	10	nurturingly enterprising in an objective-focused way
13.75	100.47	Bangkok, Thailand	92.033	4	111	108	12	is visited by all, a world city in being in touch with the beyond	7	11	12	(social) noisily enterprising in an environment-attentive way
7.02	100.47	Hat Yai, Thailand	92.033	4	111	108	12	is visited by all, a world city in being in touch with the beyond	7	5	7	proud and enterprising in an enterprising way
14.35	100.57	Ayutthaya, Thailand	91.933	4	111	108	12	is visited by all, a world city in being in touch with the beyond	7	11	5	(social) noisily enterprising in a showy way
12.93	100.88	Pattaya, Thailand	91.617	4	111	108	12	is visited by all, a world city in being in touch with the beyond	7	10	4	(not necessarily negatively) calculatingly enterprising in a concerned way
4.60	101.07	Ipoh, Perak, Malaysia	91.433	4	111	108	12	is visited by all, a world city in being in touch with the beyond	7	3	8	expressive, communicative, and enterprising in a pushy way
0.53	101.45	Pekanbaru, Riau, Indonesia	91.050	4	111	108	12	is visited by all, a world city in being in touch with the beyond	7	12	5	spacey, odd, and enterprising in a showy way
56.12	101.60	Bratsk, Irkutsk Oblast, Russia	90.900	4	111	108	12	is visited by all, a world city in being in touch with the beyond	10	8	10	no-nonsense and objective-focused in an objective-focused way
3.15	101.70	Kuala Lumpur, Federal Territory, Malaysia	90.800	4	111	108	12	is visited by all, a world city in being in touch with the beyond	7	2	6	materially-focused and enterprising in a busy way
36.63	101.77	Xining, Qinghai, People's Republic of China	90.733	4	111	108	12	is visited by all, a world city in being in touch with the beyond	9	5	3	proud and self-declaring in a thoughtful way
14.98	102.10	Nakhon Ratchasima, Thailand	90.400	4	111	108	12	is visited by all, a world city in being in touch with the beyond	7	11	11	(social) noisily enterprising in a community-anchored way

6.13	102.25	Kota Bharu, Kelantan, Malaysia	90.250	4	111	108	12	is visited by all, a world city in being in touch with the beyond	7	4	10	nurturingly enterprising in an objective-focused way
2.20	102.25	Malacca Town, Malacca, Malaysia	90.250	4	111	108	12	is visited by all, a world city in being in touch with the beyond	7	1	9	aims-insistent and enterprising in a self-declaring way
17.97	102.60	Vientiane, Laos	89.900	3	112	109	1	is a source of affairs, leads other cities in controlled thought	8	2	4	materially-focused and pushy in a concerned way
25.07	102.68	Kunming, Yunnan, People's Republic of China	89.817	3	112	109	1	is a source of affairs, leads other cities in controlled thought	8	8	12	no-nonsense and pushy in an environment-attentive way
17.42	102.75	Udon Thani, Thailand	89.750	3	112	109	1	is a source of affairs, leads other cities in controlled thought	8	1	11	aims-insistent and pushy in a community-anchored way
16.43	102.83	Khon Kaen, Thailand	89.667	3	112	109	1	is a source of affairs, leads other cities in controlled thought	8	1	1	aims-insistent and pushy in a {questing} way
1.48	103.73	Johor Bahru, Johor, Malaysia	88.767	3	112	109	1	is a source of affairs, leads other cities in controlled thought	7	1	2	aims-insistent and enterprising in a {self-value aware} way
36.03	103.80	Lanzhou, Gansu, People's Republic of China	88.700	3	112	109	1	is a source of affairs, leads other cities in controlled thought	9	4	9	nurturingly self-declaring in a self-declaring way
1.28	103.83	Singapore, Singapore	88.667	3	112	109	1	is a source of affairs, leads other cities in controlled thought	7	1	12	aims-insistent and enterprising in an environment-attentive way
13.37	103.87	Siem Reap, Cambodia	88.633	3	112	109	1	is a source of affairs, leads other cities in controlled thought	7	10	8	(not necessarily negatively) calculatingly enterprising in a pushy way
30.67	104.07	Chengdu, Sichuan, People's Republic of China	88.433	3	112	109	1	is a source of affairs, leads other cities in controlled thought	9	12	6	spacey, odd, and self-declaring in a busy way
52.32	104.30	Irkutsk, Irkutsk Oblast, Russia	88.200	3	112	109	1	is a source of affairs, leads other cities in controlled thought	10	5	10	proud and objective-focused in an objective-focused way
-2.98	104.75	Palembang, South Sumatera, Indonesia	87.750	3	112	109	1	is a source of affairs, leads other cities in controlled thought	6	9	7	confidently busy in an enterprising way
11.55	104.92	Phnom Penh, Cambodia	87.583	3	112	109	1	is a source of affairs, leads other cities in controlled thought	7	9	4	confidently enterprising in a {self-value aware} way
21.03	105.85	Hanoi, Vietnam	86.650	3	113	110	2	is a noteworthy travel destination in controlled thought	8	4	9	nurturingly pushy in a self-declaring way
29.57	106.57	Chongqing, People's Republic of China	85.933	3	113	110	2	is a noteworthy travel destination in controlled thought	8	11	7	(social) noisily pushy in an enterprising way
20.85	106.68	Hai Phong, Vietnam	85.817	3	113	110	2	is a noteworthy travel destination in controlled thought	8	4	8	nurturingly pushy in a pushy way
10.77	106.68	Ho Chi Minh City, Vietnam	85.817	3	113	110	2	is a noteworthy travel destination in controlled thought	7	8	7	no-nonsense and enterprising in an enterprising way
-6.20	106.80	Jakarta, Jakarta, Indonesia	85.700	3	113	110	2	is a noteworthy travel destination in controlled thought	6	7	12	sociable and busy in an environment-attentive way
-6.60	106.80	Bogor, West Java, Indonesia	85.700	3	113	110	2	is a noteworthy travel destination in controlled thought	6	6	8	practical and busy in a pushy way
47.92	106.92	Ulaanbaatar, Mongolia	85.583	3	113	110	2	is a noteworthy travel destination in controlled thought	10	2	4	materially-focused and objective-focused in a concerned way
16.47	107.58	Huế, Vietnam	84.917	3	114	111	3	is vocal, social, expressively unhindered in controlled thought	8	1	2	aims-insistent and pushy in a {self-value aware} way
-6.92	107.62	Bandung, West Java, Indonesia	84.883	3	114	111	3	is vocal, social, expressively unhindered in controlled thought	6	6	5	practical and busy in a showy way
16.07	108.23	Da Nang, Vietnam	84.267	3	114	111	3	is vocal, social, expressively unhindered in controlled thought	8	12	10	spacey, odd, and pushy in an objective-focused way
22.82	108.32	Nanning, Guangxi, People's Republic of China	84.183	3	114	111	3	is vocal, social, expressively unhindered in controlled thought	8	6	3	practical and pushy in a thoughtful way
34.27	108.90	Xi'an, Shaanxi, People's Republic of China	83.600	3	114	111	3	is vocal, social, expressively unhindered in controlled thought	9	3	4	expressive, communicative, and self-declaring in a concerned way
-0.02	109.33	Pontianak, West Kalimantan, Indonesia	83.167	3	114	111	3	is vocal, social, expressively unhindered in controlled thought	6	11	11	(social) noisily busy in a community-anchored way
1.57	110.35	Kuching, Sarawak, Malaysia	82.150	3	115	112	4	is tourist nurturing in controlled thought	7	1	3	aims-insistent and enterprising in a thoughtful way
-7.80	110.37	Yogyakarta, Special Region of Yogyakarta, Indonesia	82.133	3	115	112	4	is tourist nurturing in controlled thought	6	5	9	proud and busy in a self-declaring way
-6.97	110.42	Semarang, Central Java, Indonesia	82.083	3	115	112	4	is tourist nurturing in controlled thought	6	6	5	practical and busy in a showy way
37.87	112.57	Taiyuan, Shanxi, People's Republic of China	79.933	3	116	113	5	is a popular regional show stealer in controlled thought	9	6	3	practical and self-declaring in a thoughtful way
-7.98	112.62	Malang, East Java, Indonesia	79.883	3	116	113	5	is a popular regional show stealer in controlled thought	6	5	7	proud and busy in an enterprising way
-7.27	112.75	Surabaya, East Java, Indonesia	79.750	3	116	113	5	is a popular regional show stealer in controlled thought	6	6	2	practical and busy in a {self-value aware} way
23.13	113.27	Guangzhou, Guangdong, People's Republic of China	79.233	3	116	113	5	is a popular regional show stealer in controlled thought	8	6	6	practical and pushy in a busy way
22.17	113.55	Macau, People's Republic of China	78.950	3	116	113	5	is a popular regional show stealer in controlled thought	8	5	8	proud and pushy in a pushy way
34.77	113.65	Zhengzhou, Henan, People's Republic of China	78.850	3	116	113	5	is a popular regional show stealer in controlled thought	9	3	9	expressive, communicative, and self-declaring in a self-declaring way
23.03	113.72	Dongguan, Guangdong, People's Republic of China	78.783	3	116	113	5	is a popular regional show stealer in controlled thought	8	6	5	practical and pushy in a showy way
4.40	114.00	Miri, Sarawak, Malaysia	78.500	3	116	113	5	is a popular regional show stealer in controlled thought	7	3	6	expressive, communicative, and enterprising in a busy way

22.55	114.10	Shenzhen, Guangdong, People's Republic of China	78.400	3	116	113	5	is a popular regional show stealer in controlled thought	8	6	12	practical and pushy in an environment-attentive way
22.28	114.17	Hong Kong, People's Republic of China	78.333	3	116	113	5	is a popular regional show stealer in controlled thought	8	5	9	proud and pushy in a self-declaring way
30.58	114.28	Wuhan, Hubei, People's Republic of China	78.217	3	116	113	5	is a popular regional show stealer in controlled thought	9	12	5	spacey, odd, and self-declaring in a showy way
36.60	114.48	Handan, Hebei, People's Republic of China	78.017	3	116	113	5	is a popular regional show stealer in controlled thought	9	5	3	proud and self-declaring in a thoughtful way
38.05	114.50	Shijiazhuang, Hebei, People's Republic of China	78.000	3	116	113	5	is a popular regional show stealer in controlled thought	9	6	5	practical and self-declaring in a showy way
4.88	114.95	Bandar Seri Begawan, Brunei	77.550	3	116	113	5	is a popular regional show stealer in controlled thought	7	3	10	expressive, communicative, and enterprising in an objective-focused way
-8.65	115.22	Denpasar, Bali, Indonesia	77.283	3	117	114	6	pursues a quest for greater relevance in controlled thought	6	5	12	proud and busy in an environment-attentive way
-32.53	115.72	Mandurah, Western Australia, Australia	76.783	3	117	114	6	pursues a quest for greater relevance in controlled thought	4	9	11	confidently concerned in a community-anchored way
-31.95	115.87	Perth, Western Australia, Australia	76.633	3	117	114	6	pursues a quest for greater relevance in controlled thought	4	10	5	(not necessarily negatively) calculatingly concerned in a showy way
5.97	116.10	Kota Kinabalu, Sabah, Malaysia	76.400	3	117	114	6	pursues a quest for greater relevance in controlled thought	7	4	9	nurturingly enterprising in a self-declaring way
39.92	116.38	Beijing, People's Republic of China	76.117	3	117	114	6	pursues a quest for greater relevance in controlled thought	9	7	11	sociable and self-declaring in a community-anchored way
-1.27	116.83	Balikpapan, East Kalimantan, Indonesia	75.667	3	117	114	6	pursues a quest for greater relevance in controlled thought	6	10	11	(not necessarily negatively) calculatingly busy in a community-anchored way
36.67	116.98	Jinan, Shandong, People's Republic of China	75.517	3	117	114	6	pursues a quest for greater relevance in controlled thought	9	5	4	proud and self-declaring in a concerned way
39.13	117.18	Tianjin, People's Republic of China	75.317	3	117	114	6	pursues a quest for greater relevance in controlled thought	9	7	3	sociable and self-declaring in a thoughtful way
-20.32	118.60	Port Hedland, Western Australia, Australia	73.900	3	118	115	7	welcomes all in controlled thought	5	7	8	sociable and showy in a pushy way
32.05	118.77	Nanjing, Jiangsu, People's Republic of China	73.733	3	118	115	7	welcomes all in controlled thought	9	1	7	aims-insistent and self-declaring in an enterprising way
-5.13	119.42	Makassar, South Sulawesi, Indonesia	73.083	3	118	115	7	welcomes all in controlled thought	6	7	10	sociable and busy in an objective-focused way
30.25	120.17	Hangzhou, Zhejiang, People's Republic of China	72.333	3	119	116	8	is a standards setter in controlled thought	9	12	2	spacey, odd, and self-declaring in a {self-value aware} way
22.98	120.18	Tainan, Republic of China (Taiwan)	72.317	3	119	116	8	is a standards setter in controlled thought	8	6	4	practical and pushy in a concerned way
22.63	120.27	Kaohsiung, Republic of China (Taiwan)	72.233	3	119	116	8	is a standards setter in controlled thought	8	6	1	practical and pushy in a {questing} way
36.07	120.38	Qingdao, Shandong, People's Republic of China	72.117	3	119	116	8	is a standards setter in controlled thought	9	4	10	nurturingly self-declaring in an objective-focused way
24.15	120.67	Taichung, Republic of China (Taiwan)	71.833	3	119	116	8	is a standards setter in controlled thought	8	7	3	sociable and pushy in a thoughtful way
14.58	120.97	Manila, Philippines	71.533	3	119	116	8	is a standards setter in controlled thought	7	11	8	(social) noisily enterprising in a pushy way
14.63	121.03	Quezon City, Philippines	71.467	3	119	116	8	is a standards setter in controlled thought	7	11	8	(social) noisily enterprising in a pushy way
14.55	121.03	Makati, Philippines	71.467	3	119	116	8	is a standards setter in controlled thought	7	11	7	(social) noisily enterprising in an enterprising way
31.20	121.50	Shanghai, People's Republic of China	71.000	3	119	116	8	is a standards setter in controlled thought	9	12	11	spacey, odd, and self-declaring in a community-anchored way
25.03	121.63	Taipei, Republic of China (Taiwan)	70.867	3	119	116	8	is a standards setter in controlled thought	8	8	12	no-nonsense and pushy in an environment-attentive way
38.92	121.63	Dalian, Liaoning, People's Republic of China	70.867	3	119	116	8	is a standards setter in controlled thought	9	7	1	sociable and self-declaring in a {questing} way
6.90	122.07	Zamboanga City, Philippines	70.433	3	119	116	8	is a standards setter in controlled thought	7	5	6	proud and enterprising in a busy way
10.72	122.57	Iloilo City, Iloilo, Philippines	69.933	3	120	117	9	provides noteworthy sights in controlled thought	7	8	6	no-nonsense and enterprising in a busy way
41.80	123.40	Shenyang, Liaoning, People's Republic of China	69.100	3	120	117	9	provides noteworthy sights in controlled thought	9	9	5	confidently self-declaring in a showy way
9.65	123.85	Tagbilaran, Bohol, Philippines	68.650	3	120	117	9	provides noteworthy sights in controlled thought	7	7	8	sociable and enterprising in a pushy way
10.28	123.90	Cebu City, Cebu, Philippines	68.600	3	120	117	9	provides noteworthy sights in controlled thought	7	8	2	no-nonsense and enterprising in a {self-value aware} way
43.90	125.20	Changchun, Jilin, People's Republic of China	67.300	3	121	118	10	hosts cultural structures in controlled thought	9	11	1	(social) noisily self-declaring in a {questing} way
-8.55	125.58	Dili, Timor-Leste	66.917	3	121	118	10	hosts cultural structures in controlled thought	6	5	1	proud and busy in a {questing} way
7.07	125.60	Davao City, Davao del Sur, Philippines	66.900	3	121	118	10	hosts cultural structures in controlled thought	7	5	7	proud and enterprising in an enterprising way
39.02	125.73	Pyongyang, North Korea	66.767	3	121	118	10	hosts cultural structures in controlled thought	9	7	2	sociable and self-declaring in a {self-value aware} way

Conclusion

Why This Book Takes the Form It Does

In light of the intriguing results associated with 997 Priska and 26 Proserpina, I began writing this book as a way of documenting my findings regarding the first 1000 Minor Planet Center bodies (which I call "asteroids" for brevity), where the chapter which listed them would have been the entire book. While going through my asteroid files, however, I became interested in finding a an actual mathematical formula for describing the action of specific bodies in the astro chart (like the kind hinted at in the previous book *144*), and eventually discovered a basic logarithmic pattern for predicting the influence of most Solar System bodies in a 2D plane. The results of that formula supported a theory of energy flux which I had developed while writing *FSA* and *HBS*, and so I decided it was finally time to reconcile all of my findings across the *FSA* series with some known physics. Meanwhile, in order to make the asteroid list slightly easier to navigate, I spent an additional month developing a mini-icon system for describing them, and in so doing found patterns in the asteroids' naming. I also continued my side research on geographic locations and used the dense sky full of asteroids to classify cities by longitude and latitude. Thus this book grew in scope and complexity to reach its present size.

I did consider that the asteroid list and quantum theory should have been placed in two separate books. But I had two good reasons for not doing so. First, the quantum theory is just a theory, not a fact, and so did not in my view warrant its own book independent of the thing it was intended to explain—which was astrology. Second, as I've said before, I don't like conveying ideas without having some sense of what they mean, and asked myself *If a person simply handed me a list of asteroids and said 'This is what they all mean,' would I believe them?* And my answer is no. I wouldn't believe them. Way back in *FSA* I talked about how Ceres is supposed to indicate nurturing, but doesn't really. Juno is supposed to show marriage, but not in the matrimonial sense. Hera and Selene are largely ignored, but shouldn't be. And almost nobody studies the Imum Coeli, though they should. So I would need at least some reasonable basis for taking a person's word for it if he claimed not only to have an explanation for something which generations of hardened scientists swore wasn't there, but also to have a formula for predicting almost any Solar System object—including nonobjects. I would need for that basis to line up with some observed physical laws. I would need to know why it would have been unreasonable before but reasonable now to look at astrology seriously through the lens of astronomy. And I would need some tables of testable data. For me, writing a book on the asteroids without presenting such a basis would have been like writing a fairy tale. What's more, some people (including myself) might ultimately depend on that kind of fairy tale to build up an important real world view of things. I can't just put something like the asteroid interpretations out there without tying their workings back to that real world. That would deprive the user of the same tools to which I had access for drawing their own conclusions.

On Quantum Mechanics and the Assertion Structure

When I think of quantum mechanics, I tend to think of three things: stepped energy, classes of energy carriers, and the Schrödinger Equation. The Schrödinger Equation, however, provides a picture of the whole graph for a wave function without explaining what goes into making that wave function what it is. This is no different from developing a function to describe the flow of ocean waves without knowing how many factors are involved in making those ocean waves exist in the first place. So we're left with the task of explaining how the entire system may be derived from basic geometries and the fixed energy levels allowable to them—something I have sought to do here.

Normally when you do a proof in mathematics you use a standard set of propositional tools: axioms, theorems, propositions, lemmas, proofs, and several other kinds of statement which vary in their centrality to the ideas in question. I have avoided these tools and used a series of "assertions" instead because the scope of what I'm explaining is simply too tangled to employ the regular propositional tools. The first few math assertions alone have been the basis of entire books and still remain open to alternative logics. But if we use words like "proposition" and "lemma" to announce them, we also invite a standard of justification which would invariably get us into the same weeds that even the most prominent particle physicists can't get out of. So although I expect that many people might dismiss the theory herein because it doesn't enter the gladiator arena of academic verbiage, it isn't as though the theory's conclusions can't be tested. They can be tested, and there is a lot to test. It isn't as though a physics theory that explains astrology is wrong just because the word astrology was associated with its formulation. Nor can we say something as simple as "it must be bogus because we know [xyz]." You don't know. I don't know. In 2018, nobody knows. But if we start using words like "lemma" and "theorem," it *sounds* like we know. I think this is the reason why I struggled for so long as a physics major in college before eventually switching to cognition. The culture (everywhere) which teaches us physics does so which such authority, such nonchalant, how-could-it-be-otherwise style "expertness," that one feels stupid for asking for the millionth time *So why is the Solar System flat but spherical again?* You know your teachers have already told you countless times before: It's gravity. But you still don't get it. And that's because your teachers, lemmas or no lemmas, have actually *not* told you what's happening, only what was observed to happen. Largely experimentally. But not causally. The rubber sheet diagrams are made to sound so intuitive that only a fool would fail to understand them. But they're not intuitive. Their z-dimension looks nothing like the z dimension we know. My point is, use of the standard propositional tools for asserting what is known or not known, obvious or not obvious, experimentally *explained* or only experimentally supported, sends us down a slope which I think restricts genuine theoretical inquiry and confines it to a system of study which is already known, but much smaller.

Summary of This Book's Quantum Mechanical Model
I have made the following assertions:

- The nature of basic known geometries sets up a system in which it is not possible for evenly distributed repeating patterns of rational dimensions to fill anything other than irrational spaces. A circle of radius 1 has an area of π. A square of side 1 has a diagonal of $\sqrt{2}$ and is not evenly distributed. In terms of energy carriers, this means that fixed energy levels will continually flow towards other spaces in off-loading their unallowed excess, in turn destabilizing other carriers. Time is set in motion in this way as a byproduct of the paradox driven system {energy level x therefore not energy level x}.

- The geometry of ranges of effect (circles) determines the allowable ratios of energy carriers in a particular region, as well as how many other energy carriers are accessible to any one carrier. In 2D space this is 12. As we move to higher dimensions, the amount of empty space only increases, making the 2D mapping of any higher dimensional model the ideal one for maximizing energy, and the one which determines the role of key limiting values such as π, the fine structure constant Җ^2, and the speed of light c—the latter two of which I have offered explanations and calculations for, since I couldn't find a nature-simple version of either in my background research.

- The twelve dimensions <x_A, ϕ_A, z_A, t, r_B, θ_B, [ϕ_B (spherical) or z_B (cylindrical)], τ, m, Д, β, מ> are essentially the 11 dimensions of M-theory, except that two dimensions (t and τ) are temporal and most other dimensions are "quasi-spatial"—occuring in space but measurable mainly through the type of energy contained therein. The most non-spatial space-like dimension β represents temperature and measures space on the scale of pre-quantic vibration. There is also an additional 12th state "mem" מ which is also spatial in nature. If you took the 11-dimensions of string theory and included the solution function itself as a 12th dimension for providing a critical history input into the next solution, you would arrive at 12. I have proposed that all energy observable by us occurs in these 12 dimensions. Mega-collections of such energy carriers still reflect these twelve basic attributes in their macroscopic dynamics. While writing this bullet I also learned of a 12-dimensional string model called F-theory, but I don't know what it entails.

- The vacuum of space consists of regions capable of possessing certain nonzero values for the aforementioned 12 dimensions, but only up to the limit of allowable energy and only down to a scale which is still big enough to organize resonant energy flows among geometric neighbors.

- Resonance and the region-trading requirements posed above encourage quanta to pull together. The need for intervening space and the need for energetic stability within an organized region encourage quanta to push apart.

- Stable orbits of megaquanta about a central emitter are a function of the surface area flux from the emitter, obeying a derivative relationship. Powers of 2 feature heavily both about a region's cycle space and linear-radially away from that region. The same rule holds for quanta as it does for galaxies, causing alternation of spherical and flat forms for energy clusters as a function of resonance distributional differences in the bigger energetic regions surrounding any volumes in question.

- Every energy cluster is a collection of the stable vacuum resonances that passed through the region where the cluster is found. So the Sun is an aggregation of whatever predominantly hydrogen and helium cloud existed there. The Earth is an aggregation of whatever resonant quanta (in the form of elements) existed on a particular isoshell away from the Sun. All quantic and megaquantic bodies will assemble like this, so all quantic bodies, on the fundamental level, can be thought of as regions of patterned, intersecting frequencies. If everything still existed in hot-cloud form, it would be a lot easier to see the Solar System as a sphere of pulsing potential. Alas, quantization disguises such multidimensional energy in the form of delineated matter. Mainly the phases have changed. But the oscillatory influences haven't.

The above theory was put together to explain my astrology findings, and is extended into implications for the human as a kind of quantum as well—hence spirituality. The idea is that, if humans consist of quanta and planets consist of quanta, and everything we observe from quarks to galactic superclusters display certain kinds of cycles and bonding over certain fields of action beyond their confining masses, there is no reason at all to think that humans wouldn't do this too. Our own sense-blindness to things like everyday gravity and waking alpha frequencies is no evidence of a lack of the related resonant fields—especially when things both larger and smaller than us in scale continue to recognize such binding forces.

Spirituality Follows from Quantum Mechanics Rules Applied To Humans as Energy Carriers

Some might think that a discussion of spirituality should be removed from a discussion of quantum mechanics. In some cases that may be. But when we study the empty space that binds an electron to a proton or a moon to its planet, the notion of what goes on in that empty space becomes the standard elephant in the room. As soon as we talk about the kind of empty space that passes among humans in dimensions other than spatial space—as soon as we entertain relativistic speeds and the freezing of time, mass as an outer bond pattern yet charge as an inner bond pattern—the set of laws that governs the material in our bodies introduces questions regarding what our bodies are actually capable of experiencing. Many times throughout the writing of this book I thought, *The most important physics theories should not be left solely to labs for their application. That wouldn't be fair to the rest of us.* If there is a way that a person can better himself with the knowledge of resonances between himself and his interactants, he should be able to use that knowledge. But now I sound like a "New Ager" right? And that that's just too bad. Astrologers aren't stupid just because they're astrologers. Spiritual people aren't irrational just because they're spiritual. There is no tenable field of science which necessarily excludes input from other fields. Anyone who claims so does so without possibility of proof, which is itself illogical.

We know that dogs communicate with each other and humans communicate with each other, but a human who talks to dogs—a "Dog Whisperer"—is considered magical. That situation should strike you as both weird and unfortunate. We've heard of plenty of people claiming that something doesn't exist because it hasn't been verified, but of course if they thought it existed they would probably come up with the means to verify it. "It doesn't exist because I didn't see it, and I won't make the tools for seeing it because it doesn't exist."[57] And so it is for Western spirituality, astrology, and other related topics as cast through some people's lenses. People who don't know are constantly telling you that *you* don't know because they don't. (I just did it earlier!) But we hope that whatever the source of their anti-certainty doesn't spread limitation to those of us who still enjoy the exploration, and doesn't permanently dampen our search to increase our knowledge and better ourselves simultaneously. I've written this book intending for the ideas in it to give us something to test not just in astrology, but in the fields of cognition and physics broadly. Until they are tested, though, the reigning sense that we "special humans" in our "special solar system" don't follow basic physics laws can be expected to prevail. "Multidimensional people fields" will continue to be off limits but "multidimensional space rock fields" won't be. Cosmic backgrounds are good, but auras are bad. It's crazy when you think about it.

Final Thoughts

As always, I have enjoyed sharing my scholarly inquiries with you. There is always so much more to learn, and I love hearing feedback which advances the journey even farther. Visit my site at http://electricmonastery.com for the files I used to do all the work in these four books. I'd definitely welcome others' extension of the research started throughout this series.

Thanks for reading,
 ajani@electricmonastery.com

---

[57] See my website for the full version of this statement.

Appendix I: Table of Orbit Properties

Below is a list of the astronomical bodies covered in this book, along with their four most relevant orbit properties. The orbital properties, when you read them, allow you to uncover an approximate interpretation for any astronomical body within our Solar System by using math instead of collecting statistics on them from dozens of charts the way I had to. The formulae for these values were derived from those stats.

- Duodecanate span $log_2\left(\frac{aph}{peri}\right)$: tells the overall apparent character of the body.

  - When this value is less than or equal to 12, you can take the character out of 12. Venus for example, with a span of 4, feels emotional or want based

  - When the value is between 13 – 144, you take the value out of 144. Agamemnon, with a span of 28, seems associated with morals because—following the rules in the previous book *144*—after we divide 12 signs into 12 regions, 28 gives us two whole signs (24 twelfths) inward when we start at 30 Pisces and go backwards, plus 4 more out of 12 (a square) to give 28. Two signs inward puts Agamemnon's span past Pisces, past Aquarius, into Capricorn. Four duodecanates inward from 30 Capricorn puts us at a square. So 28 is a Capricorn-square, associated with structured emotions: morals.

  - When the duodecanate span is higher than 144, you take the character out of 1728. Bacchus, with a span of 153, produces a full group of 144+9, putting it past Pisces into Aquarius, then with 9 left over gives a novile. So it appears as an Aquarius-novile, broadcasting one's social attention. Sedna, spanning 514, includes 3*144+82, Putting it past the first three backwards signs into Sagittarius, plus an additional 82. In the book *144*, an 82 was a Virgo-decile, associated with eccentric attention getting. So Sedna would appear associated with a Saj-Virgo-decile: eccentric attention getting in the realm of abstract public viewers (which is basically what we interpreted it to mean in *144*).

- Perihelion argument $log_2(peri) + 7 - \frac{1}{12}$: shows (usually) the start or the end type of event associated with the body in action, corrected for the position of Earth. The value includes a fraction out of 144, which tells us the detailed 144th aspect involved.

- Aphelion argument $log_2(aph) + 7 - \frac{1}{12}$: shows (usually) the end or the start type of event associated with the body in action, corrected for the position of Earth. This one also includes a 144th fraction.

- Semimajor argument $log_2(semimaj) + 7 - \frac{1}{12}$: shows the average or central type of event around which the acting body is based, corrected for the position of Earth. This one also includes a 144th fraction.

As I learned upon recent inspection of one of the major dwarf planets, the Minor Planet Center has frequent updates of the orbital elements for these bodies, so the numbers upon which these calculations were based do change every now and then. Usually not drastically, but often enough to shift a value of, say, 21 to a value of 22 in more than a few cases. That said, you may want to look at neighboring values to the ones in the table (as in also comparing 84/144 if it says 83/144— especially if the span doesn't seem to line up with what you read in the asteroid chapter). There's nothing we can do about it. That's science for ya.

MPC#	Name	Duodecanate Span	Perihelion argument	Semimajor argument	Aphelion argument
15760	1992 QB1	28	12 39/144	12 53/144	12 66/144
677	Aaltje	22	8 58/144	8 69/144	8 79/144
864	Aase	81	7 109/144	8 9/144	8 45/144
456	Abnoba	76	8 16/144	8 57/144	8 91/144
151	Abundantia	15	8 35/144	8 42/144	8 49/144
829	Academia	43	8 19/144	8 41/144	8 61/144
588	Achilles	62	9 10/144	9 43/144	9 71/144
523	Ada	75	8 30/144	8 70/144	8 104/144
330	Adalberta	109	7 115/144	8 32/144	8 79/144
525	Adelaide	44	7 134/144	8 12/144	8 32/144
812	Adele	71	8 10/144	8 47/144	8 79/144
647	Adelgunde	83	7 128/144	8 29/144	8 66/144
276	Adelheid	29	8 66/144	8 80/144	8 94/144
229	Adelinda	59	8 68/144	8 100/144	8 127/144
145	Adeona	61	8 16/144	8 48/144	8 76/144
398	Admete	95	8 1/144	8 53/144	8 95/144
608	Adolfine	53	8 46/144	8 74/144	8 98/144
268	Adorea	59	8 48/144	8 79/144	8 106/144
239	Adrastea	101	8 14/144	8 70/144	8 114/144
143	Adria	32	8 39/144	8 55/144	8 70/144
820	Adriana	22	8 70/144	8 81/144	8 91/144
91	Aegina	45	8 18/144	8 42/144	8 63/144
96	Aegle	59	8 45/144	8 76/144	8 103/144
159	Aemilia	46	8 56/144	8 79/144	8 101/144
396	Aeolia	68	8 17/144	8 54/144	8 84/144
369	Aeria	41	8 26/144	8 47/144	8 66/144
446	Aeternitas	54	8 29/144	8 57/144	8 82/144
132	Aethra	172	7 84/144	8 43/144	8 112/144
911	Agamemnon	28	9 31/144	9 46/144	9 59/144
228	Agathe	104	7 94/144	8 8/144	8 53/144
47	Aglaja	55	8 35/144	8 64/144	8 89/144
641	Agnes	55	7 125/144	8 10/144	8 35/144
847	Agnia	41	8 36/144	8 57/144	8 76/144
645	Agrippina	62	8 54/144	8 86/144	8 115/144
744	Aguntina	50	8 58/144	8 84/144	8 107/144
950	Ahrensa	67	7 132/144	8 23/144	8 54/144
861	Aida	44	8 59/144	8 82/144	8 102/144
978	Aidamina	100	8 30/144	8 86/144	8 129/144
738	Alagasta	24	8 63/144	8 75/144	8 86/144
702	Alauda	9	8 82/144	8 85/144	8 89/144
719	Albert	256	7 25/144	8 46/144	8 136/144
465	Alekto	88	8 31/144	8 79/144	8 118/144
418	Alemannia	51	8 16/144	8 42/144	8 65/144
259	Aletheia	55	8 53/144	8 81/144	8 106/144
54	Alexandra	84	8 5/144	8 51/144	8 89/144
929	Algunde	48	7 130/144	8 12/144	8 34/144
291	Alice	39	7 134/144	8 10/144	8 28/144
887	Alinda	268	7 3/144	8 33/144	8 126/144
266	Aline	66	8 23/144	8 58/144	8 88/144
124	Alkeste	32	8 29/144	8 45/144	8 60/144
82	Alkmene	94	8 4/144	8 55/144	8 97/144
457	Alleghenia	74	8 40/144	8 79/144	8 112/144
390	Alma	56	8 17/144	8 47/144	8 72/144
925	Alphonsina	34	8 33/144	8 50/144	8 66/144
971	Alsatia	68	8 10/144	8 46/144	8 77/144
955	Alstede	124	7 116/144	8 42/144	8 95/144
119	Althaea	34	8 24/144	8 41/144	8 57/144
850	Altona	53	8 45/144	8 72/144	8 97/144
650	Amalasuntha	78	7 133/144	8 31/144	8 66/144
284	Amalia	95	7 114/144	8 22/144	8 64/144
113	Amalthea	37	8 5/144	8 24/144	8 41/144
725	Amanda	94	7 132/144	8 40/144	8 82/144
193	Ambrosia	128	7 114/144	8 43/144	8 97/144
986	Amelia	86	8 34/144	8 81/144	8 120/144
916	America	101	7 111/144	8 23/144	8 67/144
516	Amherstia	117	7 127/144	8 49/144	8 99/144
367	Amicitia	41	7 133/144	8 10/144	8 29/144
871	Amneris	51	7 127/144	8 10/144	8 33/144
1221	Amor	195	7 5/144	7 123/144	8 55/144
198	Ampella	97	7 122/144	8 31/144	8 74/144
29	Amphitrite	31	8 24/144	8 39/144	8 53/144
55576	Amycus	175	10 122/144	11 82/144	12 8/144
980	Anacostia	86	8 6/144	8 53/144	8 92/144
270	Anahita	64	7 118/144	8 8/144	8 37/144
824	Anastasia	58	8 27/144	8 57/144	8 84/144
175	Andromache	99	8 30/144	8 85/144	8 128/144
965	Angelica	122	8 14/144	8 83/144	8 134/144
64	Angelina	54	8 21/144	8 49/144	8 74/144
791	Ani	83	8 35/144	8 81/144	8 118/144
265	Anna	115	7 107/144	8 28/144	8 77/144
910	Anneliese	65	8 33/144	8 67/144	8 97/144
817	Annika	76	8 1/144	8 42/144	8 76/144
129	Antigone	90	8 14/144	8 63/144	8 103/144
651	Antikleia	43	8 52/144	8 74/144	8 94/144
90	Antiope	70	8 45/144	8 82/144	8 114/144
272	Antonia	12	8 51/144	8 56/144	8 62/144
121725	Aphidas	209	10 28/144	11 12/144	11 91/144
1388	Aphrodite	39	8 54/144	8 74/144	8 92/144
1862	Apollo	264	6 42/144	7 68/144	8 16/144
358	Apollonia	65	8 29/144	8 63/144	8 93/144
988	Appella	101	8 26/144	8 82/144	8 126/144
387	Aquitania	101	7 142/144	8 54/144	8 97/144
849	Ara	85	8 36/144	8 82/144	8 120/144
841	Arabella	30	7 142/144	8 13/144	8 27/144
407	Arachne	30	8 30/144	8 45/144	8 58/144
973	Aralia	48	8 62/144	8 86/144	8 108/144
15810	Arawn	52	12 5/144	12 32/144	12 56/144
394	Arduina	97	8 2/144	8 55/144	8 98/144
737	Arequipa	105	7 127/144	8 42/144	8 87/144
197	Arete	70	8 16/144	8 53/144	8 85/144
95	Arethusa	65	8 42/144	8 77/144	8 106/144
469	Argentina	68	8 48/144	8 84/144	8 115/144
43	Ariadne	72	7 114/144	8 8/144	8 41/144
793	Arizona	53	8 30/144	8 58/144	8 82/144
780	Armenia	41	8 59/144	8 80/144	8 99/144
514	Armida	18	8 67/144	8 75/144	8 84/144
774	Armor	72	8 37/144	8 76/144	8 108/144
959	Arne	94	8 32/144	8 84/144	8 126/144
404	Arsinoe	85	7 140/144	8 42/144	8 80/144
105	Artemis	76	7 127/144	8 24/144	8 58/144
8405	Asbolus	303	9 99/144	11 12/144	11 112/144
214	Aschera	14	8 37/144	8 43/144	8 50/144
4581	Asclepius	156	6 45/144	6 137/144	7 56/144
67	Asia	79	7 129/144	8 28/144	8 63/144
962	Aslog	43	8 44/144	8 66/144	8 85/144
409	Aspasia	31	8 25/144	8 41/144	8 55/144
958	Asplinda	79	8 89/144	8 131/144	9 23/144
246	Asporina	47	8 26/144	8 50/144	8 72/144
672	Astarte	57	8 9/144	8 39/144	8 65/144
658	Asteria	28	8 48/144	8 62/144	8 75/144
233	Asterope	42	8 26/144	8 47/144	8 67/144
5	Astraea	82	7 140/144	8 40/144	8 77/144
152	Atala	34	8 65/144	8 82/144	8 98/144
36	Atalante	131	7 123/144	8 54/144	8 109/144
111	Ate	44	8 19/144	8 42/144	8 62/144
515	Athalia	74	8 41/144	8 81/144	8 114/144
230	Athamantis	26	8 11/144	8 24/144	8 37/144
730	Athanasia	76	7 115/144	8 12/144	8 46/144
881	Athene	88	7 140/144	8 44/144	8 83/144
161	Athor	58	7 137/144	8 24/144	8 51/144
1198	Atlantis	146	7 71/144	8 13/144	8 73/144
810	Atossa	77	7 109/144	8 6/144	8 40/144
273	Atropos	68	7 133/144	8 25/144	8 56/144
254	Augusta	52	7 124/144	8 7/144	8 31/144
700	Auravictrix	44	7 132/144	8 11/144	8 31/144
419	Aurelia	107	7 126/144	8 42/144	8 89/144
94	Aurora	40	8 62/144	8 83/144	8 101/144
63	Ausonia	54	7 141/144	8 26/144	8 50/144
136	Austria	36	7 141/144	8 16/144	8 33/144
2063	Bacchus	153	6 58/144	7 4/144	7 66/144
856	Backlunda	50	8 3/144	8 29/144	8 52/144

333 Badenia	68	8 46/144	8 82/144	8 112/144	
770 Bali	64	7 120/144	8 10/144	8 39/144	
324 Bamberga	148	7 106/144	8 49/144	8 110/144	
597 Bandusia	62	8 16/144	8 48/144	8 76/144	
298 Baptistina	41	7 137/144	8 14/144	8 33/144	
234 Barbara	105	7 110/144	8 25/144	8 70/144	
945 Barcelona	69	8 8/144	8 45/144	8 77/144	
819 Barnardiana	60	7 120/144	8 8/144	8 35/144	
441 Bathilde	34	8 42/144	8 58/144	8 74/144	
592 Bathseba	56	8 45/144	8 74/144	8 100/144	
172 Baucis	49	7 143/144	8 24/144	8 47/144	
813 Baumeia	12	8 5/144	8 10/144	8 15/144	
301 Bavaria	29	8 38/144	8 52/144	8 66/144	
656 Beagle	57	8 52/144	8 82/144	8 109/144	
83 Beatrix	35	8 11/144	8 29/144	8 45/144	
943 Begonia	91	8 30/144	8 80/144	8 120/144	
178 Belisana	19	8 22/144	8 31/144	8 40/144	
695 Bella	68	8 2/144	8 38/144	8 68/144	
28 Bellona	65	8 22/144	8 56/144	8 85/144	
734 Benda	43	8 60/144	8 82/144	8 102/144	
976 Benjamina	43	8 63/144	8 86/144	8 106/144	
863 Benkoela	13	8 80/144	8 86/144	8 92/144	
776 Berbericia	70	8 30/144	8 67/144	8 99/144	
653 Berenike	18	8 65/144	8 73/144	8 81/144	
716 Berkeley	37	8 40/144	8 59/144	8 76/144	
629 Bernardina	65	8 47/144	8 82/144	8 111/144	
422 Berolina	92	7 104/144	8 10/144	8 51/144	
154 Bertha	33	8 69/144	8 86/144	8 101/144	
420 Bertholda	14	8 93/144	8 99/144	8 106/144	
937 Bethgea	93	7 104/144	8 11/144	8 52/144	
250 Bettina	57	8 52/144	8 82/144	8 108/144	
218 Bianca	50	8 22/144	8 48/144	8 71/144	
54598 Bienor	85	10 91/144	10 138/144	11 32/144	
585 Bilkis	55	8	8 29/144	8 54/144	
960 Birgit	71	7 119/144	8 12/144	8 44/144	
998 Bodea	91	8 31/144	8 80/144	8 120/144	
371 Bohemia	28	8 38/144	8 52/144	8 65/144	
720 Bohlinia	9	8 61/144	8 64/144	8 68/144	
712 Boliviana	80	7 142/144	8 41/144	8 76/144	
767 Bondia	77	8 39/144	8 80/144	8 115/144	
361 Bononia	91	8 80/144	8 130/144	9 26/144	
66652 Borasisi	38	12 33/144	12 53/144	12 70/144	
741 Botolphia	30	8 37/144	8 52/144	8 66/144	
859 Bouzareah	45	8 65/144	8 88/144	8 109/144	
640 Brambilla	35	8 65/144	8 83/144	8 99/144	
606 Brangane	94	7 134/144	8 42/144	8 83/144	
293 Brasilia	45	8 39/144	8 62/144	8 83/144	
786 Bredichina	68	8 48/144	8 84/144	8 115/144	
761 Brendelia	28	8 48/144	8 62/144	8 76/144	
450 Brigitta	41	8 53/144	8 74/144	8 93/144	
655 Briseis	37	8 53/144	8 71/144	8 89/144	
521 Brixia	122	7 128/144	8 53/144	8 105/144	
455 Bruchsalia	127	7 119/144	8 47/144	8 101/144	
323 Brucia	130	7 94/144	8 24/144	8 79/144	
290 Bruna	110	7 103/144	8 20/144	8 68/144	
123 Brunhild	51	8 23/144	8 50/144	8 74/144	
901 Brunsia	94	7 102/144	8 10/144	8 52/144	
908 Buda	63	7 143/144	8 32/144	8 61/144	
338 Budrosa	10	8 61/144	8 66/144	8 71/144	
384 Burdigala	63	8 13/144	8 47/144	8 75/144	
374 Burgundia	34	8 39/144	8 56/144	8 72/144	
834 Burnhamia	86	8 38/144	8 85/144	8 123/144	
199 Byblis	77	8 42/144	8 84/144	8 118/144	
297 Caecilia	61	8 51/144	8 83/144	8 111/144	
952 Caia	104	8 14/144	8 72/144	8 117/144	
341 California	83	7 107/144	8 8/144	8 45/144	
957 Camelia	35	8 49/144	8 67/144	8 83/144	
107 Camilla	28	8 90/144	8 104/144	8 117/144	
377 Campania	34	8 33/144	8 50/144	8 65/144	
740 Cantabia	47	8 52/144	8 76/144	8 98/144	
479 Caprera	93	8 1/144	8 52/144	8 93/144	
491 Carina	37	8 66/144	8 85/144	8 103/144	
360 Carlova	76	8 32/144	8 72/144	8 106/144	
558 Carmen	19	8 57/144	8 66/144	8 75/144	
671 Carnegia	29	8 64/144	8 79/144	8 92/144	
235 Carolina	27	8 50/144	8 64/144	8 77/144	
505 Cava	105	7 135/144	8 49/144	8 95/144	
186 Celuta	64	7 133/144	8 23/144	8 52/144	
513 Centesima	36	8 55/144	8 73/144	8 90/144	
807 Ceraskia	28	8 59/144	8 74/144	8 87/144	
1 Ceres	32	8 39/144	8 56/144	8 71/144	
65489 Ceto	489	11 11/144	13 86/144	14 67/144	
313 Chaldaea	77	7 126/144	8 24/144	8 58/144	
19521 Chaos	43	12 39/144	12 62/144	12 82/144	
10199 Chariklo	73	10 90/144	10 130/144	11 19/144	
627 Charis	25	8 53/144	8 65/144	8 77/144	
543 Charlotte	66	8 41/144	8 76/144	8 106/144	
388 Charybdis	28	8 59/144	8 73/144	8 86/144	
568 Cheruskia	72	8 26/144	8 64/144	8 96/144	
334 Chicago	10	8 122/144	8 126/144	8 131/144	
623 Chimaera	48	8 6/144	8 31/144	8 53/144	
2060 Chiron	168	9 143/144	10 99/144	11 22/144	
402 Chloe	47	8 15/144	8 39/144	8 61/144	
410 Chloris	104	7 139/144	8 52/144	8 97/144	
938 Chlosinde	83	8 37/144	8 82/144	8 119/144	
628 Christine	19	8 32/144	8 41/144	8 50/144	
202 Chryseis	44	8 54/144	8 77/144	8 98/144	
637 Chrysothemis	53	8 56/144	8 84/144	8 108/144	
34 Circe	45	8 26/144	8 49/144	8 70/144	
642 Clara	52	8 58/144	8 85/144	8 109/144	
302 Clarissa	48	8 2/144	8 26/144	8 48/144	
311 Claudia	2	8 65/144	8 65/144	8 65/144	
252 Clementina	29	8 69/144	8 83/144	8 97/144	
935 Clivia	62	7 121/144	8 10/144	8 38/144	
661 Cloelia	15	8 66/144	8 73/144	8 80/144	
282 Clorinde	35	8 3/144	8 21/144	8 37/144	
237 Coelestina	31	8 40/144	8 55/144	8 69/144	
972 Cohnia	101	8 21/144	8 76/144	8 120/144	
327 Columbia	26	8 43/144	8 56/144	8 69/144	
489 Comacina	20	8 73/144	8 83/144	8 92/144	
58 Concordia	19	8 41/144	8 50/144	8 59/144	
315 Constantia	72	7 117/144	8 12/144	8 44/144	
815 Coppelia	33	8 31/144	8 47/144	8 62/144	
504 Cora	93	8 1/144	8 52/144	8 93/144	
365 Corduba	67	8 23/144	8 58/144	8 88/144	
425 Cornelia	26	8 51/144	8 64/144	8 76/144	
915 Cosette	60	7 123/144	8 10/144	8 38/144	
644 Cosima	66	8 7/144	8 42/144	8 72/144	
83982 Crantor	120	10 105/144	11 29/144	11 80/144	
486 Cremona	69	7 129/144	8 22/144	8 53/144	
660 Crescentia	46	8 13/144	8 37/144	8 59/144	
589 Croatia	17	8 74/144	8 82/144	8 89/144	
763 Cupido	71	7 118/144	8 12/144	8 44/144	
403 Cyane	42	8 37/144	8 59/144	8 78/144	
65 Cybele	47	8 75/144	8 100/144	8 122/144	
52975 Cyllarus	166	10 135/144	11 90/144	12 12/144	
133 Cyrene	58	8 46/144	8 77/144	8 103/144	
61 Danae	71	8 33/144	8 71/144	8 103/144	
41 Daphne	119	7 132/144	8 55/144	8 106/144	
511 Davida	80	8 40/144	8 83/144	8 119/144	
541 Deborah	22	8 48/144	8 59/144	8 69/144	
157 Dejanira	83	7 140/144	8 41/144	8 78/144	
184 Dejopeja	29	8 71/144	8 85/144	8 98/144	
395 Delia	37	8 38/144	8 57/144	8 74/144	
560 Delila	69	8 18/144	8 54/144	8 85/144	
349 Dembowska	39	8 47/144	8 67/144	8 85/144	
667 Denise	81	8 41/144	8 85/144	8 121/144	
666 Desdemona	102	7 130/144	8 42/144	8 86/144	
344 Desiderata	136	7 108/144	8 42/144	8 99/144	
53311 Deucalion	28	12 42/144	12 56/144	12 69/144	
337 Devosa	58	7 138/144	8 24/144	8 51/144	
78 Diana	89	7 140/144	8 44/144	8 83/144	
209 Dido	25	8 70/144	8 82/144	8 94/144	
99 Dike	83	8 3/144	8 48/144	8 85/144	
106 Dione	71	8 46/144	8 84/144	8 116/144	
3671 Dionysus	253	6 134/144	8 8/144	8 98/144	
423 Diotima	17	8 69/144	8 77/144	8 85/144	
382 Dodona	73	8 41/144	8 80/144	8 113/144	
668 Dora	101	8 2/144	8 57/144	8 101/144	
48 Doris	31	8 64/144	8 80/144	8 94/144	

339	Dorothea	42	8 52/144	8 73/144	8 92/144
620	Drakonia	58	7 143/144	8 29/144	8 55/144
263	Dresda	33	8 48/144	8 64/144	8 80/144
400	Ducrosa	50	8 55/144	8 81/144	8 104/144
564	Dudu	119	7 130/144	8 54/144	8 105/144
571	Dulcinea	104	7 113/144	8 27/144	8 72/144
200	Dynamene	57	8 24/144	8 53/144	8 79/144
60558	Echeclus	205	9 66/144	10 48/144	10 126/144
60	Echo	78	7 127/144	8 25/144	8 60/144
413	Edburga	149	7 98/144	8 41/144	8 103/144
673	Edda	6	8 57/144	8 59/144	8 61/144
742	Edisona	51	8 47/144	8 73/144	8 96/144
517	Edith	77	8 42/144	8 83/144	8 117/144
445	Edna	84	8 40/144	8 86/144	8 123/144
340	Eduarda	49	8 29/144	8 54/144	8 77/144
13	Egeria	36	8 23/144	8 41/144	8 57/144
442	Eichsfeldia	31	8 6/144	8 21/144	8 35/144
694	Ekard	140	7 111/144	8 48/144	8 106/144
858	El Djezair	44	8 36/144	8 59/144	8 79/144
31824	Elatus	167	9 114/144	10 69/144	10 136/144
130	Elektra	89	8 33/144	8 81/144	8 120/144
354	Eleonora	49	8 33/144	8 58/144	8 80/144
567	Eleutheria	39	8 62/144	8 81/144	8 99/144
618	Elfriede	31	8 70/144	8 85/144	8 100/144
956	Elisa	87	7 113/144	8 17/144	8 56/144
412	Elisabetha	19	8 46/144	8 55/144	8 64/144
435	Ella	66	7 139/144	8 30/144	8 60/144
616	Elly	25	8 26/144	8 39/144	8 51/144
59	Elpis	51	8 25/144	8 51/144	8 75/144
182	Elsa	79	7 129/144	8 27/144	8 63/144
277	Elvira	39	8 44/144	8 64/144	8 82/144
576	Emanuela	82	8 27/144	8 72/144	8 108/144
481	Emita	67	8 18/144	8 53/144	8 84/144
283	Emma	62	8 43/144	8 76/144	8 104/144
342	Endymion	54	8 12/144	8 40/144	8 65/144
221	Eos	45	8 50/144	8 73/144	8 94/144
802	Epyaxa	34	7 134/144	8 7/144	8 23/144
62	Erato	72	8 42/144	8 81/144	8 114/144
894	Erda	47	8 56/144	8 80/144	8 102/144
718	Erida	85	8 30/144	8 76/144	8 114/144
163	Erigone	81	7 123/144	8 23/144	8 59/144
636	Erika	72	8 28/144	8 66/144	8 99/144
462	Eriphyla	38	8 44/144	8 63/144	8 81/144
136199	Eris	198	12 23/144	13	13 76/144
705	Erminia	21	8 57/144	8 67/144	8 77/144
406	Erna	77	8 25/144	8 66/144	8 101/144
698	Ernestina	47	8 39/144	8 63/144	8 85/144
433	Eros	95	7 14/144	7 66/144	7 108/144
889	Erynia	87	7 127/144	8 30/144	8 68/144
622	Esther	104	7 114/144	8 27/144	8 72/144
331	Etheridgea	43	8 52/144	8 74/144	8 94/144
181	Eucharis	87	8 34/144	8 81/144	8 120/144
217	Eudora	134	7 130/144	8 63/144	8 119/144
45	Eugenia	36	8 34/144	8 52/144	8 69/144
743	Eugenisis	26	8 45/144	8 57/144	8 69/144
247	Eukrate	104	7 140/144	8 47/144	8 99/144
495	Eulalia	55	8 4/144	8 33/144	8 59/144
185	Eunike	55	8 25/144	8 53/144	8 79/144
15	Eunomia	79	8 3/144	8 46/144	8 82/144
630	Euphemia	47	8 20/144	8 44/144	8 66/144
31	Euphrosyne	94	8 31/144	8 83/144	8 124/144
52	Europa	47	8 55/144	8 79/144	8 100/144
527	Euryanthe	64	8 19/144	8 52/144	8 81/144
75	Eurydike	132	7 117/144	8 48/144	8 104/144
195	Eurykleia	19	8 54/144	8 64/144	8 73/144
79	Eurynome	81	7 130/144	8 30/144	8 66/144
27	Euterpe	74	7 126/144	8 21/144	8 54/144
164	Eva	151	7 101/144	8 45/144	8 107/144
503	Evelyn	75	8 12/144	8 52/144	8 86/144
751	Faina	65	8 4/144	8 39/144	8 68/144
408	Fama	61	8 51/144	8 83/144	8 111/144
821	Fanny	91	8 6/144	8 56/144	8 96/144
866	Fatme	23	8 70/144	8 81/144	8 92/144
294	Felicia	100	8 28/144	8 83/144	8 127/144
109	Felicitas	128	7 121/144	8 50/144	8 104/144
72	Feronia	52	7 131/144	8 14/144	8 38/144
524	Fidelio	55	8 17/144	8 45/144	8 70/144
37	Fides	75	8 6/144	8 46/144	8 79/144
380	Fiducia	49	8 24/144	8 49/144	8 71/144
795	Fini	44	8 32/144	8 54/144	8 75/144
8	Flora	67	7 116/144	8 8/144	8 38/144
321	Florentina	20	8 54/144	8 64/144	8 74/144
19	Fortuna	68	7 138/144	8 30/144	8 60/144
982	Franklina	100	8 21/144	8 77/144	8 121/144
862	Franzia	35	8 40/144	8 58/144	8 74/144
520	Franziska	47	8 48/144	8 73/144	8 94/144
309	Fraternitas	49	8 23/144	8 48/144	8 70/144
678	Fredegundis	93	7 133/144	8 41/144	8 82/144
76	Freia	71	8 61/144	8 99/144	8 131/144
722	Frieda	62	7 117/144	8 5/144	8 33/144
538	Friederike	72	8 44/144	8 83/144	8 116/144
77	Frigga	56	8 19/144	8 48/144	8 74/144
709	Fringilla	48	8 42/144	8 66/144	8 88/144
854	Frostia	74	7 127/144	8 23/144	8 56/144
609	Fulvia	18	8 69/144	8 78/144	8 87/144
355	Gabriella	45	8 14/144	8 38/144	8 59/144
74	Galatea	102	8	8 56/144	8 101/144
427	Galene	51	8 43/144	8 70/144	8 94/144
697	Galilea	67	8 28/144	8 64/144	8 94/144
148	Gallia	79	8 13/144	8 56/144	8 91/144
180	Garumna	70	8 15/144	8 52/144	8 84/144
951	Gaspra	74	7 113/144	8 9/144	8 42/144
764	Gedania	42	8 63/144	8 85/144	8 105/144
680	Genoveva	127	8 10/144	8 82/144	8 136/144
485	Genua	82	8 10/144	8 54/144	8 91/144
376	Geometria	73	7 121/144	8 16/144	8 49/144
359	Georgia	67	8 17/144	8 53/144	8 83/144
300	Geraldina	25	8 74/144	8 86/144	8 98/144
122	Gerda	14	8 81/144	8 87/144	8 94/144
663	Gerlinde	62	8 44/144	8 77/144	8 105/144
241	Germania	44	8 53/144	8 76/144	8 96/144
686	Gersuind	115	7 121/144	8 42/144	8 91/144
710	Gertrud	57	8 51/144	8 81/144	8 107/144
613	Ginevra	25	8 54/144	8 67/144	8 79/144
352	Gisela	63	7 118/144	8 7/144	8 36/144
492	Gismonda	76	8 39/144	8 80/144	8 114/144
857	Glasenappia	38	7 132/144	8 7/144	8 24/144
288	Glauke	87	8 7/144	8 55/144	8 94/144
316	Goberta	58	8 54/144	8 84/144	8 111/144
305	Gordonia	83	8 34/144	8 79/144	8 115/144
681	Gorgo	44	8 57/144	8 79/144	8 100/144
424	Gratia	46	8 32/144	8 56/144	8 77/144
984	Gretia	84	8 12/144	8 58/144	8 96/144
493	Griseldis	75	8 40/144	8 80/144	8 114/144
496	Gryphia	34	7 135/144	8 8/144	8 23/144
328	Gudrun	45	8 57/144	8 80/144	8 101/144
799	Gudula	10	8 33/144	8 38/144	8 42/144
891	Gunhild	13	8 56/144	8 62/144	8 69/144
983	Gunila	40	8 63/144	8 83/144	8 101/144
657	Gunlod	48	8 19/144	8 43/144	8 66/144
961	Gunnie	39	8 30/144	8 50/144	8 68/144
777	Gutemberga	46	8 63/144	8 87/144	8 109/144
806	Gyldenia	32	8 70/144	8 86/144	8 101/144
444	Gyptis	75	8 16/144	8 56/144	8 89/144
682	Hagar	73	8 8/144	8 47/144	8 80/144
368	Haidea	85	8 31/144	8 77/144	8 115/144
518	Halawe	98	7 127/144	8 37/144	8 80/144
449	Hamburga	74	7 143/144	8 39/144	8 72/144
452	Hamiltonia	7	8 58/144	8 61/144	8 64/144
723	Hammonia	23	8 61/144	8 72/144	8 83/144
480	Hansa	20	8 36/144	8 46/144	8 55/144
724	Hapag	107	7 115/144	8 31/144	8 77/144
578	Happelia	82	8 10/144	8 54/144	8 91/144
40	Harmonia	20	8 4/144	8 14/144	8 24/144
736	Harvard	70	7 114/144	8 8/144	8 40/144
136108	Haumea	81	12 8/144	12 51/144	12 87/144
362	Havnia	19	8 32/144	8 41/144	8 50/144
6	Hebe	86	7 125/144	8 28/144	8 66/144

#	Name				
108	Hecuba	24	8 76/144	8 88/144	8 99/144
207	Hedda	13	8 10/144	8 16/144	8 22/144
476	Hedwig	31	8 31/144	8 46/144	8 61/144
325	Heidelberga	68	8 50/144	8 86/144	8 117/144
100	Hekate	72	8 40/144	8 78/144	8 111/144
624	Hektor	11	9 40/144	9 45/144	9 50/144
949	Hel	82	8 28/144	8 73/144	8 109/144
699	Hela	182	7 78/144	8 43/144	8 115/144
101	Helena	60	8 10/144	8 41/144	8 68/144
522	Helga	37	8 93/144	8 112/144	8 129/144
895	Helio	62	8 53/144	8 86/144	8 114/144
967	Helionape	72	7 116/144	8 10/144	8 43/144
801	Helwerthia	34	8 26/144	8 43/144	8 59/144
225	Henrietta	113	8 34/144	8 98/144	9 2/144
826	Henrika	88	8 4/144	8 51/144	8 90/144
2212	Hephaistos	505	5 58/144	8 4/144	8 130/144
103	Hera	35	8 33/144	8 51/144	8 67/144
5143	Heracles	427	5 95/144	7 114/144	8 89/144
880	Herba	140	7 135/144	8 72/144	8 130/144
532	Herculina	75	8 16/144	8 56/144	8 90/144
458	Hercynia	103	8 15/144	8 72/144	8 117/144
923	Herluga	84	7 142/144	8 44/144	8 81/144
346	Hermentaria	43	8 35/144	8 58/144	8 78/144
685	Hermia	84	7 110/144	8 11/144	8 48/144
121	Hermione	57	8 71/144	8 101/144	8 127/144
546	Herodias	49	8 17/144	8 42/144	8 65/144
206	Hersilia	16	8 46/144	8 54/144	8 61/144
135	Hertha	89	7 124/144	8 28/144	8 68/144
69	Hesperia	73	8 32/144	8 71/144	8 103/144
46	Hestia	73	7 141/144	8 37/144	8 69/144
944	Hidalgo	331	7 126/144	9 63/144	10 25/144
996	Hilaritas	60	8 47/144	8 78/144	8 106/144
153	Hilda	60	8 100/144	8 131/144	9 14/144
684	Hildburg	16	8 21/144	8 29/144	8 36/144
898	Hildegard	163	7 100/144	8 53/144	8 118/144
928	Hildrun	63	8 48/144	8 81/144	8 110/144
426	Hippo	44	8 42/144	8 64/144	8 85/144
692	Hippodamia	72	8 59/144	8 97/144	8 130/144
706	Hirundo	83	8 8/144	8 53/144	8 89/144
804	Hispania	59	8 29/144	8 61/144	8 88/144
788	Hohensteina	57	8 51/144	8 81/144	8 107/144
872	Holda	34	8 36/144	8 53/144	8 69/144
378	Holmia	55	8 27/144	8 56/144	8 82/144
236	Honoria	81	8 14/144	8 58/144	8 94/144
932	Hooveria	39	8 8/144	8 28/144	8 46/144
805	Hormuthia	80	8 42/144	8 85/144	8 121/144
260	Huberta	49	8 76/144	8 101/144	8 124/144
379	Huenna	78	8 40/144	8 82/144	8 117/144
434	Hungaria	32	7 110/144	7 126/144	7 141/144
38628	Huya	122	11 108/144	12 33/144	12 85/144
430	Hybris	109	8	8 61/144	8 108/144
10	Hygiea	48	8 57/144	8 82/144	8 104/144
10370	Hylonome	106	11 23/144	11 82/144	11 128/144
238	Hypatia	38	8 46/144	8 66/144	8 83/144
587	Hypsipyle	71	7 126/144	8 20/144	8 52/144
98	Ianthe	79	8 7/144	8 49/144	8 85/144
1566	Icarus	490	4 71/144	7 4/144	7 129/144
286	Iclea	13	8 79/144	8 85/144	8 91/144
243	Ida	18	8 54/144	8 63/144	8 71/144
963	Iduberga	58	7 126/144	8 12/144	8 39/144
176	Iduna	72	8 46/144	8 85/144	8 117/144
385	Ilmatar	52	8 35/144	8 62/144	8 86/144
249	Ilse	93	7 117/144	8 24/144	8 65/144
919	Ilsebill	36	8 38/144	8 56/144	8 73/144
979	Ilsewa	58	8 52/144	8 83/144	8 110/144
926	Imhilde	77	8 29/144	8 71/144	8 106/144
389	Industria	29	8 29/144	8 43/144	8 57/144
391	Ingeborg	132	7 87/144	8 19/144	8 74/144
561	Ingwelde	49	8 58/144	8 84/144	8 107/144
848	Inna	70	8 43/144	8 80/144	8 112/144
173	Ino	89	8 5/144	8 54/144	8 93/144
704	Interamnia	66	8 41/144	8 76/144	8 106/144
85	Io	83	8 2/144	8 47/144	8 84/144
509	Iolanda	41	8 56/144	8 77/144	8 96/144
112	Iphigenia	54	8 1/144	8 29/144	8 54/144
794	Irenaea	128	8 8/144	8 81/144	8 135/144
14	Irene	71	8 4/144	8 41/144	8 74/144
7	Iris	99	7 114/144	8 25/144	8 68/144
177	Irma	101	7 143/144	8 56/144	8 100/144
591	Irmgard	88	8 1/144	8 49/144	8 88/144
773	Irmintraud	34	8 45/144	8 62/144	8 78/144
210	Isabella	53	8 25/144	8 52/144	8 76/144
364	Isara	64	7 120/144	8 10/144	8 39/144
939	Isberga	75	7 116/144	8 12/144	8 46/144
42	Isis	95	7 121/144	8 30/144	8 71/144
190	Ismene	71	8 94/144	8 131/144	9 19/144
211	Isolda	69	8 39/144	8 75/144	8 106/144
183	Istria	153	7 112/144	8 57/144	8 120/144
477	Italia	80	7 128/144	8 27/144	8 63/144
918	Itha	81	8 19/144	8 63/144	8 99/144
497	Iva	130	7 132/144	8 62/144	8 116/144
28978	Ixion	104	11 119/144	12 33/144	12 78/144
383	Janina	70	8 45/144	8 82/144	8 114/144
526	Jena	57	8 51/144	8 81/144	8 107/144
607	Jenny	32	8 46/144	8 62/144	8 77/144
549	Jessonda	111	7 131/144	8 49/144	8 97/144
544	Jetta	65	8 8/144	8 42/144	8 71/144
726	Joella	123	7 114/144	8 40/144	8 92/144
127	Johanna	29	8 40/144	8 55/144	8 68/144
899	Jokaste	85	8 19/144	8 66/144	8 104/144
836	Jole	75	7 110/144	8 7/144	8 41/144
649	Josefa	120	7 114/144	8 38/144	8 89/144
303	Josephina	27	8 67/144	8 81/144	8 93/144
921	Jovita	78	8 42/144	8 84/144	8 119/144
652	Jubilatrix	54	8 11/144	8 39/144	8 64/144
948	Jucunda	70	8 37/144	8 74/144	8 106/144
664	Judith	98	8 31/144	8 85/144	8 129/144
139	Juewa	75	8 17/144	8 57/144	8 90/144
89	Julia	79	7 140/144	8 39/144	8 74/144
816	Juliana	47	8 48/144	8 72/144	8 94/144
3	Juno	110	7 130/144	8 48/144	8 95/144
	Jupiter	21	9 32/144	9 43/144	9 53/144
269	Justitia	91	7 138/144	8 44/144	8 84/144
605	Juvisia	59	8 41/144	8 72/144	8 99/144
22	Kalliope	42	8 44/144	8 66/144	8 86/144
204	Kallisto	74	8 8/144	8 48/144	8 82/144
53	Kalypso	88	7 140/144	8 44/144	8 83/144
818	Kapteynia	40	8 63/144	8 84/144	8 102/144
832	Karin	35	8 45/144	8 63/144	8 79/144
781	Kartvelia	50	8 61/144	8 87/144	8 110/144
114	Kassandra	58	8 19/144	8 49/144	8 75/144
646	Kastalia	91	7 114/144	8 19/144	8 59/144
320	Katharina	50	8 47/144	8 73/144	8 96/144
842	Kerstin	51	8 61/144	8 88/144	8 112/144
470	Kilia	40	8 6/144	8 26/144	8 45/144
216	Kleopatra	107	7 141/144	8 57/144	8 104/144
84	Klio	101	7 111/144	8 23/144	8 67/144
97	Klotho	110	7 130/144	8 48/144	8 95/144
583	Klotilde	69	8 47/144	8 84/144	8 115/144
104	Klymene	68	8 46/144	8 82/144	8 113/144
179	Klytaemnestra	48	8 45/144	8 70/144	8 93/144
73	Klytia	19	8 38/144	8 48/144	8 56/144
191	Kolga	39	8 45/144	8 65/144	8 83/144
940	Kordula	73	8 58/144	8 97/144	8 129/144
158	Koronis	23	8 52/144	8 63/144	8 74/144
867	Kovacia	55	8 48/144	8 77/144	8 102/144
548	Kressida	79	7 117/144	8 15/144	8 51/144
800	Kressmannia	86	7 104/144	8 7/144	8 45/144
488	Kreusa	68	8 48/144	8 84/144	8 114/144
242	Kriemhild	51	8 36/144	8 63/144	8 86/144
553	Kundry	47	7 130/144	8 11/144	8 32/144
936	Kunigunde	76	8 40/144	8 81/144	8 115/144
669	Kypria	33	8 57/144	8 73/144	8 88/144
570	Kythera	50	8 74/144	8 100/144	8 124/144
336	Lacadiera	41	7 136/144	8 13/144	8 32/144
120	Lachesis	23	8 69/144	8 80/144	8 91/144
208	Lacrimosa	6	8 62/144	8 65/144	8 67/144
39	Laetitia	48	8 31/144	8 56/144	8 78/144
822	Lalage	66	7 122/144	8 13/144	8 43/144
187	Lamberta	103	7 139/144	8 52/144	8 97/144

248	Lameia	28	8 18/144	8 32/144	8 45/144	20	Massalia	61	7 139/144	8 27/144	8 54/144
393	Lampetia	144	7 117/144	8 56/144	8 116/144	760	Massinga	99	8 27/144	8 82/144	8 126/144
683	Lanzia	24	8 68/144	8 80/144	8 92/144	454	Mathesis	47	8 21/144	8 45/144	8 66/144
507	Laodica	43	8 61/144	8 83/144	8 102/144	253	Mathilde	113	7 127/144	8 47/144	8 95/144
639	Latona	45	8 50/144	8 73/144	8 94/144	883	Matterania	84	7 110/144	8 11/144	8 49/144
467	Laura	46	8 45/144	8 68/144	8 90/144	765	Mattiaca	122	7 113/144	8 38/144	8 90/144
162	Laurentia	76	8 33/144	8 74/144	8 108/144	745	Mauritia	18	8 81/144	8 90/144	8 98/144
38	Leda	66	8 18/144	8 53/144	8 83/144	348	May	29	8 56/144	8 70/144	8 84/144
691	Lehigh	52	8 46/144	8 73/144	8 97/144	991	McDonalda	67	8 46/144	8 82/144	8 112/144
47171	Lempo	94	11 122/144	12 30/144	12 72/144	873	Mechthild	63	8 11/144	8 45/144	8 74/144
789	Lena	63	8 16/144	8 49/144	8 78/144	212	Medea	45	8 57/144	8 80/144	8 101/144
969	Leocadia	88	7 127/144	8 31/144	8 70/144	149	Medusa	28	7 135/144	8 5/144	8 19/144
319	Leona	93	8 48/144	8 99/144	8 139/144	464	Megaira	88	8 10/144	8 58/144	8 97/144
728	Leonisis	38	7 138/144	8 13/144	8 30/144	688	Melanie	59	8 19/144	8 50/144	8 77/144
696	Leonora	107	8 24/144	8 84/144	8 130/144	56	Melete	102	7 130/144	8 42/144	8 87/144
844	Leontina	30	8 71/144	8 86/144	8 100/144	137	Meliboea	91	8 31/144	8 81/144	8 121/144
893	Leopoldina	64	8 42/144	8 76/144	8 105/144	676	Melitta	52	8 50/144	8 77/144	8 100/144
1264	Letaba	66	8 28/144	8 63/144	8 93/144	869	Mellena	94	7 142/144	8 50/144	8 91/144
68	Leto	80	8 13/144	8 56/144	8 92/144	18	Melpomene	93	7 109/144	8 17/144	8 58/144
35	Leukothea	97	8 19/144	8 72/144	8 114/144	373	Melusina	60	8 49/144	8 80/144	8 108/144
954	Li	73	8 42/144	8 81/144	8 114/144	1247	Memoria	74	8 41/144	8 81/144	8 115/144
771	Libera	106	7 131/144	8 47/144	8 93/144	188	Menippe	76	8 14/144	8 55/144	8 89/144
125	Liberatrix	33	8 37/144	8 54/144	8 69/144	536	Merapi	37	8 86/144	8 104/144	8 121/144
264	Libussa	58	8 27/144	8 58/144	8 84/144		Mercury	88	5 31/144	5 79/144	5 118/144
356	Liguria	102	7 143/144	8 55/144	8 99/144	808	Merxia	54	8 26/144	8 54/144	8 79/144
213	Lilaea	62	8 22/144	8 55/144	8 83/144	545	Messalina	72	8 47/144	8 86/144	8 118/144
1181	Lilith	84	8 2/144	8 48/144	8 85/144	792	Metcalfia	55	8 15/144	8 44/144	8 70/144
756	Lilliana	64	8 52/144	8 86/144	8 114/144	9	Metis	52	7 142/144	8 25/144	8 49/144
468	Lina	84	8 35/144	8 81/144	8 119/144	878	Mildred	97	7 113/144	8 22/144	8 65/144
828	Lindemannia	13	8 79/144	8 85/144	8 91/144	93	Minerva	59	8 24/144	8 55/144	8 82/144
974	Lioba	48	8 13/144	8 37/144	8 59/144	594	Mireille	154	7 98/144	8 45/144	8 108/144
846	Lipperta	78	8 39/144	8 81/144	8 116/144	102	Miriam	108	7 131/144	8 47/144	8 94/144
414	Liriope	31	8 89/144	8 105/144	8 119/144	569	Misa	77	8 5/144	8 47/144	8 82/144
58534	Logos	51	12 34/144	12 61/144	12 85/144	4523	MIT	60	8 18/144	8 49/144	8 76/144
463	Lola	94	7 118/144	8 26/144	8 67/144	57	Mnemosyne	49	8 57/144	8 83/144	8 105/144
117	Lomia	13	8 66/144	8 72/144	8 77/144	733	Mocia	26	8 85/144	8 98/144	8 110/144
165	Loreley	36	8 62/144	8 81/144	8 98/144	370	Modestia	39	7 143/144	8 19/144	8 37/144
429	Lotis	52	8 16/144	8 43/144	8 67/144	766	Moguntia	41	8 52/144	8 74/144	8 93/144
868	Lova	64	8 17/144	8 51/144	8 80/144	638	Moira	68	8 17/144	8 53/144	8 84/144
222	Lucia	56	8 53/144	8 82/144	8 107/144	428	Monachia	76	7 121/144	8 18/144	8 52/144
146	Lucina	29	8 37/144	8 52/144	8 65/144	833	Monica	52	8 46/144	8 73/144	8 97/144
281	Lucretia	56	7 121/144	8 7/144	8 33/144	535	Montague	11	8 35/144	8 40/144	8 45/144
675	Ludmilla	86	8 9/144	8 56/144	8 94/144	797	Montana	27	8 24/144	8 37/144	8 50/144
292	Ludovica	15	8 30/144	8 37/144	8 44/144	782	Montefiore	17	7 142/144	8 6/144	8 14/144
599	Luisa	126	7 128/144	8 56/144	8 109/144	947	Monterosa	107	7 139/144	8 55/144	8 101/144
141	Lumen	92	7 141/144	8 48/144	8 88/144	787	Moskva	55	8 9/144	8 38/144	8 63/144
775	Lumiere	31	8 58/144	8 73/144	8 87/144	993	Moultona	21	8 52/144	8 62/144	8 72/144
809	Lundia	82	7 115/144	8 16/144	8 52/144	941	Murray	84	8 11/144	8 57/144	8 94/144
713	Luscinia	69	8 62/144	8 98/144	8 129/144	600	Musa	24	8 35/144	8 47/144	8 59/144
21	Lutetia	70	7 136/144	8 29/144	8 61/144	966	Muschi	56	8 22/144	8 52/144	8 78/144
110	Lydia	35	8 35/144	8 53/144	8 69/144	381	Myrrha	38	8 68/144	8 87/144	8 105/144
917	Lyka	85	7 122/144	8 24/144	8 62/144	845	Naema	30	8 53/144	8 68/144	8 82/144
897	Lysistrata	40	8 17/144	8 38/144	8 57/144	559	Nanon	28	8 37/144	8 51/144	8 65/144
510	Mabella	81	8	8 43/144	8 80/144	853	Nansenia	45	7 139/144	8 18/144	8 39/144
318	Magdalena	36	8 67/144	8 85/144	8 102/144	534	Nassovia	25	8 52/144	8 64/144	8 76/144
66	Maja	73	8 7/144	8 46/144	8 79/144	448	Natalie	80	8 38/144	8 81/144	8 117/144
136472	Makemake	66	12 27/144	12 62/144	12 92/144	811	Nauheima	31	8 50/144	8 65/144	8 80/144
754	Malabar	21	8 61/144	8 71/144	8 81/144	192	Nausikaa	105	7 112/144	8 26/144	8 72/144
749	Malzovia	74	7 116/144	8 12/144	8 45/144	903	Nealley	20	8 79/144	8 88/144	8 97/144
758	Mancunia	64	8 51/144	8 85/144	8 114/144	51	Nemausa	29	8 9/144	8 23/144	8 36/144
739	Mandeville	61	8 21/144	8 53/144	8 81/144	128	Nemesis	54	8 26/144	8 54/144	8 79/144
870	Manto	114	7 99/144	8 19/144	8 68/144	289	Nenetta	86	8 17/144	8 64/144	8 102/144
565	Marbachia	55	8 1/144	8 30/144	8 55/144	431	Nephele	72	8 43/144	8 82/144	8 114/144
310	Margarita	48	8 30/144	8 55/144	8 77/144	287	Nephthys	11	8 17/144	8 22/144	8 27/144
735	Marghanna	140	7 116/144	8 52/144	8 111/144		Neptune	5	11 117/144	11 119/144	11 121/144
170	Maria	28	8 25/144	8 39/144	8 52/144	601	Nerthus	44	8 59/144	8 81/144	8 102/144
602	Marianna	107	8 18/144	8 78/144	8 124/144	7066	Nessus	241	10 69/144	11 77/144	12 20/144
506	Marion	63	8 42/144	8 75/144	8 104/144	659	Nestor	50	9 15/144	9 41/144	9 65/144
912	Maritima	75	8 41/144	8 81/144	8 115/144	855	Newcombia	76	7 126/144	8 23/144	8 57/144
746	Marlu	102	8 23/144	8 80/144	8 124/144	662	Newtonia	93	7 132/144	8 39/144	8 79/144
711	Marmulla	83	7 110/144	8 11/144	8 48/144	843	Nicolaia	90	7 110/144	8 15/144	8 55/144
	Mars	40	7 55/144	7 76/144	7 94/144	307	Nike	61	8 34/144	8 66/144	8 94/144
205	Martha	16	8 49/144	8 56/144	8 64/144	779	Nina	97	7 138/144	8 48/144	8 90/144
981	Martina	87	8 31/144	8 79/144	8 117/144	357	Ninina	33	8 66/144	8 83/144	8 98/144

71	Niobe	74	8 15/144	8 55/144	8 88/144	189	Phthia	16	8 22/144	8 30/144	8 38/144
727	Nipponia	45	8 17/144	8 40/144	8 61/144	556	Phyllis	44	8 9/144	8 31/144	8 52/144
703	Noemi	59	7 119/144	8 5/144	8 32/144	614	Pia	47	8 25/144	8 50/144	8 72/144
473	Nolli	45	8 24/144	8 48/144	8 68/144	1000	Piazzia	111	8 22/144	8 84/144	8 131/144
783	Nora	98	7 110/144	8 21/144	8 64/144	803	Picka	28	8 71/144	8 85/144	8 99/144
555	Norma	64	8 51/144	8 85/144	8 114/144	784	Pickeringia	104	8 21/144	8 79/144	8 124/144
626	Notburga	104	7 127/144	8 40/144	8 86/144	312	Pierretta	68	8 21/144	8 57/144	8 87/144
150	Nuwa	53	8 44/144	8 71/144	8 96/144	648	Pippa	83	8 41/144	8 86/144	8 123/144
875	Nymphe	65	8 5/144	8 39/144	8 68/144	484	Pittsburghia	25	8 36/144	8 48/144	8 60/144
44	Nysa	63	7 139/144	8 28/144	8 57/144		Pluto-Charon	109	11 116/144	12 33/144	12 80/144
224	Oceana	19	8 37/144	8 46/144	8 55/144	946	Poesia	61	8 48/144	8 80/144	8 108/144
475	Ocllo	167	7 87/144	8 42/144	8 109/144	142	Polana	57	7 141/144	8 28/144	8 54/144
598	Octavia	107	7 139/144	8 55/144	8 101/144	33	Polyhymnia	145	7 123/144	8 63/144	8 123/144
215	Oenone	16	8 48/144	8 55/144	8 63/144	595	Polyxena	27	8 73/144	8 86/144	8 99/144
439	Ohio	27	8 68/144	8 82/144	8 94/144	308	Polyxo	18	8 46/144	8 54/144	8 62/144
52872	Okyrhoe	132	9 65/144	9 141/144	10 53/144	32	Pomona	34	8 24/144	8 42/144	8 58/144
304	Olga	95	7 118/144	8 26/144	8 68/144	203	Pompeja	25	8 41/144	8 53/144	8 65/144
835	Olivia	38	8 68/144	8 87/144	8 105/144	757	Portlandia	47	7 143/144	8 24/144	8 45/144
582	Olympia	95	7 135/144	8 43/144	8 85/144	547	Praxedis	101	8 1/144	8 56/144	8 100/144
171	Ophelia	56	8 52/144	8 81/144	8 107/144	790	Pretoria	64	8 65/144	8 99/144	8 128/144
255	Oppavia	33	8 37/144	8 54/144	8 69/144	529	Preziosa	41	8 52/144	8 73/144	8 93/144
90482	Orcus	94	11 124/144	12 31/144	12 73/144	884	Priamus	52	9 15/144	9 42/144	9 66/144
701	Oriola	15	8 66/144	8 73/144	8 80/144	970	Primula	116	7 118/144	8 40/144	8 89/144
350	Ornamenta	68	8 44/144	8 80/144	8 110/144	508	Princetonia	4	8 81/144	8 83/144	8 85/144
3361	Orpheus	140	6 91/144	7 28/144	7 86/144	997	Priska	78	8 6/144	8 48/144	8 83/144
551	Ortrud	52	8 43/144	8 70/144	8 94/144	902	Probitas	77	7 133/144	8 30/144	8 64/144
750	Oskar	55	8 1/144	8 30/144	8 55/144	194	Prokne	102	7 131/144	8 44/144	8 88/144
343	Ostara	98	7 117/144	8 27/144	8 70/144	26	Proserpina	39	8 27/144	8 47/144	8 65/144
913	Otila	72	7 113/144	8 8/144	8 40/144	147	Protogeneia	13	8 76/144	8 81/144	8 87/144
670	Ottegebe	83	8 13/144	8 58/144	8 95/144	474	Prudentia	90	7 126/144	8 30/144	8 70/144
994	Otthild	49	8 11/144	8 37/144	8 60/144	261	Prymno	38	8	8 20/144	8 38/144
401	Ottilia	15	8 88/144	8 95/144	8 102/144	16	Psyche	57	8 37/144	8 67/144	8 93/144
363	Padua	30	8 39/144	8 54/144	8 68/144	762	Pulcova	44	8 60/144	8 83/144	8 104/144
953	Painleva	81	8 13/144	8 57/144	8 93/144	632	Pyrrha	81	8 4/144	8 48/144	8 84/144
415	Palatia	130	7 127/144	8 57/144	8 112/144	432	Pythia	62	7 135/144	8 23/144	8 52/144
49	Pales	97	8 26/144	8 79/144	8 121/144	50000	Quaoar	16	12 44/144	12 52/144	12 60/144
914	Palisana	92	7 125/144	8 31/144	8 71/144	755	Quintilla	59	8 54/144	8 84/144	8 111/144
2	Pallas	99	8 1/144	8 56/144	8 99/144	674	Rachele	83	8 22/144	8 67/144	8 104/144
372	Palma	111	8 20/144	8 82/144	8 130/144	708	Raphaela	37	8 29/144	8 48/144	8 65/144
539	Pamina	91	8 4/144	8 53/144	8 93/144	927	Ratisbona	37	8 69/144	8 87/144	8 104/144
55	Pandora	61	8 23/144	8 55/144	8 83/144	572	Rebekka	67	7 134/144	8 26/144	8 56/144
70	Panopaea	77	8 2/144	8 44/144	8 78/144	573	Recha	49	8 48/144	8 73/144	8 96/144
471	Papagena	99	8 10/144	8 65/144	8 108/144	285	Regina	88	8 30/144	8 78/144	8 117/144
347	Pariana	71	8 5/144	8 43/144	8 75/144	574	Reginhild	103	7 100/144	8 13/144	8 57/144
11	Parthenope	43	8 8/144	8 30/144	8 50/144	575	Renate	54	8 10/144	8 39/144	8 64/144
888	Parysatis	82	8 7/144	8 51/144	8 88/144	906	Repsolda	37	8 46/144	8 65/144	8 82/144
451	Patientia	32	8 60/144	8 77/144	8 92/144	528	Rezia	9	8 94/144	8 98/144	8 102/144
436	Patricia	29	8 71/144	8 86/144	8 99/144	38083	Rhadamanthus	64	11 140/144	12 30/144	12 60/144
617	Patroclus	59	9 12/144	9 43/144	9 70/144	577	Rhea	66	8 45/144	8 80/144	8 110/144
278	Paulina	56	8 25/144	8 55/144	8 80/144	907	Rhoda	68	8 22/144	8 58/144	8 89/144
537	Pauly	98	8 24/144	8 77/144	8 120/144	437	Rhodia	107	7 109/144	8 25/144	8 71/144
679	Pax	135	7 108/144	8 41/144	8 98/144	166	Rhodope	90	8	8 49/144	8 89/144
118	Peitho	70	7 136/144	8 29/144	8 61/144	879	Ricarda	66	8 2/144	8 37/144	8 67/144
49036	Pelion	58	11 3/144	11 33/144	11 60/144	335	Roberta	73	7 137/144	8 32/144	8 65/144
201	Penelope	77	8 7/144	8 49/144	8 83/144	904	Rockefellia	38	8 53/144	8 72/144	8 89/144
271	Penthesilea	44	8 50/144	8 73/144	8 93/144	920	Rogeria	45	8 21/144	8 44/144	8 65/144
554	Peraga	65	7 133/144	8 24/144	8 53/144	472	Roma	40	8 18/144	8 38/144	8 57/144
399	Persephone	32	8 60/144	8 76/144	8 91/144	942	Romilda	73	8 44/144	8 83/144	8 116/144
975	Perseverantia	14	8 54/144	8 61/144	8 67/144	223	Rosa	49	8 53/144	8 79/144	8 101/144
482	Petrina	42	8 51/144	8 72/144	8 91/144	314	Rosalia	74	8 43/144	8 83/144	8 116/144
830	Petropolitana	27	8 74/144	8 87/144	8 99/144	900	Rosalinde	69	7 139/144	8 32/144	8 64/144
968	Petunia	58	8 32/144	8 63/144	8 89/144	540	Rosamunde	38	7 134/144	8 10/144	8 27/144
174	Phaedra	60	8 31/144	8 62/144	8 90/144	985	Rosina	120	7 93/144	8 17/144	8 68/144
322	Phaeo	105	7 142/144	8 57/144	8 102/144	615	Roswitha	47	8 21/144	8 45/144	8 67/144
3200	Phaethon	592	4 11/144	7 38/144	8 26/144	874	Rotraut	34	8 65/144	8 83/144	8 99/144
296	Phaetusa	68	7 118/144	8 11/144	8 42/144	317	Roxane	37	7 141/144	8 16/144	8 33/144
274	Philagoria	51	8 49/144	8 75/144	8 99/144	353	Ruperto-Carola	142	7 115/144	8 53/144	8 112/144
280	Philia	46	8 44/144	8 68/144	8 90/144	232	Russia	74	7 143/144	8 39/144	8 72/144
977	Philippa	12	8 75/144	8 80/144	8 86/144	798	Ruth	16	8 66/144	8 73/144	8 81/144
631	Philippina	35	8 40/144	8 57/144	8 74/144	665	Sabine	73	8 43/144	8 82/144	8 115/144
196	Philomela	8	8 77/144	8 80/144	8 83/144	120347	Salacia	47	12 20/144	12 44/144	12 66/144
227	Philosophia	81	8 39/144	8 83/144	8 120/144	562	Salome	43	8 52/144	8 74/144	8 94/144
25	Phocaea	109	7 109/144	8 26/144	8 73/144	275	Sapientia	70	8 19/144	8 56/144	8 87/144
5145	Pholus	271	10 7/144	11 38/144	11 132/144	80	Sappho	85	7 114/144	8 17/144	8 55/144
443	Photographica	18	8 1/144	8 9/144	8 17/144	533	Sara	20	8 61/144	8 71/144	8 80/144

796	Sarita	139	7 109/144	8 45/144	8 103/144
461	Saskia	60	8 49/144	8 81/144	8 108/144
	Saturn	24	10 13/144	10 25/144	10 36/144
1525	Savonlinna	113	7 131/144	8 50/144	8 99/144
460	Scania	45	8 28/144	8 52/144	8 73/144
643	Scheherezade	25	8 84/144	8 96/144	8 108/144
596	Scheila	70	8 30/144	8 67/144	8 99/144
922	Schlutia	83	8 5/144	8 50/144	8 86/144
837	Schwarzschilda	18	8 8/144	8 17/144	8 25/144
989	Schwassmannia	108	7 131/144	8 47/144	8 94/144
876	Scott	48	8 48/144	8 73/144	8 95/144
155	Scylla	119	7 131/144	8 55/144	8 106/144
90377	Sedna	514	13 24/144	15 122/144	16 105/144
892	Seeligeria	44	8 65/144	8 87/144	8 108/144
580	Selene	36	8 70/144	8 88/144	8 105/144
500	Selinur	62	8 11/144	8 44/144	8 72/144
86	Semele	91	8 29/144	8 80/144	8 120/144
584	Semiramis	100	7 112/144	8 24/144	8 67/144
550	Senta	95	7 133/144	8 42/144	8 83/144
483	Seppina	22	8 89/144	8 100/144	8 110/144
838	Seraphina	57	8 35/144	8 65/144	8 91/144
168	Sibylla	31	8 81/144	8 97/144	8 111/144
579	Sidonia	34	8 56/144	8 73/144	8 89/144
386	Siegena	72	8 26/144	8 65/144	8 98/144
552	Sigelinde	38	8 63/144	8 82/144	8 100/144
459	Signe	89	7 139/144	8 44/144	8 84/144
502	Sigune	76	7 127/144	8 24/144	8 59/144
79360	Sila-Nunam	7	12 51/144	12 54/144	12 57/144
257	Silesia	47	8 56/144	8 80/144	8 102/144
748	Simeisa	80	8 86/144	8 129/144	9 21/144
332	Siri	38	8 37/144	8 56/144	8 74/144
116	Sirona	61	8 23/144	8 55/144	8 83/144
823	Sisigambis	38	7 134/144	8 10/144	8 28/144
1866	Sisyphus	251	6 104/144	7 121/144	8 66/144
244	Sita	58	7 119/144	8 5/144	8 32/144
1170	Siva	130	7 89/144	8 19/144	8 74/144
140	Siwa	92	8 3/144	8 53/144	8 93/144
251	Sophia	42	8 57/144	8 79/144	8 98/144
134	Sophrosyne	50	8 14/144	8 40/144	8 63/144
731	Sorga	60	8 40/144	8 71/144	8 99/144
896	Sphinx	70	7 123/144	8 16/144	8 47/144
831	Stateira	62	7 120/144	8 9/144	8 37/144
707	Steina	46	7 126/144	8 6/144	8 27/144
220	Stephania	110	7 104/144	8 21/144	8 69/144
566	Stereoskopia	51	8 71/144	8 97/144	8 120/144
995	Sternberga	72	8 5/144	8 44/144	8 76/144
768	Struveana	90	8 32/144	8 82/144	8 122/144
964	Subamara	51	8 49/144	8 76/144	8 99/144
417	Suevia	58	8 28/144	8 58/144	8 84/144
752	Sulamitis	32	8 15/144	8 31/144	8 46/144
563	Suleika	101	7 140/144	8 51/144	8 95/144
542	Susanna	60	8 34/144	8 66/144	8 93/144
	Sun (Earth dist)	8	6 128/144	6 132/144	6 135/144
933	Susi	70	7 130/144	8 23/144	8 55/144
329	Svea	11	8 27/144	8 32/144	8 38/144
992	Swasey	36	8 56/144	8 74/144	8 91/144
882	Swetlana	114	8 16/144	8 81/144	8 130/144
519	Sylvania	79	8 15/144	8 57/144	8 93/144
87	Sylvia	40	8 83/144	8 103/144	8 122/144
721	Tabora	49	8 82/144	8 107/144	8 130/144
326	Tamara	81	7 119/144	8 19/144	8 55/144
772	Tanete	39	8 52/144	8 72/144	8 91/144
825	Tanina	32	7 138/144	8 18/144	8 25/144
2102	Tantalus	129	6 111/144	7 41/144	7 95/144
769	Tatjana	79	8 41/144	8 84/144	8 119/144
581	Tauntonia	15	8 80/144	8 87/144	8 93/144
512	Taurinensis	109	7 90/144	8 7/144	8 54/144
814	Tauris	133	8 6/144	8 83/144	8 138/144
453	Tea	46	7 126/144	8 6/144	8 28/144
88611	Teharonhiawako	14	12 48/144	12 54/144	12 60/144
604	Tekmessa	85	8 36/144	8 82/144	8 120/144
345	Tercidina	26	8 6/144	8 19/144	8 32/144
478	Tergeste	36	8 55/144	8 74/144	8 90/144
81	Terpsichore	90	8 13/144	8 62/144	8 102/144
23	Thalia	101	7 133/144	8 45/144	8 88/144
586	Thekla	26	8 62/144	8 75/144	8 87/144
24	Themis	53	8 54/144	8 82/144	8 106/144
778	Theobalda	108	8 25/144	8 85/144	8 132/144
440	Theodora	46	7 129/144	8 9/144	8 30/144
295	Theresia	73	8 18/144	8 58/144	8 91/144
32532	Thereus	84	10 1/144	10 47/144	10 85/144
17	Thetis	56	8 2/144	8 32/144	8 58/144
405	Thia	104	7 128/144	8 41/144	8 87/144
88	Thisbe	69	8 19/144	8 56/144	8 87/144
299	Thora	27	8 16/144	8 29/144	8 41/144
279	Thule	15	8 141/144	9 4/144	9 11/144
934	Thuringia	93	8 3/144	8 54/144	8 95/144
219	Thusnelda	95	7 113/144	8 22/144	8 64/144
115	Thyra	82	7 124/144	8 24/144	8 61/144
753	Tiflis	94	7 112/144	8 20/144	8 61/144
603	Timandra	74	7 142/144	8 38/144	8 71/144
687	Tinette	117	7 130/144	8 52/144	8 102/144
267	Tirza	42	8 35/144	8 56/144	8 76/144
466	Tisiphone	39	8 75/144	8 95/144	8 114/144
593	Titania	92	8	8 50/144	8 91/144
732	Tjilaki	19	8 22/144	8 31/144	8 40/144
498	Tokio	95	7 138/144	8 47/144	8 89/144
138	Tolosa	69	7 137/144	8 30/144	8 61/144
590	Tomyris	34	8 55/144	8 72/144	8 88/144
924	Toni	66	8 33/144	8 68/144	8 98/144
1685	Toro	195	6 78/144	7 53/144	7 128/144
715	Transvaalia	35	8 38/144	8 56/144	8 72/144
619	Triberga	32	8 20/144	8 36/144	8 51/144
530	Turandot	94	8 33/144	8 85/144	8 126/144
258	Tyche	87	7 140/144	8 44/144	8 82/144
42355	Typhon	252	11 7/144	12 25/144	12 115/144
909	Ulla	39	8 87/144	8 107/144	8 125/144
885	Ulrike	80	8 36/144	8 79/144	8 114/144
714	Ulula	25	8 25/144	8 37/144	8 49/144
160	Una	29	8 38/144	8 52/144	8 66/144
92	Undina	44	8 62/144	8 85/144	8 105/144
306	Unitas	64	7 132/144	8 22/144	8 52/144
905	Universitas	65	7 119/144	8 9/144	8 39/144
30	Urania	54	7 139/144	8 23/144	8 48/144
	Uranus	21	11 16/144	11 26/144	11 35/144
167	Urda	16	8 54/144	8 62/144	8 69/144
501	Urhixidur	60	8 52/144	8 83/144	8 111/144
860	Ursina	45	8 34/144	8 58/144	8 79/144
375	Ursula	45	8 57/144	8 81/144	8 102/144
634	Ute	79	8 33/144	8 75/144	8 111/144
131	Vala	29	8 14/144	8 29/144	8 42/144
839	Valborg	64	8 10/144	8 44/144	8 73/144
262	Valda	91	7 133/144	8 39/144	8 79/144
447	Valentine	19	8 62/144	8 71/144	8 80/144
611	Valeria	52	8 44/144	8 71/144	8 95/144
610	Valeska	109	8 18/144	8 79/144	8 126/144
240	Vanadis	88	8	8 48/144	8 87/144
20000	Varuna	22	12 38/144	12 49/144	12 60/144
416	Vaticana	93	8 6/144	8 57/144	8 98/144
126	Velleda	45	8 6/144	8 29/144	8 50/144
487	Venetia	38	8 29/144	8 48/144	8 66/144
	Venus	4	6 63/144	6 65/144	6 66/144
499	Venusia	92	8 82/144	8 132/144	9 29/144
245	Vera	83	8 34/144	8 79/144	8 116/144
490	Veritas	40	8 63/144	8 84/144	8 103/144
4	Vesta	38	8 3/144	8 23/144	8 40/144
144	Vibilia	100	7 136/144	8 47/144	8 91/144
12	Victoria	94	7 113/144	8 20/144	8 61/144
397	Vienna	106	7 130/144	8 45/144	8 91/144
366	Vincentina	24	8 70/144	8 82/144	8 93/144
231	Vindobona	64	8 33/144	8 67/144	8 96/144
759	Vinifera	88	7 140/144	8 44/144	8 83/144
557	Violetta	43	8 8/144	8 30/144	8 49/144
50	Virginia	123	7 121/144	8 47/144	8 99/144
494	Virtus	28	8 57/144	8 71/144	8 84/144
635	Vundtia	33	8 66/144	8 82/144	8 97/144
877	Walkure	68	7 141/144	8 33/144	8 64/144

987 Wallia	101	8 26/144	8 82/144	8 126/144
256 Walpurga	29	8 58/144	8 72/144	8 86/144
890 Waltraut	26	8 61/144	8 74/144	8 86/144
886 Washingtonia	116	8 18/144	8 84/144	8 133/144
729 Watsonia	42	8 34/144	8 55/144	8 74/144
621 Werdandi	59	8 50/144	8 81/144	8 108/144
226 Weringia	87	8 4/144	8 51/144	8 90/144
930 Westphalia	61	7 140/144	8 29/144	8 56/144
931 Whittemora	99	8 30/144	8 84/144	8 127/144
392 Wilhelmina	60	8 32/144	8 64/144	8 92/144
747 Winchester	148	7 130/144	8 73/144	8 133/144
717 Wisibada	113	8 18/144	8 82/144	8 130/144
852 Wladilena	118	7 100/144	8 23/144	8 73/144
827 Wolfiana	67	7 123/144	8 15/144	8 45/144
690 Wratislavia	77	8 40/144	8 82/144	8 117/144
411 Xanthe	50	8 42/144	8 68/144	8 91/144
156 Xanthippe	97	7 143/144	8 53/144	8 95/144

625 Xenia	97	7 136/144	8 46/144	8 89/144
990 Yerkes	93	7 141/144	8 48/144	8 89/144
351 Yrsa	65	8 21/144	8 55/144	8 85/144
999 Zachia	93	7 137/144	8 43/144	8 84/144
421 Zahringia	122	7 112/144	8 38/144	8 90/144
851 Zeissia	38	7 135/144	8 11/144	8 28/144
169 Zelia	56	7 137/144	8 22/144	8 48/144
633 Zelima	36	8 55/144	8 74/144	8 90/144
654 Zelinda	99	7 106/144	8 17/144	8 60/144
840 Zenobia	43	8 59/144	8 81/144	8 101/144
693 Zerbinetta	14	8 62/144	8 68/144	8 75/144
531 Zerlina	84	8 11/144	8 57/144	8 94/144
438 Zeuxo	29	8 24/144	8 39/144	8 53/144
689 Zita	98	7 109/144	8 19/144	8 61/144
865 Zubaida	83	7 127/144	8 27/144	8 64/144
785 Zwetana	90	7 135/144	8 40/144	8 80/144

Appendix II: Methodological Considerations

A seasoned researcher may have looked at the city table in Chapter 43 and asked, how can we possibly classify a city's culture without knowing its founding date—the all-important "birth time?" The answer is, we can't really. The theory behind the city table was almost entirely based on human behavioral sequences and clines of human preferences imposed upon the earth. As such, we can expect that chart to represent the view of a city only as a generic location on the map and mainly compared to other city regions broadly. For people who are into the actual internal culture, job and civic opportunities, social support systems, or governance details of a city, you'll actually need the founding date as well.

The problems of studying astrology rigorously are the same as the problems that come with studying psychology. Interestingly, those same problems are rooted in the separation of cycle, physical, and interphysical space—the mind, body, and spirit of any dynamic. For example, while working on my doctorate, I ran into all kinds of trouble early on for using the interpersonal circumplex (IPC) as a behavioral measure, since it was not commonly used in the field I majored in (Leadership Studies). Leadership Studies and much of psychology in the US relies on the more commonly known Big-5 personality system—a reflection of our tendency to equate grapefruits and oranges in matters of interaction. At heart, the Big-5 measures personality outside of the context of interaction, while the IPC measures behavior inside the context of interaction. Although there is a growing body of research which considers these areas distinct, it remains the tendency of those of us in the field to continue to fall back on the more familiar measure when the less familiar one should actually be used. A person who scores high on neuroticism and low on extraversion in the Big-5 may be antisocial in a broad sense, but super social among a close knit group which shares similar neurotic measures. I know because this applies to my own scores. Using cycle personality to make conclusions about physical interactions may be rooted in some basic correlations among the relevant dimensions, but those dimensions are in fact not the same. And then there is the matter of the interphysical body image, genetic plan (or its oft-conflated relative, ethnicity) which we carry around with us. A neurotic woman and a neurotic man are generally treated differently. A highly communal Mexican and a highly uncommunal (cold) Mexican are treated differently. That too is a separate space.

One of the most important broad lessons I learned in shifting from neuroscience to sociology to leadership was that the scope of activity matters in a study. One of the difficulties in developing a unified theory in physics is that we have long attempted to marry macro-level measures to micro-level phenomena, one of the main results being a need for extra-special math like the use of tensors and manifolds. Not that these things are wrong. They definitely tend to align with what we macro-level people have observed of micro-level space. But when we imagine the Big Bang, we tend to picture a basic explosion of energy, not an explosion of nested, looping, metasystems. In the beginning, the universe was likely simpler in its soupy state than the complex, cooled, system of waves, tides, biologies, and genetics that we have now. We could marry the micro to the macro, but in an environment where the macro is built from far simpler micro-relationships, we won't necessarily need anything more complicated than basic geometry and energy counts. We could try to cast our findings of interpersonal behavior in terms of the function that maps it to personality, but why go through the trouble of a maze of contextualizing partial correlations when you could just use the two axes of communion and agency to explain almost all of the statistical variance involved?

To efficiently study fields like astrology, psychology, history, and to a lesser extent physics and chemistry, we need data from internal, external, and interactional sources. "Proofs" of astrology have long relied on isolated game-show challenges where some debunker has set up some system and demanded the astrologer or associated data simply "make it work." This is a lot like dumping a physicist into a junkyard and demanding that he build an airplane. Where the Hubble has outstripped our big data capacity, the tools haven't been there. The data hasn't been there. And most importantly, the proper context hasn't been there—including the attitudes of people with the tools. If a lack of bias is key to any good science, then its no wonder many good hard science researchers would make bad social science researchers (including astrologers) and vice versa. Some of it stems from a lack of resources. But a lot of it is just elitism.

Reading More into Your Astrology Chart, More Formal Research

The following steps took me years to piece together. Contact me through http://electricmonastery.com if you need help with it.

For people interested in studying astrology on a PC but who don't have the luxury of sampling hundreds of students the way I did, here are some tools I recommend you use:

- **StarFisher** http://www.starfisher.cz/starfisher/EN/download.htm - an easy to modify, free chart reading program

- **Microsoft Excel** for easy data entry and manipulation

- **The Swiss Ephemeris Plugin for Excel** http://www.astrotexte.ch/sources/swexls.html – an absolutely indispensable tool for turning Excel into a kind of astrology program. The site is in German. The file you want is **orbit.xls**. You'll need to create a folder called C:\SWEPH\EPHE and put your ephemeris files (the ones from the StarFisher "ephemeris" folder) in there.

  - Unless you have some special file which already contains the orbit.xls macros, you will almost certainly need to build your database starting with orbit.xls itself. Just save a new copy. (I plan to upload such special files to electricmonastery in the future. Keep a look out for them.)

  - (Optional) Some knowledge of VBA for modifying Excel's macros to do fancier things like calculating the nearest 144th harmonic

- (Optional) For those who are extra hardcore in their statistics and think Excel is for wimps, there is always the R-Project https://www.r-project.org/. You'll need to keep updating ephemeris files for certain kinds of research, though. Regarding such a foray into the world of asteroids in particular, I wouldn't if I were you.

- (Optional) Online, Astrodatabank https://www.astro.com/astro-databank/Main_Page for obtaining information on all kinds of documented people

- **Online, astro.com's ephemeris files** ftp://ftp.astro.com/pub/swissep/ephe/ for bodies which don't come with StarFisher. These go in both your StarFisher and your C:\SWEPH\EPHE folders. The subfolders are each labeled ast# and contain all the MPC bodies numbered #XXX. So if you want to download 2063 Bacchus, for example, you'd go to the folder ast2, then download se02063s.se1. If you want 136199 Eris, you'd go to ast136, then download s136199s.se1

  - After you put the files in your two ephemeris folders, you'll need to get them working in both StarFisher and Excel. In both cases, for non-major bodies you'll need to add 10000 to the lookup call. Below is what I have in "StarFisher Settings>Bodies>Definitions" for 752 Sulamitis, for example:

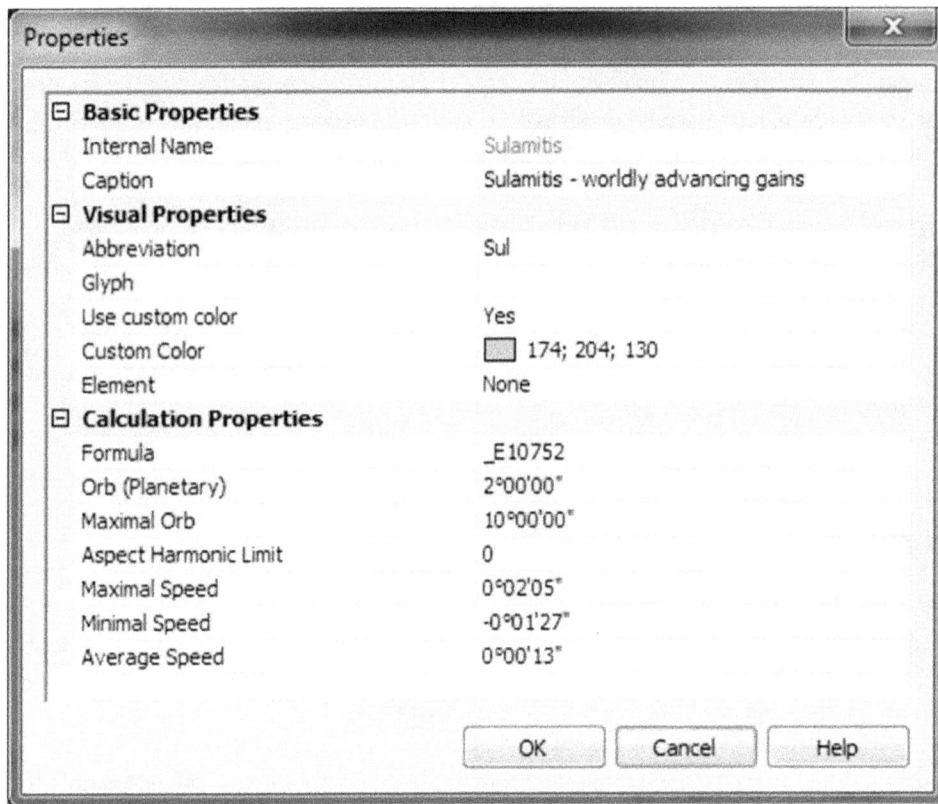

The most important thing is the Formula _E10752, which tells StarFisher to look in its ephemeris folder for body #752. Notice I needed to add 10000 to it. I'd set the orb to something small like 2° as shown, and would pay attention to the last few boxes only if you want to be extra precise and feel like calculating more stuff. Since StarFisher is only for display and not for statistics though, I ignored these. Similarly, my formula for Eris is _E146199.

○ In order to get the location of your new asteroid in Excel, use the command "=SwissCalc(MPCnum+10000,Year*1,Month*1,Day*1,Julian*1)" where MPCnum, Year, Month, Day, and Julian are all values that go with your chosen date. The file orbit.xls has a model for how to do this on the tab called "Ephemeride." Make sure your time zones are right. Compare the Excel results frequently against StarFisher in the beginning to save yourself a lot of headaches.

• In the previous book I talked about how important it is to start doing your astrology research with people you know, despite common prescriptions against this. But if you don't want to use people you know, **you'll need data**. Although astrodatabank is okay for certain biographical information, it's not good for really deep personal behaviors typically hidden from public biography. For that reason, you'll need to tap into some source of psychological knowledge. There are lots of surveys and free instruments out there. For personality, I like the ipip http://ipip.ori.org/ myself, which will give you PLENTY to chew on. That's for personality. For interpersonal behavior, you might start with the Locke CSIE http://www.midss.org/content/circumplex-scales-interpersonal-efficacy-csie. For body image or genetic data…well…eyeballing seems to be all we have for now.

• Over the course of all the research throughout the *FSA* series' four books, I created several special mutations of orbit.xls: FamousOrbit (the *FSA* and *144* database), FullSynastric and TIY_Composite (the *HBS* databases), Serennu1020, MPAsteroids, and (the admittedly misnamed) Astrocartography (the Laurentia databases). After removing the copious private data from these files, I plan to upload them to electricmonastery for general research purposes. Anyone interested in pursuing these topics further should check the site for updates.

Sources

Bruce, Robert. (1999) *Astral Dynamics.* Hampton Roads Publishing.

Hesse-Biber, N. Sharlene. (2006). *Handbook of Feminist Research: Theory and Praxis.* Sage Publications.

Krantz, Steven. (1995) *Elements of Advanced Mathematics.* CRC Press.

Roberts, Thad. (2016) *Einstein's Intuition.* Quantum Space Theory Institute.

Strang, Gilbert. (2010). *Linear Algebra.* Obtained from https://ocw.mit.edu/courses/mathematics/18-06-linear-algebra-spring-2010/ MIT Open Courseware.

Virtue, Doreen. (2002) *Messages from Your Angels.* Hay House.

15.18	145.75	Saipan, Northern Mariana Islands, United States	46.750	2	129	126	6	pursues a quest for greater relevance in the bearing of people in it	8	12	1	spacey, odd, and pushy in a {questing} way
-16.93	145.78	Cairns, Queensland, Australia	46.717	2	129	126	6	pursues a quest for greater relevance in the bearing of people in it	5	10	5	(not necessarily negatively) calculatingly showy in a showy way
-19.25	146.82	Townsville, Queensland, Australia	45.683	2	129	126	6	pursues a quest for greater relevance in the bearing of people in it	5	8	7	no-nonsense and showy in an enterprising way
-9.52	147.22	Port Moresby, Papua New Guinea	45.283	2	129	126	6	pursues a quest for greater relevance in the bearing of people in it	6	4	4	nurturingly busy in a concerned way
-42.88	147.33	Hobart, Tasmania, Australia	45.167	2	129	126	6	pursues a quest for greater relevance in the bearing of people in it	4	1	8	aims-insistent and concerned in a pushy way
-35.30	149.12	Canberra, Australian Capital Territory, Australia	43.383	2	130	127	7	welcomes all in the bearing of people in it	4	7	9	sociable and concerned in a self-declaring way
-23.38	150.52	Rockhampton, Queensland, Australia	41.983	2	131	128	8	is a standards setter in the bearing of people in it	5	5	3	proud and showy in a thoughtful way
59.57	150.80	Magadan, Magadan Oblast, Russia	41.700	2	131	128	8	is a standards setter in the bearing of people in it	10	11	7	(social) noisily objective-focused in an enterprising way
-34.43	150.88	Wollongong, New South Wales, Australia	41.617	2	131	128	8	is a standards setter in the bearing of people in it	4	8	5	no-nonsense and concerned in a showy way
-33.87	151.22	Sydney, New South Wales, Australia	41.283	2	131	128	8	is a standards setter in the bearing of people in it	4	8	10	no-nonsense and concerned in an objective-focused way
-32.92	151.75	Newcastle, New South Wales, Australia	40.750	2	131	128	8	is a standards setter in the bearing of people in it	4	9	7	confidently concerned in an enterprising way
7.45	151.85	Weno, Federated States of Micronesia	40.650	2	131	128	8	is a standards setter in the bearing of people in it	7	5	11	proud and enterprising in a community-anchored way
-27.47	153.03	Brisbane, Queensland, Australia	39.467	2	132	129	9	provides noteworthy sights in the bearing of people in it	5	2	12	materially-focused and showy in an environment-attentive way
-28.02	153.40	Gold Coast, Queensland, Australia	39.100	2	132	129	9	provides noteworthy sights in the bearing of people in it	5	1	7	aims-insistent and showy in an enterprising way
6.92	158.17	Palikir, Federated States of Micronesia	34.333	2	134	131	11	shows lots of activity in the bearing of people in it	7	5	6	proud and enterprising in a busy way
53.02	158.65	Petropavlovsk-Kamchatsky, Kamchatka Krai, Russia	33.850	2	134	131	11	shows lots of activity in the bearing of people in it	10	6	4	practical and objective-focused in a concerned way
-9.47	159.82	Honiara, Solomon Islands	32.683	2	134	131	11	shows lots of activity in the bearing of people in it	6	4	5	nurturingly busy in a showy way
-22.28	166.45	Nouméa, New Caledonia, France	26.050	1	137	134	2	is a noteworthy travel destination in social innovation	5	6	2	practical and showy in a {self-value aware} way
-0.55	166.92	Yaren District, Nauru	25.583	1	137	134	2	is a noteworthy travel destination in social innovation	6	11	6	(social) noisily busy in a busy way
-29.07	167.97	Kingston, Norfolk Island, Australia	24.533	1	138	135	3	is vocal, social, expressively unhindered in social innovation	5	12	8	spacey, odd, and showy in a pushy way
-17.75	168.30	Port Vila, Vanuatu	24.200	1	138	135	3	is vocal, social, expressively unhindered in social innovation	5	9	9	confidently showy in a self-declaring way
-46.42	168.35	Invercargill, New Zealand	24.150	1	138	135	3	is vocal, social, expressively unhindered in social innovation	3	10	10	(not necessarily negatively) calculatingly thoughtful in an objective-focused way
-45.87	170.50	Dunedin, New Zealand	22.000	1	139	136	4	is tourist nurturing in social innovation	3	11	3	(social) noisily thoughtful in a thoughtful way
7.07	171.27	Majuro, Marshall Islands	21.233	1	139	136	4	is tourist nurturing in social innovation	7	5	7	proud and enterprising in an enterprising way
-43.53	172.62	Christchurch, New Zealand	19.883	1	140	137	5	is a popular regional show stealer in social innovation	4	1	2	aims-insistent and concerned in a {self-value aware} way
1.43	173.00	South Tarawa, Kiribati	19.500	1	140	137	5	is a popular regional show stealer in social innovation	7	1	1	aims-insistent and enterprising in a {questing} way
-41.27	173.28	Nelson, New Zealand	19.217	1	140	137	5	is a popular regional show stealer in social innovation	4	2	11	materially-focused and concerned in a community-anchored way
-36.83	174.73	Auckland, New Zealand	17.767	1	140	137	5	is a popular regional show stealer in social innovation	4	6	6	practical and concerned in a busy way
-41.28	174.78	Wellington, New Zealand	17.717	1	140	137	5	is a popular regional show stealer in social innovation	4	2	11	materially-focused and concerned in a community-anchored way
-37.78	175.28	Hamilton, New Zealand	17.217	1	141	138	6	pursues a quest for greater relevance in social innovation	4	5	9	proud and concerned in a self-declaring way
-39.65	176.83	Hastings, New Zealand	15.667	1	141	138	6	pursues a quest for greater relevance in social innovation	4	4	3	nurturingly concerned in a thoughtful way
64.73	177.52	Anadyr, Chukotka Autonomous Okrug, Russia	14.983	1	142	139	7	welcomes all in social innovation	11	3	9	expressive, communicative, and community-anchored in a self-declaring way
-18.13	178.45	Suva, Fiji	14.050	1	142	139	7	welcomes all in social innovation	5	9	5	confidently showy in a showy way
-8.52	179.22	Funafuti, Tuvalu	13.283	1	142	139	7	welcomes all in social innovation	6	5	2	proud and busy in a {self-value aware} way
-16.43	179.37	Labasa, Fiji	13.133	1	142	139	7	welcomes all in social innovation	5	10	10	(not necessarily negatively) calculatingly showy in an objective-focused way
-9.38	179.85	Nukulaelae, Tuvalu	12.650	1	142	139	7	welcomes all in social innovation	6	4	5	nurturingly busy in a showy way

37.97	126.55	Kaesong, North Hwanghae, North Korea	65.950	3	121	118	10	hosts cultural structures in controlled thought	9	6	4	practical and self-declaring in a concerned way
45.75	126.63	Harbin, Heilongjiang, People's Republic of China	65.867	3	121	118	10	hosts cultural structures in controlled thought	10	12	7	spacey, odd, and objective-focused in an enterprising way
37.48	126.63	Incheon, South Korea	65.867	3	121	118	10	hosts cultural structures in controlled thought	9	5	11	proud and self-declaring in a community-anchored way
37.57	126.98	Seoul, South Korea	65.517	3	121	118	10	hosts cultural structures in controlled thought	9	6	12	practical and self-declaring in an environment-attentive way
39.15	127.45	Wonsan, Kangwon, North Korea	65.050	3	121	118	10	hosts cultural structures in controlled thought	9	7	3	sociable and self-declaring in a thoughtful way
26.22	127.68	Naha, Okinawa, Japan	64.817	3	122	119	11	shows lots of activity in controlled thought	8	8	11	no-nonsense and pushy in a community-anchored way
-3.70	128.17	Ambon, Maluku, Indonesia	64.333	3	122	119	11	shows lots of activity in controlled thought	6	9	12	confidently busy in an environment-attentive way
35.87	128.60	Daegu, South Korea	63.900	3	122	119	11	shows lots of activity in controlled thought	9	4	8	nurturingly self-declaring in a pushy way
35.18	129.08	Busan, South Korea	63.417	3	122	119	11	shows lots of activity in controlled thought	9	4	1	nurturingly self-declaring in a {questing} way
62.03	129.73	Yakutsk, Sakha Republic, Russia	62.767	3	122	119	11	shows lots of activity in controlled thought	11	1	7	aims-insistent and community-anchored in an enterprising way
41.80	129.78	Chongjin, North Hamgyong, North Korea	62.717	3	122	119	11	shows lots of activity in controlled thought	9	9	5	confidently self-declaring in a showy way
33.58	130.40	Fukuoka, Fukuoka, Japan	62.100	3	123	120	12	is visited by all, a world city in controlled thought	9	2	10	materially-focused and self-declaring in an objective-focused way
-12.45	130.83	Darwin, Northern Territory, Australia	61.667	3	123	120	12	is visited by all, a world city in controlled thought	6	2	12	materially-focused and busy in an environment-attentive way
43.13	131.90	Vladivostok, Primorsky Krai, Russia	60.600	3	123	120	12	is visited by all, a world city in controlled thought	9	10	6	(not necessarily negatively) calculatingly self-declaring in a busy way
34.38	132.45	Hiroshima, Hiroshima, Japan	60.050	3	123	120	12	is visited by all, a world city in controlled thought	9	3	6	expressive, communicative, and self-declaring in a busy way
67.55	133.38	Verkhoyansk, Sakha Republic, Russia	59.117	2	124	121	1	is a source of affairs, leads other cities in the bearing of people in it	11	6	12	practical and community-anchored in an environment-attentive way
7.37	134.48	Koror, Palau	58.017	2	124	121	1	is a source of affairs, leads other cities in the bearing of people in it	7	5	10	proud and enterprising in an objective-focused way
7.48	134.60	Melekeok, Palau	57.900	2	124	121	1	is a source of affairs, leads other cities in the bearing of people in it	7	5	11	proud and enterprising in a community-anchored way
34.68	135.20	Kōbe, Hyogo, Japan	57.300	2	125	122	2	is a noteworthy travel destination in the bearing of people in it	9	3	8	expressive, communicative, and self-declaring in a pushy way
34.70	135.50	Osaka, Osaka, Japan	57.000	2	125	122	2	is a noteworthy travel destination in the bearing of people in it	9	3	9	expressive, communicative, and self-declaring in a self-declaring way
35.02	135.77	Kyoto, Kyoto, Japan	56.733	2	125	122	2	is a noteworthy travel destination in the bearing of people in it	9	4	12	nurturingly self-declaring in an environment-attentive way
35.18	136.90	Nagoya, Aichi, Japan	55.600	2	125	122	2	is a noteworthy travel destination in the bearing of people in it	9	4	1	nurturingly self-declaring in a {questing} way
-34.93	138.60	Adelaide, South Australia, Australia	53.900	2	126	123	3	is vocal, social, expressively unhindered in the bearing of people in it	4	8	12	no-nonsense and concerned in an environment-attentive way
35.45	139.63	Yokohama, Kanagawa, Japan	52.867	2	126	123	3	is vocal, social, expressively unhindered in the bearing of people in it	9	4	4	nurturingly self-declaring in a concerned way
35.52	139.70	Kawasaki, Kanagawa, Japan	52.800	2	126	123	3	is vocal, social, expressively unhindered in the bearing of people in it	9	4	4	nurturingly self-declaring in a concerned way
35.68	139.70	Tokyo, Japan	52.800	2	126	123	3	is vocal, social, expressively unhindered in the bearing of people in it	9	4	6	nurturingly self-declaring in a busy way
-2.53	140.72	Jayapura, Papua, Indonesia	51.783	2	127	124	4	is tourist nurturing in the bearing of people in it	6	9	11	confidently busy in a community-anchored way
38.27	140.87	Sendai, Miyagi, Japan	51.633	2	127	124	4	is tourist nurturing in the bearing of people in it	9	6	7	practical and self-declaring in an enterprising way
43.07	141.35	Sapporo, Hokkaido, Japan	51.150	2	127	124	4	is tourist nurturing in the bearing of people in it	9	10	5	(not necessarily negatively) calculatingly self-declaring in a showy way
-38.15	144.35	Geelong, Victoria, Australia	48.150	2	128	125	5	is a popular regional show stealer in the bearing of people in it	4	5	5	proud and concerned in a showy way
13.48	144.75	Hagåtña, Guam, United States	47.750	2	128	125	5	is a popular regional show stealer in the bearing of people in it	7	10	9	(not necessarily negatively) calculatingly enterprising in a self-declaring way
13.52	144.83	Dededo, Guam, United States	47.667	2	128	125	5	is a popular regional show stealer in the bearing of people in it	7	10	9	(not necessarily negatively) calculatingly enterprising in a self-declaring way
-37.82	144.97	Melbourne, Victoria, Australia	47.533	2	128	125	5	is a popular regional show stealer in the bearing of people in it	4	5	8	proud and concerned in a pushy way
43.33	145.58	Nemuro, Hokkaido, Japan	46.917	2	129	126	6	pursues a quest for greater relevance in the bearing of people in it	9	10	8	(not necessarily negatively) calculatingly self-declaring in a pushy way